Juliette Gordon Low

Juliette Gordon Low

The Remarkable Founder of the Girl Scouts

Stacy A. Cordery

VIKING

VIKING
Published by the Penguin Group
Penguin Gr[illegible]SA) Inc., 375 Hudson Street, New York, New York 10014, U.S.A.
Penguin Group (Canada), 90 Eglinton Avenue East, Suite 700, Toronto, Ontario,
Canada M4P 2Y3 (a division of Pearson Penguin Canada Inc.)
Penguin Books Ltd, 80 Strand, London WC2R 0RL, England
Penguin Ireland, 25 St. Stephen's Green, Dublin 2, Ireland (a division of Penguin Books Ltd)
Penguin Books Australia Ltd, 250 Camberwell Road, Camberwell, Victoria 3124, Australia
(a division of Pearson Australia Group Pty Ltd)
Penguin Books India Pvt Ltd, 11 Community Centre, Panchsheel Park,
New Delhi – 110 017, India
Penguin Group (NZ), 67 Apollo Drive, Rosedale, Auckland 0632, New Zealand
(a division of Pearson New Zealand Ltd)
Penguin Books (South Africa) (Pty) Ltd, 24 Sturdee Avenue, Rosebank,
Johannesburg 2196, South Africa

Penguin Books Ltd, Registered Offices: 80 Strand, London WC2R 0RL, England

First published in 2012 by Viking Penguin, a member of Penguin Group (USA) Inc.

1 3 5 7 9 10 8 6 4 2

This book is not licensed or endorsed by Girl Scouts of the USA.

PHOTO CREDITS:

Courtesy of the author: insert 1, p. 1 top; *Courtesy of the Library of Congress:* insert 1, p. 1 bottom, p. 2 top, p. 3, p. 7 bottom, p. 16 top; insert 2: p. 3 bottom, p. 4 bottom, pp. 6–8, p. 9 top, pp. 10–11, p. 12 bottom, p. 13, p. 16; *Girl Scouts of the USA–Juliette Gordon Low Birthplace. Used by Permission:* insert 1: p. 2 bottom, pp. 4–6, p. 7 top, pp. 8–9, p. 10 bottom, p. 11, p. 12 top, p. 13, p. 14 bottom; insert 2: pp. 1–2, p. 3. top, p. 4 top, p. 5, p. 9 bottom, p. 12 top, pp. 14–15; *Courtesy of Preserve Rhode Island:* insert 1: p. 10 top; *Courtesy of Margaret Seiler:* insert 1: p. 12 bottom; *Courtesy of Clive Hanley:* insert 1: p. 14 top; *Country Life:* insert 1, p. 15 top; *@ National Portrait Gallery, London:* insert 1: p. 15 bottom; *Courtesy of Girlguiding UK:* insert 1, p. 16 bottom

LIBRARY OF CONGRESS CATALOGING IN PUBLICATION DATA
Cordery, Stacy A.
Juliette Gordon Low : the remarkable founder of the Girl Scouts / Stacy A. Cordery.
p. cm.
Includes bibliographical references and index.
ISBN 978-0-670-02330-1
1. Low, Juliette Gordon, 1860–1927. 2. Girl Scouts of the United States of America—Biography.
3. Girl Scouts—United States—Biography. I. Title.
HS3268.2.L68C67 2012
369.463092—dc23
[B] 2011036177

Printed in the United States of America
Designed by Nancy Resnick

To S.C.E.C.

". . . the means of grace . . ."

Author's Note

Note on names: Juliette Gordon Low's father, brother, and husband were all named William. For the sake of clarity, Willie refers to her father, William Washington Gordon II. Bill refers to her brother, William Washington Gordon III. Willy refers to her husband, William Mackay Low.

Preface

Juliette Gordon was born just as the Civil War ripped the United States in half. When it ended, her father, a third-generation Georgian, returned from the fighting and the family quickly patched itself together. Daisy, as Juliette was always known, grew up as one of five siblings in a beautiful Savannah home rich in love and material comforts. Her irascible mother hailed from Chicago's founding family. The Gordons gave their children a cosmopolitan upbringing, a good education, and a sense of duty.

Daisy was an extroverted, popular girl, excelling at art and enjoying outdoor amusements. Chafing only a little at nineteenth-century society's restrictions on young women, she fell in love with a man who failed her completely. William Mackay Low was a wealthy Englishman with Savannah roots. He stepped in to comfort her upon the death of one of her sisters, and Daisy lost her heart to him. Unfortunately, just before their 1886 marriage, a physician's error damaged her ear and her hearing, and not long after, a piece of wedding rice thrown at the couple stuck painfully in the same ear. The other ear deteriorated, leaving Daisy to cope with compromised hearing for the rest of her life.

The Lows lived among the British aristocracy, and their circle of friends included titled nobility with mores very unlike her own. Her husband's infidelity shocked and wounded her. She bravely chose the scandalous option of divorcing him, but he died before she could complete the process. From beyond the grave he added to her humiliation by leaving the bulk of his considerable estate to his mistress. With her sisters-in-law, Daisy fought successfully to regain her share. Though she found temporary comfort in travel and visiting friends, Daisy could not immediately solve the riddle of what to do in her widowhood.

The answer came when she met British war hero Robert Baden-Powell. He had just created two organizations, the Boy Scouts and the Girl Guides, which combined duty and play in a fashion Daisy found compelling. She threw herself into the formation of Girl Guide patrols in Scotland and England, learning much about the program. Encouraged by Baden-Powell's support, in 1912 Daisy Low returned to the United States and founded the single most important organization for girls in the history of the nation. For eight years she led the Girl Scouts of the United States, until it grew from a handful of girls and a few adult leaders in Savannah into a nationally known, highly respected, self-supporting organization with a membership in the tens of thousands.

In 1920 she traded the title of president for founder but continued for seven more years to be the voice and the face of Girl Scouting. Her unceasing efforts produced hundreds of experienced adult leaders who shared her vision. Once her organization had matured, Juliette Low turned to the nascent challenge of developing global Girl Scouting in the face of American isolationism. She died beloved of her Girl Scouts in 1927, her name forever associated with them.

The creation of the Girl Scouts was, at first glance, the most extraordinary and uncharacteristic act of her life. Though her family members were initially dubious, Scouting celebrated everything that Daisy had been taught to prize: duty to country, civic participation, joy in nature, and a cheerful spirit. Girl Scouting also imparted ideals that Daisy knew, from sad experience, were imperative for girls to learn: chiefly, the importance of independence and the value of sisterhood. Daisy's nine-year marriage was the unhappy aberration in her life, but without Willy's death, it is doubtful that she would have moved with such swiftness to involve herself in Baden-Powell's program.

Girl Scouting was one of many institutions attempting to assist youth during the Progressive Era. But Daisy Low and her organization were not consciously part of this larger movement. She neither knew the reformers nor took much notice of their work, beyond initiating Girl Scout patrols at Hull House. Daisy drew on her own familial and social contacts to establish and run Girl Scouting, seldom turning outward to network with recognized reform leaders. She was in the reform movement but not of it.

She was not an intellectual or a deep thinker. She did not confide to paper any rationales or philosophies for her actions, because she operated intuitively. A fundamentally happy childhood gave her an innate trust in and liking for people, and they generally rose to her expectations. She admitted that it was improbable that someone like her should have begun such a great movement. She frequently compared herself to Saint Denis, who, after his beheading, plucked his head from the ground, tucked it under his arm, and walked up Montmartre. It was only the first step that was hard, she would laugh—after that, the rest of the journey was easy.

Juliette Low was neither methodical nor predictable. She was the visionary leader of an organization that is still thriving one hundred years later. Her sense of humor first drew her to Baden-Powell's emphasis on fun. Girl Scouting had an earnest agenda, but it had to be enjoyable. Juliette Low saw enormous potential in girls and knew women had few outlets for personal and professional development. In 1916 she explained, "Our purposes are analogous to those of the Boy Scouts. They aim to make better men, we to make better women. They are made better housewives if they are to remain in the home, for they are taught practical and useful things, or, if they have to go out in the world, they will learn self-reliance as well as being helped to a means of livelihood."

Only Daisy Low could have created the Girl Scouts of the United States. Had she been a trained, earnest reformer, she would have neglected the fun at the heart of Girl Scouting. Had she been less patriotic and duty driven, she would have discounted Scouting's emphasis on civic preparedness. A traditional woman would have stressed only the homemaking side of Girl Scouting, but Juliette's disastrous marriage made her prize the organization's unconventional offerings. Her enormous charisma, her storytelling abilities, her youthfulness and joie de vivre complemented her hugely effective persuasive skills. She converted her disability into an advantage, conveniently turning a deaf ear to those who would say no to her.

No one who knew the young Daisy Low—when she was the age of a typical Girl Scout—would ever have dreamed she would create an organization that would affect millions and millions of girls around the world. The story of the Savannah belle who transformed into a uniformed leader of one hundred thousand girls gladly donating millions of hours of service to the United States during the First World War is an unlikely one. The tale of a romantically inclined dreamer who devoted her last decade to peace through international understanding seems improbable. That a near-deaf fifty-one-year-old childless widow began the Girl Scouts is preposterous. To have done so with neither a network of social reformers nor experience in any pertinent fields is unbelievable. But that is precisely the story of Juliette Gordon Low's remarkable life.

Contents

Juliette Gordon Low

CHAPTER 1

Civil War and the Problem of Loyalties

The enemy occupation had begun. Union general William Tecumseh Sherman and his formidable army ended the siege of Savannah after a three-hundred-mile march through Georgia during which, he observed, "All the people retire before us and desolation is behind." Yet some elite Savannah families welcomed these conquerors into their homes. Heedless of the baleful stares of her hard-eyed Confederate neighbors, Eleanor "Nellie" Kinzie Gordon pulled her tea set out of hiding and threw open her parlor doors to men her family had known long before the terrible Civil War began. Generals Sherman and Oliver O. Howard sat in the elegant house she shared with her husband, William Washington Gordon II, and their daughters, Eleanor, Daisy, and Alice. Willie was still off fighting for the Confederacy, so the Union officers enjoyed Nellie's hospitality. Three-year-old Daisy perched on Howard's knee, eyeing him curiously. With a child's candor, she asked what had happened to his arm. "Got it shot off by a Rebel," he told her. Daisy brightened. "I s'pose my father did it," she enthused. "He shot lots of Yankees."[1]

The adults present surely smiled at this earnest expression of a daughter's loyalty, and Daisy could not have been expected to understand the complexities of war. These nice men were friendly. They brought candy, visited often, and "made a great pet of [Daisy], roaring at her comments about Yankees," Nellie recounted. Yet they were adversaries, dressed in blue uniforms far different from the resplendent, familiar gray her father wore. And it wasn't a desire to catch up with old family friends that brought them to town, but rather the relentless Union offensive that pushed the Confederacy one step closer to defeat. After the city fell to the Union forces that December 20, 1864, Daisy's father mourned privately, "Savannah evacuated last night. . . . This seventh anniversary of my wedding day ends seven happy years! The future is very dark."[2]

Willie Gordon was right. As the "mystic chords of memory" binding the United States together unraveled completely in 1861 and Northerners and Southerners took up arms against one another, Willie and Nellie found themselves straddling the divide. He was a third-generation Georgian. Her ancestors had founded Chicago. They had personal and business connections north and south. Daisy's father could not be a fire-eating, radical secessionist, but the righteousness of the Southern cause was unambiguous to Willie. So was his duty.

Gordon men had a long history of military service. Ambrose Gordon, Daisy's great-grandfather, migrated to Georgia from New Jersey to settle the land he had earned fighting in the American Revolution as a cavalry lieutenant under George Washington's nephew, William Washington. Gordon so admired Washington that he and his wife, Elizabeth Meade Gordon, named their son after him. When it was time, they sent William Washington Gordon north to be schooled. He was the first Georgian to graduate from the United States Military Academy at West Point, ranking seventh in a class of forty. His stint in the army was brief, because William Gordon preferred law books to firearms. He married Sarah Anderson Stites, whose grandfather had been George Washington's aide-de-camp in the American Revolution. Like his father, a federal marshal, Gordon earnestly performed his public duties. He served as an alderman and mayor of Savannah and as a representative and senator in the Georgia legislature. In the 1830s, he founded what eventually became the Central of Georgia Railway, an important economic link between Savannah's deepwater ports and the state's interior.[3]

William Washington Gordon II—known as Willie—was the son of Sarah and William Washington Gordon. Born in 1834, Willie was only eight when his father died, but he grew up knowing that honor, masculine pride, and defending the family businesses predestined his service in the War Between the States. Willie, too, had been educated in the north. At Yale College in the winter of 1853 he met a charming boarding school classmate of his sister Eliza's. Eighteen-year-old Nellie Kinzie slid gleefully down the banister at the Yale library and landed with a self-assured bounce directly in front of the astonished Southerner. Opposites attracted. The mature, self-possessed, duty-bound college senior fell in love with the irrepressible Nellie.

Raised in the frontier town of Chicago, Eleanor Lytle Kinzie was the only daughter among seven sons, three of whom died very young, born to Juliette Magill and John Harris Kinzie. Life was precarious; this sad truth might have liberated Nellie, who viewed her reputation as a mischief maker with satisfaction. She recorded in her memoirs tales of her "naughty" ways, including a lifelong and most unladylike tendency to curse—which she could do expertly in more than one language. Nellie loved the outdoors, trounced the boys at marbles, and kept up with them easily in sledding, horseback riding, and ice-skating. In Chicago's public and private academies she mastered Italian and French. From her mother she learned how to keep house, play the piano, nurse the sick, grow a garden, sew, and make shoes. It was, she recalled, "everything which might be required of a woman separated from the conveniences of civilization."[4]

At Madame Canda's finishing school in New York City, winsome Nellie Kinzie became friends with a number of young women, including Savannahian Eliza Gordon. Nellie met Eliza's brother Willie in December 1853. During their three-year engagement, Nellie explained to Willie her family's pivotal role in the founding of Chicago, including how the first Episcopal service had been held in the Kinzie home in 1835, the year before her birth. They and their fellow parishioners then erected Saint James, the city's earliest Episcopal church, in 1837. Nellie had been baptized and confirmed there. The church and her religion were extremely important to her, as she emphasized to Willie before their marriage: "I feel anything like a *slur* on my church far more than you ever did my remarks on *slavery*." Despite his Presbyterianism, they wed at Saint James. After a honeymoon at Niagara Falls, they settled in Savannah, and Nellie worked hard to fit in as a transplanted Northerner. It was trial by fire.[5]

Nellie's mild antislavery sentiments presented a stumbling block to full acceptance in Georgia, where her new husband's family was in the cotton brokering trade. In 1857, Willie's firm, Tison & Gordon, was a year old. With other cotton factors, his office was located on Bay Street, high on the bluff above the Savannah River, where businessmen kept a close eye on water traffic. Tison & Gordon's profits depended on the system of slavery, because slaves grew and harvested the cotton that Willie bought and sold. His family owned Belmont plantation in Jefferson County, which similarly depended on the work of slaves. Every material comfort Willie would provide for his new wife was produced through slave labor.

More pressing for the Gordons than their cultural and political differences was Nellie's first pregnancy. In an era when motherhood was a woman's highest calling, she was conflicted about the role. She sent her mother scorching missives about the constriction of her time and whims. Nellie had been a flirtatious, happy belle and a joyful young bride. She quickly made a name for herself in Savannah for having courageously and publicly ridden the untamed horse of a local patrician. Pregnancy curtailed such exploits. Nellie also feared that a baby would come between her and Willie, and separate them even more than his time-consuming livelihood did. Her mother had scant sympathy for the "unreconciled spirit" Nellie evinced. "Do not," Juliette cautioned her daughter, "give way" to mutinous feelings. "They are wrong—every way wrong." She suggested that Nellie lean on God and on her husband.[6]

Savannah's Christ Episcopal Church welcomed Nellie. But leaning on her husband was not easy. His cotton factor firm kept him busy. Nellie complained about the "many lonely and gloomy hours" she spent without him. And when he was at home, they were not alone, for they had moved in with Willie's mother, Sarah Gordon. No matter how kind Sarah might have been, Nellie was no longer the center of attention as she had been in Chicago as an unmarried woman. Nellie longed for a dwelling of their own, where she would not have to share her husband's focus. Juliette took a mother's part and emphasized that it was crucial for Willie to contribute to his wife's happiness, especially in her condition: "He ought to take care that everything should be planned and provided as you think will be most conducive to your comfort. . . . [H]is duty is to see you saved from every annoyance and unpleasant anticipation."[7]

Just in case Willie did not fill that tall order, Juliette swept into Savannah in time to sustain Nellie for the birth. Her daughter's adopted city was more than one hundred years older than the town the Kinzies settled. Savannah's busy wharves gave the elegant town a cosmopolitanism lacking in Chicago. Nearly twenty-two thousand people lived there, including seven hundred free blacks and more than seven thousand slaves. At the time Juliette arrived, Savannah was in the throes of another yellow fever outbreak, a deadly viral illness spread by mosquito bites. Its symptoms included a high fever, headache, vomiting, and jaundice, which gives skin a yellowish cast, hence its name. There was no vaccination and no cure for yellow fever in the nineteenth century, and the death rate was generally very high. Memories of the 1854 epidemic caused Sarah Gordon to flee to her daughter Gulielma, in New Jersey, in hopes of escaping the danger. Juliette and Nellie, however, professed "little fear of epidemics," and so the two were together when Eleanor was born on September 27, 1858.[8]

Nellie's concerns about the baby's interfering with her marriage proved groundless, and her relationship with Willie grew stronger. When Eleanor was almost a year old, Nellie took her to Illinois to introduce her to the Chicago relatives. The letters between husband and wife attest to their deep commitment to each other, rooted securely in a mutual physical attraction that continued unblushingly throughout their lives. Nellie's love for Willie was the bridge between her family's ardent Republicanism and his devotion to the Southern cause. Yet unpleasant politics were a constant backdrop. After Nellie returned to Savannah, her mother missed her tremendously, but, she wrote, she understood that Nellie had to get back to Willie: "for I would not want him to think that I am trying to *abolish* him, or deprive him of his *white* property."[9]

In the spring of 1860, Nellie was pregnant with their second child. Her ambivalence resurfaced, but neither Juliette nor Willie sympathized with her defiance of a woman's essential nature. "For you I grieve," Willie wrote sadly, "not only because of your present inconvenience, but because of the repugnance you have always felt lest such a result should be brought about." Why Nellie voiced such complaints, when the evidence points to her having been not only a good mother but an interested and involved parent, is unclear. The burdens of child rearing were eased by servants in Chicago and slaves in Savannah. Perhaps it was because Nellie was happiest when her parents and her husband indulged her.[10]

As the birth neared, her apprehension decreased markedly, as did the frequency of discussions about the moralizing of abolitionists and the future of slavery. On the last day of October 1860, Nellie and Willie welcomed the arrival of Juliette Magill Kinzie Gordon. The "fat, hearty little stranger" was named for her maternal grandmother and dubbed Daisy—a common nickname of the time. In an attempt to quell the fussing of new parents about the infant's ill-favored appearance, Grandmother Kinzie counseled patience: "I am sure that after a very little while she will cease to look like a 'freak' and do credit to the stock from which she is descended." Very quickly they came to describe Daisy as "a beautiful baby," with "a sweet disposition," who gave them "very little trouble."[11]

The trouble came instead from national crises. Between Eleanor's and Daisy's births in 1858 and 1860, cataclysmic events made war all but inevitable. The fuse was lit just seven days after Daisy was born, when Illinois politician Abraham Lincoln won the 1860 presidential election. Lincoln's name had not even appeared on the ballot in most Southern states, his victory making white Southerners feel unrepresented and impotent. Fragile compromises worked out by Washington legislators rapidly unraveled. The Confederate States of America took up arms against the United States, federal forces readied to stop them, and the American union dissolved.

Once Confederate troops fired on Fort Sumter in April 1861, Bishop Stephen Elliott felt compelled to make it the topic of a celebratory, pro-war sermon at Christ Church. "Georgia expects every man to do his duty," Elliott thundered. He insisted the prayer for the president of the United States should be changed immediately to "Thy Servant, the Governor of the State of Georgia." Elliott's exhortations spurred Willie to leave his family and "go to the front at once," Nellie seethed. She did not want to be without her husband. Daisy was barely six months old in April 1861; like her sister, a child of the North and the South. Two-and-a-half-year-old Eleanor might have sensed their mother's ire, because Nellie described herself being "violently" against Willie's joining up: "Not from any sentiment as to whether the South was right; I didn't care a fig for that. I simply did not want him to run the chance of getting shot."[12]

Family funds helped Willie equip a company of the Georgia Hussars. Willie's father and grandfather had served with the 125-year-old cavalry unit, and so his service was foreordained. They trained on Skidaway Island, not far from Savannah. There, through directives home, he continued to manage the family's finances. Willie and his men lived on bacon, beans, and hoecakes. He begged Nellie to send him "bread or rusks or cakes every chance you hear of," and some fabric so he could make a proper mattress. Sandflies and midges were eating him alive. In mid-June he had to tell Nellie that the original plan of thirty days at Skidaway would lengthen, as he would be sent off to Virginia. "I love you with all my heart and soul," he assured her. "Kiss" the girls "for me," Willie continued, "and don't let them forget about me." Not long after, Second Lieutenant Gordon and the rest of the Hussars went to fight in Virginia as Company F of the Georgia Hussars, Jeff Davis Legion.[13]

They spent the fall outside of Richmond, but by mid-October Willie relayed their orders to march six days north to Manassas Junction. But the time away from Nellie was wearing on him, as much as on her: "God bless you my dearest, darling wife. I love you with all my life strength. Rest assured I will take good care of myself. Imagine yourself being kissed a thousand times for I could almost devour you with kisses were I with you now."[14]

Nellie remained at home with Eleanor, Daisy, her mother-in-law Sarah, and the slaves. She hated being apart from Willie. Her letters, full of the children's doings, contained equal measures of consolation and courage: "I am sorry, darling, that your journey has been so unpleasant;—either raining or hot, all the time;—I trust its after results, will repay you for your present discomfort."[15] She followed the war news closely and began a journal into which she poured her frustration, descriptions of the people she met, and notes about household troubles. Nellie might have been born and raised in Chicago, but she soon adopted her husband's feelings about the necessity of Southern independence. She grew livid thinking that the North did not take Southern resistance seriously, even after four states of the upper South joined the cause in the spring of 1861. Although the Confederacy won the first major battle of the war when Union troops broke ranks and ran away at Manassas, Virginia, Nellie felt Northerners still denigrated Southern unity and seriousness of purpose:

> Truly, if this is a Rebellion it is a gigantic and unanimous one. The North still whines out its old tune of "crushing out the Rebellion." They are either willfully blind—or woefully ignorant—for they cannot yet, after nearly a year's struggle—wherein they have wasted all their strength, and energies, and resources, in vain—realize that this is not the uprising of a few who have in some mysterious manner overawed and cowed an immense Union Party! Fatal—absurd—insane delusion! I am disgusted at the course pursued by the government of the North! Such blindness! Such folly! . . . They will never never conquer the South, nor subdue the so-called Rebellion.[16]

It was just as well that Nellie felt that way living as she did in Savannah, for in January, while Willie was freezing in a hard eastern

Virginia winter, two of her close relatives accompanied their forces en route to Georgia smartly dressed in Union blue. In early 1862, Nellie's uncle, Major General David Hunter, led a force of Northern troops to gain control of Fort Pulaski and the Savannah River. Located on Cockspur Island, Fort Pulaski guarded the entrance to Savannah. It was considered invincible because of its seven-and-a-half-foot-thick masonry walls. Nevertheless, in fewer than two days and with minimal casualties, Union artillery, with new rifled cannons, compelled a wholesale, "disgraceful surrender"—as Nellie called it. To make matters worse Nellie's own brother, Arthur Magill Kinzie, was Hunter's aide-de-camp.[17]

Hunter was an abolitionist. He was also a general with a shortage of manpower. So, after Pulaski fell, he unilaterally freed the slaves on Cockspur Island. Then he went further and freed all the slaves in Florida, South Carolina, and Georgia. He expected they would take up soldiering gratefully, and he assumed President Lincoln would follow his lead and proclaim the end of slavery. Hunter was stunned when neither outcome occurred. Instead, North and South alike condemned his high-handedness. Lincoln disowned responsibility and repudiated Hunter's order—but never punished him. In Savannah, his niece suffered guilt by association.[18]

Nellie endured the constant tension of having loved ones on both sides of the battle lines. She confessed that it was "delightful" and "a comfort" to hear from Illinois relatives, particularly so after long periods of silence when the fighting interrupted the mail. Nellie was not shy about asking Georgia friends in the military to ferry mail between her Chicago relations and her uncle David. At the same time, Nellie bragged to her diary about the large numbers of boxes of "clothes and necessaries" that she and other women had packed to send off to Confederate soldiers. Bishop Elliott blessed their efforts, preaching on "Women's Heroism in War" and "God's Presence with Our Army at Manassas."[19]

While Nellie always used "we" to refer to the Confederacy, her loyalties lay less with the South or the North than with her husband and family. Neither side fully understood her dilemma. When a cousin of Willie's waved Uncle David Hunter's "outrageous proclamation" before Nellie's face, condemning him roundly, she shot back that she "didn't care what kind of proclamation he had made," insisting, "I knew and loved him well enough already." Sarah interrupted passionately: "I wish to heaven no son of mine had ever married a Northerner!" Nellie huffed that she could "not be on friendly terms with any one who talks to me in that style!" Eventually, Sarah apologized, but the chill between them was slow to thaw.[20]

When her own mother wrote excitedly to say that Arthur was outside Savannah, preparing to visit her, Nellie was impatient. She mused to her diary that her brother was "Willie's open enemy, and yet expects me to be delighted to meet him, when he comes under such circumstances! Opposed to each other at a distance, I could stand it, but to come against his home? No, I love Arth dearly, but to meet him under such circumstances would only give me pain, not pleasure." Nellie had been the target of whisperings—and worse—of Savannahians who suspected her of treasonous divided loyalties. She returned home one time to "buckets of filth from a cess pool . . . dashed all over the front door, porch and steps." She recognized that this "charming specimen of the refinement of Savannah residents" had been thrown "as a protest against us." It was lucky that her fellow citizens did not know her cousin Henry H. Wolcott was president of the Starr Arms Company in New York, where his six hundred employees churned out weapons to equip the Union army.[21]

Nellie tried to maintain a normal existence. Though Savannah was depleted of its white male population, the fighting was far off, and those left behind were safe enough. After Fort Pulaski fell, a Union blockade closed off Savannah's Atlantic side. The commodities available early in the war became scarcer. Local travel was still possible, and Nellie escaped Sarah's home and the city whenever she could. She amused herself by writing pen portraits of her friends. She delighted to see her daughters recovered from croup and measles and grow "so well and fat!" But she missed Willie. In early March, Nellie left the children in Savannah with their grandmother and set out on a mission to find him. Though some Georgia Hussars escorted her,

Nellie was annoyed at her inability to track down her husband. She did locate her old friend General Robert E. Lee, whom she had known a decade earlier when he was superintendent of West Point and she had been a debutante attending dances there. Lee could only guess where Willie was bivouacked, but eventually the couple found each other. "Weren't we glad!!" rejoiced Nellie. Their precious harmony was interrupted by a courier who, Willie wrote his mother, "arrived at camp with orders for every well man to start for the front at daylight." Willie left his wife's side and handed out ammunition until dawn, when he roused Nellie and sent her on an eventful trip through hail and snow back to Savannah. She was thrilled to receive a blissful welcome from Eleanor and young Daisy, who "is so Sweet!" she confided to her diary.[22]

Uncle David's siege of Fort Pulaski happened not long after Nellie's return in early April 1862 and it changed her experience of war entirely. Letters "from home," as she called Chicago, stopped arriving and so mostly she stopped writing. Every so often a welcome package would get through by messenger. In June of 1862, Andrew Low, a wealthy Savannah businessman and neighbor, brought her mail from her mother—once he had gotten out of military prison in Boston for suspicion of treason. Nellie began to lose faith in the conflict's rapid conclusion. Her despair at long separations from Willie grew. She gave in to "the most violent fit of grief," which she knew upset her daughters. Nellie grew more critical of the Confederates, too, and when she did, she did not use "we." "The Southerners, as I tell them all the time," she wrote in her diary, "can whip twice their number in a fight. Fighting is their element. But when it comes to 'pitching in' and *working* hard to secure means and advantages or even to turn to account those natural blessings and gifts they have, they are too lazy, and inefficient to do it. They're so used to being worked for, that they don't know what it means to work—and they won't do it."[23]

Willie, one of those "Southerners," meanwhile withstood twelve hours of being "under fire of shot, shell, and musketry" before escaping from the Union forces in the retreat from Yorktown to Richmond.

His assessment of the battlefield remained positive, and Nellie could not have missed that he called it "a beautiful sight to see the working of Artillery on each side and to see our Infantry march to the front. . . ." A practiced soldier, his lengthy report to her from the field acknowledged Union military skill. Willie "narrowly escaped capture" from "five or six Yanks" while he was about the important task of "buying some cornbread." Whether she concluded that was courage or folly must be left to the imagination.[24]

For Nellie, the hardest blow resulted from Confederate "barbarity," as one observer called it. Gray-clad sharpshooters killed her brother John while he was wounded and defenseless. A sixty-nine-pound shell caused a boiler explosion on his ironclad, the *Mound City,* and the impact hurled a scalded John Kinzie into Arkansas's White River. He floundered in the water, an easy target for the sniper who picked him off. Kinzie was one of 105 men out of a crew of 175 who died in the battle at Saint Charles. "Oh, my poor Father & Mother . . . How can I help to comfort you so far away, so cruelly separated from you!" Nellie cried to her diary.[25]

She begged Willie to allow her to go north to console her family, but was downcast at his "abrupt and unkind refusal." Only the receipt of a package from Chicago, containing a photograph of John and the reassurance that her mother had "not sunk under this blow," mollified Nellie. Nellie thanked God: "Oh, I have been *so* blessed that I feel as if I must spend the whole night in prayer and thanksgiving. What am I that God is mindful of me! and yet 'He has raised me out of the horrible pit!' for truly I was in a state of the utmost distress. Faithless Heart! Why did you despair? This mercy is but a specimen of all thy life!" She resumed writing to her mother, confident that some of her notes would get through.[26]

As the war dragged on, Willie's correspondence dwindled. Brief bouts of battlefield illnesses meant he could not write. In October he cast a farmer's appraising eyes over Maryland's mountains, valleys, houses, barns, stock, crops, and towns, and liked what he saw, even though the people were Yankees. He sensed they were more anxious for the war to end than they were zealously partisan. Nellie felt the same way. Daisy had turned two by then, and was talking "quite sweetly," yet Willie had yet to hear her voice. Recent mail contained money from her parents, but Nellie had no way to spend it for what they needed, as goods became ever more scarce.[27] She was fed up with Willie's absence and with having to make do. "What do you think of the state of affairs at present?" she demanded:

> I think we are pretty badly off, myself! Just whipped at Corinth and all but whipped at Sharpsburg—the North is getting the best of it and what's more will get the best of it, with all their men and resources—This secession Willie is going to be a failure I am afraid and whether it is or not I wish to Heaven you would leave fighting to those who have nothing better to do, and come home! I am tired out with being lonely and unprotected and uncomfortable. I am cut off from all I care for and my only comfort, you, are off the Lord knows where, "Fighting for your country." What do you care for your country in comparison to your wife and children? Or rather what ought you to care? It's all a delusion—an absurdity, my darling!—and I wish to Heaven everybody would come to their senses! I am cross, as you will not need to be told, but there's enough to make me so, I am sure. If I could see what good there was to be gained even after the war was over I would not care—but I don't—and it will last forever and you will be killed and I shall be left alone wretched and miserable on the earth! Come home, Willie, do come home if you can![28]

Nellie's ardent plea, however self-serving and unpatriotic, nevertheless moved Willie. Six weeks later he had found a way to rejoin his family in Savannah, if only briefly. He attended his sister Gulie's wedding, played with Eleanor and Daisy, and reestablished his intimacy with his wife. When he left again, it was with a promotion to assistant adjutant general, serving under his uncle Hugh W. Mercer.[29]

By June 1863, Willie earned a place on the Confederate Roll of

Honor "for meritorious service during operations in the Richmond campaign," and promotion to captain. In September of that year, while fighting at Frederick's City, Maryland, a bullet came so close to Willie that it left a hole in the rim of his hat. One year later "a stray ball" wounded him at Lovejoy's Station, but not badly enough to send him home. Instead, he transferred with his Hussars to Anderson's Brigade of Wheeler's Division of Cavalry. Joseph Wheeler's forces fought hard to halt General Sherman's advance through the Carolinas. Willie commanded the rear guard as the Confederates retreated, blowing up bridges as they went to thwart Sherman.[30]

Willie was luckier than two of Nellie's brothers, Arthur and George, who were captured and sent to the Confederate prison at Cahaba, Alabama. When she learned of her brothers' imprisonment, Nellie immediately set off to see how she could help, taking clothing and food. Meanwhile, Nellie's distraught parents worked through their circle of acquaintances—which extended to President Lincoln—to construct a successful prisoner exchange.[31]

By March 1863, Willie had missed most of his second daughter's life and nearly all of her childhood "firsts." Nellie's letters never began with the children and their activities, but she did relate that Daisy was "very good and no trouble." The three-year-old had taken to calling herself "Daisy Dordon." She made sure to send "Sarther" her love every time Mama wrote to him. Willie asked to have Daisy sew a handkerchief for him, "to be ready to give me when I come home." Daisy was a tiny girl during the fighting, but she understood that a crisis was ongoing because of the absence of her father, her mother's anxiety, the cruel death of her uncle John, and ubiquitous discussions of war. In such strife, children typically cling to their familiar toys and games, like make-believe house and school. Eleanor recalled how "the young Negro children of our servants were our constant playmates." But wartime games often turned into childish reconstructions of battles reflecting the social upheaval around them and the patriotism they assimilated. The Gordon girls were lucky to have the stability of their home, their mother, and the slaves. There were things to celebrate, too, especially the birth in 1863 of their little sister, Sarah Alice, usually called Alice. Daisy and Eleanor gave her the nickname Skinny, which may have been an indicator that the Gordon household was feeling the bite of war.[32]

Certainly other Georgians were. As the Union forces moved inexorably southward in 1864, Willie's sisters, Gulie and Eliza, thought it best to stay with their mother in Savannah. Nellie tried to take her daughters to safety in Chicago, but Willie forbade her sheltering in enemy territory. Juliette Kinzie thought it "sad and strange . . . that your husband should pursue in refusing you a privilege. . . ." Eventually Willie declined even to listen to Nellie on the subject. She took it upon herself to leave her mother-in-law's rapidly filling home. She moved with her three girls to a bungalow near the new town of Thunderbolt, located five miles from Savannah on the Wilmington River. Her happiness at being in her own home, surrounded by picturesque live oak trees, and having the ability to provide "plenty of good plain food" from local gardens for their daughters, was clear from her letters to Willie. She described for him how the girls worked up an appetite feeding the chickens and pigs. They all kept Willie in mind, even Daisy, who found his razor one day and exclaimed, "Oh, Mama, look . . . here's what Papa skins his face with!" Nellie was content in her "snuggery" with her books and her piano. But her rural idyll did not last, for General Sherman's forces had begun their march through Georgia and the noose was tightening around the South. Willie was "continually skirmishing and under fire of shell, shrapnel, and bullets . . . getting no sleep at night, retreating or should I say 'retiring to a new position' three times" in four days. Nellie, the girls, and their nurse returned to Sarah's home, causing an even greater paucity of space and food for all.[33]

Before 1864, Savannah was barely touched by the war, beyond the obvious absence of white men and a decrease in the availability of consumable items. The marketplace flourished, cotton mounted at the depot waiting mostly in vain for the blockade-runners who attempted to sell it in England, and people went about their business. City fathers even allowed the enfeebled Union League to continue meeting. That all changed when Sherman marched south from

Atlanta. He aimed "to whip the rebels, to humble their pride, to follow them to their inmost recesses, and make them fear and dread us." His sixty thousand Union troops foraged, living "sumptuously—turkeys, chickens and sweet potatoes all the way," Sherman wrote to his wife, "but the poor women and children will starve. All I could tell them was, if Jeff Davis expects to found an empire on the ruins of the South, he ought to afford to feed the people. . . ."[34]

In desperation, the Georgia legislature, on November 18, passed an act compelling all white men between the ages of sixteen and fifty-five to fight. Legislators reminded citizens of the danger: "Our cities are being burned, our fields laid waste, and our wives and children mercilessly driven from their homes by a powerful enemy." Confederate general P. T. Beauregard urged all patriotic Georgians to "obstruct and destroy all roads in Sherman's front, flank, and rear, and his army will soon starve in your midst!"[35]

To Georgian William J. Hardee fell the unenviable job of defending Savannah. Knowing he was unlikely to halt Sherman with his small force, Hardee abandoned the city to keep his army intact. Savannahians who could escape did so. The siege of Savannah began on December 10, 1864. Sherman sent his army to attack by land, and after a fifteen-minute battle on December 13, Fort McAllister, "the guardian of the Ogeechee River," fell to Union forces, who were rewarded with the capture of ammunition, food, and wine.[36]

Nellie did not join the long line of men, women, carts, carriages, and livestock hurrying across the pontoons and out of Savannah. She wrote Willie on December 20 about the "perfect rush now, to get off. People are such fools!" Two of their slaves "cleared out," Nellie divulged, but she and her family stayed, waiting for what would come after Mayor Richard D. Arnold proffered the city's surrender. A generally amicable takeover began under the U.S. flag. "The citizens mostly remain, and the city is very quiet," Sherman noted. On December 22, he sent his famous telegram to President Lincoln: "I beg to present you as a Christmas gift the City of Savannah with 150 heavy guns & plenty of ammunition & also about 25,000 bales of cotton."[37] In Washington, three hundred cannons sounded to celebrate the fall of Savannah, and the new cotton agent in the Treasury Department laid plans to confiscate and sell the harvest, worth approximately "twenty eight millions of dollars," to the profit of the federal government. Some of those twenty-five thousand bales belonged to Nellie, and some were Tison & Gordon's.[38]

As the enemy lines closed around his family, Willie worried. Nellie tried to placate him. Her note, written with the battle so near that the house was shaking, encapsulated their troubles and laid bare his suspicions:

> I am sure I have always proved myself ready and willing to do all for [your mother] in my power—and in this case, I have more power to serve her, than if I were her own child. As long as I have a cent, or a mouthful to eat, I promise you she shall share it. And if she survives this war, surely she can have a home and comforts with us; My property will always avail you to start again in business and my only pleasure in its possession is the thought that it will help you to build up a fortune which you can enjoy. May God grant that we may live to enjoy it together.
>
> Why do you harp so continually upon the idea that I shall compromise you in some way if the Yankees come here? Do not fear. Neither I, nor the children, will associate with them, or have anything to do with them save what is actually necessary. I tell you this now, for the last time to re-assure you, my Darling. I will never take the oath [of loyalty to the Union] under any circumstances. If we are compelled to go away from here, I will take [your] Mother with me and go to Chicago—but not otherwise, and I shall promise to do nothing without consulting her and following her advice. Does that satisfy you? And do I make a sufficient negation of myself by such promises?
>
> I must say Willie, that I do not think in some things you have had as much consideration for me, as is your wont. For a married woman, who has got some sense, my

> hands are as completely tied, as they could be if I were a child—You make everything in my plans or desires, give up to either your Mother or yourself—and you do not I think reflect upon all I have borne with patience which [your] Mother might have prevented if she had dared to make [your sister] behave with common civility. Much as I love your dear Mother and I do love her dearly, as you know, I really think that she might have stood my friend in some matters, where she was blameably silent.
>
> As to giving up my will to yours, my own darling, that is not a trial to me. I love you so much Willie, that I could do anything and everything for you! And I am heartsick at the idea of a restricted correspondence and a long separation. Be sure your children will be as great "Rebels" when you see them again as they are now.[39]

Money, his mother, her loyalty, the children's loyalty, her independence: these vexing concerns could hardly be solved by letter. Juliette begged her daughter and granddaughters to come north, tempting them with the question, "Could we live through the happiness of such a meeting?" But Nellie had promised Willie, and so they stayed despite the Union occupation, until such time as they'd be forced to leave.[40]

Sherman made his first headquarters in an imposing Gothic Revival house on Madison Square. Charles Green, the wealthy business partner of cotton factor Andrew Low, owned the home and offered it to the general for his use. Sherman turned reflective on Christmas morning as he surveyed his surroundings. He wrote to his wife, "This house is elegant and splendidly furnished with pictures and statuary. . . . There are many fine families in this city, but when I ask for old and familiar names, it marks the sad havoc of war. The Goodwins, Teffts, Cuylers, Haberhams, Laws, etc., etc., all gone or in poverty, and yet the [women] remain, bright and haughty and proud as ever. There seems no end but utter annihilation that will satisfy their hate of the 'sneaking Yankee' and 'ruthless invader.' They no longer call my army, 'Cowardly Yanks,' but have tried to arouse the sympathy of the civilized world by stories of the cruel barbarities of my army. . . ." Lincoln's attorney general Edwin M. Stanton concurred with Sherman's assessment. He told cabinet members in January that he found "little or no loyalty in Savannah," where "the women are frenzied, senseless partisans."[41]

Food was a woman's domain, and women had been trying desperately to feed their loved ones on little more than local rice and fish since the fall of Fort Pulaski. To make matters more trying, war refugees swelled the city's population to bursting. Rationing had been in effect for a year before Sherman's forces arrived. The poor suffered earliest and most, but even members of polite society had to ignore the rumbles from one another's empty stomachs. Sherman allowed a warehouse full of rice to be sold in Boston under Mayor Arnold's auspices. Arnold purchased "flour, hams, sugar, coffee" and other goods to distribute to Savannah's hungry for free, Sherman noted approvingly.[42]

The general knew that the lightest hand would secure the quickest allegiance. The mayor believed that nearly all Savannahians just wanted the war to end. Besides, Arnold felt, "where resistance is hopeless it is criminal to make it." So the general and his staff shined their shoes and polished their buttons and made social calls to demonstrate that they did not intend to punish the city unduly. For some of Savannah's matrons, the pragmatic embrace of the enemy's presence ensured a measure of peace in the short run and perhaps better terms from the Union when the war was over. Sherman's military career had brought him to Georgia in the 1840s, when he first met several Savannahians. Nellie and Sherman were familiar, as he was friends with her brother. He kindly brought her letters from Chicago, and spoiled the children with sugar. Sherman and Howard missed their own children and delighted in the Gordon girls' antics.[43]

As somber Christmas celebrations began, the women of Savannah reconciled themselves to the presence of the Northerners. Nellie assured Willie that "Sherman's troops have treated the citizens and private property well here." The city's white inhabitants as a whole showed their gratitude for the peaceful transition by entertaining the invading forces at the Freemasons' Lodge. Within a week, seven hundred Savannahians had openly cast their lot with the Union.[44]

This rankled Willie. He knew the war was a lost cause for the South. While his family clung together in the besieged city, he had been on the move for three years. He worried about money, cotton sales, the ignominy of losing to the Yankees. The end of the war occasioned a brief but profound crisis of faith for Willie. "I pray constantly, earnestly, but it does no good," he wrote Nellie morosely. "I can't feel that God has given me his Grace and I cannot amend without it." Under the guidance of the Right Reverend Henry C. Lay, Willie was eventually confirmed in the Episcopal Church. "I can't realize that I have become a Christian," he rejoiced. To his apprehensive mother, he was careful to explain that he saw "but very little" difference between the "Episcopal and the Presbeterian [sic] forms of worship. The latter is endeared to me by associations connected with you, the former by associations connected with Nellie. I consider the form but of little consequence."[45]

Willie's concern about betraying his mother paled beside his belief that his wife had betrayed *him*. Despite her promise, Nellie was consorting with his adversary. He could not have been in Savannah to protect his family, and thus was not there to forbid her from opening their home to his foe. He had fought in hopes of "annihilating Sherman." Willie wrote to her in January 1865, "What really galls me is that you should associate with my enemies upon any other terms than those politeness demands from every lady."[46]

The visiting came to an end in March, when General Sherman ordered the removal of the families of Confederate officers from Savannah. Nellie kept her word and did not take the oath of loyalty to the Union. Sherman told her to join her family in Chicago. Nellie secured his promise to watch over her mother-in-law's house, but she would not leave until she had seen Willie. Sherman, knowing something about Nellie's temperament, provided a flag of truce so that she could await the rendezvous. After several attempts, the couple finally met, whereupon Nellie and the children—with escorts personally arranged by General Sherman—made their way to Illinois. Watching them leave, under the protection of the Union forces, Willie wrote, "was like tearing my heart out by the roots. It has haunted me like a nightmare ever since and will . . . to the end of my life." Her actions left him "humiliated, crushed, and stung."[47]

En route to Chicago, Daisy, Eleanor, and Alice met their uncles and saw their first snowfall, and generally bore up well until someone on the train began to sing "We'll Hang Jeff Davis to a Sour Apple Tree." Proudly, the girls began to shout a popular ditty:

> Jeff Davis rides a milk-white horse
> And Lincoln rides a mule—
> Jeff Davis is a gentleman,
> And Lincoln is a fool!

As her mother tried to shush her, Daisy said tearfully, "They shouldn't hang Jeff Davis on a *sour* apple tree . . . 'cause he's my papa's friend. I wouldn't care if they hung him to a *sweet* apple tree, but they shouldn't hang him on a *sour* one." Young Daisy, fervently attached to her father and his cause, was on her way to see her grandparents in the land of the enemy. Exhausted, weak from a near starvation diet, and confused, Daisy Gordon sobbed in her mother's arms.[48]

CHAPTER 2

A Savannah Childhood

The Chicago sojourn did not make a Yankee out of four-year-old Daisy Gordon, as her father feared it might. She was too ill to think about much else except how bad she felt. She and her sisters were so thin and malnourished upon arriving in Chicago that one of Nellie's friends described the girls as having "tow-colored hair and clay-colored skins," and looking "like poor Southern white trash." Rather than being insulted, Nellie shrugged concurrence. Weak and vulnerable physically, Daisy could not fight off an attack of what her mother called brain fever. This might have been encephalitis or meningitis, or something else altogether. "Brain fever" referred to several dire conditions that often resulted in blindness, deafness, insanity, or death. So it was not surprising that Nellie stayed glued to Daisy's bedside for two weeks. Everyone feared for her life. By March 1865 the delirium had passed, and Nellie reported that Daisy was improving. She particularly missed Willie. "Daisy says 'she loves her Papa,'" Nellie recounted, "'because he's been in the Rebel Army so long!' There's 4 year old patriotism!!" But the young Confederate was slow in recovering, and the attending doctors advised the family to coddle and cosset her to avoid a relapse. Daisy ultimately escaped the worst ravages of brain fever. When she was finally able to leave the sickroom, she began to learn about her very different Northern relatives. Daisy's grandmother Juliette Magill Kinzie had written down some of the family chronicle in a book entitled *Wau-bun*, published in 1857.[1]

Daisy's great-grandfather John Kinzie was the son of a Scottish immigrant, born in Canada in 1763. That same year, Great Britain secured the vast wilderness of the Northwest Territory, where Kinzie would make his living trading with Native Americans. In 1804, he and his wife, Eleanor Lytle McKillip Kinzie, acquired the first house in Chicago, from a French Canadian trader. It sat in a bend on the north side of the Chicago River, just opposite the newly garrisoned American frontier outpost Fort Dearborn. The Kinzie homestead was easily identifiable from the four Lombardy poplar trees in the front yard, and from the fact that it was "the only home of a white settler in Chicago for many years." Five Kinzie children grew up in the wilds: Margaret, Eleanor's daughter from her first marriage; John Harris Kinzie, born the year before the family moved to Chicago (and fated to be Daisy's grandfather); Ellen Marion, who married into the Wolcott family; Maria Indiana, who became David Hunter's wife; and the youngest, Robert Allen.[2]

From the tiny settlement in the shadow of the fort, John Kinzie carried on a thriving business with Native Americans over vast areas, while selling farm produce and other wares—including, briefly, slaves—to local settlers. Until the War of 1812 began, Kinzie also gained, probably through bribery, the exclusive contract to supply Fort Dearborn. He murdered one of his customers for threatening to expose him. The family story claims it was self-defense, and notes that Kinzie cared tenderly for his victim's grave ever after.[3]

Great-grandfather Kinzie had a secret life. During the War of 1812, he might have been a spy for England, and then a spy for America, or perhaps a double agent. Daisy's mother published the biography of John Kinzie, and even she had to admit that his murky maneuvers were ultimately "inexplicable." After some dislocation caused by the War of 1812, the Kinzies resumed their lives in their Chicago house, which, by 1816, had been joined by four others. Kinzie put his past behind him. His various jobs made him, Nellie wrote, "rich" in real estate, "for he owned nearly all the land on the North side of the Chicago River, and many acres on the South and West sides, as well as . . . over one hundred acres of land surrounding the original Kinzie homestead." When John Kinzie died in 1828, Chicago had fewer than one hundred residents, no newspaper, school, or church. But John Kinzie was honored as the "father of Chicago," respected for his good relations with Native Americans and acknowledged as the first white settler to establish a home inside what became the city limits.[4]

Daisy's grandfather John Harris Kinzie was a pillar of Chicago. He took up his father's profession of working with Native Americans before becoming personal secretary to Governor Lewis Cass of Michigan. John Harris Kinzie reportedly spoke Winnebago and thirteen other Indian languages. In 1827 he married Juliette Magill of Connecticut, an educated woman who read French, Latin, Spanish, and Italian; painted in watercolor and oil; did fine needlework; and played the piano.[5] Juliette had studied with noted educator Emma Willard, who taught that women were equal to men, and surely it was because of her influence that Juliette packed her piano and enthusiastically accompanied John in 1830 to the hinterlands of what would be south-central Wisconsin. Her remarkable journey is the centerpiece of *Wau-bun*. After a harrowing but successful time in Wisconsin, made more lucrative by the five-thousand-dollar federal award given to each of the four Kinzie siblings for claims stemming from the Blackhawk War, the two built their own Chicago home.[6]

John Harris Kinzie engaged in the wild land speculation of those days, and eventually owned valuable property in Chicago and significant farmland outside the city. He increased his wealth through investments in railroads, a copper mine, and a speedy ferry boat across Lake Michigan. In 1835, the year their daughter Eleanor, Daisy's mother, was born, Kinzie was president of the Chicago branch of the Second State Bank. Later in his career, he would help organize the Chicago Board of Trade and serve as the first president of the Illinois Saving Institution.[7]

His interests extended beyond economic development, however.

Kinzie was a founding member of the Chicago Athenaeum and the city's public schools, a manager of the Orphan Benevolent Association, president of the board of the volunteer fire department, and vice president of the Fireman's Benevolent Association. Saint James Episcopal Church so regularly benefited from Juliette and John's generosity that people called it the Kinzie Church.[8]

The Kinzies lived among Chicago's elite on the desirable north side. John hoped his associations and his wealth would make him the city's first mayor. His Democratic neighbor, William B. Ogden, defeated him and his Whig ticket, but four years later Kinzie proudly celebrated the election of Whig William Henry Harrison to the U.S. presidency. After the demise of the Whigs, Kinzie served as the chairman of the executive committee of the Republicans of Chicago. Too old for battle when the Civil War began, Kinzie became a U.S. Army paymaster.[9]

When Daisy was a girl and visited her grandparents, she witnessed gorgeously arrayed American Indians calling on Agent Kinzie to trade information and to seek his assistance before taking their concerns off to Washington. The meetings occurred on the front lawn, the participants sitting solemnly and thoughtfully on the ground, with her grandfather perched on a soapbox. Daisy—a hidden observer—found the assemblage strange because there was more silence than talking, at least until Grandma Kinzie served up refreshments.[10]

Though it is impossible to know how closely she herself encountered them, Daisy's family certainly respected Native Americans. According to British writer Harriet Martineau, who visited the Kinzies in 1834, they were "absolutely Indian in their sympathies and manners" and "the only persons I met with who, really knowing the Indians, had any regard for them." Daisy always felt herself to be more than usually connected to the nation's past, both through her family's extensive involvement with Native peoples and through her own youthful experiences. She idealized "Indian culture" as a healthy alternative to cramped urban living, and never forgot the family tales of the generous, brave, and compassionate Native Americans who were friends and comrades.[11]

Daisy's other great delight in Chicago was the block-long garden that lay between her grandparents' house and her great-uncle Robert's home. There the children ran and played, picnicked, told stories, and rested under the shade of tall trees. In 1865, Nellie enjoyed this time with her relatives, but she missed her husband. He could not leave the South yet—and even though the Civil War was over, it still divided them. The half dozen Kinzie servants left her little to do, and Nellie's active mind shifted from domestic life to national politics. Never a shrinking violet, Nellie traveled alone to Washington, staying with Aunt Maria and Uncle David Hunter. She meant to seek redress for the cotton belonging to her that Union forces had seized in Savannah.[12]

Exploiting family ties helped her gain reimbursement from the federal government, but it set her starkly against her Confederate husband. A man with a less finely honed sense of honor than Willie Gordon might have been glad of his wife's ability to employ her network of family and friends to recoup money owed, but Willie wrote her wrathfully that he "would be humiliated beyond endurance" at receiving "favors . . . through *your* influence and the Federal authorities, military or civil." He wanted nothing to do with those who defeated the South. Tension mounted between husband and wife.[13]

Nellie accused him of not trusting her. He could not make her understand his position, and her collusion was like a viper in his gut. Desperate to disprove her complicity, hoping he had misunderstood her, Willie opened Nellie's letters to his business partner, William Hayes Tison, and the children's nursemaid's notes to her sister. These confirmed that General Hunter had helped Nellie in her quest for federal compensation. Willie's scorn was stinging: "Pardon me, I humbly beseech you. I constantly forget that I am subjected and barely realize that besides country, cause, [and] hope, I seem about to lose (or have already lost) the love, honor and obedience once pledged me. What a pity that one so talented and so highly connected should have thrown herself away on a creature so stupid as to prefer honor and principle to interest and success!"[14]

As he suggested, Willie's trials went beyond his wife's disloyalty.

The Confederate surrender in April 1865 would prey on Willie's mind for decades. His pride in his military labor and the bonds formed with his fellow soldiers never dissipated, but the mortification of defeat hung about him like a dark cloud. Through it, he had to reestablish his business and reunite with his family. He let Nellie know in May that she and the children should remain in Chicago, "for I don't know where to get bread for my mouth and for the present am helpless to fill four or even one more." His depression colored everything, and the forced separation from Nellie and the girls increased his suspicions about their love for him. "Kiss the chicks and never let them forget," he warned, "that the word 'rebel' means an unfortunate man whom success would have made a hero and a patriot." Their daughter remained true, Nellie assured him: "Daisy says, she loves her dear Papa, she is a rebel, and he is a rebel. . . ."[15]

Willie, at least, had a home. He was lucky to be ensconced in his mother's house while she was with relatives in Macon, though he shared it with his fellow veteran David Waldhauer, and a destitute Savannah family, the Tatnalls. Waldhauer and the Tatnalls were without "a cent in the world, liv[ing] on rations received from the City," and without any future prospects, he told his mother sorrowfully. Sarah did not concur with her son's charitable view on the Tatnalls. She was frantic, lest she find herself unable to dislodge them all when it was time for her to return. The Tatnalls, she fretted, were "a slow family. . . . They stick like leeches." She wanted to be in Savannah, but Willie persuaded her to remain in Macon. "There is positively no money here. . . . ," he averred. "You have no conception of things. Actual starvation stares in the face persons even who have property but who can't sell it." The lack of money haunted him. He was internally torn about his wife and children—glad they were eating better and safe but desirous of their company, despite the humiliations. "We are, my dear Mother," Willie admitted, "poor indeed now and we must all prove our blood and our breeding by not being ashamed to own it or afraid to endure its privations & sufferings." Despite this sermon to Sarah, Willie's desperation drove him to consider a job in China.[16]

In June, while traveling with her parents, Nellie sustained a terrible blow: the unexpected death of her father. Arrangements fell to Nellie, and she entreated Willie to join her: "My Husband, I beseech you do not write cruelly to me! My heart is too sore. My poor mother is almost crazy." Luckily, events worked in their favor. President Andrew Johnson had recently proclaimed "amnesty and pardon" for most Confederate soldiers, which allowed Willie property, political rights, and the ability to travel freely. When Nellie sent him sixty dollars, he raced to her side, and finally, their physical proximity cleared the air between them. Willie was a savvy businessman who knew that while he was up north for his father-in-law's funeral, he could "raise money enough to enable me to go into the Country and get some of our Cotton into Market. If I fail," Willie confided to his mother, "God knows what will become of us all."[17]

By summer's end, the family was reunited in Savannah. The Tatnalls were banished, the house was put to rights, the girls found their former playmates, and Willie's cotton factor firm began to buy and sell the South's staple crop again. Belmont plantation slowly became productive once more. Not long after their return, Nellie was pregnant—evidence, perhaps, that the couple had well and truly overcome their own divide.

The birth of William Washington Gordon III in April of 1866 prompted a celebration, and the family focus shifted to the firstborn son. Daisy was a delighted big sister, interested in all the fuss. Uncle George Gordon waxed rhapsodic. He credited the baby's existence to Willie's wartime confession of faith. Like saints of old, Willie had "united [him]self with His Holy church . . . that His face was turned in love to you and your hopes fulfilled." Nellie prepared to show off young Bill in Chicago that autumn. She planned to take all the children except Daisy, who would be left with a cousin. It is not clear why.[18]

Family letters rarely mentioned Daisy, and then usually in association with some mishap. Willie and especially Nellie could fill four pages with vignettes of Eleanor's maturity, Alice's illnesses, and the baby's antics without mentioning Daisy. Willie devoted just one line to an accident. On August 4, 1865, he reported that "Daisey [sic] was pushed off the [railroad] cars and fell between them and [the] platform." Nellie noted briefly in July 1866 that "Daisy fell out of bed—on her head, as usual. . . ." She was perhaps more accident-prone than her sisters. That same year, a windowsill dropped on her hand, breaking two fingers badly enough that the adults considered—but rejected—amputation. When the physician completed his treatment, four-year-old Daisy said, "Well I *do* hope we are not going to have any more performances like this one!" Her response, which the family recorded as endearing, is more telling about Nellie's mothering than Daisy's ability to bear pain.[19]

Though seldom at the center of family life, Daisy was not a "problem child." One of her siblings commented that the feeling of being spoiled was "entirely absent from Daisy's lot at home." There was one time, however, when Daisy was physically very different from other girls: she had short hair. Neither choice nor aesthetics explained it, but rather a young cousin, who cleverly observed at a taffy pull that Daisy's hair was precisely the same color as the candy. He suggested braiding the taffy into the plaits that hung down her back. Daisy thought it a wonderful idea. The taffy stuck fast and hardened into the hair. Both had to be chopped off.[20]

As adults, the Gordon children attested to Daisy's lifelong "brilliant eccentricity." When her two youngest siblings were born, Mabel in 1870 and Arthur in 1872, Daisy was old enough to have to take some responsibility for them. Her "experiments in child raising," as Arthur termed it, often went awry. He compared Daisy's "absolutely illogical" reactions to "a weird dream." She was often late, because "time meant nothing in Daisy's scheme of things." Arthur insisted that "two and two by no means made four to her," and she was often "killingly funny" when she didn't mean to be. In the large Gordon family, with a remote father and an often self-absorbed mother, Daisy carved out her own niche, purposefully or not, with her eccentricities. Her brother said that "she had extraordinary intuition and very little logic." Her relatives dubbed her "Crazy Daisy," and to a degree, that became her role.[21]

She might have been unconventional, but Daisy was also kind. From an early age, she showed great sympathy for humans, animals, and even inanimate objects in distress. Eleanor remembered that Daisy felt so sorry for their china dolls one cold evening that she tucked them inside her nightgown and slept with their hard heads against her body to warm them. On another winter night, Daisy decided the family cow must be freezing. She plucked the blankets from the guest-room bed, ran outside, wrapped them around the surprised animal, and used safety pins to secure them. Unfortunately, not securely enough. The blankets slipped to the mud and were trampled. One day, Daisy and her mother saw a dog that had been killed on the road. The young altruist ordered the carriage to a stop. She gathered the dog in her arms, took it home, laid it on her mother's bed, and tried to revive it with Nellie's medicinal electric wand. She could not be convinced that the dog "was beyond resurrection."[22]

Nellie liked to entertain people with a story of the unexpected consequences of Daisy's nocturnal act of benevolence.

DAISY: Oh Mama you had better keep that $3.00 you owed me, because I spoiled one of your best embroidered linen pillow-cases.

MAMA: Why Daisy, how did you do that?

DAISY: It caught fire from the blue blanket. I'm so sorry! It was one of your handsomest blankets, too—one of the new ones. Too bad!

MAMA: But how did the blue blanket catch fire?

DAISY: Why the alcohol lamp fell over into the bed the other night.

MAMA: But what in the world were you doing with an alcohol lamp in the middle of the night?

DAISY: I was making a cup of tea. You know I came into your room at 4 o'clock the other morning, and woke you up, and asked if you would have a cup of tea?—and you said "Yes," and so I started to make the tea, and the lamp fell over on to the bed, and the blue blanket caught fire, and set the pillow case on fire, and the pillow case set the bed on fire, and it nearly set me on fire, too! But I put it out, and I made the cup of tea. You got that all right, didn't you?

MAMA: Oh yes, I got the cup of tea, Daisy. Thanks very much.[23]

While Nellie was involved in the children's upbringing, motherhood did not absorb her every moment. She entertained with the purpose of promoting her husband in Savannah society, followed current events diligently, and maintained a daily schedule of reading and correspondence. Nellie found time to write to prominent American author and women's rights supporter Great-aunt Sarah Josepha Hale. Mrs. Hale was also famous as the editor of *Godey's Lady's Book,* a popular periodical. Nellie suggested that the magazine's readers would enjoy Emily Dickinson's poem "The Lost Jewel." Hale dismissed it as already too familiar to subscribers but encouraged Nellie to write again "often," and to "keep the National Thanksgiving." Thanksgiving had long been the focus of Hale's energies. If all Americans concentrated on a common heritage for one day, Civil War wounds would surely begin to heal. Hale's argument convinced President Lincoln, who, in 1863, had proclaimed the last Thursday in November a nationwide holiday.[24]

Unlike the children, who seemed to be getting on fine, the family's financial situation remained critical. A day of national thanksgiving could not revitalize the cotton market in a state where the cotton crop had fallen from a high of seven hundred thousand bales produced in 1860 to fifty thousand five years later. Tison & Gordon managed to remain open and retain a reputation as a firm with "excellent factors and responsible men," but William Tison was no more flush than Willie. The partners had similar understandings of politics and gentility. During the Union occupation, Tison alone had the presence of mind to rescue the wife and children of Confederate president Jefferson Davis. He cleared a path through a legion of armed Yankees and starstruck Savannahians, installed them at the Pulaski House Hotel, and promised to cover their debts. Chivalrous, maybe, but Nellie thought him spineless. "He's a fool—a slow, hesitating, pokey creature! How can you stand him," she demanded of Willie. "I can't. I wanted him to borrow from the bank—today he had a splendid offer for the 62 bales—[and] instead of taking it and sending you 13, or 14,000 to reinvest, he refused."[25]

She kept her ear to the ground, recommending once that Willie buy corn on his travels because it would fetch a premium in Savannah. When Willie was away, Nellie was a frustrated go-between to Mr. Tison. "I wish I were your partner," she fumed. "I'm not fit for quiddling about a house—and I hate it." Nellie's peevishness was born of a feeling of powerlessness and the ache of missing him. "Daisy and Alice are both sleeping with me, but I wish it was you instead," she confessed. She also worried that the stress would make Willie ill, and offered equal measures of advice and adulation: "Do not apologize my love for telling me of your business troubles. I wish to share all things with you—and if I can not remedy evils, at least I can sympathize with and perhaps comfort you."[26]

The climb out of what Arthur Gordon recalled as "financial ruin" was slow going. Willie remained pessimistic about the future of the South, regularly betting against its full recovery. For example, he recorded: "Jonathan W. Anderson bets me one box (100) cigars there will be 2,000,000 Bales cotton more this year. . . ." In his tiny, leather-covered pocket diaries, Willie scratched down notes to himself, recipes for medicines, contracts with gardeners to keep Laurel Grove Cemetery lots weed-free, and Civil War poetry. But the diary also provided proof that the Gordons' finances did improve. It contained records of money he borrowed and lent, sums he spent regularly on pew rents at Christ Church, on "candy," "whiskey," "cigars," the "orphan asylum," "Mrs. Kinzie," "church" (five dollars to the "African church," and two dollars to the Baptists, for instance), "Nellie house" and "Nellie allowance," and "Mother."[27]

Oblivious, at age five, to family worries about money, Daisy had no reason to believe she lived in anything other than a secure and prosperous world. While she was growing up, the Gordons vacationed at resorts and hotels in the North and in the South. When

Daisy was older, especially memorable were the summers spent in the foothills of the Appalachian Mountains of northeastern Georgia. There, at Etowah Cliffs, the home of Aunt Eliza and Uncle William Henry Stiles, scads of relatives gathered to swim, fish, play dress up, pick flowers, and explore. There might be as many as twenty cousins—enough for wonderful games of Indians, of Yankees and Rebels, or playacting. Daisy's cousin Caroline Couper Stiles described her as "very small" and "very plucky," and therefore, Daisy often wound up in stunts that were physically challenging or hurtful. As a "Yankee spy," she was once "crammed . . . through a knot hole in an oak tree," where she stayed, defiant, until "at last her prison-keepers relented and hauled her out." Another turn in the same role found her concealed under a bed, until "she was dragged out by the hair of her head," only to conclude the ordeal with a flourish by singing "'Hang Old Jeff Davis on a Sour Apple Tree,' as she was hung off the bedpost."[28]

Everyone liked pretending that the schoolhouse among the walnut trees was a hotel that served the delicious and imaginative concoction called Peach Gobble, paid for in paper money expeditiously cut out and colored the night before. For the price of more handmade dollars, cousins driving festive goat- and donkey-powered "streetcars" carried the others to the Etowah River for a swim. They "lived in trees," Caroline recollected: in the roots of the huge oaks, where they each had their own "special room"; in the fruit trees they raided for snacks; and among the scuppernong arbors laden with plump, round, green grapes. Daisy wrote to her father ecstatically that "the playhouse is finished, it is a nice little house in the grove and we have one half for a playhouse and Miss Atternay the governess has the other to teach school in. . . . We have white washed our playhouse and put little curtains to the window." The girls divided it up into "a dining room, three bedrooms, a pantry, and a kitchen," and stocked it with lovely things to eat, given to them by indulgent adults.[29]

So many cousins together meant enough people to participate in and be an audience for amateur theater. Daisy wrote scripts, planned costumes, and played as many parts as the others would let her. She excelled at acting. The girls particularly liked to perform a vivid Mary Queen of Scots, with a gruesome but audience-pleasing beheading, complete with purple pokeberry juice at the appropriate moment. They charged admission and sent the proceeds to Indian charities. Making paper dolls was similarly absorbing, and the cousins acknowledged Daisy's artistic skills as she elaborately painted the figures that Caroline sketched. A crowning achievement was the "Reynard the Fox Dinner" that Daisy dreamed up. The cousins drew the Etowah family dining table and then crowded it with the animal representations of the family from the book *Reineke Fuchs*. Daisy was the "most gifted writer and illustrator" for the *Malbone Bouquet,* a summer newspaper the children produced in which her first poems appeared. Poetry was important to every member of her family, and Daisy never stopped creating poetry for solace and for amusement.[30]

Like her sisters, Daisy learned to read and write with the help of her family and Lucille Blois, who taught the oldest Gordon girls "in the garret room of [her] house on Chippewa Square" in Savannah. Fellow pupil Caroline Couper remembered her as "a dried-up but very sprightly old maid." Although Miss Blois was listed as a "high school teacher" in the Savannah city directory, she could not improve Daisy's innovative spelling, a lifelong source of vexation to her family. Her niece, Daisy Lawrence, implied that Daisy suffered from a reading disability. Seeking a reason for "Daisy's weird spelling," Lawrence concluded that it "stemmed from the same emotional complex as her equally weird reasoning methods." Daisy's misspellings could be quixotic, but her mistakes were not consistent, and learning disabilities are not flawlessly diagnosed from the distance of more than a century. On the other hand, research today suggests that abundant inventive talent often attends dyslexia, which can be accompanied by poor spelling. Daisy's creative abilities were obvious, even in her childhood, and art would be her avocation in later life. Perhaps Daisy's spelling was caused by disinterest. Eleanor recalled that her sister "was conscientious about her lessons" but not "especially enthusiastic about any one of them."[31]

Daisy much preferred to play. At one summer vacation on the Isle of Hope, south of Savannah, she and her siblings fished, caught crabs, sunbathed, sailed, swam, and practiced the piano, which Nellie made sure accompanied them. Daisy once acquired a gray rabbit, "not as big as a little kitten," and tamed it. Being outdoors with friends and animals was her favorite way to spend time—even when she had to be brave. There is some evidence that Daisy rescued a three-year-old child from drowning when she herself was only eight. This was taken in stride in the duty-bound Gordon family, but surely the wisdom of being prepared for an emergency was not lost on her. Growing up after the war, with the luxury of carefree summer holidays, Daisy forgot neither the curative power of the outdoors nor the sheer bliss of sharing those joys with her companions. Cousin Caroline remembered Daisy as a girl with self-confidence, courage, perseverance, and a great love of doing and being involved—but also as "maddeningly erratic." "While you never knew what she would do next," Caroline recalled, "she always did what she made up her mind to do. . . ."[32]

Her childhood lessons went far beyond Miss Blois's teaching. Daisy grew up in a large, generally happy household led by a narcissistic mother and a taciturn father. She was part of a wider social fabric stretching from Chicago to New England to Savannah and its environs. Once the anxieties and fears of Civil War were behind the Gordons, she lacked for nothing material. Daisy's brother later stated that she "learnt the self-reliance acquired when playthings and luxuries are absent, and parents must be helped instead of leaned upon." The wartime jumble in her child's mind of gallant men in uniform, an absent father, a willful and independent mother, the family's financial worries, and securing the center of attention only when ill left a curious and lasting impression.[33]

CHAPTER 3

Schooling in the South and Beyond

Daisy's youth fostered wonderful memories. Her hometown was breathtakingly beautiful, an attractive city with leafy parks, gorgeous architecture, and refined emporiums. Savannah's population was profoundly civic-minded. The Gordons had deep roots in Georgia and Daisy's early years were fundamentally happy. Following the Civil War and her brief stay in Illinois, she experienced a sheltered and privileged childhood in an environment that quickly put depravation behind it and looked forward. The family regained its comfortable lifestyle and Daisy, though seldom the cynosure, was well loved.

Identifying strongly as a Southerner, she enjoyed a sense of place in her community. As she grew older, Daisy reaped the benefits of having a Chicago-born mother and a father whose business travel took him outside the region: she would be sent to boarding school in the North, and she journeyed abroad before marriage. Thus Daisy approached travel fearlessly, encountered other cultures appreciatively, and made lifelong friendships with people from outside Georgia.

But Savannah was her home. Established in 1733 by James Oglethorpe, the founder and one of the trustees of the British colony of Georgia, the city began as a fortress on a bluff forty feet above the

Savannah River—placed to avoid flooding and to observe approaching Spanish invaders. Oglethorpe established Savannah's unique town plan with four wards, or neighborhoods; the centerpiece of each was a public square. Each square was surrounded by building lots: four trust lots for public structures and forty house lots for settlers. This orderly layout ensured that each ward would be home to at least forty soldiers to subdue any potential Spanish threat. And because this urban design was repeated in twenty additional wards for more than a century after Oglethorpe's departure from Georgia, modern Savannah was given its most famous features: inviting, parklike squares. The early colonists expected to grow silkworms to export cloth, or grapes to make wine, yet like so many plans concocted in England by those with little experience of America, these schemes came to naught. But the surrounding land was fertile and the winters mild, and immigrants from Scotland, England, France, Portugal, and Germany arrived, bringing an entrepreneurial spirit and faith traditions that ranged from Judaism to Methodism. Oglethorpe cultivated amicable relationships with the Native American populations in the area, primarily with Tomochichi, the leader of the Yamacraw.

Oglethorpe resisted the encroachment of slavery into Georgia because he wanted Georgia to be the place where England's hardworking poor could become wealthy. Until 1750 the practice was outlawed, but by then the settlement was in decline, and slavery seemed to assure the desirable but elusive economic success. Thus it was that when Georgia became a royal colony in 1753, one-third of its inhabitants were enslaved. After the American Revolution and the first siege of Savannah in 1779, the city served as the new state's first capital, until Augusta replaced it in 1785. President George Washington noted during his triumphal visit to the city in 1791 that Savannahians exported rice, tobacco, lumber, and indigo, and to a lesser extent, hemp and cotton.[1]

The first half of the nineteenth century was a time of growth, due in part to the invention of the cotton gin. It mechanized the extraction of cottonseeds from the cotton boll and thus greatly sped up a very labor-intensive task. Slavery and the cotton gin allowed the crop to be "king" across the South. Production of cotton increased so rapidly that, along with Savannah's lucrative rice harvest, the town became one of the nation's busiest export cities. When railroads like Daisy's grandfather's Central of Georgia opened the interior of the state, more cotton could be brought to port, adding to the concentration of wealth in Savannah. With this, citizens overcame yellow-fever epidemics and terrible fires, and built mansions, schools, hotels, theaters, lecture halls, and all the appurtenances of polite society to entice investors and visitors. The latter often commented on the Spanish moss that draped artistically from the live oak trees, one calling it "drooping funereal lichen resembling a perpetual downpour of rain," but most thinking it added to the city's romantic charm. As modern improvements rose around them, city leaders founded the Georgia Historical Society in 1839 to preserve their ancestors' achievements. But when the Civil War came and white men left to become soldiers, the town fell into disrepair. At war's end, clearing out the Savannah River, rebuilding the port, and selling the cotton that Sherman had not commandeered helped Savannah pay off its four-hundred-thousand-dollar debt and reestablish itself as an important regional center.[2]

In Daisy's youth Savannah was a city in transition. All around her the social fabric of the South was changing. Slaves were freed, made citizens, and the men given the right to vote. The Gordons had to decide whether to pay their former slaves wages or look for white help. Uncle William Stiles decreed that his family at Etowah Cliffs would not hire any African Americans, but Nellie's servants were black. To run a house as large as hers, Nellie depended on the cooking skills of Eliza Hendry and the myriad talents of other African Americans.[3]

The Gordons' status insulated their children from many unsettling aspects of postwar Savannah. Squabbling among fractious dock workers, prostitutes plying their trade, the cries of the pushcart vendors on Broughton Street, and the tragedies affecting those confined to the poorhouse and the jail were all kept from Daisy and her siblings. She would not have seen much of the bittersweet conversion from bondage to freedom for the city's black population. While she might have noticed the presence of the Freedmen's Bureau, mutual aid societies, Republican political clubs, schools, and churches that endeavored to meet the needs of the freedmen and women, the confusion, dislocation, intimidation, riots, and murder of African Americans by white supremacist groups would not have been discussed in front of children. Indeed, Willie Gordon left a record of giving that suggests generosity on his part toward freedmen and women.

His growing brood of children, his wife, and his business were his main occupations. In the summer of 1867, as he kept an eagle eye on the cotton crop, Nellie and the children traveled to Chicago for a holiday. Her household responsibilities decreased in her mother's home, and it was "not the custom" there, as it was in Savannah, for children "to dress up and parade out every afternoon." Nellie visited friends but mostly spent time with her brothers and her mother. The widowed Juliette was the family's inveterate communicator, full of financial updates, neighborhood news, and worries about her sons' monetary failures and disastrous love lives. She was the driving force keeping *Wau-bun* and her other books in print.[4]

The Kinzie family matriarch maintained a close relationship with her only daughter and kept abreast of her grandchildren's lives, particularly Eleanor (the eldest) and Daisy, her namesake. On All Saints' Day in 1868, the day after Daisy's eighth birthday, Grandmother Juliette penned a prayer to Nellie: "May God spare her to be a pride and a comfort to us all as we tread the down-hill path of life! If she is to her Mother what that mother has been to her parent, she will knit in that blessed fellowship with the holy ones whose anniversary we this day commemorate."[5]

The unexpected death of such a vital element of the family was a grievous blow. It began with one of Juliette's frequent headaches. In mid-September 1870 she and a pregnant Nellie were otherwise savoring a vacation together in Amagansett, Long Island. To alleviate the pain, the women sent out to the local pharmacist for her usual medicine, quinine pills. When the package of drugs arrived, Juliette hesitated, because it was unmarked. In an attempt to assuage her mother's worries—and with a rashness that her daughter Daisy would often duplicate—Nellie popped a tablet into her own mouth. Quelling her reservations, Juliette then took her normal dose of two pills. Unluckily, Juliette's fears were realized. The women had not swallowed quinine. The unmarked package of pills contained morphine, a strong painkiller derived from the poppy. One morphine pill made Nellie ill, but two killed Juliette Kinzie within hours.[6]

Depression followed bereavement. As she did when her father died, Nellie sought solace in Willie and in her faith. It was the practical Eleanor who proved the most helpful as their mother mourned, while the youngest provided distraction. Daisy was nine years old, an intuitive and sensitive girl who felt her mother's distress. Her Crazy Daisy role had a use. She could offer comic relief, and in this way ease Nellie's heartache. It gave her a niche in the family, a role to play. It also allowed her happy spirit to bubble up even when those around her were gloomy.

Willie and Nellie ruled the home with unquestioned sovereignty and drilled into their progeny the importance of duty, obedience, loyalty, and respect, while simultaneously demonstrating such qualities in the care of their own parents. Daisy imbibed these values no less than her siblings, but she learned at this time that her actions, even when not intended to cause amusement, sometimes did. And sometimes there could be a value to that. When Daisy left home, she took the family's ethics with her to boarding schools chosen to reinforce, not challenge, those principles.

Because Nellie came from a line of educated women, she made certain that her daughters were properly schooled. At age twelve, Daisy followed Eleanor to Miss Emmett's school in Morristown, New Jersey, and a year later she again tailed her sister, to the Virginia Female Institute (VFI) in Staunton. VFI was an Episcopal school founded in 1844, to which the venerable Robert E. Lee had sent his daughters, thinking it an "admirably conducted and superior Institution for Young Ladies." When Daisy attended, from 1874 to 1875, the curriculum included traditional subjects such as mathematics, social studies, French, English grammar, spelling, religion, and elocution. Daisy continued her piano studies and especially loved the drawing classes.[7]

She returned home for idyllic holiday breaks, during which school friends might visit and interesting scrapes ensue. Once Daisy promised her friend Bessie that she could remove her unsightly freckles and it wouldn't hurt a bit if Bessie just sang through the process. When "wild sounds" and "shrieks of agony" were heard instead, the family flew upstairs to see Daisy urging "sing, Bessie, sing," as she bent over her, picking out the freckles with a needle.[8]

Summers filled quickly with gatherings as Nellie continued her efforts to build up Willie's stature in the community. She included the older children in special dinners with elite guests, such as the one she hosted for Georgia's second Episcopal bishop, John W. Beckwith, and Savannah philanthropist George W. J. DeRenne. Bishop Beckwith had been a Confederate chaplain, and he and Willie enjoyed each other's company. DeRenne was an Englishman who lived nearby at the lush Wormsloe plantation and who, at the time of the Gordons' dinner, was considering deeding land to Savannah for the education of African American children.[9]

Nellie went all out, serving, as she described to Alice, "Oysters on the half shell, Strained tomato soup, Broiled shad, and potato balls, White fricassee of chicken with asparagus, Tenderloin of beef . . . cooked with Mushrooms, rice, new potatoes with parsley sauce and spinach, Stewed shrimp, venison shanks and green peas, Dressed lettuce and dressed tomatoes, Orange sherbet, strawberries and cream, nuts, candied ginger and prunes, cake—Then cheese and crackers—then black coffee." Accompanying this was "champagne, hock, Chateau Lafite of 1864, [Chateau] Yquem [a dessert wine], pear sherry and Old Madeira, and Burgandy."[10]

Perhaps spurred by DeRenne's example, Daisy created the Helpful Hands Club—her first foray into organizing a group of girls. Established with the assistance of her cousins, the club's purpose was "to help others." The enthusiastic members made plans via that mainstay of children's communication, the tin-can telephone. One cousin shouted into a can, and at the end of the string, in the house next door, the other girl held another can to her ear. As a contingency, they sent servants scuttling between the houses with the same message. The club had a grand idea—to assist an immigrant family of fruit sellers by making clothing for the children. Alas, none of the Helpful Hands could sew. Not daunted, Daisy decided to lead them in learning. Although she unaccountably forced "them all to thread their needles with their left hands," the girls persevered. The poorly sewn clothes they produced could not withstand the rough-and-tumble life of the Italian children, and the girls became known as the Helpless Hands Club. The Gordons laughed at another of Crazy Daisy's stubborn schemes, but the good-heartedness behind it was plain.[11]

When she was a young teen, the thought of leaving for boarding school took the gloss off the end of summer break. "Do let me stop school," Daisy beseeched, "I hate it so and I don't believe I learn a thing." Her message was mixed, at best, for her postscript read, "Do please let me go to school, I mean stop school." Her letter came from Etowah, where she and her cousins were happily absorbed in a charity performance of a tableau called "The Sister Spirits."[12]

Daisy was at home when a horrific yellow-fever epidemic struck among the twenty thousand Savannahians in the late summer of 1876. Nellie's friend Belle Spivey quickly succumbed. When a young cousin next became sick, the family held a conference. Willie insisted that Nellie take the children and leave the city. Nellie refused—unless he went with them. Conscientious Willie would not desert the Savannah Benevolent Society as he and other members moved swiftly to assist the suffering. At that point, Nellie recorded in her lengthy account of the contagion, "All the children were willing to stay in Savannah with the exception of Daisy. She wanted to leave at once. I reproached her," Nellie wrote. "'Would you not want to stay here,' I asked, 'and die with your family?' 'I would like to live anywhere with my family' said Daisy 'but I don't want to die with my family here or anywhere else.'" The opinionated girl could not be dissuaded. A compromise was reached. Daisy's brother Bill went to the home of cousins in Morristown, New Jersey, taking a gun and his Bible, his two most prized possessions. The other five children went to Etowah Cliffs. Nellie stayed closer, in Guyton, because Willie promised to join her regularly. The epic proportions of the outbreak meant he was seldom with her. She complained irately. "[M]y place is right here with you," she swore. Willie urged her to think of their children. "Not at all . . . they can stay here and get yellow fever," Nellie insisted, "What do I care for them in comparison to you!"[13]

The five-month ravage killed 1,594 people, or 1 in every 15 Savannahians. The parents of the Italian children for whom the Helpful Hands Club made clothes both died. Thirty-three people expired on one September day, Nellie wrote to Alice. Willie saw this all first-hand, as his intrepid work with the Benevolent Society took him among the poor, both black and white. He visited the segregated hospital to make sure the African American patients were being tended. His hands were full at the office, as a number of his clerks came down with the disease. He stinted his own sleep and gave barely a thought to his own health as he made twice-daily rounds of his district, where he nursed the sick, called in physicians (when they could be found), comforted the grieving, and made arrangements for disposition of the bodies. When the illness reached Guyton, Nellie also gave of her time and energy to care for the dying.[14]

So certain was Willie that the 1876 outbreak would prove cataclysmic that, as soon as Belle Spivey passed away, he wrote a will leaving everything to Nellie. His letter informing her of this fact was full of tenderness and advice: "Educate our children as well as your means will allow. Teach them never to go in debt and that labor is honorable. Impress upon the girls that an honest man who has learned to work and support himself is preferable for a husband to a man born rich, and that a wife, to be a helpmeet, must conform to the means of her husband." Whether or not Nellie ever read the letter to their children, it seems likely that the warnings against indebtedness and husbands with inherited wealth were conveyed to the girls throughout their youths, since they were among Willie's guiding principles.[15]

Etowah escaped the yellow fever. The Gordons regrouped in

Savannah and grieved for their losses, including Willie's business partner, William Tison. Daisy recalled "a perfectly silent, almost deserted city, nothing to be seen in the streets except hearses carrying away the dead." Perhaps she was ready, then, to leave for Edgehill School in Albemarle County, Virginia, and to make new friends.[16]

Edgehill's curriculum included geography and German, and Daisy learned to write home in tolerable French. Her drawing talent was evident with every letter that included dress designs. An intricate "calisthenics dress" adorned one note, while a detailed bodice took up most of another. At both VFI and Edgehill, Daisy earned prizes and top marks in some subjects, including piano, speech, drawing, and French. Though she proudly wore her medal on a gold necklace chain, the academies emphasized the social graces. The idea that an elite Southern girl would prepare for a profession was nearly unthinkable. Even Nellie expected boarding school to make her daughters into scintillating hostesses and good wives. While Elizabeth Cady Stanton, Susan B. Anthony, and others had laid out the reform agenda at the first woman's rights conference at Seneca Falls, New York, twelve years before Daisy's birth, the apex of the women's rights movement was still decades ahead.[17]

And so Daisy harbored no thoughts of a career or agitated for women's rights, even while attending a Northern school. It was not her lot in life that she kicked against as a young woman; it was boarding-school rules of conduct that frustrated her. Girls were required to be ladylike at all times and leave school grounds only with prior permission. Daisy yearned to roll down hills, investigate interesting paths, ride horseback, and pick wildflowers, regardless of fences. "I can't be good in this old school," she moaned. "I don't do all my duty, and when I say my prayers at night, I'm so, so tired, and sleepy, that I can't pray for all I want, and in the morning I don't have time, and I fly into passions, and do bad things. . . ." From Edgehill she declared, "Mama, I can't keep all the rules, I'm too much like you."[18]

She stoutly professed herself ready to pay the price for her high spirits. Bursting for adventure, Daisy described how she and a girlfriend once ducked out of their room after hours and made straight for the spookiest place in the school—the shadowy corridor "on the one-eyed French teacher's floor"—there to terrify themselves with ghost stories until midnight. But, "oh, how I suffered for it," Daisy reported to Nellie. The canny teachers discovered them "of course," and she "caught it." It was the *worst* kind of punishment: a gang of teachers looming over her, cataloging her sins, and reading chapter and verse from the Bible to nail their points home. "I'd rather," Daisy groused, "have had you swear at me for an hour." Still, she felt she'd withstood the chastisement nobly: "I smiled a little sickly smile / And went out the door / And the subsequent proceedings / Interested me no more!" Daisy wrote her story so amusingly that she seems to have escaped maternal scolding for using "subsequent" when she really meant "previous."[19]

Money and clothing were all-consuming topics in Daisy's letters home. The Gordon children were sent funds, but it was never enough for Daisy. She often asked for more, and angrily blamed her younger sister Alice for financial misdeeds. In Daisy's eyes, Alice burned through their allowance and was untruthful about where she spent it. Daisy pointedly reconstructed her own expenses for her grandmother and for her parents, especially when she thought she might persuade one of them to underwrite her. A typical letter would find her needing $1.40 for travel, $.75 a week for washing, a quarter for shoe polish, and $.40 for two yards of "ruffling." This sort of list could move her "darling Sweet Granny" to send Daisy a few spare cents.[20]

As she aged, she developed a sense of style and strong ideas about outfits that suited her. She sketched for Nellie her preferred bodice or skirt designs. "My precious Mother," one letter began, "this is how I want my blue bunting, please if you have not commenced to make it this way the skirt only takes 5 yards (!) and there is very little silk on it only the under vest and sash, the plaited skirt must be plain around the hips but the plaits commence under the sash a dark blue silesia skirt will go under the skirt instead of silk and never shown." Accompanying this were four intricate drawings. All the Gordon women could wax eloquent about lace or ribbon or beautiful fabric. Daisy yearned for modish clothing purchased in New York or Paris, but the creations of local dressmakers or Gordon family servants were more affordable. Yet weekend trips away from boarding school called for the latest fashions. While Nellie understood the importance of good clothing, she and Daisy tangled about the cost.[21]

They also squabbled over spelling. For Daisy, "calisthenics" had two *l*'s, and "soirée" was "suarray." She mixed up *s*'s and *c*'s. Sometimes her letters contained extraordinary errors; for example, the way she worded her hope "to pass in my Guid to Knoledge exination." Such mistakes earned her tart rebukes, which then called forth heated explanations or penitent promises. "Mama, I am going to try to be very good, and practice and study hard, so you won't be disappointed in me again, after today." This fear of disappointing Nellie prompted Daisy to include in nearly every letter an accounting of her transgressions, however slight, with a pledge of better behavior in the future. Eventually, Daisy grew impatient with the reprimands. Because letters were passed around the family, she once insisted that her mother write "strictly private" on those containing a dressing down, so that she could keep them away from her sisters.[22]

Sometimes Nellie softened her lectures with humor. "Please remember . . . ," she admonished, "that a person's bust means both their bosoms and according to your description of Alice's 'busts' the unfortunate child has four—two in front I suppose and two behind, I conclude, which is certainly more than her share and I don't wonder her dress had to be let out." On occasion, Nellie could be tender. For her birthday in 1874, Daisy thanked her mother for the gift of a Bible, and for "such a funny little letter, about your loving me. I love you too my own mama, more than I can tell. . . ." Yet every time Daisy erred, she feared more than anything the loss of Nellie's affection. "I'd rather have you scold me to death," she wrote plaintively, "than not take any notice of me."[23]

Tableaux and skits offered some relief from bothersome school rules and strict parents. Daisy's enthusiasm for theater had not decreased. She gave elaborate attention to her costumes. Because she was short and thin, Daisy was cast as Little Boy Blue and as a hunched-over old man. Overcome again by apprehension at the possibility of Nellie's disapproval of the fun she had been having, she penned an ardent justification: "Mabbey you think that we have too much playing in this school, but we don't, we have to study so hard, and oh they are so strict that we have very little play at all."[24]

Occasional outings and good friends enlivened her days. One January term began with a "bilious" fever, but, "oh, Mama," Daisy related, "Miss Burn was so good to me, she took me down in her room, and I had everything I wanted, she always takes me down there when I am sick." Miss Burn was likely to have been a teacher, but she could have been an older student. It was lucky for Daisy to have such a harbor, for illness—especially earaches—struck frequently. Sometime in her youth she caught malaria, which was not uncommon in the South, and then suffered recurring bouts of it. The bilious fever subsided, and Daisy recovered enough by February to enjoy the cold snap: "Just think I went skating the other day, and have been sleigh riding four times, and made a snow man, since the snow has lasted so long."[25]

One lingering winter freeze claimed a robin's life, moving the girls to tears and Daisy to the vigorous organization of a proper funeral. She made a "shroud and a little cap" for the dead bird. The young mourners laid him in a box decorated with pins exactly "like silver-headed nails" for a stately coffin. Daisy made herself the officiating minister, and conducted six pallbearers as they recited in turn the long poem "Who Killed Cock Robin?" In lugubrious tones the girls sang "The North Wind Doth Blow" for his elegy. Filing out, they gazed one last satisfied time at the tombstone. The neat hand-lettering proclaimed: "Here lies Cock Robin / Snug as a Bug in a Rug."[26]

Daisy was a popular girl. She joined Theta Tau, a secret group akin to the sororities multiplying on college campuses at that time. Theta Tau supplied the sense of belonging Daisy liked and provided the absorbing activity of acquiring badges. Badges seem to have been unique to Theta Tau; it is a mystery where or with whom the idea originated. When Alice obtained the L.U.V. badge (the girls never spelled out the esoteric abbreviation) before Daisy did, it drove the impecunious older sister to distraction. Long and bitter protests flew to Mama about the unfairness of Alice never paying for the soap, pins, shoe polish, and clothes mending they both required. Saving up for the L.U.V. badge was making Daisy seem like a miser in front of her friends, she objected. Still, it was worth it. Whatever their backgrounds or differences, when they came together for meetings, when they worked toward earning their badges, when they shared confidences, the Theta Tau sisterhood eased her homesickness and felt like a family.[27]

During an era when the sexes were separated and girls spent most of their time in one another's company, same-sex crushes were commonplace. Using flowery language, adolescents described flirtations and special friendships, which were frequent and generally accepted in boarding schools then. Daisy's extravagant 1875 Valentine's Day haul at VFI proved several classmates held her in particularly high regard. She crowed about "three valentines, beauties, every one, and the largest came in a box, and is the prettiest one in school, and two lovely little ones." Ashamed then of boasting to her parents, Daisy was careful to add, "Nell got one very pretty one, prettier than mine." In 1874, Daisy's best friend was Lelia Gittings, and while she doesn't appear to have kissed and "slobber[ed] with" Lelia the way Daisy reported Eleanor did incessantly with Ida Ewing, Daisy did have what Alice called a "spoon" at Edgehill. It might have been Lucie Berrien McIntosh, for whom Daisy composed a poem in November 1877 that concluded:

> I'm sure there's not a wish that's new,
> That, Lucie, I can breathe for you,
> But this, I'll promise, dear, to pray
> That you may love me more each day!

The girls sometimes "slept out" of their own rooms and spent the night with their spoons. Alice wrote of sleeping out two nights in succession, "because Daisy wanted to sleep with one of her spoons."[28]

Another great pal at Edgehill was bad-girl Belle Cross. "Built in splendid proportions" and standing six feet tall, Belle was the adopted daughter of Maryland banker John S. Giddings. The wealthy Giddings family knew the Lincolns and owned an estate near Baltimore. Regardless of her family, Nellie disapproved. Daisy and Belle both loved fun, but Belle seems to have lacked the sense of propriety inculcated into the Gordon children. Belle came near to expulsion, as Daisy related, for "shooting a pistol and writing 'Come in Students' on an old tumble down gate." Only Belle's penitent spirit saved her. When Nellie warned against the friendship, Daisy's defense tumbled out in a touchingly honest letter not expressly calculated to calm Nellie's fears. "I am devoted to her," Daisy declared. "She is the most fascinating creature I ever met . . . her great fault is carrying on with men, and I know you can trust me for not doing that, and also from doing anything I think wrong (against God, I mean). I can never be more than a friendly schoolmate of Belle's for in the first place she don't like me enough and in the second place she talks ('vulgar') to other girls though never to me and that is a thing I never could stand." Yet clearly something drew Daisy to this appealingly wayward friend. It is impossible to know how much time Daisy spent with Belle Cross, but it is just as easy to imagine Daisy dutifully spurning Belle as it is to imagine the friendship—fueled by her mother's censure—continuing in secret.[29]

That year of Belle was Daisy's "happy, happy [time] at Edge-hill." At term's end she wondered "how any mortal could have managed to squeeze as much pleasure in so short a space of time. I can hardly realize that I will never see some of the girls again. School girl love is called silly, but I feel that in all my after life I can never love as warmly and purely as I do now." With youth's rapid rebound, Daisy described in the same letter to her mother a dance she attended where she did not know any of the men there, but bravely "went in heart and soul" and "never had a better time in my life." Her dance card was full, and she received other invitations, too. A Mr. "Cockral" paid court to her, telling her that she was "the prettiest girl at Edge-hill" and that "one glance of my eye was more piercing than a thousand words," and that she was "the light of the room, etc." He frightened her a bit, she confessed, because he was "not a boy but a man and he has never fallen in love with anyone yet." Daisy held him off, as she knew her father "would not like" Mr. Cockerel flattering her in such words.[30]

Daisy's lessons in courtship and love came from her sister and older girls at school, and from observing her parents and reading novels. Willie's love for his wife remained strong throughout their marriage. When Daisy was fourteen, he wrote to Nellie: "On this, the eighteenth anniversary of our marriage, permit me to say what I have always felt,—that no man was ever blessed with a more loving and devoted wife,—that you have labored and contrived and economized unceasingly to promote my welfare and that you have sacrificed your own wishes and pleasures to further mine." Nellie's tart tongue and tempestuous nature balanced her milder husband. Daisy was a witness to their love and the negotiations of their relationship.[31]

Alternative approaches to love could be found in novels. Novel reading was considered risky for girls, because love stories were thought to awaken sexual desires best kept dormant. Nellie absolutely forbade Daisy to read *Hester Morley's Promise,* a popular novel of that era. If Daisy had dipped into it, which seems likely, she would have encountered the tale of the strong-willed daughter of an Anglican vicar, Miss Waldron. It was she who actually ruled the church through her father. She felt the seminary was her "true home, and the pulpit was her sphere." The heroine's assertiveness was almost certainly not as troubling for Nellie as the subsequent romance between Miss Waldron and a priest. Though Daisy had successfully received "a great many callers" on New Year's Day in 1878, it was not until her season at a New York boarding school—or more precisely, not until her holidays *from* her New York boarding school—that she encountered young men outside of fiction.[32]

The Mesdames Mathilde and Fannie Charbonnier ran the boarding school bearing their surname at 36 East Thirty-fifth Street. The eighty young women who attended nicknamed them and it "the Chars." In September of 1878, at the age of seventeen, Daisy trailed

Eleanor to the Chars, where students were strictly forbidden to be seen with a man unchaperoned—not even, as Daisy discovered, a relative. The pupils wore uniforms like French schoolgirls, and in their classes attended to skills that would make them suitable partners for ambitious men.[33]

Daisy, who idealized her father, was certain she would loathe her Yankee classmates. Her first report was as caustic as her initial impression of Edgehill. "Nannie Brigham is on one side of me and for the rest of the girls—they are as 'ugly as the devil before day,' but 'polite as punch.' I am determined to hate them all except [roommates] Nannie [Brigham] and Georgia [Lamar] . . . ," she insisted.[34]

Daisy could not have been more wrong about her Northern classmates. She quickly fell in with two new "spoons," women who would remain friends for life: Abby Lippitt and Mary Gale Carter. Daisy and Mary met on Daisy and Abby's shared birthday, October 31, in 1881. The three became inseparable, communicating through "weeklies"—letters sent off on staggered days so they could all respond to one another's notes—when summers scattered them to their own pursuits. Daisy was the creative, spontaneous, imaginative one leading them into scrapes. Abby was acerbic, reserved, at odds with her family, methodical, a scorekeeper, and a talented athlete. Mary was poised, gracious, dutiful, and thoughtful—but she could be moody and insecure. Daisy viewed the world in living color, Abby discerned only black and white, while Mary could not help seeing mostly shades of gray. The three friends would support one another, keep one another's secrets, celebrate victories, and mourn losses, their friendship only slightly weakened by time until death finally separated them.[35]

Abby Lippitt's ancestors arrived in America in 1638 and helped organize the colony of Rhode Island. In 1807, Lippitts built the third cotton mill in the state. Abby's father, Henry Lippitt, was a partner in the Quinebaug Manufacturing Company, which erected the Globe Mill, a five-story landmark housing an enormous steam engine and three water wheels that turned a mind-boggling forty thousand spindles and nine hundred looms. A Civil War veteran, Henry Lippitt parlayed his extensive network of contacts into a successful run for the governorship of Rhode Island in 1874. After serving one term, he returned to his very profitable business.[36]

In 1856, scarlet fever claimed three of Abby Lippitt's four brothers and rendered her sister Jeanie deaf. Left with Charles, Jeanie, and infant Henry, their mother, Mary Ann Balch Lippitt, dedicated her life to Jeanie. In the mid–nineteenth century, provisions for deaf children were few. They mostly lived in asylums, where they learned how to sign, but not to speak. Mary Lippitt believed that sign language would divide Jeanie from her family, so she painstakingly—and successfully—taught Jeanie to speak herself. Aided later by two local families with deaf daughters, Mary Lippitt's efforts culminated in the creation of the Clarke School for the Deaf in Northampton, Massachusetts, and the Boston School for Deaf Mutes.[37]

While Mary's work with Jeanie continued, the Lippitt family added four more children: Mary (called May), Lincoln, Abby, and Alfred, who died in infancy. Abby was the youngest, but, like Daisy, never the center of attention. That special place was always occupied by Jeanie. Abby also shared Daisy's fondness for arguments, but hers were more often about current events, as she grew up in a family well versed in contemporary politics. One observer concluded that "Lippitt arguments are a form of indoor sport. A sort of whetstone on which to sharpen keen intellects." Abby loved outdoor sports, too. She was an avid tennis player and golfer, ice skater and tobogganer. She enjoyed the winter, hated to rise early, and was an unwilling traveler, but most of all declared over and over again that she had no time for young men. Her friends laughed merrily about this, and Daisy dubbed her the Icicle. Abby was not amused.[38]

Nicknames delighted Daisy. Among the girls, she was "Flower." Abby was also "Lippy," and Mary Gale Carter was "Gale." But Daisy had another appellation for Mary: Venus de Milo, for she embodied the same timeless elegance as the famous sculpture. Mary's origins were as far from classical Greece as possible: she was a transplanted New Yorker, born in 1862. Her father's family lived in Ohio, because her grandfather, the Reverend Lawson Carter, served as rector of Grace Episcopal Church in Cleveland. Four of Mary's Carter uncles and one brother-in-law were Episcopal priests. It is unsurprising, then, that Abby described Mary as "religiously inclined." Abby—the Unitarian among them—noted drily, "I am not that kind."[39]

Mary's father, William Lawson Carter, appears to have been a little less religiously inclined as well, for he graduated from New York University with a law rather than a theology degree. Mary's mother, Jane Russell Averell, descended from one of Cooperstown's earliest settlers. When she was twenty-four years old, Jane married William Lawson Carter, and the couple had five children: Jane Russell (1860), Mary Gale (1862), Anna Grace (1864), Marcia Holt (1866), and Lawson Averell (1869). During the Civil War, the Carters lived in Ohio, where Jane was a member of the Soldiers' Aid Society, but afterward moved back to Jane's hometown of Cooperstown, New York. They took up residence in a grand house with a lawn that sloped down to the very edge of Lake Otsego. The catalyst for the move might have been Mary's father's depression. It propelled him to his death, by suicide, in 1872, when Mary was ten years old. Other members of the Carter family also appear to have suffered from depression, particularly the youngest two children, and ultimately Mary herself. How evident this was when Daisy and Abby met her at the Charbonniers school is very difficult to ascertain.[40]

Mostly the three young women concentrated their energies on having a good time and outwitting the strict boarding-school regime. Abby bewailed the fact that the Chars were uninterested in games for the girls, not even serendipitous snowball fights, and were merciless upon discovering some infraction, like secret midnight feasts. The girls created their own culture, full of slang like "flush," for having enough cash on hand to not have to beg Mama for it, and "hooked out," for skipping classes or duties. Daisy's letters home soon included stories of her adventures with Mary and Abby, such as sleigh rides, walking in New York, and meeting young men on weekends away.

But all that was possible only when they were "up to snuff" in their courses of study. Daisy described her curriculum to her grandmother: "I rise at six study one hour before breakfast which is at eight, during the morning I have nothing but French studies, historie

Romaine, Historie francais, historie du Moyen age, literture francais and anglais, german twice a week grammair, verb et analyse compositroic and poesie. Tadrictiou, Lexicologie these things all come on different days in the week, at twelve we have lunch, three times a week I go to my drawing." She was generally a good student. After Christmas in 1879, Daisy learned she was "first in my French History and literature" and received the highest mark for her composition. Daisy exulted: "Snub me no more, my precious Mother, about my spelling for my French dictee. I came out first!" Now, she winked, she should "be considered a mistress of French orthography."[41]

Daisy particularly liked her art teacher, "a perfect character, a little funny gray headed man who has a pile of anecdotes which he trots out on all occasions." He might have been that, but Samuel Frost Johnson was also an internationally known still life and portraiture artist with exhibitions at the 1869 Paris Salon, the National Academy of Design, and the Brooklyn Academy of Art to his credit. In the 1880s, Johnson taught at St. John's College (now Fordham University) and the Metropolitan Museum of Art. While not remembered in the front rank of artists today, Frost Johnson was a professional painter taken seriously by his peers.[42]

Her dancing master was the renowned child prodigy Allen T. Dodworth. Born in 1822, young Allen played the piccolo, cornet, and violin but also composed and arranged music, directed bands, and was much in demand as a musician. In 1848, Dodworth committed himself to dance and became the most famous dance instructor and inventor on the East Coast. The jocund, bearded Mr. Dodworth trained legions of elite New Yorkers at his studios on Fifth Avenue. "Whew," Daisy recognized, the other pupils "are so 'swell.'" Still, she enjoyed the dancing and soon knew "lots of people there." Dodworth made classes fun. In his authoritative dancing text he described many of his popular tricks. "The Butterflies" was a movement he created for a fashionable dance called the german. In "The Butterflies," "each lady is provided with a butterfly attached to a piece of wire, about three feet long; three gentlemen are furnished with short hand nets such as are used to catch insects with; each endeavors to catch one of the butterflies; if successful, he dances with the lady, yielding his net to another gentleman."[43]

The Chars allowed Daisy to attend the theater, and her father paid for the tickets. The actress who moved Daisy to superlatives was Helena Modjeska, a Polish immigrant celebrated for her critically acclaimed renditions of Shakespeare's heroines. "Whenever I see Modjeska," Daisy avowed, "I feel as if I wanted to be either a man or an actress. If I was the former I would make love to her, if the latter I would imitate her. . . ." Modjeska "is perfect," Daisy sighed, after seeing her in the title roles of Alexandre Dumas's heartrendingly sad *La Dame aux Camélias* and Henri Meilhac and Ludovic Halévy's *Frou Frou*. The second play features a young, irresponsible wife who lives only for herself. Like the Prodigal Son, she eventually returns repentant and is forgiven. True to Victorian sensibilities, however, Frou-Frou—like Camille—dies spectacularly in the end. This was exactly the sort of drama that teenagers with the sheltered upbringings of Daisy, Abby, and Mary loved to watch.[44]

The scrupulous supervision of the Mesdames Charbonnier stopped men from consorting with their scholars, but Daisy and her friends escaped regularly to the balls and parties in Washington, D.C. It was not far by train, and many students had family connections in the capital, thus facilitating entrée to amusements. "Six little cadets from West Point" turned Daisy's head over the 1877–78 winter break. They were "the most perfect gentlemen" she'd ever met, "except at home," she added loyally. She saw them off and "really felt quite sad!" That same holiday, the son of Maine's powerful senator James G. Blaine was "very attentive" to her, but she knew it could never become serious. "I just thought to myself," Daisy wrote to Nellie, "<u>what would my father say</u> if he saw me talking to this <u>red republican</u>!!!"[45]

Nellie and Willie would have been intimately involved with Daisy's choice of suitors. The era of arranged marriages was long over in the United States, but Willie, as patriarch, could give or withhold his blessing. Since marriage and motherhood were the goals of nearly all women then, introductions to eligible bachelors were made whenever Daisy was home from school. The social ritual of her debut, which

Daisy dreaded, occurred in Savannah when she was eighteen. This symbolized her availability for serious courting. Daisy was a convivial creature who loved the parties and balls, rides, and other exhilarating get-togethers with potential suitors. Only Lent and family tragedies interrupted the social season. Just as her fascination with men was beginning, however, another death in the family changed everything.[46]

CHAPTER 4

Emotional Upheaval

In 1880, Nellie and Willie Gordon had been married nearly a quarter of a century. They remained deeply in love, tolerating each other's foibles and supporting each other's strengths. Although Willie's father had passed away decades earlier, Sarah Gordon, Willie's mother, was a living and loving presence in their lives. Nellie and Willie shared a devotion to their family, an attachment to their church, and a commitment to their community. Willie's career was on the rise. His firm, renamed W. W. Gordon and Company after William Tison's death, was thriving. Esteemed by his colleagues, Willie had been elevated to Captain of the Georgia Hussars and made a director of the Central of Georgia Railway.

Nellie's primary concern was the children. She loomed large in their lives, her exacting expectations of behavior often communicated sharply. But she could also be warm and spontaneous, encouraging their independence as the children grew up. Aged twenty-two in 1880, Eleanor was absorbing art and culture during her European tour. Nineteen-year-old Daisy, finished with formal schooling, spent the summer vacationing in New England with cousins and friends involved in the happy socializing preliminary to serious courtship with young men. Seventeen-year-old Alice was completing her time at the Chars. Bill was fourteen and off at boarding school. At home full time were the youngest children, Mabel, age ten, and Arthur, the baby, at eight.

With Eleanor out of the country, Daisy became Nellie's factotum, a role that did not come naturally to her. She preferred people her own age and found mothering her younger siblings a trial. In Eleanor's absence, there was no peacemaker between the volatile Nellie and the headstrong Daisy. Their frequent clashes sprang from three unavoidable difficulties and wrecked family harmony. First, Nellie had been the original pampered and indulged belle of the Gordon household. She found it vexing to lose the spotlight as Daisy grew into a graceful young woman with suitors lounging on the veranda, hoping to squire her around Chatham County. Second, as Daisy matured, she questioned authority more. Nellie was accustomed to obedience and did not like being challenged. Daisy believed that Nellie was less draconian with the other children, and interpreted this as a lack of love toward herself. Third, Daisy enjoyed a good fight. She had a keen sense of justice and a ready sympathy for the underdog. Their battles of will were fraught with guilt for Daisy, who knew well the commandment to honor her mother and father—yet she chafed at the constant berating.

Eleanor was her empathetic ear. Of all her siblings, Daisy was closest to Eleanor then. Their circles of friends overlapped, and they shared similar school experiences. The elder understood Daisy's frustration that Nellie spoiled "the children" and did not keep up Eleanor's regimen of discipline, to the especial detriment of Arthur, "who is," Eleanor conceded, Mama's "heart's darling." Nellie was "awfully unfair" to Daisy, her sister agreed, "especially so, because you are touchy and she thinks you imagine things."[1]

Daisy longed to escape just as Eleanor had. She knew by this time that her real love was art and pursuing advanced studies appealed to her. After a successful scuffle with Mama about the cost, Daisy returned to New York in the fall of 1880 to take painting lessons along with her friend Maria Higginson.[2]

Art was one of few appropriate pastimes for young women of her background. It was also a hobby that set her apart from her mother, because writing was the calling of the female Kinzie relatives. Art lessons legitimated Daisy's absence from the close parental oversight in Savannah and allowed her more freedom with her friends. She occasionally toyed with the notion that painting could turn into a way to augment her finances. She expected to marry, of course, but in the event that she did not, or in case she was somehow widowed and penniless, painting for commissions and galleries could mean the difference between independence and reliance on her family's resources. And being busy made Daisy happy. From New York she wrote home contentedly of her packed schedule: classes with Mr. Weir from nine a.m. to one-thirty, lessons with Mr. Volkmar from three to five p.m., and "[a]fter tea in the evening" came instruction from Mr. Lycett.[3]

Her teachers were justly renowned in their respective spheres. The famous Robert W. Weir was a landscape painter best known for his *The Embarkation of the Pilgrims,* which today hangs in the Capitol Rotunda in Washington, D.C. While a drawing professor at West Point, he mentored James McNeill Whistler. A genial, white-haired octogenarian by the time Daisy studied with him, Weir taught from his crowded studio among "its easels, its casts of arms and legs, its pictures on the walls and on the floor, its large cabinet of carved wood, its high-backed comfortable chairs, its rug before the cosy fire place, its loaded book cases, its store boxes for paints and brushes, its standing groups of spears, swords and bows, its collections of armour. . . ." Robert Weir thought highly of Daisy's work: he "says I'm doing splendidly, have a good eye for color, and," she reported, "though Maria took all last winter and a year in Dresden, he said I could paint from life and she could not." He taught them from living models and conveyed his belief that art should serve "a strong incentive to good." Daisy knew that she'd "never learned as much in as short a space of time," as she had with Mr. Weir that month of November.[4]

Daisy studied ceramic painting with the Baltimore-born Charles Volkmar. In 1861, facing accusations that he was a Confederate sympathizer, Volkmar fled to France. He honed his abilities at transferring his nature studies to pottery and learned new techniques that became all the rage on his return to the United States. Pupils like Daisy flocked to Volkmar as his fame grew steadily during the last two decades of the nineteenth century.[5]

Her third main art teacher, Edward Lycett, was perhaps the best-known porcelain painter in the United States in the nineteenth century. Growing up in England, Lycett trained at the Spode china works, and like Volkmar's, his work was exhibited in Europe. Once in America, the Lincolns commissioned Lycett to paint their White House china. When the Civil War ended, china painting became a fad, and Lycett was a magnet for affluent women who took up the hobby. According to *The New England Magazine,* Lycett was the "pioneer of china painting in America," an artist who eschewed commercial profit and instead "produced conscientious work of a high order of artistic merit." His designs ran the gamut from silhouettes to delicate flowers to landscapes on china—including plates decorated with fish that burst their gold-rimmed borders to leap toward the viewer. [6]

In Lycett, Daisy had a teacher supportive of female ceramic painters. He postulated that women made more sensitive artists than men because their innate moral purity inclined them to art for art's sake, rather than for profit. Lycett proclaimed to an interviewer: "The women decorators in all parts of the land are rapidly elevating the standard of this beautiful art. . . ." By the end of the 1880s, women's names became more commonplace in exhibit notices in newspapers, but only a rare few made a career of it. The caliber of the craftsmen with whom Daisy studied marked her as both a serious and a talented artist at this point in her life.[7]

She became proficient in the art of painting on Limoges china, a special type of very white porcelain used for dinnerware. Limoges "blanks" were made in Limoges, France, and sold in America. Blanks could be any sort of tableware—bowls, platters, vases, pitchers—which artists purchased to paint. Usually the entire piece was given a background color or wash, and then the artist either traced a design or drew freestyle on top of the wash. The decorated pieces—no longer blanks—were then fired, and sometimes painted and fired again to create deeper perspective and more resplendent color. Daisy painted, among other things, a porcelain milk pitcher for her father and twelve dessert plates with the nature scenes that Lycett and Volkmar favored.[8]

She was so busy that even the theater, which she loved, hardly made an impression. She did see the incomparable Sarah Bernhardt on her first American tour—so magnificent that Daisy thought she'd "never see such a superb performance again, in all my life!" But very little could pull Daisy from her work. She vowed she would "cut my Washington and Baltimore [social] visits short and spend all my energies painting." The autumn in New York bestowed tremendous self-confidence upon her. She thought of herself as an artist, and dismissed much less quickly suggestions that she sell her work in galleries. It had been a good fall. Daisy was happy and absorbed as Christmas neared, planning to give nearly everyone she loved something she'd made herself.[9]

But tragedy struck first. At the Charbonniers School, just before the holidays, her little sister was struck down by scarlet fever. After a brief rally, Alice died. Nellie's despair knew no bounds. As one relative put it, she "surrendered to grief completely [and] mourned ceaselessly and would not be comforted." Nellie's greatest consolation, Willie, was mired in his own sorrow. The ever-dependable Eleanor was still abroad and battling her own terrible remorse for having neglected to send Alice a birthday card. "It is sad to think," Eleanor lamented, "what sharp thorns little things may become." Daisy believed that Alice was Sarah Gordon's "favorite granddaughter," and so she spent as much time as possible with her disconsolate grandmother, in her "great lonely house," where she lived all by herself across the street. To Daisy fell the hopeless task of comforting them all: Nellie, Willie, Eleanor, and Sarah. As Nellie's lassitude deepened, Daisy also had to manage the mundane domestic chores for which she had been trained, including overseeing the family's needs and supervising the servants.[10]

For the first time in her young life, Daisy was in charge. But it was not because Nellie had deputized her with full faith and confidence—it was because Nellie could not function. "It seems to get worse and worse," Daisy wrote in February—and for long months after that Daisy bore the brunt of Nellie's grief. There was no jollying Nellie along; Crazy Daisy antics were stowed away. Daisy endured the emotionally difficult task of parenting her parent, alone, with no one to care for her. Nellie was so beside herself that she lashed out at Daisy, accusing her of shallowness: of not loving Alice enough, of not mourning deeply enough. This was callous, as it tapped into Daisy's own remorse about years of petty bickering with Alice.[11]

Daisy discovered the inner strength to reject her mother's accusations: "There is no need to analyze what I feel, and it is only when by myself that I feel most. . . . When you or Nell give way [to your pain], you comfort each other. But I have so long controlled myself before you that it is not possible for me to cry or see you cry without wishing to go away or get alone. . . . [T]here is more than one kind of sorrow, and that borne in silence is not less genuine because it is not always seen. To have you judge me thus is terrible. . . ." At this point, Daisy divulged the source of her own shame: "suppose, oh suppose somebody thought you did not love her?" This awful belief seared Daisy, who knew the chance to reassure Alice was gone forever.[12]

Since Mama had abrogated her role as her daughter's comforter, Daisy was lucky to have a friend who understood the hollowness at her center. Mary had lost her younger sister Marcia only seven months earlier. The circumstances were much different, for, just like her father, Marcia Carter had committed suicide. While those who mourn a suicide must withstand unique agonies, Daisy and Mary drew together over the loss of their younger sisters. "I sometimes long for you, old girl," Daisy confided, "just to have a little talk and give way to my feelings, for Mama is so broken down that anyone else's grief distresses her too much for me to indulge in mine before her." It was only to Mary that Daisy could ask anguished questions: "Does the doubt ever come to you, 'Can time ever heal?' because I go almost frantic with the thought that life is so long and it can never again seem desirable to me."[13]

Daisy escaped her mother's neediness for a time by spending some of April 1881 with cousins and friends on the Sea Islands outside of Savannah. Still, she felt terrible. "A year—" Daisy wrote pensively, "how much sadness that little space may hold." She sent William Cullen Bryant's "Death of the Flowers" to Mary. It begins famously, "Where are the flowers, the fair young flowers . . . ?" But it must surely have been the final verse that consoled Daisy and that she hoped would hearten Mary:

> And then I think of one who in her youthful beauty died,
> The fair meek blossom that grew up and faded by my side.
> In the cold moist earth we laid her, when the forests cast
> the leaf,
> And we wept that one so lovely should have a life so brief:
> Yet not unmeet it was that one, like that young friend
> of ours,
> So gentle and so beautiful, should perish with the flowers.

Perhaps that poem was on her mind when Daisy designed a marker for Alice's grave and decorated it with carved flowers. As she continued to care for her family, Daisy encouraged both Mary and herself when she penned, "The only way we can kill for a moment our pain is by unselfishness." Lean on God, she counseled her, and take heart that Marcia, like Alice, would never age or feel physical pain. Nor would she marry and grow to love "others better than those in your little family circle." Just writing to each other helped Daisy: "If it affords you as much relief to talk of your sweet little sister as it does me to talk of mine, I hope you will do so as freely as I am doing." Five months after Alice's death, Mary remained Daisy's primary comfort. "If we could not pray for, and grieve with one another, what a barren land this would be," she conceded.[14]

Desolate in spirit and unsettled by the ferocity of Nellie's grief, Daisy needed comforting. Into this miasma stepped an old acquaintance, William Mackay Low, the "strikingly handsome" son of their neighbor and family friend Andrew Low. Willy was in town from England, revisiting his boyhood home. The two young people felt an immediate affinity. Daisy fell quickly, and as she put it, "madly and unreasonably in love with him." She could unburden her heart to Willy, and in his presence relinquish her taxing role of household head. They were so close that she compared their bond to that between "two confidential girl friends." Offering a sympathetic shoulder, he tended to Daisy with his "little careful way of reading my wants and supplying them." She found him a "graceful prepossessing person" with a "joyous boyish manner." Willy took her mind off the relentless grief in the house and reminded Daisy that the world still held happiness.[15]

The two traveled in the same set of Savannah family and friends. Their relationship intensified, because Willy, Daisy acknowledged, managed "always to be my cavalier in every riding party, tennis, dinner or excursion. . . ." Their flirtation was subtle, hidden, known only to themselves, which Daisy recognized as a "more dangerous form of intimacy in which every look was like a caress." It went on, unseen, right under Nellie's nose.

When Daisy offered to paint his portrait, Willy responded ecstatically: "Now we will be able to spend the mornings together too!" Those were evanescent "days of sunshine" for Daisy. He read to her as she worked. She gazed absorbedly at her beau, brush lingering on the palette as they laughed easily together. One day when Willy couldn't model, he obligingly let her cut off a lock of his hair to use to match the tint. Daisy placed it "in the back of her watch," a tactile reminder of him that she carried with her. The two sweethearts hiked together, dined together, shared poetry and secrets. He was courteous and solicitous. Willy Low was a dashing horseman, elegant in dress, and aristocratic in mien. He was somehow more of a gentleman than her father and wittier even than her mother. Willy brought back the joie de vivre that had been missing since Alice took sick.

But Daisy was ashamed. They had fallen in love less than ten short weeks after her sister's death: it was unseemly. She should be drowning in grief, not in the depth of Willy's eyes. And she knew, neighbor though he might be, that Willy did not meet her father's standards. Willy was lazy. He had no job. He had no work ethic. He was the sole male heir to the three-million-dollar fortune made by his autocratic father. Facing the certain disapproval of society and of her parents, their love had to grow clandestinely. Daisy told no one, not even Mary and Abby.[16]

Willy, too, kept the secret. His father would not approve, either—at least, not at first. Sometime in the early summer of 1881 Willy returned to Europe. Only the notes he sent thrice weekly relieved the pain of their separation. But suddenly, unaccountably, his letters stopped. A heartbreaking silence was all she heard from Willy once his classes began again at Oxford. For a time, she continued writing to him.

Eventually it dawned on Daisy that Willy's father had intervened to quash the budding romance. Andrew Low's sorrows had made him hard, unsympathetic, and determined to control everything around him. An immigrant to Georgia from Scotland at the age of sixteen, he eventually became the wealthiest cotton factor in the city. His 1843 marriage to Sarah Cecil Hunter produced a son and two daughters. The Lows hired architect John Norris to build their home on Lafayette Square, just a few minutes' walk along Drayton Street from the Gordons', but neither Sarah nor their son lived to see the house completed. Andrew Low and his daughters, Amy and Harriet, moved in during the mourning period.

Five years later, the red-bearded, "stout old gentleman" possessed of a voice "like a growl" wed Savannah belle Mary Couper Stiles, the daughter of Elizabeth Mackay and William Henry Stiles. Stiles was a former U.S. congressman, chargé d'affaires to Austria, and Georgia state Speaker of the House. Their home was at Etowah Cliffs, and Daisy knew them well, because her father's sister, Aunt Elizabeth Gordon, had married Mary Couper's brother, Henry Stiles. Even though Mary Stiles was much younger than Andrew Low, their marriage was considered a very good one, uniting two fine Georgia families.[17]

The Lows entertained visitors such as Robert E. Lee and William Thackeray. Lee had formerly been Elizabeth's suitor, and remained a friend of the family. Thackeray sojourned there in the 1850s, already famous as the author of *The Luck of Barry Lyndon, Vanity Fair,* and *Pendennis.* He called the Lows' home "the most comfortable quarters I have ever had in the United States" and wrote glowingly about "these tremendous men, the cotton merchants," like his friend Andrew Low. Thackeray was just one of many interesting Europeans the Lows knew. They traveled often to England to check on their business interests. Andrew Low was a Confederate sympathizer and (probably) financial backer. Smuggling papers for the Confederate general staff earned him a brief prison term in 1862. But because so much of his capital was based in England, Low came through the Civil War without significant financial reversals.[18]

Andrew and Mary Low eventually had four children of their own: Katherine, Mary, Willy, and Jessie. In 1864, when Willy was only four, his mother died. Andrew was bereft again. Because his cotton empire could be managed from either side of the Atlantic, Low moved with his children to Royal Leamington Spa, an old English resort town. The Lows lived there more or less permanently from the late 1860s, returning to Savannah occasionally for business. Andrew Low did not chance a third marriage. Instead, he kept a tight rein on his children—so tight, Daisy believed, that he had tried to impede the wedding plans of Harriet Low and George Robertson, and Amy Low and Harry T. Grenfell.

Thus she suspected Andrew Low had read her letters to Willy. She knew it was "commonly his custom" to peruse his children's mail. Daisy concluded that Andrew simply did not forward her notes to Willy, "especially as he lives in mortal fear lest some of his children should marry in America and above all a poor girl." An American wife might mean his only son would live in the States, far from his father. The Gordons were not poor—unless compared to the Lows. As letter after letter went unanswered, Daisy could no longer be wholly sure that the silence sprang from the tyrannical deception of old Mr. Low rather than the fickle betrayal of young Mr. Low.

She was spared a single-minded obsession with this question by the welcome arrival of Eleanor, home from Europe. Her sister's very presence made her "happier than I ever expected to be again. I have been morbidly, darkly, and bitterly grieved at times this Winter," she allowed. While Daisy almost certainly never mentioned her uneasiness about Willy to Eleanor, at least they could finally mourn for Alice and band together against Nellie's depression. In a self-defense pact, they laid plans to leave Savannah for the remainder of the summer of 1881. Abetted by their father, they visited friends and relatives in Rhode Island and New York. Daisy wanted especially to go to Cooperstown, so she and her "sweet Venus" could comfort each other.[19]

Compelled to return to Savannah, Daisy's spirits sank again. Two late-summer visitors helped relieve the bleakness: first Bessie Hazelhurst, and then Mary Carter. Daisy described herself at that time in "such a state of abject misery" that she "could have committed suicide cheerfully." Either Nellie allowed the visits despite the family mourning period, or Willie noticed his daughter's dejection and intervened to bring her some pleasure.

Elizabeth McKim Hazelhurst, a friend from school, was the daughter of widower Henry R. Hazelhurst, a civil engineer who made a fortune in the railroad and iron industries in Baltimore. They lived with Bessie's sisters Julia and Margaret at Lilburn, a gorgeous mansion in Ellicott City, Maryland. Daisy and Eleanor spent many happy occasions there, picnicking, cantering on horseback over the endless acres of hilltop land, enjoying quiet talks in the tastefully appointed rooms, and calling on nearby Cylburn, home of Jesse Tyson, an amiable older, wealthy bachelor who had his eye on Eleanor.

Halfway though Bessie's six-week Savannah sojourn, she fell in love with Daisy's cousin, twenty-six-year-old Beirne Gordon. By the time Bessie left Georgia, the two had an understanding. Mr. Hazelhurst thought their actions "precipitate" because of Bessie's age and the little time they'd known each other. Bessie's father decreed a three-month cooling-off period, with no communication between the pair at all.[20]

Watching a romance develop between her cousin and her friend did not cheer Daisy. She spent her days nervously awaiting the post, ready to pounce on letters from Willy that never came. Nevertheless, she did her best to "strangle" every trace of her love affair to keep it a secret. When Mary finally arrived, Daisy wanted to open her little box with Willy's photographs and letters and confess everything to her Venus, but could not, "for very shame." Even without the balm of unburdening her soul, Mary's visit did Daisy good. Abby wrote jealously, "I suppose by this time you and the Flower are spooning to your heart's content."[21]

Time alone with Mary was precious, and hosting her school chum took Daisy's mind off Willy and forced her to reenter society. She introduced the New Yorker to Savannah's young men, one of whom, Willy's cousin Fred Habersham, became such an earnest suitor that he mailed a stream of love letters to Cooperstown and then found reason to call in person. But Beirne became Mary's fast friend. He disclosed his love affair to her, who sympathized absolutely with "the two B's." Venus turned out to be a curative for both Gordons. Daisy declared that Mary "broke the spell of helpless despondency which had settled upon me, and kept my mind from dwelling on my woes."[22]

The early winter months dragged on inexorably toward the one-year anniversary of Alice's death. Daisy tried to be positive for her mother and Eleanor. Alice was at peace and in heaven, she reminded them. To Mary, though, Daisy divulged that she was "so unhappy Christmas week that I almost wished no more to wake and that my hold on life would break." And still the silence from England continued. Unwilling for this to carry into the new year, Daisy made up her mind to confront Willy. She pressed her case to her parents—not mentioning him at all but touting the incontrovertible cultural benefits of a European trip for a budding artist. Besides, Eleanor had had her tour. It was Daisy's turn.[23]

Her supplications were rewarded. In midsummer 1882 her parents found suitable chaperones in the Parkers of New Jersey. First came the excitement of shopping in New York for provisions. Then not even the death of her grandmother could stop Daisy from tracking down Willy. Fred Habersham broke away from proclaiming his love for Mary Carter long enough to report that "Granny Gordon" was so ill that the family held no hope for her recovery. Sarah's daughter Eliza Stiles and her daughter-in-law Nellie Gordon were caring for her, but Willie was on cotton business, "so far in the wilds of Texas that he has not been heard from." He returned in time for his mother's funeral, but Daisy was already en route to Europe.[24]

Without familial support, Daisy's mourning barely dented her preoccupation with the monumental decision of whether to fight for or give up Willy Low. Continuing to love him despite silence, distance, and parental disapproval was foolish. Asking him to be true to her while he completed his education at Oxford would be too much to ask. Torn, Daisy made what she felt was the selfless choice to give him up—but she told herself she must see him just once more in order to do it. That's why, she explained to Mary, her "feverish desire for a sight of him" propelled her to call on the Low daughters. They welcomed her, but disappointingly, Willy was away playing cricket. Recklessly, Daisy prowled around Beauchamp Hall, looking for clues. She found what she sought: "proof of the Governor's little trick." The mirror in Willy's room bristled like a porcupine with the drawings she had sent him in the summer, but all her notes and sketches from the fall were missing. This was proof positive for Daisy that Andrew Low had censored his son's mail.

She was unable to locate Willy and confirm her suspicions before the Parkers left for the continent. They were "traveling fast," according to Abby, who was surprised by an unexpected visit from Daisy on a July afternoon in Munich. "The only thing we could do was talk as fast as possible until the evening," Abby complained; "I feel as if I had hardly seen Daisy at all." She begged her to accompany the Lippitts to Switzerland, since Daisy was headed there with her chaperones anyway, but Mrs. Lippitt made it plain that she was tepid about the idea. Daisy failed to divulge to Abby her desire to speed back to London in search of Willy Low.[25]

The wondrous beauty of the Alps briefly stilled Daisy's restless spirit. From Chamonix, France, Daisy wrote of the enthralling vistas she witnessed, telling Mary rapturously, "I never saw anything like the color and the atmosphere of the whole scene." With an artist's eye, Daisy described how "[t]he Mts. of Savoy were crimson with sunshine, and the lake lay at their feet like a great blue green jewel (did you ever see anything more perfect than the color of the Swiss lakes?). Above the sun-touched mountains, the sun glared coldly down, and as it grew stronger and streamed out over the lake, I thought of it in Cooperstown and how it shines over your lawn and lake and I fancied you near the rose bed where we used to stand to count our 9 stars each night. . . ." That same moon illuminated her view of the "simply ravishing" Castle of Chillon on the banks of Lake Geneva, which inspired Lord Byron's poem "The Prisoner of Chillon." Daisy felt a communion with the lonely Prisoner who had "learned to love despair."[26]

Her own despair dissipated temporarily as she stood awestruck and nose to canvas with paintings she had studied and admired for years. Everywhere she went—Geneva, Dresden, Paris, and London—she visited the great art galleries, sometimes criticizing and more often marveling at the works of Murillo, Carlo Dolci, Raphael, Titian, and others.

From the continent, Daisy urged Jessie Low to persuade her brother to chaperone a meeting in London, but the plan fell through. Daisy went nearly mad with disappointment, unable to fully take in that she wouldn't see Willy. She was desperate to tell him that she had been faithful, and that his father was to blame for the letters that never reached Oxford. Daisy's sole purpose for conniving to get to Europe was to admit her love to him in person before fully and freely letting him go. So urgent was this compulsion in her that she nearly telegraphed Willy directly to ask him to meet her, but her upbringing would not allow it: "I would rather have been tortured in the Inquisition than give him cause to think me 'fast.'" Instead, defeated, the only telegraph she sent him was "Goodbye, I sail on the *Gallia*." The emotional roller coaster was enervating. "I was so tired of loving him," she recalled, "and so weary of life that I entered the *Gallia* with almost a prayer that I might be drowned."

Then, hopes revived! Moments before the ship weighed anchor, the purser handed her a lengthy telegram from Willy. He had heard she was in Europe; he had tried to find her. He was on his way to her when he received her farewell telegram. Although she never actually set eyes on Willy, she had the reassurance she craved with his closing: "Cum optimo amore. [With the best love.] Goodbye and don't forget W. M. Low." She pored over his message for two hours in her stateroom, alternately laughing and crying. Then she formulated what she told herself was a final communiqué. "Every word," she related later to Mary, "was written in a kindly friendly spirit, but I told him I thought it best all things considered that I should not write again. Thus it all ended. If we meet again it will be a mystery how either of us will act. I have buried my love, yet his memory is so fresh and green that twice when Mamma has spoken unkindly of him, the quick tears have come to my eyes."

And so it was a heartbroken twenty-one-year-old who sailed for home after a month abroad. Daisy was resigned to a life without true happiness. She believed she would never marry. She did "not think such a love ever comes twice in a life time," and she wouldn't compromise and marry someone she didn't love. It felt as if "all the shining paths and the warmth and color have faded away." Thus, when Captain Henry Sandford Pakenham-Mahon began a shipboard flirtation with her, Daisy, recklessly, as she later admitted, "dared [to] be saucy." Mahon was a decade older. She assumed he was just trifling with her. It assuaged her vanity to toy with the Englishman in return. As they spent time together on the journey to New York she found to her delight that the captain "did not seem to hold as his creed that to be happy one must give one's self up to amusements and let one's brain rust." Daisy was interested to hear about his collections of engravings and antique books. She so thoroughly approved of one of his hobbies that she let him teach it to her: shorthand.[27]

Mahon was a master at this system of speed-writing using an abbreviated language of symbols and letters. Shorthand was undergoing a resurgence in popularity, with a journal (*Shorthand: A Scientific and Literary Magazine Devoted to the Interests of the Art*), a society (The Shorthand Society), and adherents who used shorthand not as a secretarial skill but rather to record their own private thoughts.

Until the very end of the nineteenth century, shorthand was considered a masculine skill, which didn't deter Daisy one whit.[28]

One of those shorthand lessons led to a confession of devotion from Mahon by way of some "very sentimental poetry" he chose as their text. Daisy was stunned, then angry. He had crossed a line. She "shut him up pretty successfully," she thought, but to her chagrin he found it impossible to stop voicing his admiration for her. Daisy still believed he was using her just to pass the time, and that hurt her feelings: "It stung me to think anybody dared to try to flirt with me, when my heart was dead and all lover's dreams forever a thing of the past to me." Mahon could not have known this. He might have received an inkling when she told him "in an unlucky moment" that she so "hated demonstrative people" that she planned to "pick out a husband who would not expect to be kissed but twice a year, once on Christmas and once on his birthday." Mahon couldn't help himself: he doubled over laughing.

It was not until Mahon inadvertently read Willy's love letter that he understood. The note, written in Latin, fell out of Daisy's book. The doughty captain swooped down and teasingly began to translate out loud. When he saw her face register a thousand different feelings, Mahon drew close and "said softly and suddenly—'Dear little child, I hope you will never be unhappy.'" But he could not help himself. A few days later, apropos of nothing, Mahon admitted that he loved her. His intensity frightened Daisy, but she remained calm enough to register how as his passion grew so did her disinterest. When he begged to know why she could not return his love, she lectured him: "Because I don't love you. You are a man of the world, and you think because I am inexperienced, that you can flirt with me; but I know what your pretty speeches are worth and I value them accordingly." He tried to kiss her gloved hand, and she was so incensed that she instantly removed the glove and threw it overboard. "Am I so vile in your eyes that my touch should contaminate even your glove?" Mahon choked. Daisy knew then that "if he did flirt at first, he is horribly earnest now." The irony depressed her: she longed for such depth of feeling—but it was coming from the wrong man.

This shipboard encounter was Daisy's first intimate friendship with an officer. All her life she was overawed by men in uniform, the esteem rooted in her earliest days in wartime Savannah. Daisy was notoriously naive where men were concerned. Family stories center on her misapprehension of male actions because of a lifetime of dire warnings against suitors "taking liberties." Once Daisy demanded to be rescued—and with a shawl—from an evening out. The Gordons laughed for years, because Daisy's gallant escort, responding to her complaint of being cold, had "taken the liberty" of removing his jacket. For his sacrifice, he gained only her indignation and an early end to the evening.[29]

Mahon was not, however, Daisy's first serious flirtation. She had been smitten by a man named Alexander Gregor, who was, as Daisy described him, "an emotional young Russian," "rich as Croesus," whom she "could not repress" and who "probably imagined" his feelings for her. In the late nineteenth century, when gentlemen professed their love, they were expected to propose. Gregor did not. This was a mystery, or "a poser," in Daisy's words. She thought, in 1882, that the answer was that he didn't want to marry her. When they parted that year, he "deluged" her with "flowers and original poetry," and she expected never to see him again.

The Gordon family knew about Gregor and worried about his intentions. They did not know about Pakenham-Mahon, although word of him reached Mary. Daisy denied her friend's charge that she had surrended her heart shipboard. Indeed, Daisy swore the only thing she fell in love with was shorthand! She promised to teach it to Mary so they could use it in their correspondence. She did admit to having had "a most beautiful time" crossing the Atlantic, because she "was never such a belle." Daisy continued to keep the facts about Willy away from her friends and her family.[30]

She had formed an opinion of her ideal man. It came from the romantic poetry and novels she read, from watching her idolized father, and from warnings and suggestions from female relatives. At seventeen, Daisy had written a paper titled "Who Is a Gentleman?" in which she pondered the virtues and vices of the male of the species. On the one hand she thought it the epitome of a gentleman "to dress in the fashion, to be witty, accomplished and full of tact; to be graceful, and gay, and fascinating; to hold current opinions upon all topics; to understand perfectly the details of social etiquette; to acknowledge the necessity of occasionally fighting a duel; to gamble, to know horses and be interested in races; . . . to know wines and mingle easily and brilliantly in fine society. . . ." But she believed that these sorts of men often "treat women with the utmost external courtesy while . . . constantly insult[ing] them in thought." In this class of gentlemen she put the dandy Beau Brummell; the traitor Aaron Burr; and the hedonist Charles the Second.

She posited a different definition: "to be an honest, simple, modest man; conscious of your own fallibility and therefore very charitable to other people; heartily respecting nobility when ever you find it and as sincerely detesting meanness however polished and graceful; easily dispensing with convention and elegance of manner for the sake of an earnest and humane intention; and not caring that a man shall wear the finest cloth, so long as you feel that he is honorable at heart; not according to the 'code of honor' but according to moral principle. . . ." Although her teenage essay did not fully reject the first definition, she did conclude that "a man may be mean, proud, inhuman, false, dishonorable toward God and his country, yet wear proper clothes and be of that indescribable manner that we call high-bred. . . ."[31]

Willy Low was certainly high bred. In 1882, as she steeled herself to let him go forever, Daisy also believed him to be honest, modest, charitable, and moral. He remained her ideal. Daisy never lacked for suitors, but she remained steadfast in her love for him, doomed though it was.

CHAPTER 5

Broken Hearts

Daisy's dejection puzzled her friends, because she did not explain it. Abby and Mary assumed she resented such a brief time in Europe. But Daisy was mired in a potent pother of lovelorn sanctimoniousness. Despite Willy Low's dockside telegram, she felt their courtship could never withstand the triple threat of distance, time, and his father. Bravely putting aside her love for the sake of his family harmony, Daisy suffered in silence, expecting to live out her days as a spinster.[1]

If Mary did not probe too deeply, it was because she was keeping her own secret: she had fallen in love with the son of a Cooperstown millionaire. In the last sultry days of August 1882, George Hyde Clarke had proposed, and she had consented. Daisy did not know Hyde—although Fred Habersham had met him—and the engagement was kept under wraps until Hyde could secure permission from Mary's mother. Too soon, and terribly, the word came back: Mrs. Carter had heard undefined rumors. Forbidding the match, she swept Mary off to Europe and mandated a twelve-month probationary period. Mrs. Carter maintained she would rather see her daughter dead than locked in an unhappy marriage.[2]

Of the three, the Icicle refused to lose her heart and scoffed at the "romantic nonsense" emanating from her two friends. "Don't worry about my finding a Captain Mahon over here," Abby wrote from Brussels. "I don't know of any better way to keep a girl from getting married than by sending her to this side of the water. No sensible girl would marry a foreigner . . . and the specimens of Americans, in the way of youths, I mean, you meet are something pretty bad."[3]

Abby's opposition notwithstanding, marriage was very much in the air that fall of 1882. Daisy's cousin Beirne Gordon wed Bessie Hazelhurst at Lilburn, in Maryland. Mr. Hazelhurst gave his permission when his three-month testing period expired. Daisy and Eleanor had been staying with friends and made the trip from Newark accompanied by Wayne Parker. Eleanor served as a bridesmaid, while Daisy looked on, gasping when sunshine flooded the room at the very moment the vows were completed.

The night before the ceremony, Daisy observed age-old rituals connected to All Hallows' Eve—which was also her twenty-second birthday. Several ancient celebrations conjoin between October 31 and November 2, when, for centuries, young people sought to divine the nature and name of their future spouses. That year, Daisy, with twenty acquaintances, read Robert Burns's famous poem "Halloween" before trooping out to the garden "hand in hand" to pick a cabbage by moonlight. Daisy explained that "[t]he size of the cabbage indicated the size of your future husband, the taste of the skin, his disposition, whether sweet or bitter. Thereafter taking off the leaves we put the stem over the door, and the first name of the first person who walked in the door was the name of your future mate." They used nuts and bowls for other sorts of divining, and Daisy learned that she was to have a "tranquil" courtship, and a "happy marriage" to a man named George. Alas, George would die, leaving her a widow. Since her cabbage had a unique double stem, she would "marry twice." This was startling news, indeed, for someone who intended never to wed.[4]

Superstitions served a purpose for many young women of Daisy's era. After their debuts, finding a husband became a full-time job. Everything led to this crucial pursuit. Art classes, French lessons, and dance academies made women socially desirable. Foreign travel created better conversationalists. The boarding-school curriculum of history, literature, classics, and a smattering of science prepared them for partnership with industrious men. Socializing showcased women's intellectual achievements as well as their physical attributes. Chaperoned parties, picnics, sporting events, and balls brought the sexes together in elaborate courtship rituals. Yet almost none of it was in the young woman's control. She could not pursue partners, make overtures, flirt, appear forward, or propose marriage. Parents had the final say over the appropriate spouse and could erect barriers, such as waiting periods, to test young lovers.

Daisy and her friends sought to influence their fates through superstition. The three companions consulted horoscope readers, read apple peels, and searched for four-leaf clovers to discover the identity of their future mates. Mary possessed a particular power of augury, they just knew. She taught Daisy to count "nine stars for nine nights" so that the first man she shook hands with afterward would become her husband. They followed some superstitions simply for luck. Mary put so much stock in horseshoes that her dresser, piled high, tested the strength of her floorboards. Daisy gave Mary a knife for Christmas, forgetting the old shibboleth that unless she "sold" it to her, it would sever their friendship. Daisy pleaded with Mary to send her a coin. When she received it, Daisy carried it for decades as her lucky penny.[5]

Mostly, though, Daisy and Mary were interested in husbands. In the spring of 1883 both women were deeply in love—but not confessing fully to each other. Instead, coyly, they availed themselves of another old folk belief: that donning a yellow garter on Easter Sunday guaranteed a marriage proposal before Easter returned again. Daisy quickly knitted two garters out of yellow silk in time to mail to Mary for the holiday. This was quite an accomplishment, considering that fiber arts were not Daisy's special provenance, and she told Mary she "look[ed] at each stitch with pride." That Easter morning, Daisy and Mary secretly pulled yellow garters onto their left legs. Daisy, at least, wore hers for the entire year.[6]

The young women knew by then precisely whom they wanted to

marry. Each would need extraordinary luck to make it come true. The ache of giving up her love and the sadness of being unable to talk about it prompted Daisy to ask Mary to agree to the only scheme whereby she could unveil the full story. Daisy wanted them to exchange candid letters about their romances—but to put them away, unread, for thirty years. She wrote hers immediately, gave it to Mary, and then kept up a steady prompting to get her friend to do the same.

Abby had no love affair to confide, and she had not enjoyed her European tour. She loathed living out of a trunk and abhorred being away from her friends. Most of all, she hated being so close to her mother, or "Mrs. L.," as she called her. Abby's European missives contain very little of the appreciation of art, architecture, and culture that run steadily through Daisy's and Mary's. The time with Mrs. L. was so disagreeable that it colored Abby's entire trip. She was deliriously happy to be home again and among her pals.

Home only reminded Daisy of Willy, and it was an effort to remain cheerful in front of her parents. She fled to Etowah Cliffs for "a good rustification" and threw herself into punishing riding lessons. Like nearly all Southerners, Daisy knew how to handle a horse, but she set herself the arduous tasks of learning bareback riding and governing spirited horses. She managed to stay upright even when the train spooked her recalcitrant mount so severely that it ran pell-mell through the streets of a town at such a pace the locals assumed her neck would be broken before it stopped.

Partridge hunting provided another outlet for her pent-up emotions. Cousin Hamilton Stiles taught her how to spy out partridge habitat and drilled her in proper firearm usage until she quit "leveling my gun at the horizon and sweeping it around shooting at every object with in my radius." Pinning up her riding habit "as high as decency would permit," Daisy shouldered her shotgun and gave chase to the swift birds.[7]

For calming interludes, she learned to milk cows so she could milk Lilburn, their cow at home, named for the Hazelhurst mansion. "This is just the kind of life I like," Daisy professed, "providing I did not always have to live it. Jolly walks in amongst the most romantic hills, a good selection of books to read aloud . . . and as much horseback riding as I can stand."[8]

Back in Savannah, Daisy's thoughts returned to art. If she was never going to wed, then perhaps she should reacquaint herself with her palette and brushes. She began grandly, by creating a new studio. She painted her dressing room walls deep red, and hung portraits of absent friends on the walls for the mute inspiration they would offer. The large window provided good natural light, and oversize mahogany furniture offered space to critique her works in progress. She dubbed the studio "cozy and sweet," and planned for the time Abby would be curled up in one of the big chairs, chunnering away, while she painted at her easel.[9]

That was not to be. Mrs. L. nixed the idea. Abby believed her mother took a malicious pleasure in refusing anything that she liked. "I can't tell you," Abby wrote sarcastically, "what a pleasant feeling it is to know that the people who naturally would think the most of you, care as little about giving you any pleasure as the man in the moon." Daisy worried about it. "I don't think Mrs. L. realizes how very wrong she is," she confided to Mary. "If she had only arranged to let Abby come there would have been more good will than has existed in that family for years." What Abby did not have the heart to tell Daisy was that her father "hates the south and Southern people" and would not let Abby go, for fear she would fall in love with a Southerner.[10]

While Abby was forced to renew Provincetown friendships and Daisy painted alone, a calamity was unfolding in Mary's life. In March 1883, Jane Carter received a letter from a man named David Gregory that accused Hyde Clarke of illicit relations with his daughter. This was so shocking that it was grounds for dissolving any understanding with Mary. Only her anguished faith that it was a lie gave Hyde any hope. He was contrite. He denied hiding anything and iterated that Mary knew he had lived a riotous life before they met. To Jane Carter, whose own husband ultimately surrendered to his demons, Hyde's actions must have bespoken a similar kind of madness. Hyde's confession reinforced her bedrock belief that a miserable marriage was a living death. Mary loved Hyde but had been taught a moral code that contained no room for behavior like his. She teetered on the brink of serious depression as Daisy's yellow garter arrived. Mary donned hers with a dread urgency.[11]

Mrs. Carter invited Daisy to join them in Rome, hoping she would be a palliative for her otherwise inconsolable daughter. Unaware of the impetus for the invitation and feeling "like a champagne bottle with all the wires cut, ready to go off," Daisy wrote jubilantly of how her mother's intervention turned her father's initial no into yes. Daisy did not believe that Mary could "realize my joy unless you have ever hoped for anything intensely and after utterly abandoning all idea of getting it suddenly find your wish about to be fulfilled." Poor Mary certainly must have wept bitter tears upon reading that sentence. But when no chaperone could be found, Daisy's trip was canceled. Mary was left seeking comfort from God.[12]

Perhaps as consolation, Papa and Mama took Daisy and Eleanor to New England to enroll Bill at Yale. They said farewell to their daughters with a "champagne supper" as Daisy and Eleanor made haste to join Abby in Mount Desert, just off the coast of Maine. With August stretching before them, lots of friends and family to swell the crowd, and a goodly number of swains, the girls had all sorts of adventures. Joining amateur thespians from Baltimore's Wednesday Night Club, they acted out sketches for fun. Daisy caught a nine-pound cod. Balmy weather drew them to "two water parties where we had refreshments and with a glorious moon, congenial people and a banjo. . . . I just would like to see anyone," Daisy wrote appreciatively, "ask for more pleasure." The men of the party grew in number as Fred Habersham joined them, nursing a broken heart. Wayne Parker paid court to Eleanor, competing with her "ancient admirer" from Maryland, Jesse Tyson, the Baltimore Chrome Works magnate. George Hazelhurst, Courtland Parker, and Billy Nelson turned up. Daisy met Yale graduate Arthur Ryerson, who became quite attentive to the twenty-two-year-old Georgian. "We do not lack beaux at present," Daisy confirmed. None of them measured up to Willy Low.[13]

Daisy's life, between her debut and her wedding, was very much like the lives of other young women of her age and class. The winter social season began in mid-November and ended on Ash Wednesday. Socializing during Lent was frowned upon. Activities were fewer and more austere until after Easter, when the summer season started. In an era before telephones, televisions, radios, computers, and other electronic means of communication, there were only letters and visits. Because the Gordons were affluent, they could send their unmarried daughters wherever friends or family resided.

With a chaperone as a moral guardian, young women attended entertainments where they could mingle with potential suitors. Athletic competitions were mostly for men, but women participated in tennis, archery, and croquet. Women observed polo matches and yachting, sailing, and horse races, where young men strove to demonstrate their prowess. Picnics, rowing parties, hikes, and horseback rides took place in mild temperatures, while inclement weather moved courtship indoors to balls, theaters, operas, and concerts.

Such socializing was fraught with worry. The slightest deviation from the strict code governing behavior for young women could result in disaster. One's reputation could be ruined and shame brought upon the family if a woman was seen alone with a man, was too flirtatious, or rejected too many proposals. Males were assumed to be naturally licentious, and thus females had to be reserved so as not to tempt them beyond their ability to resist. Women should be interested but demure companions. Voices should be moderated, emotions kept in check, tempers never raised, and deference shown to men. This was not always easy.

Sometimes things went unwittingly and embarrassingly wrong, as happened one day for Daisy, when she was exhibiting her tennis skills at the navy yard. On the court, in front of many spectators, Daisy ran to her shot, but her bustle stayed behind. Held by strings around her waist, it had come untied, and quivered forlornly on the court. She had no choice but to pick it up—play could not go on—and remove it. She was mortified. Not only had her undergarment come off in front of all those sailors, but it was filthy. Her mother had warned her! At least Daisy could joke about it in her weekly. One of her most enduring traits was her sense of the absurd. It allowed her to laugh at her wildest predicaments, such as parting company with her bustle on a tennis court, which was definitely not the shortest route to a husband![14]

The crowning event of the fall for Abby was the very first exposition sponsored by the National Horse Show Association of America. Five thousand observers—half of whom were women—swarmed into Madison Square Garden for the mayor's opening speech and the exhilarating sight of "thoroughbreds, trotters, and Arabs, . . . hunters, saddle-horses, . . . roadsters, . . . fancy breeds," small ponies, and huge Percherons, all parading in the ring, some of them ridden by professional horsewomen. Between the judging were exhibits to see and people to meet. The National Horse Show grew beyond equestrian lovers and became the place to see and be seen for American elites. In fact, in only a few years, as it increased in prestige, the Madison Square Garden Horse Show opened the fall social season.[15]

Incredibly, Daisy and Abby were also present at the start of what would become another New York institution: the Metropolitan Opera House. The idea came to wealthy New Yorkers who did not have entrée to the established Academy of Music. Like the National Horse Show, the Met surpassed the wildest dreams of its creators. On the inaugural night in October of 1883 Abby and Daisy saw Charles Gounod's *Faust* with Christine Nilsson as Marguerite and an aging Giuseppe Del Puente as Valentin. "The cast was splendid," a "collection of stars," Daisy swooned, and "the house is superb." She loved opera as she loved theater. Daisy had seen legendary actors of the era, including Ellen Terry and Henry Irving. With Abby, Daisy once went to the theater fifteen times in twenty days, "and instead of being satiated," Daisy related, she felt "more wild about plays than ever."[16]

Good Episcopalian that she was, Daisy admitted to some ambivalence about spending too much time in society—especially after her father won election to the Georgia House of Representatives. Since the Helpful Hands Club, Daisy's charitable works consisted of fundraising by charging admission to plays. For example, while taking the waters at Old Sweet Springs spa in West Virginia, Daisy discovered that local farmers were destitute from two years of crop failures. "You never saw such misery in your life, it makes my heart sick to see great men almost starving," she wrote Mary. She and a friend worked together to put on tableaux vivants. These were groups of costumed people with props arranged to look like scenes from paintings, mythology, the Bible, novels, or history. Those in the tableaux remained frozen, and people paid to come look at them. Daisy and Mabel participated in a tableau called "The Last Days of Pompeii" and brought Edward Greene Malbone's *The Hours* to life. "It was my first attempt as manager," Daisy explained, "and I am awfully pleased that [we] succeeded, though the sum of $31.90 was not great it was something to start with."[17]

But these philanthropic forays were rare. "The harm of having too much pleasure," Daisy ruminated, is that "[o]ne never wants to settle down. Now when one is travelling and improving one's mind it seems a most desirable life to lead, but when I feel that for six months I have lived a thoroughly hollow and useless existence it is enough to leave a bad taste in my mouth, and it requires a strong jerk into the right groove to ever enable me to make good resolutions for the future." She had inherited her parents' commitment to social uplift, but it had not yet taken deep root. Although she was aware of injustices, Daisy had not been seized with an ardor to amend them. But her family and her church had impressed upon her the sin of a life lived selfishly. Daisy pledged to trade the winter's amusements if she could only take art lessons. She conceded that a career in art would result in "something solid and wholesome," but the cost would be a terrible solitude. She was just twenty-three years old, and her conclusion was perhaps to be expected: "Well after all, one should begin I suppose by 'doing their duty in that state of life into which it has pleased God to call them' and it is foolishness to cry out because the prospect seems too gay."[18]

Too much gaiety also caused a resurgence of malaria and earaches, both of which had bothered her for years and returned predictably when her immune system was weakened. By November

1883, Daisy weighed only 111 pounds and could not sit up for more than fifteen minutes at a time. She went to Etowah to convalesce, with castor oil making a pitiful Thanksgiving feast. There was nothing else but "quinine and patience"; the former for the recurring symptoms of malaria, and the latter for the temporary hearing loss caused by ear infections. "As far as I can see I shall continue to take them until I become stone deaf," she wrote sadly.[19]

She indulged in a longer-than-usual weekly to Mary, recalling the art she had loved in Dresden, where the Carters were spending Christmas. "Such quantities of pictures troop through my mind," she wrote, as she recalled the Virgin Mary's hair in Caravaggio's *Rest on the Flight into Egypt* and the drunken work of Guido Reni. Reni had two artistic styles, one produced when he was sober and one when he was not. Daisy admitted puckishly that she preferred the latter. But she hated to impose her views on Mary, for "no two people ever like the same pictures best, nor think the same things about them. The same pictures even appear differently at different times, the light one sees it in, the people with whom one sees it, and above all the mood of one's own mind all influence the impression a picture makes on one." Slowly she gained nearly ten pounds at Etowah, so that her fighting spirit was matched by her physical strength again. While recuperating, she painted, studied German, and longed for her friends.[20]

Part of what caused Daisy's breakdown in health was the paralyzing knowledge that her dear sister would soon exit the family home forever. "[W]hat a nuisance it is any way this getting married and leaving everybody just for the sake of a man," the Icicle fumed. Daisy was more melancholic. She believed that marriage changed the totality of a woman's world, and that it separated her from her former life like an unscalable wall, transforming forever the landscape of her social relations and her private life. Eleanor had fallen in love with Wayne Parker. Abby met him in October 1883 and pronounced him "first rate." Daisy liked him because she saw his "goodness" and recognized that he would make Eleanor happy, but she recognized, too, that in Eleanor's absence she would be needed more at home.[21]

Wayne Parker was a decade older than Eleanor, already a practicing attorney with an interest in Republican politics, and related to the Gordons through his mother, Elizabeth Wolcott Stites. Within the year, he would enter the New Jersey Assembly. A passionate reader with a philosophical bent, the Gordon family depended on Wayne for assistance with chaperoning and legal matters. The wedding occurred in January 1884 at Christ Church. Nellie redecorated the home for the two hundred guests who came to the reception. Eight bridesmaids formed a circle around Eleanor, who, blindfolded, threw a handkerchief to see who would be the next bride. Wayne did the same thing for his ushers. There were a number of couples pairing off at Eleanor and Wayne's wedding, but not Daisy. Spending every morning sobbing "unfits one for brilliant conversation," she noted.[22]

Daisy was desolate. Eleanor felt as lost to her as Alice. In an era when women spent most of their time with other women, the marriage of an older sister was wrenching for her siblings. Women taught other women, counseled them, cheered them on, assisted them in every facet of their lives, and provided their closest comfort. Daisy confessed glumly to Mary: "I cannot bring myself to visit Eleanor until I get myself more used to her being married. Next fall, perhaps, I shall be more resigned but at present I spend my time when with her, shedding buckets full of tear[s]. . . ."[23]

Eleanor's wedding turned Daisy's thoughts to Willy and the old sore of never actually having seen him while abroad. A trip to England would allow her finally to be able to tell Willy good-bye in person and close that festering chapter of her life. At the same time, she could get used to the idea of Eleanor's marriage and spend time with her Venus, who was suffering from the "blue devils." Manipulating just a bit, she invited herself to visit Mary in England. It took some doing. She begged Mary to ask her mother to write the Gordons. Since Daisy had failed to take advantage of Mrs. Carter's last invitation, she could not count on another.[24]

As she waited, she kept busy in her usual fashion, reading romantic poetry, acting in plays, attending the Calico Charity Ball, and designing her own daisy dress to wear to a ball at the Hardees' home.

The white satin skirt was overlaid with white petals made of soft silk "plush." The bodice was green satin, "but with small white satin petals coming out at the neck and sleeves." A wide-brimmed daisy hat with long white petals finished the effect. She was so pleased with the costume that she drew a picture of it for her weekly to Mary.[25]

On a boating party Daisy met a Mr. Comstock, and found his treatment of women so rare that she described him to Mary approvingly: "he was nice, however more of a man's man and had a way of treating women that was very courteous. . . . He had a chivalrous idea of them that was very old-fashioned and rare in the present race of men, who fold their hands and expect the women to entertain them." Her definition of the ideal man at that point seemed to encompass the antebellum stereotype of the passive, adoring woman.[26]

On the other hand, Daisy's fascination with ne'er-do-wells continued. Belle Cross had intrigued her in boarding school. Mr. Gregor was a cad. Willy Low could manifest a devil-may-care stance. Daisy and Mary enthused over the scoundrel protagonist in Caroline Norton's *Stuart of Dunleath,* whom Daisy labeled utterly "fascinating." They also oohed and aahed over the real-life romance of the author "who gave up her 'first love'" and wed another. As a widow, Daisy narrated, Norton "then married her early love, although they had both grown old." Daisy teetered on the disappointed lover's treacherous threshold, one day certain of her decision to release him, the next hoping against hope he would return.[27]

Daisy held fast to her belief that she would never tie the knot. She did not lack opportunities: the yellow garter worked. Since Easter 1883, Daisy reported confidentially to Mary, she had received two marriage proposals. Well, in the end she decided it was three—the first one came within the year, just as it was supposed to—but it was a little vague. Her suitor never uttered the word "marry." In retrospect, Daisy counted it. The other two came the following year, and Daisy declined them both. "It is very unfortunate," she concluded, "for one to form an ideal." Suitors could never measure up to Willy Low, because Daisy found it impossibly "hard to like every day young men, when one has had vague ideas of a superior being. . . ."[28]

When Mrs. Carter sent the longed-for European invitation, Eleanor kindly volunteered to take Nellie and the younger children to her home in New Jersey. Relieved of their care, Daisy sailed in May 1884 and reunited with Mary and her sister Grace. The girls mingled among eligible young men at Lord's Cricket Ground, and thrilled as hundreds of carrier pigeons were released to carry the news of the first-ever dead-heat 1884 Derby finish. Daisy visited the Inns of Court and marveled at the living quarters of former residents Samuel Johnson, Oliver Goldsmith, Charles Lamb, and William Blackstone. She stood at Runnymede, where King John signed the Magna Carta in 1215. She strolled through Hyde Park, revisited the paintings in the National Portrait Gallery, and reveled in the Tower of London, where so many momentous events in Britain's history had played out.[29]

A real-life secret drama even more exhilarating than the ones she had read about was unfolding in London: finally, Daisy saw Willy. She accepted an invitation to visit the Lows. She claimed to be going to Beauchamp Hall to save money, a lie that angered the Carters. A tart letter found her there, and her contrite reply followed. She admitted, "I have appeared perhaps to you to be absolutely indifferent to whether I saw much or little of you and I don't blame you for thinking so." She assured Mary that it was not the case, but Daisy's mind was fixed on Willy and their fleeting time together.[30]

Three years after those "days of sunshine" when they fell in love, Daisy and Willy "could not help the past so sweet and dangerous coming back to us." They talked things through. She understood finally what she did not know for certain in 1881: Willy loved her. She was at last able to tell him plainly that she loved him in return. They had both been acting selflessly. Willy had confided to his cousin Caroline Stiles that it was futile to pursue Daisy, because attending Oxford would prevent them from seeing each other, probably for years. He felt he could not ask Daisy to wait. That's precisely what she felt—that she loved Willy too much to "let him tie himself down."[31]

What's more, she learned she had been right about Andrew Low. He had decreed that his son could not marry while he was alive. She intuited that her own father's pride would keep her from marrying into a family whose welcome would be lukewarm at best. Knowing the "sin of a secret engagement" would aggrieve all three parents and believing it was her duty, Daisy—for the second time—let Willy go.

His innate cheerfulness would help him recover, Daisy felt sure, and someday he would be grateful for what she had done. As usual, she trusted God to help her past her own sorrow. "Though harder now to take up my life," she sighed, "it will be sweeter for having known of his love." Such long-sought joy buried alive under such valiant self-sacrifice! The rest of her visit with Mary took place beneath a gloomy pall. Daisy tried to confide in her, crediting her Venus with exemplifying "perfectly unobtrusive unselfishness and patience during a time when every girl is excused from being self absorbed and forgetful of other people's comfort." But she told Mary later, "if you have any little feeling of resentment that I was not as explicit in London about someone I cared for . . . please trust me, and believe me it is easier for both of us that you wait and read my letter—thirty years hence."[32]

To her parents she wrote only that she had seen Willy in London. "Mr. Low seems feeble," she reported to her mother. "He wept when he saw me because he mistook me for <u>you</u> and he considers himself a dying man, although doctors say he may and probably will live twenty years." Daisy pitied the Low daughters for the difficult responsibility of caring for Andrew. It made her appreciate her own parents more. Still, the Lows were kind and treated her like a sister. They all had a "jolly time" together. She repaid their hospitality by painting a portrait of Mary's dog. Daisy had only the briefest of time with Willy before his commitments took him away. Her love was rekindled—even as she was willing the fire out—so Daisy resisted accompanying her chaperones for a trip through Scotland and the continent, just in case Willy reappeared. The Low daughters made her swear to return to them before sailing for home.[33]

Once she'd conceded to rejoin her chaperones, Daisy fell unexpectedly and completely in love with Scotland. She saw it all through the desperate heroism, selfless romance, and passionate tales of Scottish bravery of Sir Walter Scott. "The Lady of the Lake" echoed in her mind as she surveyed Loch Katrine, and mysterious Loch Lomond was "teeming with the relics" of *Rob Roy*. She read *The Heart of Midlothian* in Edinburgh and made a pilgrimage to Jeanie Deans's small cottage at the edge of Holyrood Park. In Melrose Abbey she murmured aloud Scott's fantastical epic *The Lay of the Last Minstrel*, partially set in that "holy pile." The tempestuous Scottish Highlands as she sat drawing made her "thank God for being alive, and that there are such beautiful things on earth. . . ." Daisy claimed to have "broken the 10th commandment by coveting all that" lay within view. The wildness of it somehow released her from her doldrums. A "patriotic feeling," enveloped her, "as if I was a Scot myself in some distant way." Like the Lows, the Kinzies and the Gordons did hail from Scotland, but her father scoffed that the Gordon ancestors were almost certainly servants. This hardly deterred her. "The meanest peasant in this land has as much loyalty for his country as the highest born noble in England," she insisted—this from the erstwhile daughter of the Confederacy who grew up immersed in the importance of allegiance.[34]

From the peaceful Highlands to the bustle of Glasgow and Edinburgh, Daisy left part of her heart in Scotland, forever colored by the glow of so recently uncovering Willy's love. That warmth remained with her in Belgium and the Netherlands. She was an appreciative traveler, enjoying Waterloo and the vista from the top of the Lion's Mound, but her compass point was fixed always on art or literature. In Brussels, she valued the extraordinary fifteenth-century Town Hall chiefly because she could imagine the Duchess of Richmond's ball described in *Vanity Fair*. In Antwerp she "wept" before the "first and greatest" painting: Peter Paul Rubens's triptych *Descent from the Cross*. She sketched the windmills, traveled by canal boat, and appreciated Holland's "flat as a flounder" countryside. The Dutch she applauded because of "the plucky way in which they fought and the persevering way in which they have clung on to their little muddy meadow of a country. . . ."[35]

Avoiding a cholera outbreak in Paris, Daisy briefly met up with Mary in Wales before the Carters went to Germany and she returned to England. Seven young women, mostly friends from her chaperone's Charbonnier days, accompanied her to London. It was difficult to remain reverent even in magisterial Ely Cathedral because the girls, as Daisy put it, were full of "petty squabbles and tittle tattle." In exasperation, she wrote to Mary, "I always did like men better than women." Still, as she calmed down she admitted, "in a more violent way I probably am just as faulty."[36]

She made her way back to the Lows' as promised, and he was there. Delectable days with Willy followed. Something shifted. Realism replaced selflessness as the couple looked squarely at their love and decided waiting for each other was preferable to ending the relationship. But to Mary, Daisy made light of it, putting Willy in the same category as another gentleman caller in London, Jesse Tyson. One suitor too young, Daisy laughed, the other too old. Lingering as long as possible at Beauchamp Hall, she reluctantly left Liverpool for the homeward voyage.[37]

Daisy and Willy named and cemented their commitment in England that summer. He visited Savannah just a few months later. By then she had confessed their relationship to her parents, who must have been cool to the idea but considerate of their daughter. To avoid suspicion or perhaps to placate her family, Daisy would not let Willy escort her to a local dance, but it hardly mattered. Like Shakespeare's Hermia and Lysander, they understood "the course of true love never did run smooth." And if Daisy doubted it, she had only to consider Mary and Hyde, for whom hope finally triumphed over parental objections. Daisy and Willy were alive with the same fierce optimism. They had no specific plan beyond trusting to fate.[38]

CHAPTER 6

Omens and Weddings

The new year of 1885 promised to be lively. Daisy was about to become an aunt, because Eleanor's first child was due in early January. Willy Low arrived from England, as it had been three long months since he had last seen his sweetheart. She, meanwhile, was preparing for another triumph on the stage at Savannah's amateur theatrical group, the Garrick Club, made sweeter by Willy's presence. Mabel and the boys returned to school, and Nellie hurried off to usher in the first Gordon grandbaby, leaving Daisy in charge of her father and the home. Nellie had her doubts, as usual, about the decision-making abilities of her "pig-headed fool" of a daughter, who, she felt, seldom listened to her and usually lacked sense.

While she might have been a scatterbrain, Daisy knew when to take herself off to the doctor. Changeable winter weather, or perhaps the frenetic pace of socializing, brought a recurrence of her old nemesis, earaches. Late Monday afternoon, January 19, 1885, the pain became so intense that Daisy left off preparations for her father's dinner party and flew to Dr. James P. S. Houston on nearby Harris Street. He treated her earache with silver nitrate, a liquid compound with many medical applications usually connected to disinfection or cauterizing. It was not a new cure for ear ailments.[1]

Unfortunately, Dr. Houston's use of the silver nitrate caused Daisy tremendous agony and set in motion a series of complications from which she would never fully recover. By the time the soreness finally subsided, Daisy Gordon's hearing was significantly impaired. The intensity of her pain after the silver nitrate prompted Dr. Houston to bring his colleague, Dr. James B. Read, on to the case. The two physicians gave Daisy an injection of morphine and a dose of Dover's powder, an opium-based sedative. They told her to rest her ear on a pillow filled with heated hops. Both men returned the following morning. While her discomfort had abated somewhat, they insisted she remain in bed.[2]

Willie blamed his daughter for the ruin of the dinner party and the feckless use of silver nitrate. His initial letters to Nellie suggested that Daisy's willfulness brought her little more than she deserved: "She . . . insisted upon his injecting nitrate of silver for her ear, as I understand it through the nose, being the same treatment as that of some New York doctor. H[ouston] protested ignorance but yielded to Daisy's importunities and as soon as he had injected the stuff it became evident that something was wrong from the intense pain she suffered." Yet Daisy's explanation of the event to Mary suggests the fault was the physican's. She told her friend that "the Dr. who was treating my ear put too strong an acid in it and burned a hole through the drum. . . ." Later she wrote that "Dr. Houston blew me up with that acid," and never hinted the treatment was her idea, or that she'd heard about its having been used in New York. Daisy was so used to taking the blame in the family and admitting her shortcomings to her best friends that had she demanded the silver nitrate, it seems probable she would have confessed that fact.[3]

On the afternoon of January 20, Daisy was able to sit up in her room and paint, even though her ear was bleeding. Her father thought this suggested her eardrum had been pierced, "either recently or from the reopening of the [scar] that formed when there was an abscess there 6 or 8 years ago." Still, the patient was comprehensively miserable. "Daisy is low in her mind," Willie wrote, "because she is lonely and because I have felt it necessary to forbid positively her acting tomorrow night in the Garrick Club play."[4]

Twenty-four hours later, Drs. Houston and Read concluded that the swelling of the eardrum was nearly gone and it would be back to normal in less than a week. Willie did not share their optimism: "Her deafness is much increased and she talks habitually in the low voice usual in such cases." He urged Nellie not to mention that to Daisy, already morose, for fear of making her withdraw further. Yet his refusal to let Willy Low visit, or even to let her beloved dogs come inside, exacerbated her situation. Mr. Gordon did have the grace to concede that it was all "a miserable muddle anyway it may eventuate."[5]

The pain returned, and Dr. Read insisted Daisy see a specialist, but Willie was too busy with work to take her to Atlanta. January 24 brought a slight improvement in her pain and her hearing. Willie concluded that his daughter was suffering from "another abscess which has at last broken through the drum, as it did before. If my theory is correct Dr. Houston was right when he wanted to lance the bulging drum some days ago. That would have relieved her at once and a cut with the lance would (so says Dr. R and Dr. H) have healed better than a break by an abscess. If also there was an abscess, then I have blamed Dr. H too much for injecting the nitrate of silver, and it only aggravated what already existed." Nellie's furious letters from New Jersey were full of criticism of Dr. Houston and impatience with Daisy. Eventually Willie had to remonstrate with his wife and remind her that their daughter felt bad enough already.[6]

This recognition led Willie to allow Willy Low to call on her, which surely brightened her mood. Daisy also had a girlfriend visiting. She asked permission to put together some sort of amusement for her. Her father, however, was not fooled. He knew the festivity was really for Willy. "Poor child," he told Nellie, "I am only too glad she can have this scrap of comfort—for I very much doubt his constancy standing the test of years of delay and separation and by the time Daisy realizes the situation she will be too old to nurse a new flame." Nellie was pleased that the two were allowed to meet. "After all, she may never see him again and if she doesn't make herself conspicuous to the Savannah public, what odds does it make whether she sees him now or not? She will not love him any the less if she don't see him, and if he should prove inconstant she will have had this much brightness in her poor little ruined life!"[7]

Nellie pitied her daughter because of her doomed romance, not her ear. Daisy's hearing was improving, and after all, Daisy had been living with ear infections and their concomitant temporary hearing loss for some years by this time. She had apprised her parents of her feelings for Willy Low and her awkward position of being in love with the son but lacking the father's endorsement. While they appeared receptive, it was not because they approved of the match. Neither of the Gordons had confidence in Willy's ability to remain faithful to her while completing his university degree and awaiting his father's permission to wed. The money Willy would inherit did not endear him to Willie Gordon, regardless of his fervent wish to see his daughter well provided for. Of much greater importance to him was that she wed a morally and fiscally responsible man with a strong work ethic. He believed that Willy Low fell short on all counts.

Eleanor and Wayne's healthy twelve-pound daughter, Alice Gordon Parker, was born on January 27, freeing Nellie to race to the daughter who now needed her most. At Dr. Read's urging, Willie redoubled his efforts and took Daisy to the Atlanta specialist Dr. Calhoun, because another swelling had arisen behind her ear. On January 30, Willie wrote that Dr. Calhoun was happy with Daisy's progress. He kept Daisy so highly sedated that she could barely talk. Nellie arrived, Willie returned to work, and Daisy slowly recovered.[8]

It was a harrowing time. "It seems something more than my hearing was involved," Daisy explained to Mary, "if the infections had penetrated the bone which is only as thick as a sheet of paper it would have gotten to my brain and I would have had meningitis. . . . There was a hole in the drum of my ear as big as this black hole [she drew a dot about half an inch across] now it is the size of the little hole here [about one quarter of an inch across]. . . ." Improvement continued. By early February, the doctor assured her that her "hearing will not be affected."[9]

It is impossible to diagnose accurately a medical complaint more than a hundred years later. It can be illuminating, however, to apply contemporary knowledge to offer an educated guess. In Daisy's case, it is likely that she suffered from a painful, chronic middle ear infection described by otolaryngologists today as causing "hearing loss, and spontaneous rupture (tear) of the eardrum." A really sizable hole in the eardrum can bring about complete deafness, but most perforations close without intervention. Once they do, hearing improves, but recurrent infections "can cause persistent or progressive hearing loss."[10]

The assumption has been that the episode with the silver nitrate made Daisy deaf in one ear. Yet the assertion by Daisy's niece that "Daisy lived the greater part of her life in nearly total deafness as a result of this particular escapade" is an overstatement. Daisy's audible range was impaired temporarily: as her father noted, for a time she could not hear herself well and spoke in a low voice. Her hearing was compromised, but she regained some of her auditory powers over time, suggesting the perforation in the eardrum did heal.[11]

Daisy's niece also reported that Dr. Houston, not long after this, committed suicide. The Gordons had indisputably called his credentials into question—because he unaccountably bowed to the impassioned plea of a medically unschooled young woman or because he simply bumbled the treatment that day, or both. Daisy felt it important to set the record straight for Mary. Dr. Houston was a trained physician, she emphasized, "not a quack" but "only a blunderer."[12]

Daisy's full recovery was slow. When she could go out for drives again, she was delighted to find a horseshoe on one of her outings. Surely that accounted for the amazing luck of all parents involved agreeing to a visit to Savannah by Abby, Mary, and the latter's younger sister Grace. "Wild were the ecstasies on all sides!" Mary recalled. She drove Abby out to Bonaventure Cemetery one March afternoon. Her description for Hyde was poetic: "Avenues of old gnarled live oaks with sweeps of the soft gray moss add a beauty and solemnity for which I can find no words. It was just before sunset and the mellow, golden, Southern sun cast the most exquisite lights and shadows imaginable. . . . Looking across the river you can see the marshes, with their delicate sweet mists softening the outlines and fading into the sky." Every night brought visitors eager to glimpse the three Northerners who were glad to meet or reestablish acquaintanceships with the city's young male "fascinators," the Gordons' superannuated cook Liza Hendry, and other family members. Mabel was now fifteen, nearly the age Abby and Mary and Daisy had been when they met. Thirteen-year-old Arthur made himself useful to Mary by running to the post office with her love letters to Hyde.[13]

The four friends went riding past antebellum plantations in the afternoons. "Very little remains of the ancient grandeur" except ghosts, Mary wrote to her sweetheart. On other days, the women took their sewing to the park and chatted or read aloud John L. Motley's "intensely interesting" history, *The Rise of the Dutch Republic.* They attended theater performances at the Garrick Club and a dance at Rose Dhu plantation. Daisy painted Mary's portrait for Hyde, finally discharging the promise she had made before the year of separation. After a dinner in the home of Savannah's most eligible bachelor, admiralty lawyer William Garrard, Mary related to Hyde that she "slept with Daisy and we talked until the small hours grew a very respectable size and in consequence have now at one o'clock only just breakfasted!" To Mary's annoyance, they seldom got to church, even though it was Lent.[14]

Then followed a summer full of sweet connections, for not long after Easter, Daisy was in Abby's part of the world, enjoying champagne and clambakes, and revelries with Brown University students. The death knell of such times for the three best friends sounded when Venus announced her engagement in September. With persistence, patience, and prayer, Mary and Hyde had finally overcome Mrs. Carter's reservations. The wedding was planned for November 10, 1885, and, putting away their "dread" for the future of their friendship, Daisy and Abby converged on Cooperstown in late October to assist the bride-to-be. Both friends became better acquainted with Hyde, known as "a man of wide reading and culture, an exceedingly good talker, and a delightful social companion."[15]

Mary Gale Carter married George Hyde Clarke at Christ Church on a day, as Daisy described to her mother, "dull and snowy enough to dampen the most ardent spirits and make any one in full dress look pinched and chill." At least Mary resembled "a saint" in her white bridal gown. After the honeymoon, Mary moved into Hyde Hall, the magnificent Clarke family home with a stunning view of Lake Otsego. Hyde preferred agriculture to the bar. Mary relished the quiet life. Her inheritance helped the family hold on to the striking neoclassical mansion and its three thousand acres of land despite the mismanagement of Hyde's father. The couple would devote much of their time to the restoration of "that tumbledown mansion at Cooperstown," as Abby called it.[16]

Apparently, the first days of the Clarkes' marriage were successful: "If incoherence is any sign of happiness," Daisy teased, "you must have been in the seventh heaven while writing your last. I think I could read between the lines that your life is 'colour de rose.'" Mary set about arranging her new home. As the house was considered the realm of the wife, Daisy was keen to know all about how her old friend was faring. She asked for details about paint colors and furniture placement, including "the nocturnal depositary," by which Daisy coyly meant beds. She had specific questions: What was the difference between "grained oak" and "stained cherry," and where should each be used? "What is the best way to decorate a reception room . . . can it be done with cabinet sized photographs or should they all be of the <u>largest</u> size[?] Should they be partially concealed or ought they to stand out in conspicuous positions[?]" Daisy chided Mary not to forget to send the old, newsy letters that kept their contact alive despite distance, even if she had to "send Hyde away long enough to write."[17]

Daisy had good reason to immerse herself vicariously in home renovation, for she hoped that same venture awaited her. Willy Low returned to Savannah not long after Mary and Hyde's nuptials. His purpose was to ask Mr. Gordon's permission to marry Daisy and, once gained, to beg his assistance in persuading his own father to allow them to wed. Willie Gordon mandated two stipulations: that Willy "would settle down and live within his income, and that they should live for six months of the year in Savannah." The younger man agreed. Considering the misgivings that Willie Gordon had about Willy Low, it was a testament to his love for his daughter that he then negotiated with Andrew Low himself. Mr. Gordon's letter made clear that without Andrew's guarantee of support for his son, Daisy would not be allowed to wed.[18]

It was a difficult situation. The families had known each other for decades. The fathers served together on the board of directors of the Central of Georgia Railway. Willy was the nephew of Willie Gordon's sister. No matter how much Willie and Nellie might disapprove of the fact that Willy had no job, he did have an enormous fortune. Willy had attended Winchester College, one of the best private schools for boys in England, as well as Oxford University. He had no specific occupational preparation, but he insinuated to Eleanor that he wanted a proper career and had approached his father's friends in London about training. But Willy made little further effort toward this end, and nothing concrete resulted. His real love was horses. He enjoyed the English racing circuit, and buying and selling fast horses was well within his means.

Had the Gordons but known it, Willy Low's reputation would have put Hyde Clarke to shame. In England, Willy was thought to have consorted with society women whose upbringings had not been as sheltered as Daisy's and whose permissive ethics would have shocked her. Willy's circle of friends revolved around Queen Victoria's eldest son, Edward Albert, the prince of Wales. Before he ascended the throne in 1901, Bertie, as he was known, was famous neither for his intellect nor for his diplomatic abilities but for a series of extramarital affairs with famous actresses (Lillie Langtry and Sarah Bernhardt), with Jennie Jerome (who was Lady Randolph Churchill), and with courtesan Alice Keppel, among others. Bertie's reputation was so wicked and widespread that in America, Abby and Mary joined with others in snubbing an acquaintance entirely because of rumors that Bertie had glanced her way. They blamed her imprudent mother for "allowing the Prince of Wales to be introduced to her daughter." When he wasn't flirting, the prince of Wales was a fixture at the tracks. Waiting nearly six decades for the throne, he whiled away his time with gambling, fine dining, and the other accoutrements of the high life, interrupted by the occasional ceremonial duty.[19]

What Bertie's friend Willy Low saw in the ingenue Daisy Gordon is open to speculation. Perhaps he craved a link to the mother from Savannah he'd barely known. Possibly Daisy would be such an oddity in his circle that she would draw the prince's attention—always a scant but welcome commodity—to Willy as a result. Maybe "the love of a pure woman," as Hyde had once put it, touched Willy's deepest reformatory desires. He might have found Daisy's differences provocative. Perhaps his choice was a way to assert his independence from his father—who would disapprove but who could not very well stop the union. Willy did not require Daisy's dowry, as he stood to inherit the lion's share of Andrew Low's fortune. But he did need that promised inheritance, which is precisely what his father threatened to keep from him. Willy's sister Jessie hoped that marrying Daisy would "keep him straight," force him to remember his bills, and "turn over a new leaf."[20]

The letters from his son and from Mr. Gordon, plus some inveigling by his daughters, convinced Andrew Low to capitulate. He "behaved most generously and kindly," Daisy reported to Mary. Mr. Low promised to give Willy the family property in Savannah to provide sufficient revenue for them, and the Low home as their own. His price? A year's delay before marriage, to begin when Willy left Georgia, around February 7, 1886. Daisy professed them both "Oh, so happy" with the arrangement. "It is just like a fairy tale," she fluttered.[21]

In common with many young women of her era, Daisy worried that she could not live up to marital expectations. The late-nineteenth-century wife was supposed to be pious, pure, domestic, and submissive. She was considered closer to God, morally superior to her husband but obedient to his will, and "the angel of the home." Her greatest calling and profoundest joy was motherhood. A devoted wife should tactfully instruct a husband in right living, but her job was to create a "haven in a heartless world" where he could relax without distraction, enjoy the sanctity of the home, leave behind the amoral world of work, and rule unchallenged. Once the children were grown, a woman could dabble in philanthropy. She should keep her mind sharp in order to be a sparkling hostess for dinner parties. This was the ideal. Real women seldom met it.[22]

Daisy's appeal to her best married friend suggests that she had absorbed the ideal and wanted only advice to meet it. She was extremely self-critical, the result either of Nellie's disparagement over the years or of the Christian belief that all humans are sinners. The contemporary model of a good wife required that she "set him an example and make him like religion," which she felt incapable of, because she always acted on impulse, and "human impulses are usually so base." Daisy tried to locate a good advice book to help her, but Willy dissuaded her, telling her not "to copy books etc. He liked me to be myself." Mary's matrimonial counsel was critical as Daisy fretted about binding herself to one man. What should she do, she asked? "I would hate to feel that I am not free, and obeying Papa is such a very different thing from obeying W." She took heart that "[f]ortunately W. has the very qualities that I lack, common sense, and judgment." These were common premarital jitters. Since patience was the cardinal virtue of a good woman, Daisy would spend the year's waiting period decreed by Mr. Low in the useful occupation of working out how to think and act as a married woman.[23]

Then, like a bolt out of the blue, in June, Andrew Low died. The waiting period was over. Willy gained his inheritance, the major portion of 750,000 pounds. Daisy no longer faced the prospect of a cantankerous and, as Mabel felt, "tyrannical" father-in-law. Tradition decreed a mourning period to honor Andrew Low, but the young lovers defied social convention by choosing to marry before the prescribed year of mourning had ended. Contrariwise, Daisy set the wedding date for later that year to honor her parents: December 21, their anniversary.[24]

The next step was the arduous task of informing extended family and friends of the engagement. At last, those who had known since

January, such as Abby and Mary and Fred Habersham, could speak freely. Willie Gordon was disappointed but not surprised to find that "the congratulations apropos to Daisy have been very 'tepid.'" This could have been because Willie's business colleagues shared his disapprobation of Willy Low. But there were other reasons why friends might be wary. "Your polite note of Independence Day announcing that you have reversed the order of the day and succumbed to a British is at hand. As a good American," wrote Jesse Tyson, "you can hardly expect me to refer to it as an occasion for sky rockets." The Lippitt sisters approved of him but feared, as did most of Daisy's acquaintances, that marrying an Englishman meant she would move to Great Britain. Daisy reiterated Willy's promise that they would live in the States at least six months a year.[25]

Everyone had to be notified, from former teachers such as the Mesdames Charbonniers and Sarah Randolph (who was thrilled that Daisy would marry for love) to former suitors. Alexander Gregor was a case unto himself. Mabel had learned the shocking news that Gregor was married—and had been married all along—to a woman in Russia. It was appalling. The reputation of a woman, once harmed, could seldom be restored. Had the news come out while he was paying court to Daisy, it could have made her instantly unmarriageable. Luckily, this did not happen. Nellie informed Gregor of Daisy's engagement, but Willie fretted that her being married would not make the unscrupulous Gregor desist in his attentions to his daughter. "I can tell you, your 'idle Englishman' will have hard sense enough to take care of Daisy when he gets her, and not let any Russians . . . prance around after her! You need not fear that Daisy will want to have them do so, either," Nellie insisted.[26]

Once the banns were announced, trousseau shopping began. By the late nineteenth century, the trousseau no longer consisted solely of linens made and decorated by the bride to supply her new abode. Instead, Daisy and Nellie accumulated garments from ball gowns to peignoirs, and necessary goods, such as handkerchiefs, underclothes, and stockings. Sheets, tea towels, bath towels, tablecloths, and the like were bought at Lord & Taylor department store in New York or sewn by the Savannah seamstresses to whom Nellie sent designs. The Gordons gave their daughter a lavish sum for trousseau purchases. Daisy interspersed this happy task with jaunts to see Abby and Mary and trips to Clifton Springs, a spa town in New York, to tend to the persistent pain in her back, which she had wrenched in a horseback riding accident earlier that spring.[27]

When urgent business concerns in Georgia connected with his father's death brought Willy unexpectedly to America, he met up with Daisy in New England. She welcomed his assistance in choosing new furniture for the Low home in Savannah. Mostly, though, as Nellie shrewdly guessed, Daisy wanted to take her fiancé to Cooperstown "to show him off." Nellie was "blistered" by the giddiness of a daughter in love, who let quotidian things like travel arrangements and chaperones slip her mind.[28]

Then Willy made a mistake. He placed a bet at a New York polo match so large it made the newspapers. His future father-in-law saw red. Daisy tried to smooth things over by suggesting that the newspaper had inflated the figure and by assuring Willie that the bet was not Low's alone—instead, "he laid one big wager for the team, on commission." His paternal protectiveness aroused, Willie Gordon lectured Daisy, "I am glad Willy was ashamed and indignant at getting in the papers, but I think it was his own fault, and betting thousands of dollars whether for himself or on commission is neither reputable nor is it calculated to give me confidence in his future." The isolated event was bad enough, but, he continued, "A man who can under any circumstances be induced to bet large sums may be sure he will constantly be tempted to do it again. . . ." Gambling sharks would encircle him, Willie warned, and entice him into bad decisions. Finally, the chiding concluded, if this was the first act of a man just come into his inheritance, it did not bode well for the future. The fortune-teller Daisy and Abby consulted around this time underscored her father's admonition. Daisy marked well the divination that she "would shed tears soon on account of sickness."[29]

Mary could not accompany them, because she was pregnant and due in a few weeks. The pregnancy was untroubled, and Venus expected to travel south to see her Flower wed. But the birth of Anne Hyde Clarke, just four days before Daisy and Abby's shared birthday on October 31, was difficult and scary. The baby was fine, but Mary was extremely sick for three days. To everyone's relief, she recovered in time to make the trip.[30]

As Daisy set out upon the expected final rounds of her friends during what Mary called "the last summer of your maidenhood," Nellie took charge of all manner of decisions regarding the remodeling of the Low house. New York wallpaperers should be hired. Rugs ought to match carpet. Curtains should be replaced. Bathrooms must be refurbished. Daisy had to decide on patterns and colors, and when she hesitated, Nellie was quick with an opinion. Nothing escaped her attention: chandeliers, chamber pots, bathtub surfaces, dumbwaiters, soup tureens, upholstery, calling cards, monograms on napkins, music racks, bedroom chairs, smoking-room shades, washstands, dressing tables, and on and on. Daisy was grateful, and expressed her appreciation in a way that pleased Nellie, easing the ongoing tensions between them as the wedding approached.[31]

The day Mary touted as "the most important day of a woman's life" finally arrived. Surrounded by eight bridesmaids dressed in white and wearing hats, Daisy and Willy were married at noon at Christ Church, by Bishop John W. Beckwith. During the vows, Jessie Low recorded, Daisy "looked up in Willie's face all the time." The bridal bouquet was composed of Alice's favorite flowers, lilies of the valley, a touching remembrance of the absent sister. Willy gave the bridesmaids pins in the shape of a daisy with heart-shaped petals made of silver and forty-four diamonds. Along the stem of the flower was "1886." He lavished his bride with diamonds also. Too few photographs were taken, but the wedding party paused on the piazza, and family gathered at the wedding breakfast following the ceremony to commemorate the occasion.[32]

Family friends opened their home on Saint Catherine's Island for the honeymoon. As the newlyweds waved from their carriage, wedding guests showered them with rice, a conventional symbol of fertility. Somehow a piece of rice flew right into Daisy's bad ear and stuck there. After the six-day honeymoon, Daisy was in such pain that Willy took her back to Dr. Calhoun in Atlanta. Nellie described for her cousin how the doctor "with great difficulty extracted the rice grain which was already partly overgrown by a sort of fungus of flesh and would have produced serious results if it had remained any longer." When the couple returned, they opened their house and began entertaining. Not long after, Daisy contracted a lengthy case of bronchitis followed by an unpleasant boil on her leg that had to be lanced and took almost two weeks to heal. The physical ordeals left her fifteen pounds lighter. The fortune-teller was right: Daisy did "shed tears soon on account of sickness." It was an inauspicious beginning. She embarked upon her wedded life with a wealthy rogue plagued by a physical handicap that would prove to be only one of the challenges in her marriage.[33]

CHAPTER 7

The Whirl of Married Life

The new Mr. and Mrs. Low spent only a short while in Savannah after their December honeymoon. They had barely settled into Willy's refurbished boyhood home before leaving for England in the early spring to a rented house in Leamington Spa. When Nellie went to visit at the end of April, she found her daughter "very weak but improving" and longing for her father's presence. A fortnight on and Nellie was more optimistic. Daisy's color had returned. She was finally strong enough to manage stairs. Nellie, hating as always to be away from her husband, curbed her impatience and waited until she could accompany the couple back to Georgia. Daisy submitted to the ocean crossing but acknowledged she was "a fading flower." Touring New York and New Jersey, the Lows visited Eleanor and Wayne and their baby, Alice, saw a play on Broadway, and spent quietly happy hours with Abby and with Mary, Hyde, and young Anne.[1]

More time resting in Savannah did not cure Daisy. Regardless, the Lows recrossed the Atlantic. Warned by her worried family to take care of herself on the journey, Daisy dutifully dressed in her heaviest clothes. She prepared to meet London's damp, chilly fog in flannels, skirts, drawers, and a woolen dress. Alas, in 1887 the city witnessed one of the hottest, driest summers in its history and the weather felt "warmer than the tropics." When Daisy finally unbundled, her misery was complete: itchy red prickly heat bumps covered her from head to toe.[2]

The couple arrived to witness one of the great celebrations of the century, Queen Victoria's Golden Jubilee in 1887, marking fifty years on the throne. Daisy, Willy, his sister Amy, and her husband, Sir Harry Grenfell, took the steam train to Portsmouth for the grand naval review. Battleships and cruisers made a double row four miles long in the waters off the Isle of Wight. Journalists splashed the spectacle on front pages of newspapers the world over. Artists such as James McNeill Whistler, the former student of Daisy's art teacher Robert Weir, arrived to immortalize the festivities. European nations sent delegates, and the U.S. secretary of state represented President Grover Cleveland. European aristocracy looked on—many, like the prince of Wales, from their own vessels—while locals jostled to find a viewing spot.[3]

Daisy and Willy experienced the two-day exhibition of British sea power from the luxurious 1,500-ton *Alva*, William K. Vanderbilt's new yacht. It was one of hundreds of private craft joining, the *New York Times* reported, "pleasure boats of all nations and climes, [that] darted about like birds of different plumage. . . ." The newspaper described the *Alva* as "conspicuous in the marine procession" and "beautifully decorated with flags." Daisy remembered the *Alva* as the only unornamented vessel—but "the minute the illuminations began at night," she snorted derisively, "he had his yacht grandly illuminated, which shows he was simply trying to be talked about and make himself conspicuous." But perhaps her memory was impaired. So deep was her exhaustion that she slumbered through part of the naval review. In the train station, on their return after the transatlantic trip, the lethargy lingered. She had fallen asleep while sitting on her brother-in-law's luggage. When the suitcases toppled over, Daisy tumbled with them and didn't even awaken.[4]

The excitement of the wedding, the honeymoon, and the sea voyages certainly wearied Daisy, but the chief culprit was her ears—both of them. By early May 1887, Daisy had gone "somewhat deaf in her good ear." She consulted one of Britain's foremost physicians, Sir William Bartlett Dalby. Featured in *Vanity Fair,* the forty-seven-year-old specialist had among his patients Oscar Wilde, who later died of "chronic middle ear disease."[5]

Sir William could wax poetic about ears. He maintained that eardrum punctures had "individualities of their own, as exhibiting various moods, or showing a diversity of behaviour under treatment." Some healed quickly, others took "long life-times." All "perforations of the tympanic membrane" were differently affected by climate, age at which the ailment began, diet, and remedies applied. He held emphatically that there was "no best treatment" overall, which may partially exonerate Daisy's Georgia physicians.[6]

Dalby's 1873 book, *Diseases and Injuries of the Ear,* suggested an opposing strategy for the treatment of the rice in Daisy's ear. If forceps did not easily extract a foreign object, then a puncture would likely occur. The physician should instead use intermittent syringing, which might take up to several months. If syringing failed, the foreign object should be ignored, for "left alone it will do no harm." If Dalby was correct, then it is probable that Dr. Calhoun in Atlanta tore the tympanic membrane while grappling with the rice. Puncturing the eardrum, Dalby noted, "is generally followed by suppuration [festering] in the cavity of the tympanum, a discharge from the ear lasting a long time, and more or less permanent deafness." Daisy seemed to have experienced a more profound deafness in that ear after the rice, caused probably by Dr. Calhoun's use of forceps.[7]

Her good ear had suffered no incident but was going deaf from what Sir William called sympathetic hearing loss and "general ill health." Almost certainly her chronic earaches had resulted in decreased hearing in both ears. He expected "to permanently cure" one ear. He did not. From that point on, Daisy had only partial hearing in both ears. Weather conditions, her health, and other factors affected the degree to which she could hear from day to day.[8]

Deafness was more common in the late nineteenth century than it had been one hundred years earlier. The crowded cities of the industrial revolution assisted the rapid spread of infectious diseases, such as the scarlet fever that deafened Jeanie Lippitt. Factory machinery clacked and clanged, and laborers were susceptible to noise-induced hearing loss. Loud, recurring gunshot blasts brought about the same in military combatants and among men, such as Willy, who hunted frequently. The prince of Wales's wife, Alexandra, was hearing impaired because of an inherited condition called otosclerosis that worsened after pregnancy's hormonal changes. The lack of treatment options and the relative paucity of knowledge of the workings of the ear hindered physicians' efforts to reverse hearing loss. So many people in the Victorian era were hard of hearing that despite the increasing stigmatization of people with disabilities, deafness did not necessarily make one conspicuous.[9]

Several factors assisted Daisy's ability to maneuver through her world. Not growing up deaf gave her an advantage in lipreading, much of which depends on "skillful guesswork . . . being able to predict what's coming next, and filling in blanks." Because Daisy could speak so well, and did not depend on sign language, her hearing problems could often go unnoticed. When she misheard and acted illogically—as judged by those who had heard perfectly—her class excused her behavior. Daisy's social status exempted her from the middle-class culture of conformity. Eccentricities among elites were accepted among peers and across class lines. Daisy's hearing loss might have exacerbated what companions—especially family who knew her before she lost her hearing—called her "craziness," but her circle of friends tolerated irregular behavior.[10]

Her acting experience also abetted her ability to funtion in hearing society. From her earliest amateur theater experience, she was attuned to other people and used to watching for their responses. Actors are trained to analyze expressions and body language for clues and to react naturally. This would have been an asset in situations where she did not understand the conversation. Acting, in other words, probably made her a better bluffer. Further, to create a character, actors must try to empathize with other people and to understand their motives. When Daisy's fluctuating hearing loss was nearest to complete deafness, then her world narrowed to the imperative of trying to make others understand her. Short of that, there were ways to compensate.

Daisy probably turned her better ear toward conversations, scanned faces for inklings of what she might have missed, sat near her conversational partners, and avoided rooms filled with ambient noise. She rarely complained. She wanted to be a happy hostess and a cheerful companion for Willy. Gregarious by nature, Daisy avidly joined in amusements and did not let her deafness inhibit her socializing. Throughout her marriage she investigated cures, and new treatments and hearing aids always intrigued her, even after she had become accustomed to her hearing loss.

Worsened hearing was only one facet of her new life. An inexperienced wife, she had to study her husband—with whom she had spent very little time before the wedding. An American in England, she had to learn the ways of British culture and society. An untested housekeeper, she had to figure out how to hire and treat English servants, where to procure domestic necessities, and how to entertain Willy's circle. As a jejune woman from a sheltered background, she wasn't sure what to make of Willy's companions and their habits and hobbies. Her old friends were far away. While her letters remained upbeat and there were good times, Daisy's first year of married life was characterized by physical pain, adjustment to significant hearing loss and unfamiliar situations, and the absence of those she knew and loved best.

Because Willy did not have a career, the new couple was free to pursue pleasurable pastimes. Early in their marriage, Willy wanted Daisy to meet his acquaintances, members of the so-called smart set. One summer day, she and Willy went boating on the River Thames with Lord James Douglas and Angel Maxwell. Daisy wanted to learn how to maneuver their flat-bottomed boat, called a punt. It was difficult, Daisy explained to Abby, because "the punt is propelled by a long pole six times as [tall] as your humble servant, and several times it stuck in the long reeds and mud and the punt moved on." She was relieved to report that she stayed with the punt, not the pole.

The object of the boating trip was a day at Lord Douglas's twin sister's riparian home. Daisy saw what she "thought was a small boy in a Sailor hat and shirt, closer inspection proved it to be the queerest little figure you ever beheld! Lady Florence [Douglas] Dixie." Poet, essayist, rationalist, and proponent of home rule for Scotland, Ireland, and Wales, Lady Florence had hunted big game across Patagonia, supported women's rights, and championed Oscar Wilde. She was a true free thinker. Only three years older than Daisy, she had already published several books, including the one she bestowed upon her American guest about her time as a journalist in Africa during the 1880–1881 Boer War, *Defence of Zululand*. Florence kept her hair defiantly short. And she wore that day, Daisy described, "the scantest apology of a skirt." But Daisy quite liked her. She found her "clever, jolly, and kindhearted." Lady Florence took Daisy in hand and taught her "scientific punting." But not everything about Florence was easy for the Savannahian to understand. Daisy related that "[Florence] and her husband go by the nick name of 'Sir Always and Lady Sometimes Tipsy' instead of Sir Beaumont and Lady Florence Dixie." Alexander Beaumont Churchill Dixie, also called Lord ABCD, was a high-stakes gambler and an adventurer. Daisy found him "one of the most repulsive men" she'd ever met.[11]

The Dixies were Daisy's introduction to the type of aristocrats who peopled Willy's world. Because Willy was a member of the smart set, their lives were governed by the pattern of the social seasons, and those had been defined by a small and closed group of landed British patricians who barred entry to outsiders until they had been scrutinized and vetted. Presentation at court assisted one's entrée. Mostly, though, one had to come from or marry into an ancient British family, or have connections to one.

These same elites controlled the British government. The aristocracy sat in the House of Lords and held positions close to the monarch and the prime minister. Part of the social season occurred in London, because "high society was an essential adjunct to political life where dinner parties might be as important as cabinet meetings." The London season also allowed for proper chaperoning of young people, since making the right match was critical.[12]

The prince of Wales was at the center of the very smartest set, named for Marlborough House, his London abode. He might have been heir to the throne, but he was already, as a contemporary noted, "the king of the social system." Bertie surrounded himself with such "raffish members of the titled classes as Lord Charles Beresford, Lord Blandford, Lord Aylesford, and Lord Randolph Churchill. But by the 1880s, he was much more captivated by 'plutocracy, Semitic or American,' and with 'the modish smartness that is its product.'" Among the "plutocracy" were wealthy business magnates like W. W. Astor, Sir Thomas Lipton, Baron Hirsch, the Rothschilds, and the Sassoons.[13]

Willy Low did not have a country estate, but he did have money. This made him useful, as the prince was always short of funds and sought out those who were not. Willy also enjoyed the things Bertie liked: horses, gambling, hunting, and women. Several of Bertie's intimates followed his notorious example and had love affairs with actresses or with women known as "professional beauties," whose primary activities revolved around making themselves attractive and being on display. Thanks in part to the prince's lead, "By the 1890s, the aristocratic 'man about town' was a well-known phenomenon. He spent his days (and nights) in sporting clubs and near the stage door, mixed with book-keepers and racing journalists, squandered his allowance, and got into all kinds of mischief." In many ways, Willy Low fit this description.[14]

The prince of Wales and his diligent avoidance of boredom shaped the social calendar. The London season covered winter and spring, and summers were spent in the country. Autumn was the best time to hunt, and throughout the year, occasional trips to spas or foreign countries provided diversion. For members of the faster set who forsook drawing-room intrigue for the more bracing pleasures of horses and hounds, the hunting season assumed special importance in the year's rhythm. Hunting was a masculine culture; women were to look on approvingly from a distance. Draped in diamonds and attractively attired, these women brought dowries and connections that often mattered more than their conversational abilities or their interest in sport or spas.[15]

Lacking an ancestral home in which to host their friends, the Lows leased suitable residences. In Scotland, Willy and Daisy first took Lude House in the Perthshire highlands. Lude, in the parish of Blair Atholl, sat on a rise among nine thousand acres, with panoramic views in every direction of purple heather stretching to the Beinn a'Ghlo Mountains in the Grampian Range. There were red deer to be stalked in the Forest of Atholl, grouse to be flushed on the moors, salmon to be teased from the River Tilt, and brown trout to spirit out of the lochs. Daisy glimpsed partridges, rabbits, and deer on walks across the countryside, where exquisite spiderwebs wet with Highland dew clung to the saffron-colored gorse. Lude House was known for its formal gardens and its proximity to Blair Castle (also called Atholl House), instantly recognizable because of its unusual white exterior.[16]

The isolated cluster of homes at the village of Blair Atholl was easier to reach after the railway entered Inverness in 1863. Guests stayed at Lude House for weeks at a time. The Lows invited nearly everyone—including American friends the Clarkes and Abby, of course, but also Beirne and Bessie Gordon, Georgia Chisholm, even Bishop Beckwith. Wayne's brother, Courtland Parker, visited in the fall of 1887 and thought Highlands life agreed with Daisy. She was "looking better and prettier than he ever saw her and her deafness was <u>much</u> better. . . ." Parker observed her "smoking a pipe with a lot of [medicinal] chemicals in it" prescribed by a doctor who promised "she would be entirely over it in time." He was wrong.[17]

As she packed up Lude to return to England for the winter social season, Daisy felt unnerved and fretful. The transition to her new life was not perfectly smooth, and her ears were troublesome. She sought assistance from yet another physician, Morell Mackenzie. Dr. Mackenzie was not just a giant in his field of laryngology—he had helped to create it. He had studied in London, Paris, Prague, and Vienna; was known as "one of the most gifted specialists in Europe, with one of the shrewdest heads on his shoulders"; and at the time Daisy consulted him, practiced at London's Royal National Throat, Nose and Ear Hospital. Like Dalby, Mackenzie wrote extensively, publishing textbooks and guides. One of his high-profile patients was Bertie's brother-in-law, the German crown prince Frederick.[18]

Daisy spent a dreary fall separated from Willy, "shut up in a foggy hotel" in London while Dr. Mackenzie "blistered . . . behind my bad ear." She was "awfully uncomfortable" and "very blue." Mackenzie and Dalby both believed that after hearing declined in one ear, the second became more susceptible to infection. This appeared to be true for Daisy. She explained that in seeing the laryngologist she was "having my ear treated—or rather my throat which is the cause of my good ear sympathizing and becoming affected also." Daisy was frustrated. She longed to be done with doctors and "settle down and begin some regular occupations."[19]

Those would not include one of Willy's regular pastimes: cross-country fox hunts. Willy forbade it. Women did ride to the hounds—Warwickshire boasted several "hunting ladies," so gender was not the crux of Willy's argument. He had ridden with Daisy and knew her for a trained horsewoman, so her skill was not sufficient reason for denying her participaion. His objections must have had one of three sources: worries that her lack of hearing would compromise her safety on the fast-moving hunt; concern that she would aggravate the back injury from her earlier riding mishap; or a desire to keep her separate from his set, with whom she had little in common beyond a love of Willy and an appreciation of fun. But Willy's injunction at the start of their marriage comprehensively shut her out of an important part of his life, leaving her home alone during daylong and sometimes weekend-long hunts while he and their guests socialized and amused themselves.[20]

Willy did not prohibit her from shooting. This elite sport consisted of stalking the fields for game and lunching in luxury under tents set up by servants. Shooting provided, Daisy thought, "exercise and the chance of knowing other women well in a way one can't do at balls or hunting." Her quirky personality impressed the British. For example, back at Beauchamp Hall, she and four female companions (with Willy to assist them) made up an impromptu cricket team. The other side was all male. Their bats were tree branches, and walking sticks made wobbly wickets. It was an uproarious game. "You perceive," she suggested in her weekly to Mary, "I have given up trying to be dignified, after a lamentable failure. I played the heavy hostess with great effect when [Lady Hertford and Lady Aylesford] first arrived. I sat in the drawing rooms, toying with a piece of knitting. I made conversation [and] in all respects conducted myself in an exemplary manner, but in one inadvertent moment I undid all my work, by rashly standing on my head in the Maxwells' room one night, where Lady Hertford caught me doing it. I think she was shocked but fascinated for she wanted to know how it was done, and made so many inquiries that I began to think she was going to try it herself. Since then I follow my natural bent, and have led Lady Aylesford into such exhibitions. Why, she actually rolled down the terrace with the rest of us."[21]

Daisy's silliness was an endearing part of her naïveté and charm, understood as such by the aristocrats she knew. Rolling down a hill, however, could not compare to the "disagreeable and scandalous" contretemps, as the *London Daily News* once described it, between Lord and Lady Aylesford. It had happened before Daisy's marriage, but it's a sure bet that someone, sometime, imparted the lurid details to the young American, which included prostitution, drunkenness, adultery, and suicide. While the Aylesford scandal was extreme, people with similarly checkered pasts and presents dotted Willy's social circle. They were not the sort of people to cleave to her father's standards of propriety.

Widely publicized scandals coupled with the prince of Wales's unpalatable choice of friends contributed to the steady decline in the power, wealth, and influence of England's traditional aristocracy. It is doubtful that Daisy would have seen it quite that way from her place in the middle of it. She did not commit her attitude toward the Marlborough set to paper. She rejected their morals, but she clearly enjoyed friendships with many of them, and she gamely tried to keep up with the lifestyle. Gone were the art classes, the German lessons, the letters of exegeses on books she'd read. Instead, she told Mary, she was "just rushing at pleasure, without time to breathe!" Daisy's part in her husband's world was to be a sparkling chatelaine of the homes they occupied, to see to the comfort of their guests, and to follow the social seasons uncomplainingly.[22]

Into this she folded her own friends as they visited. Daisy took them to Oxford to gape at the great university and the punters on the Isis, to Anne Hathaway's tidy cottage in Stratford-upon-Avon, to the romantic, foxglove-strewn Kenilworth Castle ruins, and to nearby Charlecote Park, the Lucy family country estate lit still by candles rather than gas. But to join Willy on the hunt proved impossible. She remained intensely fascinated by foxhunting, yet, she wrote desolately, "nothing goes right in that line. Willy has made up his obstinate old mind not to be interested in my hunting." Daisy stubbornly sneaked out on her own, trying to learn, because "[t]hey have laughed so at my hunting experiences. . . ."[23]

Forced to remain at home, Daisy sought distraction from Willy's sisters, particularly Katie and Mary. Mary had recently become engaged to Willy's close friend, Major Green. She planned gatherings that did not include hunting or racing. But it was difficult to deny that Daisy and Willy were frequently apart. In his absence she fell into a "depressed state of mind." Letters from loved ones in America were "the best part of my life now," she told Mary, "except Willy," she added loyally.[24]

So her friends redoubled their efforts at their weeklies. Abby agreeably gossiped about friends' marriages, including Jesse Tyson's. He had finally found the young woman of his dreams, which provoked an outburst from Abby: "Really, though, is it not disgusting, this selling yourself for filthy lucre[?] I thoroughly appreciate the good of this same filthy lucre, but I confess it is one too many for me to marry a man seventy years [too] old for it." Abby was not alone in noticing the age imbalance as the wealthy Tyson wedded the ravishing Edith Johns. The succinct, front-page *New York Times* headline read: "Fifty and Nineteen."[25]

Other news from home was sad. Mary's mother succumbed to a series of illnesses. "I feel as if I had lost my own mother," Daisy wrote sympathetically. "The happiest moments of my life were spent under her roof, and I reverenced and loved her as one of the best women that ever lived." Daisy reminded Mary to "trust in God's mercy and love" but to stay busy: "nothing but active work can dull the edge of grief."[26]

By then it was early spring in England, and crocuses and snowdrops were gracing the garden's "moist dark nooks." She took long walks in the Midlands just to see the new lambs, whose antics made her smile. She grew closer to her sisters-in-law: Daisy helped Mary after the sudden death of her fiancé. Katie stood by Daisy as she faced a phalanx of fifty local women when she hosted a tea party to pay back all of her social debts at once. Katie and Daisy redecorated the Leamington Spa home, making silk lampshades and "draping any number of chairs" to keep busy. One special decoration must have come as a result of Katie's influence. It was the stuffed and mounted head of a fox, which Daisy treasured as "a memento of my first day's hunting." Willy relented, at least once, and that might have been the time Daisy ran afoul of the English custom of signifying a kicking horse by tying a ribbon around its tail to warn other riders. After watching Daisy's mount misbehave, an irate huntsman asked with asperity why she had failed to put a ribbon on her horse's tail, because the horse obviously kicked. With unerring logic, Daisy responded, "That is just the reason that I would *not* tie a ribbon on his tail."[27]

That spring included the excitement of a presentation at court. Only those with connections and flawless public morals were invited to Queen Victoria's drawing room in Buckingham Palace. Daisy's sponsor was Lady Emily Murray, the marchioness of Hertford. She was the widow of Sir Francis George Hugh Seymour, fifth marquess of Hertford, whose ancestral home, Ragley, was located in Warwickshire. The marchioness's daughter, Lady Mary Margaret Seymour, was fond of Daisy, and attended the presentation with them.[28]

After procuring the appropriate gown, rehearsing the curtsy, and memorizing everyone's advice, it turned out to be a most undignified event. There was a terrible "rush and tear" on the way to the queen, which reminded Daisy, thinking of London's famous fish market, more of "Billingsgate than Buckingham." She summoned "what few wiles I possess[ed] to keep my clothes on my back and myself on my legs," as the crush of the crowd was overwhelming. The sight of a Low cousin who was a lord-in-waiting braced her. His job was to arrange the lengthy trains on the women's expensive court dresses. The line moved ponderously; people jostled one another amid apologies. The initial excitement turned sour as Daisy's heavy gown and oversize spray of flowers weighed her down unmercifully. Seeking to ease her burden, Daisy placed her bouquet "on the bustle of the lady in front of me, and quite unconscious of the service she rendered, she carried it the length of all the rooms!" But the pushing and waiting and anticipation were for naught, because the audience ended before Daisy made it to the queen.[29]

Also disappointing was the decline in her hearing that spring of 1888. Her friend Angel Maxwell and Katie Low accompanied Daisy to Paris for shopping, before she was exiled to the care of an "aurist" in Dresden. That German physician held "no hopes" of her "ever recovering normal hearing." Only slight improvement could be expected, and he insisted on two weeks of treatment immediately followed by a month in a "high, dry" place, such as Switzerland.[30]

This meant that from May through mid-July, Daisy would be apart from Willy, who could not accompany her because he was camping with the Warwickshire Yeomanry, his volunteer cavalry unit. Instead, Daisy met up with Mary's sister, Grace Carter, who was recovering from chaperoning her clinically depressed brother Averell across Europe. Grace thought Daisy looked thin but was hearing "very well—even low sounds." The damp English weather played havoc with Daisy's auditory abilities, causing uncontrollable variations. Hearing was easiest "on clear bright days" and when she was "excited," but mundane conversations were difficult.[31]

Two years into her marriage, Daisy had learned much about her husband, some of it disturbing. The Willy who had courted her was a man with a modest allowance, but she married a millionaire. The heady combination of access to funds and no parental oversight allowed for perpetual sprees by a young man whose father's controlling behavior had taught him little about how to be an independent, responsible adult. With each passing month, Willy's time and priorities shifted away from his wife and toward accumulating extraordinary toys—like racehorses—and unmatched experiences with his friends. No children had yet been born to the Lows to help anchor him to home. Daisy, meanwhile, fought to amend her hearing, and the search for cures took her away from him just as his racing, gambling, and hunting trips took him away from her. The relationship was strained by their diverging schedules and concerns.

In acknowledgment, Willy made an ill-fated attempt to join his wife in Germany but was stopped at the French border and accused of smuggling the five hundred cigarettes in his luggage. Even though he swore he meant to declare them, customs officers did not believe him. He protested his 120-franc fine and blamed the confusion on his inability to be understood by the guards, who spoke no more English than he did French. Annoyed, Willy went back to England, "hired a courier [to ferry the cigarettes] and joined me in triumph at Lucerne," Daisy related. Just what Willy was doing with five hundred cigarettes his faithful wife did not explain. Though he was entranced by unforgettable views from six thousand feet above Lucerne, he did not linger. He was having trouble selling some of his horses. The fact that his Hallmark won a cup Daisy called "only a tiny exception that proves the rule of his invariably bad luck where racing is concerned." Her brother Bill was in Europe, and joined them on Mount Rigi. No doubt Bill carried these stories back to Savannah.[32]

The aurist had been right about the salutary effect of Alpine air on Daisy's hearing. But by the end of the summer Daisy had more physical problems. She conferred with renowned Dr. Lawson Tait, a professor of gynecology at the Birmingham Women's Hospital. Pugnacious, ambitious, and egotistical, Tait's peers dubbed him "the greatest gynecologist of [his] time," and William J. Mayo called him "the father of modern abdominal surgery." Tait believed ovarian cysts should be removed as soon as they were discovered, which set him in opposition to London's most famous gynecologist, Sir Spencer Wells, who felt cysts should be left alone until surgery was the last option. Their feud was well known, and Daisy's body became their battleground.[33]

She seems to have suffered—not for the first time—from abdominal or tubo-ovarian abscesses, and probably ovarian cysts. Daisy explained that she "had the sac of the old abscess cut out, and the shock set another abscess going, in or near a vital place, the London Doctor and Birmingham Doctor differed as to where it was, only they all agreed that it was too deep to lance, and yet that it might break internally and give me blood poisoning so the Birmingham man, Dr. Lawson Tait, who was rather a butcher, wanted to cut me open from the outside, and cut out the abscess, but the London Dr. would not countenance the operation, in fact they were all at loggerheads. Willy feared the shock and decided not to have me cut open. The abscess fortunately broke in a safe place. . . ."[34]

It was a grave crisis. Daisy fully expected to be an invalid for life. Her family thought she would die. When the threat passed, family and friends took her to Scotland to convalesce. Daisy wanted the details of her ordeal kept private. Tell only Abby, she directed Mary, "as I am rather ashamed of having so many abscesses, it appears to me that I must be very rotten." Abby wondered on paper what others were thinking silently: Why did Daisy blame herself—and where was Willy Low in this crisis? He was certainly not in Scotland.[35]

Persistent abscesses probably explain why Daisy and Willy never had children. According to one of her physicians, Daisy had what might have been a malformed, unicornuate uterus. Nellie illustrated her letter to her cousin to help her understand the condition. She drew a normal uterus as a lightbulb with a long neck. Daisy's unicornuate uterus looked like the lightbulb had been stretched out and bent over to the right so that the bulb rested on the top of its head, which was level with the bottom of the bulb: rather like an underpass bloated on the right side. A unicornuate uterus would not necessarily rule out childbearing, but combined with abscesses, it might have in her case.[36]

Childlessness carried a terrible social stigma; it was a reflection on the woman, who deserved pity for being denied the most fundamental female role, or scorn for rejecting it. Victorian society considered childless women to be—through perversity or frigidity—negligent of their duty, and thus socially useless. By failing to provide a namesake or an heir, she had not fulfilled her part of the marital contract. Men expected sons to carry on their family name, and couples looked forward to raising children as part of their married life together. Daisy felt all of this. She believed she had let the Gordons down and disappointed the entire Low family. She could never compare herself favorably to her sisters, because she had not achieved the first and most basic function of a wife. This shame and the sorrow of childlessness were always raw.

From Scotland, Nellie brought her ailing daughter back to America. Daisy spent her twenty-eighth birthday with Abby, just like old times. Though they pleaded, Mary had to remain with her guests at Hyde Hall. Daisy returned to Savannah by Christmas to wait for Willy, but he could not tell her when to expect him or how long he might stay. He asked her to open the Lafayette Square house, but, as she put it, "Until I set eyes on that husband of mine I shall not know what my plans are." She knew Willy was tempted to join his friends Sir Francis Grenfell and Jack Maxwell in Egypt, fighting in the colonial wars with the British Army. She missed him. They had been separated for most of four months. His letters did not bridge her loneliness: "They are so unsatisfactory that all I can glean from them is that he was frightened to death at meeting 34 strangers at Sandringham, on the Princess's birthday!"[37]

With her older sister present, Mabel made her debut in January 1889. A pregnant Mary protested that her presence at the ball would shock Georgians. Nonsense, Daisy wrote. "I agree with the ancient Greeks who always made a low salutation to any woman in that condition, whether she was princess or peasant, so much was it esteemed an honor!" Mary and Hyde made the trip and returned to New York before their second child, George, was born. Willy did turn up in Savannah, and the winter went well and happily. Friends and family had been pleased to see their own Daisy still charming and uncorrupted by London living. They noted, too, how affable Willy was. Daisy had recuperated so thoroughly that Nellie was no longer frightened to let her return to England.[38]

As the English horse-racing season began—and Willy's poor luck continued—Daisy and her sister-in-law Hattie were wild to cross the English Channel and join the hullabaloo of the 1889 Paris Exposition, which marked the centennial of the French Revolution. Willy, Daisy bemoaned, "refuses to improve his mind and French conversational powers," despite the border squabble over the cigarettes, and so stayed behind. Daisy and Hattie were two of thirty million visitors who marveled at paintings, cultural pavilions, industrial exhibits, and agricultural accomplishments from around the world. The stupendous hydraulic railway ferried them across the massive grounds as they ate unusual food and pondered the future made present in demonstrations of electric light, the telephone, moving pictures, and the first gas-powered horseless carriage.[39]

Daisy appreciated the music and paintings sent by countries proud of their artists. She remarked on the "villages with the inhabitants and trades of China, Japan, Java, Borneo," and other nations. Like fellow guests from Europe and America, Daisy found the exotic fascinating. She thought the "little Japanese ladies" danced in a "most seductive manner." Appraising like a sculptor, Daisy noticed their "most shapely bodies, very plump and rounded arms and legs and tiny waists and ankles." She especially liked the "history of habilitations, which represented the earliest dwellings of savages, also facsimiles of Egyptian architecture [from] 4000 B.C.," and "a Roman house built in Gaul in the time of Clovis."

The pièce de résistance was the brand-new Eiffel Tower. Many artists loathed the monstrosity that shot like a malevolent needle over Paris. French novelist Guy de Maupassant wrote memorably of the "tall, skinny pyramid of iron ladders, the giant and disgraceful skeleton with a base that seems made to support a formidable monument of Cyclops and which aborts into the thin, ridiculous profile of a factory chimney." Others, like Daisy, loved it, and could envision tremendous possibilities for the use of metal in inspired ways. Drawn inexorably to the architectural sculpture, Daisy waited for two hours to reach "the top in elevators which look like a crab." She feared the climb—but she did it. In jest, she averred, "if one must ascend into heaven, I hope to do so in a state of unconsciousness, for anything more terrifying I never experienced than the last elevator of all where one simply rises in the air. . . ."[40]

Returning to England held the great charm of finally settling into her own home. Willy bought, for a great deal of money, Wellesbourne House in rural Warwickshire. Set on fifty-five acres, it met his needs with room to entertain, meadows for grazing his mares, and three wine cellars. Daisy described it as small but comfortable and "beautifully furnished with real old Chippendale furniture while the paper and paint is modern and in very good taste." An indication of life with her profligate husband came from her admission to Mary that she "had imaginary scares about Bailiffs on Willy's account." But she feared also an "intense loneliness if I do not hunt" while living in the "inaccessible" Midlands, so far from London. Daisy taught herself to follow the British parliament and swore she would "devote my self to a dairy, garden, and the poor of the parish!" As it turned out, she was so busy with visitors that she got around to only the poor of the parish.[41]

Society friends came after the Lows converted what Wellesbourne historian Peter Bolton called "a jumped-up hunting box into a house on the grandest of scales." At Willy's direction, Wellesbourne grew to twenty bedrooms, with stables for forty horses. Near the home, he constructed a cottage for the gardener, separate laundry facilities, and a garage to hold the very first automobiles in Wellesbourne, which soon became the talk of the village and beyond. One of Willy's cars was large enough to ferry Londoners from the Warwick train station. The Lows dug a sunken garden, converted the old gaslights to electricity, added an electric generator, and built a "private sewage plant." Daisy procured a pair of stone lions like those welcoming visitors to the Low home in Savannah. Warwick Castle, Leamington Spa, Stratford-upon-Avon, Compton Verney, Charlecote, and the home of Sir Charles Mordaunt, Walton Hall, were nearby.[42]

Daisy came to love Wellesbourne House. It "is like a bourne," she told Grace, "which I've at last reached, where I am at anchor. It has made the most tremendous difference to me, I begin to identify myself with this land."[43] She identified with the people of the village of Wellesbourne, too. Willy could not tolerate the thought of a zealously philanthropic wife who was self-righteous about his indolent friends. Though he discouraged her from participating in organized charity work, Daisy could not restrain her altruistic bent, and quietly contributed to Warwickshire life, spending one afternoon every week with a woman who was ostracized because she had Hansen's disease, or leprosy. Daisy visited with the destitute men and women of No. 50 Arden Street, the term preferred by the sympathetic director for the Stratford-upon-Avon workhouse. Daisy fed and tried to care for vagrants who happened upon Wellesbourne House. She donated flowers from her greenhouse and pitched in to help dress Saint Peter's Church for Christmas services. Daisy joined the local nursing association, attended village concerts and summer fetes, gave to the Parochial Tea when she was in residence, and served sweets as a patroness of a charity bazaar alongside Lady Jane Seymour, the marchioness of Hertford, and her American friend May Cuyler, Lady Grey Egerton.[44]

Willy, too, could be generous beyond his immediate family circle. In 1895 he purchased coal from a rural merchant teetering on the brink of bankruptcy and then doled out the fuel to nearly two dozen impoverished families. This "became a fairly regular event," according to Bolton. By 1905 the Lows supplied "fifty widows and infirm old people" with enough coal to heat their homes until springtime. Willy also paid for the community observance of the queen's Diamond Jubilee, including a fireworks display so fabulous that it "bewildered" one venerable resident. Willy was president of the Wellesbourne Cricket Club, although perhaps more patron than organizer, and was a director of the Birmingham Race Course, where spectators could watch traditional racing as well as Willy's favorite, the steeplechase.[45]

The vicar's wife, Valentine Eliot, was a particularly interesting addition to the village of Wellesbourne. Mrs. Eliot was an accomplished woodworker with her own workshop. Her display area held the "nearly 200 pieces she produced ranging from humble carved picture frames to oak linen presses as well as . . . carved hymn boards," which stood in the nave to announce that day's songs. Indeed, the size of some of Valentine Eliot's works, like the vicarage doors, suggests that she might have been an inspiration and perhaps a colleague as Daisy took up art again, beginning with a carved wooden mantelpiece for Willy's smoking room. She filled Willy's absences with the physical labor of woodworking and created the clawed feet for a bed, dragon heads and other designs carved into a mahogany highboy, and a "leaf cradle" she designed and built to hold the extra leaves from her dining-room table.[46]

Daisy also found a way to craft metal, for she created an exquisite set of gates for Wellesbourne House. Metalworking by women was exceptionally unusual, then and now. In the Victorian era, the few females who did so typically made jewelry out of soft gold and silver, usually because their husbands were metalworkers. Not until the 1890s, late in the Arts and Crafts movement, did female artists both design and create jewelry themselves.[47]

Women very rarely became farriers. The job demanded physical strength and a tolerance for burns and grime. It was a masculine occupation. Blacksmiths required long apprenticeships. How, therefore, did Daisy come to make the gates for Wellesbourne? As an artist, designing the gates would have been second nature. The Eiffel Tower might have inspired her. But from design to reality involved several steps generally inaccessible to women—principally forging. While industrialization made possible the purchase of iron bars for the uprights, those would still have to be welded together. The decorations on the gates entailed shaping the metal also.

There are three possible places where Daisy might have learned to heat and bend metal. While in London, she could have encountered the Women Metal Workers Company. This unique group produced not jewelry but bellpull chains, doorknobs, clocks, chandeliers, fingerplates, door locks, and picture frames. Encountering their workshop and showroom in Mayfair would have been simple for Daisy, who knew people living in that upscale neighborhood. Seeing the women working on large projects, such as gates, might have contributed to her determination to acquire the necessary skills.[48]

Surrounding Wellesbourne were several foundries, the best known in Leamington Spa. Foundries in the 1890s were bastions of male work. It is possible but unlikely that Daisy could have had the idea for the gates, taken herself off to a foundry, and asked for training from the men. A more likely scenario would be that one of the three ironmongers in the village of Wellesbourne had instructed her. Chedham's Yard was a local wheelwright and a blacksmith shop, and William Chedham might have taught Daisy before his death in 1889.[49]

More probable still, someone came to her home to teach her. Fewer social rules were broken that way, and Willy might have been persuaded to allow his wife to engage in such untraditional behavior in the privacy of their own home. The Lows hired the son of a Wellesbourne village blacksmith, John Thomas Thorpe, to fix whatever broke around their house or stables.[50] Daisy thus encountered him frequently. Thorpe had the skills, the tools, and the opportunity during his visits to the house. He could easily have built a forge for Daisy (or resurrected one already there), taught her how to heat and shape metal, and been close at hand for questions. Thorpe could have welded the uprights together and attached the decorative bits she made, or he could have taught her how to manage it. She did enough of the work herself to expand the muscles in one arm, making the sleeves of her gowns difficult to wear. Daisy Low was deterred neither by the difficulty of metalworking nor by the fact that women seldom went near it.[51]

The Gordons came to see for themselves how their daughter was faring in the early summer of 1891. Aboard the S.S. *Saale* bound for Southampton, Nellie, Willie, Mabel, Bill, and Arthur spied a pod of one hundred whales and passed four serene icebergs. Nellie's continued ability to find fault with Daisy was evident in her complaints about the hotel and her daughter's appearance despite the fact that Daisy and Willy both had the flu. Willy's doctor sent him to sunny Brighton, warning that "any imprudence in eating, drinking, or catching cold again may kill him." Daisy was too sick to go, and the doctor ordered her home. She dragged herself from Southampton to Wellesbourne. Luckily, Grace Carter was visiting and able to help with the most laborious tasks.[52]

Daisy aimed to keep her family busy, even after she was later sent to Brighton to regain her health. Jessie Low Graham played hostess while Mary Low offered her opera box. Among the visitors was Rowland Leigh, a young barrister from an old English family. His ancestral home was nearby Stoneleigh Abbey. "Rowley" Leigh, who was soon to take a three-year position as the private secretary for the secretary of state for war, was just then busy falling in love with Mabel. Willie Gordon went to Ascot with some of Willy Low's friends, but Willy dashed to the deathbed of his oldest half sister, Harriet Coke-Robertson, in Nottinghamshire. Her passing was "a great blow to Daisy," Nellie noted. Harriet's husband, George, commissioned a marble memorial sculpted by Edouard Lanteri for the Church of Saint Peter and Saint Paul, Widmerpool, where she was buried.[53]

Time with friends and family remained important for Daisy, and so she made a point of returning to the United States yearly, and always for important events, such as the wedding of the Icicle to Duncan T. Hunter. Once both of Abby's parents had passed away, the Lippitt daughters married in rapid succession: May in 1892, then Abby and Jeanie in 1893. Abby's husband was born in London to Scottish parents in 1863. After his father, Archibald Hunter, died in 1868, Duncan's mother, Mary Jane Hunter, returned to Scotland to raise her children. Duncan had older siblings, twins Archie and Nellie; sisters Janet, Ann, and Marion; and a younger brother named George. When his mother married again in 1871, there were two half brothers and another relocation, this time west to the Ayrshire coast, where Duncan's stepfather imported rum from, and exported coal to, the West Indies.[54]

Educated in Scotland and England, Duncan sought his fortune in the American West at nineteen. Pooling his money with four other Englishmen, they bought a six-thousand-acre cattle ranch and land near the Missouri River that they incorporated into the town of Three Forks, in the Montana Territory. The killing winter of 1886 depleted their stock, their funds, and their enthusiasm. In 1889, Duncan sold his investment at a great profit to William Rockefeller's Amalgamated Copper Company and relocated to the frontier city of Helena to be the western representative of the Equitable Life Insurance Company of New York. Duncan immersed himself in the life of his adopted town by joining the Shriners, the Masons, and the exclusive Montana Club.[55]

Before meeting Duncan, Abby had been finding joy in the relatively untrussed life of the female athlete. She played tennis and golf, ice-skated, and rode horses. Abby's adventurous streak took her to Helena, where she met Duncan. After a Scottish honeymoon, they returned to Montana in search of gold. Abby described it as "rustl[ing] for our 'million' in this desolate country." There, two daughters (Mary Lippitt and Frances Grahame) were born, and two more (Janet Malise and Marion Amcotts) followed after the family returned—without gold—to Providence in 1897.[56]

Daisy's situation was very different from Abby's. The absence of children and the presence of wealth, servants, and the Marlborough set meant that Daisy's life resembled her Southern belle upbringing. Entertaining occupied most of her days, and her talents made their very busy social life possible. When Nellie scolded her for writing infrequently, Daisy impatiently explained that "decorating the dinner table and writing the menus in French everyday" took time. Her handwritten place cards were works of art. Travel was such an ordeal that visitors always stayed between three nights and a fortnight or more. Feeding and amusing guests left little private time. She accompanied them to tourist sites, inspections of Willy's horses, rowing parties on the River Avon, or strolls in the garden. London dressmakers or jewelers were de rigueur for Americans. In inclement weather they read aloud or played whist while Daisy's Georgia mockingbirds serenaded them. Even surrounded by guests, a hostess could not neglect her village commitments. Daisy knew that letter writing to absent loved ones was an expected part of a woman's day, and the larger the family, the more one had to dip one's pen into the ink pot. But it was never easy to find the time, she insisted to her mother.

Willy Low swung between extravagance and economy, presumably because of his continuing bad luck at the racetrack that Daisy mentioned with depressing regularity. She felt she lacked enough servants and sought cost-cutting measures to please him. At least guests usually brought their own maids to see to their clothing and toilette, decreasing the strain on the hostess's staff. The unpacking and ironing of gowns and the washing and styling of hair could take hours of a maid's time. Even Daisy's "nice fat little cook" felt the pinch, and was reduced to weeping by Willy's "mania of economy." To save money, Daisy purchased groceries locally rather than from London. Guests requested the peach-fed Georgia hams her mother shipped to her, and many delectable—and to the British, unusual—recipes from her Savannah cook, Mosianna Milledge.[57]

Daisy's occasions ranged from a race party luncheon of one hundred people to dinner for as many as thirty guests at Wellesbourne. The more who came, the greater the number of rooms to be prepared, the larger the number of diversions to be planned, and the higher the financial cost. But as one's standing with one's friends rose or fell based in part on one's ability to entertain well, the Lows considered the fuss and frustration worth it.[58]

Willy invited the prince of Wales to the Warwickshire Yeomanry dance in May 1895. On his arrival, the prince noticed Daisy while she was dancing and asked to be presented to her. Daisy was proud to tell her mother that "H.R.H. was very gracious, said he had known Willy for years and didn't . . . know I existed. It was a great shame to hide me away, etc! He sent for Willy and said the next time he came to Newmarket, I was to be taken there also. Then, to everybody's amazement, he asked me to dance . . . and I was the only woman in the room he danced with. . . . Willy was very pleased so I am glad I was noticed." Newmarket was the least respectable racecourse, which may be why Willy forbade Daisy to attend. Or perhaps Willy hoped to keep his comely wife away from Bertie's roving eyes.[59]

Bertie was fond of Americans. In 1896 he visited the Lows at

Wellesbourne House. In his party was his mistress, the Brooklyn-born widow Lady Randolph Churchill. Lord and Lady Warwick joined them. Daisy presided over the luncheon table, and the prince, she related to her mother, "made himself most agreeable." What she thought of her compatriot she did not say.[60]

Since both Bertie and Willy delighted in the new and the fantastic, Willy almost certainly entertained his royal guest with his fifteen-foot-tall giant orchestrion. This mammoth mechanical instrument was related to an organ, but with its one hundred wooden pipes, it could make nearly all the sounds of an orchestra as it played symphonies and waltzes. A day of shooting or a trip to Birmingham Race Course would have rounded out Bertie's visit.[61]

Another extraordinary guest was a relative. Nellie was related to Carrie Kipling, who lived in Sussex with her husband, renowned author Rudyard Kipling. Once the connection was established, the Kiplings became great friends of Daisy's. Rudyard left an evocative description of Wellesbourne in which Willy "went in for horse-racing and had thirty brood mares on the premises." Kipling enjoyed the "big old country-house full of butlers and valets and electric lights and hot house plants—the regular gilt-edged show," but most of all he praised "the sweetest American hospitality and genuine kindliness," and concluded, "I'd visit round a good deal if all folks were like that." The Kiplings were very different from the Marlborough set, and Daisy enjoyed them.[62]

Wellesbourne House was Daisy's home, and she was devoted to it and to their Warwickshire friends. Willy was glad to have a country place to entertain his set and exercise his horses. When he left to go hunting, she returned to the States or channeled her energies into art and furtive acts of charity. Their marriage held tensions she worked hard to disguise. Extroverted and interested in everything, Daisy was not the type to sit on her hands and mope. She found new friends of her own, and learned to become braver in Willy's absences.

CHAPTER 8

Wars, Colonial and Domestic

Egypt was an exotic holiday site for the wealthy, and Daisy was determined to go. She had been hearing friends describe the Sphinx, the blazing-hot sand, and the bizarre customs, and she was insanely curious. In 1891, she got her chance. The commander in chief of the Anglo-Egyptian Army, Sir Francis Grenfell, and his wife, Evelyn, invited the Lows to Cairo. Daisy drank in the colors and the hospitality. "Every other man one meets is a Duke," Daisy exclaimed. The couple mingled with the Grenfells' set of friends, and Daisy found them infused with "a sociable warmheartedness, that reminded me of Savannah." And to her satisfaction, the Egyptian climate made her deafness "almost disappear."

Daisy couldn't wait to see everything, but Willy preferred to hole up at Cairo's horse races with two sisters whom Daisy found "rather rowdy and bad form." Since, Daisy explained scathingly to Mary, he "refused to improve his mind at the expense of bodily fatigue," she had no one to sightsee with. Preparing to make the best of it, she unexpectedly encountered the Mesdames Charbonniers. Even after a decade, Daisy found the Chars "as unaltered by time as the pyramids." The three women went adventuring on donkeys to explore the ruins of ancient Memphis. Daisy was humbled by the vast reserves of historical details her old teachers were able to summon.[1]

Four years later, Daisy returned to Egypt on a medicinal trip for Willy. In the late fall of 1894 he suffered from malaria and influenza so badly that he swore off alcohol. It profited him, Daisy thought, but it was also brave, because all his men friends "drink a lot." Willy's physician prescribed salt air to strengthen his weakened lungs, so he and some of those hard-living friends chartered a yacht and sailed to Albania on a lengthy hunting expedition. Willy requested that Daisy and eighteen-year-old Mabel join him in Cairo after the shoot. Daisy was eager to show her sister around. The best part of the trip was meeting Abby's brothers-in-law, Colonel Archibald Hunter and Captain George Hunter, both stationed there. As governor of the Sudan, Archie had access to everywhere they wanted to go.[2]

Riding camels, with, as Daisy put it, "ease if not grace," they saw the irrigation project called the Barrage, built in 1863 to help cotton farmers along the Nile. In March, when Daisy visited, the fields were freshly planted with Ashmouni or Sakellaridis, cotton varieties so fine they challenged the long-staple Georgia Sea Island cotton of her father's business. She also viewed the site of the proposed dam outside Aswân, where the Nile became rocky and full of rapids, called cataracts. Construction of the Aswân Dam would not begin until 1898, so Daisy had the rare and thrilling experience of going over the first cataract. Hunter took them on the government steamer up the Nile to a British garrison and staging point called Wadi Halfa. Too new to have a hotel, and seldom visited by women, Hunter gave up his quarters to Mabel and Daisy. "Two ladies made a ball on this occasion," Daisy said with a laugh, when she and her sister led a dance for all sixteen men stationed there. The British soldiers tried hard to please these unusual guests, who surely did not understand Daisy's rage when a rousing rendition of "Marching Through Georgia," depicting General Sherman's destructive Civil War offensive, was struck up in their honor.[3]

"We have seen more than any other tourists and in the pleasantest way and Col. Hunter is a sort of Grand Mogul here and he <u>is</u> so nice, quite the nicest man Mabel and I have met for years!" Daisy boasted in her letter to Mary. In fact, both Archie and George Hunter were as enchanted with the Gordon sisters as the sisters were with them. Daisy invited the brothers to Wellesbourne, and Archie appeared in 1895 while her parents were visiting. It pleased her immensely that they could all know one another. Archie, Willie, and Arthur especially enjoyed one another's company.[4]

The idyllic time in Egypt began a long and important friendship between Archie and Daisy. After Archie's only trip to Rhode Island to see the Hunter family in October 1895, Abby wrote knowingly that Daisy had "taken a tremendous fancy for Archie." But Archie suddenly became affianced to a Scotswoman. Archie's great-nephew suggested it was a result of coveting Duncan and Abby's domestic bliss and being "on the rebound" from loving a married woman: Daisy. Archie and Daisy kept up a correspondence wherein he included confidential information about the undertakings of the Egyptian Army and she apprised him of the activities of mutual acquaintances. Whenever he returned to Europe, Archie made a point of seeing Daisy, so their communication was regular and their visits as frequent as his schedule would allow.[5]

Archie was a successful officer with the Egyptian Army. He earned promotion to major general at the young age of forty. He understood the drawbacks of such a rapid rise but appreciated his good fortune. Archie broke off his engagement at this time. He blamed it on his promotion, the life of a military man posted beyond the pale of civilization, and the wait of seven or eight years before he could marry. The truth was that Archibald Hunter was wedded to the army.[6]

More and more of Daisy's friends came from the military. "I can always get on with soldiers," Daisy wrote once, "their lives are so interesting." These men were certainly not all Willy's cup of tea, but Daisy became engrossed in their careers. The British Empire was at the height of its power then, spanning the globe with colonies on nearly every continent. Such a far-flung empire took watching by the British Armed Forces, as the tendency of occupied peoples was to prefer independence.[7]

In 1898, Daisy herself participated in a colonial conflict. Nearly her entire family served in the Spanish-American War, born from a sympathetic desire on the part of Americans to help Cubans throw off the yoke of their overlord, Spain. In February 1898, 266 Americans died when the U.S.S. *Maine* exploded in Havana harbor, and the United States issued a declaration of hostilities against Spain. President William McKinley tapped former Confederate William Washington Gordon II to serve the United States as head of the Second Brigade, Second Division, Seventh Army Corps, USV, with the rank of brigadier general.[8]

Duty motivated Willie. One of his favorite poems was "What I Live For," written by the contemporary English journalist George L. Banks. The final lines described Willie's life's mission:

> For the cause that lacks assistance,
> For the wrongs that need resistance,
> For the future in the distance,
> And the good that I can do.[9]

It was duty—no more and no less—that moved him to agree to McKinley's request, because unlike the Civil War, Willie did not consider the Spanish-American War a "patriotic war." Nevertheless, his two sons longed for military glory. Because he knew that "no Colonel can favor or help an enlisted man, unless as his orderly," Willie dismissed Arthur's desire to join up as a private with Lieutenant Colonel Theodore Roosevelt's Rough Riders as "raving madness." Instead, Arthur and Bill both served on their father's staff.[10]

Remembering the painful separation from Nellie during the earlier war and probably knowing a little about his daughter's marital woes, Willie secured Willy Low's permission for Daisy to summer with her mother. Before her arrival, General Gordon received orders to proceed to Camp Miami. Nellie accompanied him, meaning to stay until the directive for embarkation came. Daisy then altered her plans and joined the family in Florida.

Camp Miami was hot, dusty, and swarming with mosquitoes. Worst of all, the drinking water was contaminated. Assembling and training the troops proved difficult, as diarrhea thinned the ranks alarmingly. "Camp Hell," as it was soon called, became overtaxed as seven thousand men packed into a space for five thousand. Other diseases developed, and afflicted men filled the hospital. Lacking recourse, the physicians released them early, forcing Willie to muster men unfit for duty. Disgusted at the woeful conditions and the poor care given at the camp hospital—and fearing a yellow-fever epidemic if things didn't change—the Gordons decided to open a convalescent hospital for men who were too sick to serve but not ill enough for the hospital. Nellie cajoled the Red Cross to provide ice, sweet-talked the chaplain for an icebox, wheedled male nurses from the army brass, and wrote home to her friends in the Colonial Dames, who proffered financial donations Nellie used to purchase mosquito netting.[11]

The couple even spent their own money on this endeavor. Nellie moved new cots, chairs, washbasins, and towels into a vacant warehouse, opening the convalescent facility on July 20. Daisy arrived the next day and immediately began caring for the men. She comforted the ailing, who suffered from dysentery, malaria, measles, mumps, and typhoid fever; purchased fans for the soldiers and foraged for milk, a rare commodity (at one point she milked the cow herself) that she made into brandied milk punch; brewed batches of broth and beef jelly; and chatted with soldiers as she poured chocolate drinks for them. Supplies were scarce and difficult to locate. Since clean water was still nowhere to be found, Nellie and Daisy kept vats of water boiling to sterilize it. As more and more men became ill, the hospital had to send them its overflow, until it was less a recovery center than "an intensive care unit." The convalescent facility soon outgrew its ninety beds and spilled over into an Episcopal church.[12]

Daisy had never encountered anything like the chaos and raw need of an army hospital. She was a long way from court presentations and fancy dress balls. To serve among the ailing, sweaty, miserable, homesick men meant tapping her untested reserves of emotional strength and physical stamina. Daisy's behavior won high praise from her mother, who admitted that she worked "like a little Brick." The soldiers' gratitude made Daisy feel valued and wanted. Her abilities broadened, and her independence increased. Daisy tucked away for future use the lesson she learned from observing her parents: when the need is great, improvise and do the job.[13]

Every part of her experience stood in stark relief to Daisy's life in England, where she was alternately a social butterfly and a lonely wife. Surely she saw Archie Hunter and other friends from British colonial wars as she looked into the faces of the men at Camp Miami. While the soldiers Daisy treated had not yet been off to fight, the worth of her endeavors was self-evident. So meaningful was her work that when her father was called to Jacksonville, where her mother planned to establish a new convalescent ward, Daisy volunteered to remain with the men. As it turned out, Daisy and Nellie went together to Jacksonville in early August. Nellie supervised the transfer of patients to what was known as Pablo Beach, an hour's train ride away, while Daisy—by then with managerial skills—had charge of the hospital. Within two weeks the United States declared victory over Spain and President McKinley reassigned General Gordon to diplomatic service as a member of the Puerto Rico Evacuation Commission charged with removing Spaniards from the island.[14]

Daisy readied herself mentally to return to England, where she seldom saw Willy and could not countenance all of his activities. She would have to make the transition from adrenaline-charged nursing, and the good feeling of being of service, to society wife. In contrast, Nellie continued her selfless work and vaulted to national fame. As she boarded the car for Savannah she was stunned to see soldiers in "a state of collapse and delirium" stagger to the train. Realizing they needed hospitalization, she tried unsuccessfully to stop their ingress. Once under way, Nellie took it upon herself to tend to them. They had no accompanying physician, no rations, and no medicine. She summoned brandy, milk, ice, water, food, and pillows for the comfort of the soldiers, natives of Goshen, Indiana.

Private Charles Perry was dying. His anxious brother prayed with Nellie as she cared for Charles until he expired. Nellie sent telegrams ahead with instructions to make sure that a railroad official bearing provisions and an undertaker with a coffin met the train in Savannah. Nellie brought the Perry brothers home, one to be embalmed and the other to have a bath and an uninterrupted night's sleep. Nellie's heroic treatment of U.S. soldiers made the front pages across America. She was not done yet, however. She wrote the head of the Goshen regiment to chastise him, and as a credible, firsthand witness, she also fired off letters to the president, the surgeon general, and members of Congress, describing the deplorable state of the Camp Miami hospital. Her words buttressed a newspaper editorial Willie wrote, and the Gordons were briefly national celebrities, the pride of Savannah and their children.[15]

No less than her siblings, Mabel applauded their parents' actions. But uppermost in her mind was her wedding, which couldn't occur until they were both back in town. Mabel and Rowley Leigh had been in love for years. Daisy opened the door for her sister to wed an Englishman, but their husbands were very different men. Willy had investments and property in America that routinely called him back to the United States, and Daisy returned annually. Rowley had no such ties. The son of William Henry Leigh, the 2nd baron Leigh of Stoneleigh, and Lady Carolyn Grosvenor, Rowley was educated at Cambridge and trained as a barrister. He soon traded lawyering for horses and became one of England's best race handicappers. While Willy and Rowley both loved the racetrack, it was Rowley who made a successful career there.

By late October 1898, all the Gordons were assembled. On Daisy's thirty-eighth birthday, Mabel and Rowley were wed at Christ Episcopal Church in Savannah by the rector. His co-presider was the Very Reverend Honorable James Wentworth Leigh, dean of Hereford Cathedral in England and Rowley's uncle. Rowley's aunt, Frances Butler Leigh, was the daughter of famous British actress Fanny Kemble and Georgian Pierce Butler, and had spent part of her youth on nearby Butler Island. Family members toasted Mabel and Rowley at a wedding breakfast following the ceremony, just as they had Daisy and Willy.[16]

Mabel was the last of the Gordon daughters to wed. Eleanor and Wayne Parker, who married first, had five children. Wayne, an attorney, was elected to the New Jersey Assembly in 1885 and 1886, and then to the U.S. Congress in 1895. He won eleven out of the next thirteen elections and served until he died in 1922. The greatest sorrow for the Parkers was the death of their son Wayne at age seven.[17]

Following in his father's footsteps, Bill Gordon graduated from Yale and joined the Georgia Hussars. His career was the law. He had married Ellen Buchanan Screven in 1892, and they had two children at the time Mabel married, William Washington IV (called B) and Ellen. B was born with some sort of hearing disorder. "He hears when his name is called," Grandfather Willie Gordon wrote concernedly to Nellie, "and hears some other loud noises and he scrapes his throat just as I do whenever he hears me do it. But he doesn't say a word." Bill and Ellen brought B to Europe, seeking the most up-to-date treatments. Aunt Daisy was always an interested observer. Two more children would complete Bill and Ellen's family: Margaret (called Daisy Doots) and Franklin. Like the Parkers, Bill and Ellen would suffer the loss of a son. Frank died in 1908, when he was only three.[18]

Arthur, the baby of the family, attended Yale, then returned to Savannah and apprenticed at W. W. Gordon and Company. He became president of the Savannah Cotton Exchange in 1896, inaugurating a long career of civic service. He also joined the Georgia Hussars and later the Oglethorpe Light Infantry. Arthur would not marry until 1906, to Virginian Margaret Cameron McGuire, with whom he would have four children, Mary, George, Arthur, and Edward. Long before he met Margaret, Arthur was the steady rock among the Gordon children, the uncomplaining Johnny-on-the-spot, sagely and humbly doling out advice on all subjects. Completely conscientious and possessed of sound judgment, he had the implicit trust of the whole family. While the Gordons habitually passed their letters around to one another, there are notes to Arthur from just about every family member marked "private."[19]

In her sixties, Nellie maintained an active life. She helped establish Savannah's Telfair Academy of Arts and Sciences, remained dedicated to Christ Episcopal Church, and joined the Huntingdon Club. Her pride in her family origins led her to organize the Georgia Society of the Colonial Dames in 1893, and to serve as its first president. She threw the weight of the organization behind a legislative battle to allow women to attend the University of Georgia. In 1906, Nellie would organize Georgia's first Red Cross chapter. For two decades she worked to keep the Kinzie name before the public. She reissued *Waubun,* supported Chicago's Kinzie Elementary School, entered into lengthy correspondences with amateur historians about the role of the Kinzies in the founding of the city and the Fort Dearborn massacre, and later took great pride in being recognized as the oldest living white Chicagoan.[20]

All of Daisy's siblings were favored with marriages as solid as their parents'. All would know the joys and sorrows of parenthood. Only Daisy, who had been wed for more than a decade by 1898, was disillusioned by her spouse and unhappily childless. She surrounded herself with animals—dogs, cats, and birds that became like children to her. But they could not substitute for sons and daughters at a time when a woman's highest priority was motherhood. Without the option of a career, Daisy pursued art only sporadically. She enjoyed socializing but was never without a simmering torment that such a life was superficial and good for ultimately nothing. Despite the reform fever that was beginning to stir in America and England in the 1890s—so much of it led by women—Daisy engaged in no organized charitable work. It was seldom done by women of her class, and Willy would not have let her had she wanted to. Instead, she was "dragged," as she usually phrased it, to horse races. Willy left her alone as he drilled with the Warwickshire Yeomanry, went to the racetrack, trained his horses, and took long hunting trips. It was, she confessed in 1895, "a rare occurrence" for them to be alone together. He had begun to drink excessively. Coldness, distance, and occasional mean-spiritedness replaced the tender attention he had paid to Daisy in the early days of their marriage.[21]

Children generally grow up studying their parents' relationship. When they marry, they strive either to replicate it or reject it. Daisy observed an exceptionally strong bond between Nellie and Willie, one that had been tested more than once. The Gordons were kind to each other, reveled in a physical relationship their entire lives long, and agreed on fundamentals such as religion, finances, child rearing, and the importance of duty. They shared an understanding of their roles in the marriage. Willie fully supported Nellie's community work and tolerated her foibles. She understood that he was quicker to criticize than to praise. Nellie's short temper and sharp tongue were balanced by his gravitas.

Daisy's marriage was nothing like her parents'. The physical proximity, mutual respect, and shared sense of purpose were all missing. Nellie fought to be by Willie's side, but Willy Low kept Daisy at arm's length. Daisy liked horses and enjoyed the trackside socializing—although not the gambling—so it was not a case of a wife refusing to participate in her husband's world. There is no evidence that Willy appreciated Daisy's art.

Mabel believed that "all nice men are influenced by their wives and the Gordons, beginning with Papa, have always been absolutely governed by theirs!" But this was not true of Daisy, who never governed her husband. At some point, Willy stopped being gentle about Daisy's disability and began making fun of her in front of their friends. Neither of them acted as a brake on each other's impetuous streaks. Daisy wasn't a girl who married her father, as the old aphorism goes. Instead, she wed a man much like Nellie. Willy Low had Nellie's impulsive temperament rather than her father's sober demeanor. Nellie was the queen bee in the Gordon family, just as Willy was the sun around whom his sisters orbited. Nellie did not appreciate competition, and her emotions ruled the family. Daisy, too much like her mother herself, could not restrain Willy the way her father could delimit her mother.[22]

In practical terms, the purely social life Willy enjoyed would never truly fulfill Daisy, because the Gordon emphasis on duty was too strong. Even as a young woman, Daisy had a low threshold for idle frivolity. "Society," she knew, while enticing, "is very hollow, very unsatisfactory and a very shaky nail on which to hang one's happiness." As a married woman she wrote, "My life is such a busy one, that I sometimes long to stand aside and get a view of it and try to get in some solid work but as years roll on, and I become more worldly and more of a butterfly, I think I deteriorate day by day." Daisy often felt, just as her mother did, the dinners and teas and parties of London to be "a very unsatisfactory mode of life—it is nothing but a rush after amusement and you don't get a great deal out of it either." Nellie was dramatic and had to be the center of attention, but when push came to shove, she did her duty: to yellow-fever-stricken neighbors, to her family, to the Colonial Dames, to the Red Cross, to soldiers and veterans, even to history. Daisy took note.[23]

Willy resembled the prince of Wales in his unwillingness to allow his wife to engage in social reform. The countess of Warwick wrote that her paramour Bertie "praised all philanthropic and educational efforts but expressed himself plainly on the subject of public women who seemed to ape men in their utterances. He would say that God put women into the world to be different from men and he could not understand why women did not recognize this instead of trying to copy men's pursuits." While Daisy grew up in the postbellum American South, where women of her class outwardly obeyed their husbands and men gallantly protected their wives, she also grew up with a mother whose charitable works did not make her "mannish."[24]

But Daisy was younger and lacked daily supportive contact with the close circle of her family. The times were against her, too. The prudery of the Victorian era was under attack by the prodigious sensual appetite of the heir to the throne. Politician T.H.S. Escott observed in 1885 that "London society in its anxiety to secure prophylactics against boredom has run into a dangerous excess. . . ." One such excess, he wrote, was "to ignore . . . the distinction between virtue and vice." Willy was a destructive whirlwind, and Daisy could not stand up to him. Her good deeds were mostly done in secret. She could not keep him home more. He would not be separated from his friends. Daisy failed to summon a firm resolve with Willy until his actions had so thoroughly violated her sense of decency that she could no longer tolerate his presence.[25]

But why did Willy essentially abandon Daisy? Maybe Daisy's deafness made Willy fear negative public repercussions. Her speech was unimpaired, but she could and did misunderstand conversations. A wife mirrored her husband: Did he perceive her as a less-than-ideal reflection of himself? The prince of Wales escaped his wife's deafness with extramarital affairs. Willy did the same. Even though the two men were not close friends, Bertie was his model. Daisy could not have been entirely comfortable with the lax morals of their acquaintances, and did not like being left alone so much. She longed for a way to be of use or to do some practical work. As Lady Warwick put it, however, high society "did not like brains" and only understood how to spend, not make, money. Further, "We considered the heads of historic houses who read serious works, encouraged scientists and the like very, very dull."[26]

Daisy and Willy lived in two different worlds almost from the start. Part of it could not be helped. From the first day of their honeymoon, he was robust, while she was burdened by the isolating fact of illness. He did not often accompany her to spas or physicians. Eleanor was convinced that Daisy and Willy's relationship was impossible to understand without taking into account how Willy manipulated their lives so that he was her only priority. Eleanor was suggesting that he needed to be everything to her and simultaneously despised her for it. Eleanor asserted, "He has always felt that it gave him the right to—well to treat her as a dog." By 1900 it was an old pattern: on one of their earliest Atlantic crossings together, Abby related, Willy "played all the way over on the steamer and . . . he hired the Captain's stateroom and spent most of his nights playing cards there while Daisy had a room below. He evidently is a very gay youth."[27]

Daisy kept her troubles to herself, making it difficult to identify exactly when their marriage began to deteriorate. Hints appear nonetheless. A melancholic letter in 1894 to Mary concluded, "I did not half let myself out to you, there was much I left unsaid. . . ." In 1896, Willy took Mabel Gordon to the countess of Warwick's famous costume ball. Because she had been spending part of the year in England with the Lows, Mabel knew their friends. The countess of Warwick was the statuesque Frances Evelyn Maynard, wife of Francis Greville.

She was also a late-life mistress of the prince of Wales, and she considered Willy Low "a dear friend." Countess Warwick did nothing halfway. Her ball was set in the era of Louis XVI, and even her servants were bewigged appropriately. The extravagance of the night was reported in breathless detail by the newspapers. The countess's former and present lovers attended, including Bertie. Willy came as the actor David Garrick, wearing all purple: velvet frock coat, satin vest, and silk stockings. Mabel's white dress was lined with blue satin and decorated with dainty pink roses that matched the wreath in her hair. In the columns and columns of fine print, Daisy was not mentioned.[28]

By 1900 Daisy was more open about her unhappiness. Willy Low, she told Arthur, "was a very bad husband." How bad was not clear, but three months later Daisy wrote to wish her parents "all the joy, success, and happiness possible in this 1st year of a New Century." She filled her note with the gaieties of her life, including hosting a New Year "ball party" at Wellesbourne, where the guests included one "very handsome Mrs. Bateman."[29]

Mrs. Bateman was Willy's mistress, though Daisy did not know it then. Attractive enough to be featured on the cover of *Country Life* magazine, Anna Bridges Bateman turned heads. She was married to Sir Hugh Alleyne Sacheverell-Bateman and lived in Morley Manor, Derbyshire. A sportsman like Willy Low, Sir Hugh had learned to sleep upright while riding, trusting his horse to return him safely home. One terrible day, Sir Hugh must have been dozing, or at least daydreaming—pipe in mouth—for, according to a relative, the horse went too near an ancient oak. A tree limb slammed into Hugh's face, and the force of the blow propelled the pipe stem "through the roof of his mouth and into his brain." He died within a few months from the complications of an infection caused by the wound. Sir Hugh was thirty-six years old and left an estate of just over eighty-four thousand pounds. Anna Bateman dedicated some of it to a Gothic-style mausoleum with stained-glass windows at the local churchyard. Then, three years later, she built a single-story, much smaller lodge on the grounds of the manor, either for herself or for friends, such as Willy, who came to hunt in Derbyshire.[30]

The start of the affair cannot be pinpointed. Mabel thought they had met in 1895, soon after Sir Hugh's demise. Historian Peter Bolton maintains they encountered each other first in 1899 at a spa in Wales, where Willy took his grieving sister Jessie after the death of her son. Whatever the truth, Jessie described Willy as "under her spell" and his conduct, decisions, and actions no longer his own. The affair was almost certainly not Willy's first, but it was the one that doomed the marriage. Anna Bateman and Willy were together often enough, and frequented the same watering holes as the Lows' friends, so that it was not long until the whispering started.[31]

Daisy may or may not have understood how dangerous Mrs. Bateman was in 1899, but at some stage Anna Bateman turned from just another woman into a clear threat. While Daisy's letters provide hardly a clue to her emotional state, she behaved defiantly—volunteering in precisely the sort of charitable work Willy would have forbidden: a working-girls' club in a poor district of London called Camberwell. This club, which probably met at the Talbot settlement house, was part of a larger reform movement whose members sought to ameliorate the lives of urban working-class children. What Daisy actually did with the Camberwell factory girls and how many times she went there is not clear. Nellie's letter mentioning that Daisy was "interested in" the club displayed no shock or surprise, and the very ordinariness of the reference suggests that Daisy assisted in Camberwell more than once.[32]

At about this time, Daisy's great friend Archie Hunter returned to England. He had been with Kitchener's forces, moving up the Nile to defeat forty thousand Dervish troops at Omdurman, near Khartoum, "bringing peace to the Sudan." He explained to his brother Duncan that he was "commanding the Infantry of the Egyptian Army & 2nd in command of the whole business." The British had celebrated Omdurman, but Archie was downed by an abscess that required three surgeries and six weeks in a Cairo hospital. By January 1899 he was well enough to be feted in his hometown and knighted by Queen Victoria.[33]

Sir Archie's next posting was to India, but he was almost

immediately transferred to South Africa, where Dutch settlers, called Boers, disputed British sovereignty. On November 2, 1899, the Boers laid siege to the settlement of Ladysmith and trapped the British, including Archie Hunter, inside. Archie capably administered the town, arranged the defenses, and led an intrepid raid on Boer artillery. A relief column arrived in Ladysmith on February 28, 1900, 118 days after the siege began and just as supplies were running out and morale deflating.

A simultaneous and storied siege was under way several hours north at Mafeking. Daisy and the rest of the English public anxiously read every scrap of news while Colonel Robert Baden-Powell and his forces held out against the Boers for seven long months. Archie Hunter devised a strategy to end the siege by engaging the Boers at Rooidam, allowing the relief column under Colonel Bryan Mahon to march virtually unmolested to Mafeking.[34]

The jubilation in England at Baden-Powell's heroic leadership during Mafeking assumed mythic proportions as celebratory echoes reverberated around the globe. His phenomenal fame overshadowed that of all other men who served in the Boer War. He was promoted to major general, replacing Hunter as the youngest holder of that rank when Hunter became lieutenant general. In 1899, Baden-Powell had published *Aids to Scouting for N.-C.O's. and Men,* intended to explain military scouting and to teach boys how to hone their skills in preparation for that career. Now that he was a household name and the toast of the Western world, his book became a best seller. Children read it and began to play "scouts" in respectful homage to their idol. Daisy was less than reverent about Baden-Powell. Though she did not know him in 1900, nor could she intuit what a pivotal role he would play in her future, she resented his fame. In her eyes, the real hero of the Boer War was Archie Hunter.[35]

Daisy was devoted to Hunter. Her entire family enjoyed the passionate, thoughtful, circumspect, mustachioed military leader. He knew Kitchener and dined with the queen. His brother was her dear friend's husband. He flattered her by writing confidentially to her. His enthusiasm to see her was a fillip to her bruised vanity. When

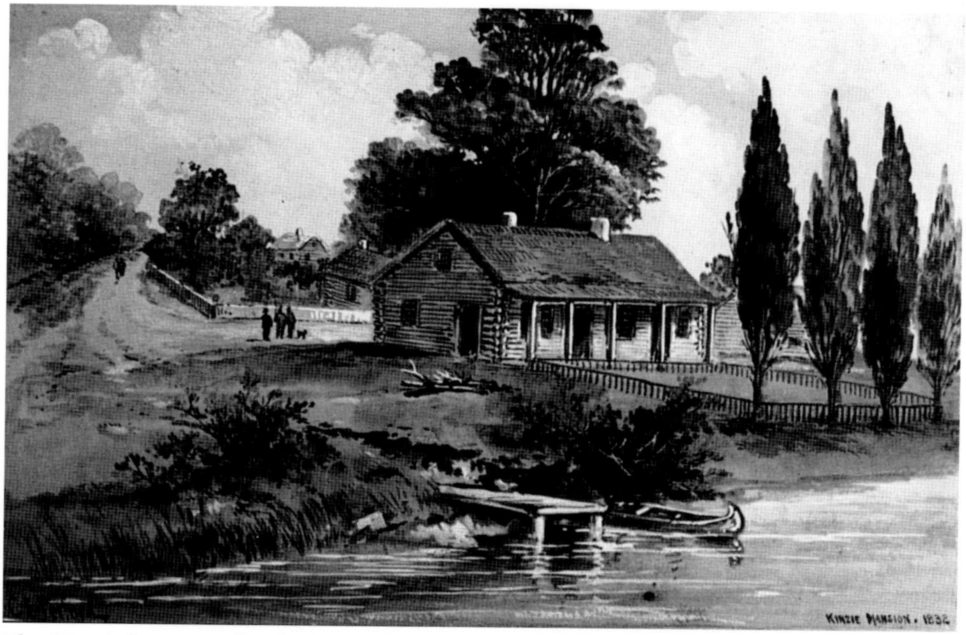

The Kinzie homestead, which Daisy's great grandparents acquired in 1804. It sat in the bend of the Chicago River.

An engraving from the January 21, 1865 issue of *Leslie's Illustrated Weekly* showing the aftermath of the capture of Savannah. Union General John W. Geary is issuing passes to the defeated Southerners.

Evidence of the destruction caused by the Civil War in Savannah, 1865.

The six Gordon children: Mabel, Eleanor, Daisy, Arthur (on the table), Bill, and Alice.

The Savannah home where Daisy was born, 1860.

The three Gordon sisters—Eleanor, Mabel, and Daisy.

Daisy, wearing her pin from the German Society, a dancing and cultural club in Savannah.

School chums and lifelong friends Abby Lippitt, Daisy Gordon, and Mary Carter.

William Mackay Low with his sisters, Mary, Katie, and Jessie, taken during a visit to Savannah in the mid-1870s.

Willy resplendent in his Warwickshire Yeomanry Guards uniform, around the time Daisy fell in love with him.

The wedding of Willy and Daisy, December 21, 1886, Savannah.

The Low house in Savannah. It was built by Andrew Low, lived in by the young Willy, redecorated by newlywed Daisy, occupied occasionally by Willy and Daisy, and in her widowhood used for rental income. Daisy died there in 1927.

A portrait of Daisy wearing the diamond-encrusted swallow pins, one of the many wedding gifts Willy presented to her.

Daisy in London, c. 1890, in a photograph taken by Alice Hughes.

Abby Lippitt's wedding party, 1895. Daisy, center; Abby Lippitt, standing, second from the right. In front of Abby is Jeanie Lippitt. Mary Carter, with the light muff, is seated center front. Seated in the front, far left, is Grace Carter.

Nellie and Willie Gordon posing in front of their Savannah home.

Three generations of William Washington Gordons: Daisy's father, brother, and nephew in their Spanish-American War uniforms, 1898.

Mabel, the youngest Gordon sister, who married Englishman Rowland Leigh, with her children, Peggy and Rowland.

G. Arthur Gordon, Daisy's levelheaded, pragmatic younger brother.

Daisy with one of her beloved dogs, during the years of her marriage to Willy.

Replicas of the gates Daisy had had made for Wellesbourne House, the Lows' home in Warwickshire. The originals are at the Juliette Gordon Low Birthplace in Savannah.

Daisy as the Marlborough set knew her in England in the 1890s. She is standing in the back with the fishing pole. Willy is seated in front in the light suit. The women are Mary (far left), Amy, and Katie.

COUNTRY LIFE

Vol. XXI.—No. 537. [Registered at the G.P.O. as a Newspaper.] *SATURDAY, APRIL 20th, 1907.* [Price Sixpence. By post, 6½d.]

H. S. MENDELSSOHN. *MRS. SACHEVERELL-BATEMAN.* 14, Pembridge Crescent, W.

Anna Bateman, the "other woman," featured on the cover of *Country Life* magazine.

General Sir Archibald Hunter in 1899, when he and Daisy were close friends.

General Sir Robert Baden-Powell, founder of the Boy Scouts, c. 1919.

Olave St. Clair Soames at the time she became engaged to Robert Baden-Powell.

Daisy and Mabel bumped into him in 1899, Daisy rushed to alert Arthur that Archie "told Mabel he was so glad to see us both he felt like 'stroking us.' He carried us off to lunch at the Hyde Park Club and we had a little talk." Daisy was proud of Archie and fretted lest he fail to receive the public acclaim he deserved. "I really love him, and wish him every success," she explained, though if there was a physical attraction, Archie and Daisy would never have given in to it, driven as they both were by duty and propriety. But the temptation must have been strong. Archie Hunter was the antithesis of Willy Low, and his attentions provided some balm as Daisy's marriage slowly collapsed.[36]

About the time Archie left for Cairo at the end of January 1901, still suffering from what his sister thought was another internal abscess, Willy became quite ill. It had been more than a fortnight since Daisy had unknowingly entertained Willy's lover at Wellesbourne. His fever and chills suggested influenza. By doctor's orders, he could not take fluids and he could not smoke. Since Willy had a thirty-cigarette-a-day habit, the restriction was significant. The physician's demeanor was grave, which made Daisy, nursing her husband alone, uneasy.[37]

He rallied, and his recovery released Daisy to travel. She spent two days with Mabel, whose daughter Peggy had been born on January 24, and then left for a trip to the United States in the early spring. Willy was to join her several weeks later.[38] If Daisy had a romantic second honeymoon in Savannah in mind, Nellie quashed it. In a "mental aberration," she invited all of the Colonial Dames to a reception and entertained houseguests in addition to the Lows. It was "complete topsy turvey-dom" in the Gordon house, Mabel was sure.[39]

Back in Britain, the rest of 1901 held the sort of painful tension that made Daisy thin and exceedingly miserable. She wanted the consolation of family. "I wish," she wrote Arthur, "I was a self-reliant person, but although I ought to make my self do without any special human affection, I find my self each year craving it more." His visit to her was "worth a fortune . . . I don't believe you will ever know how much good you have done me both in health and spirits." Her brother relieved her of such unhappiness that Daisy thanked him twice: ". . . it was not what you said but simply a tacit understanding and sympathy. I was awfully blue and discouraged and you were like a nice fresh bracing air."[40]

Daisy soon needed a stronger curative than the sight of her brother. She opened Meallmore, the home she and Willy rented, in mid-August, readying for the usual crowds of visitors for the Scottish hunting season. A week after Daisy's arrival, Willy appeared, fourteen pounds heavier and looking better from his time at the spa in Nauheim. Daisy apprised Mabel that there were "[n]o women here except Ota [Wilton]. Mrs. Bateman comes Friday." Something significant appears to have happened at this point. Probably she learned that Anna Bateman and Willy were lovers, and perhaps that they had "stayed in the same hotel" at Nauheim, for after that passing reference to her on the 21st, Daisy began sending what Mabel described as "frantic telegrams" summoning her to Meallmore. "I need you," she importuned, without elaboration. Mabel agreed to join her on Saturday and stay until Tuesday, before going south to see friends Robert and Alexandra Beech at Meggernie Castle in Glen Lyon, Perthshire.[41]

On Monday, September 2, 1901, Mabel wrote that among the guests at Meallmore was "a Mrs. Bateman." She was just one of eight people Mabel listed off to Arthur, with no special inflection. Daisy "looks pretty well," and planned to join her at Meggernie for a week on September 7, Mabel reported. For Arthur, Daisy also cataloged the guests, including Anna Bateman, with no emphasis or qualifier.[42] Mabel moved on as scheduled to the Beeches and wrote Arthur with greater elaboration but no suspicion: "I found [Daisy] tired out (getting the house in order) and bored with the women; but Katie Low is there now, also Elspeth Campbell, May Egerton, and Romaine Turnure, all of whom are devoted to her, and I left her rested and in good spirits. Willy looked very well."[43]

Daisy Low and Anna Bateman were together at Meallmore as they had been at Wellesbourne, but this time Daisy knew the latter was not just an innocent friend of Willy's. But what could she do?

Departing was ceding the field; staying with her there was impossible. It was, Daisy wrote later, "Mrs. Bateman's presence [that] obliged me to leave Meallmore." Once her sister-in-law Katie arrived to be hostess in her stead, Daisy exited Meallmore forever.[44]

At Meggernie the Beeches took her in, and Mabel comforted her. To her intense delight, Archie Hunter was there, a bulwark of reticence, his propinquity reassuring. Mabel laid plans for Daisy to spend October and November with the Leighs in order to keep her away from Meallmore and Anna Bateman for two-thirds of the hunting season. As it turned out, Mabel had an acute "gastric attack," and Daisy remained at Meggernie to nurse her. Then Lady Ota Wilton, who had been both at Wellesbourne and at Meallmore, asked the Leighs and Daisy to come to her for a month. Like Mabel, Ota understood Daisy's predicament. By December, Nellie and Willie had been apprised. "I knew she was ill and down-hearted and needed our letters and our sympathy. . . . I <u>try</u> not to worry about our poor Daisy—but how can I help it?" Nellie brooded.[45]

The January after Anna Bateman set foot in Wellesbourne, the catastrophic results of 1901 were clear from Daisy's anguished letter to her father:

> Dearest Papa: What I regret most is the trouble and anxiety I am causing you. From what I have heard since I came back here—I fear Willy is quite under Mrs. Bateman's influence and has made up his mind to chuck me [out] or rather when I go home to force me to divorce him. . . . I have absolutely declined to discuss my affairs with anyone but I think Mrs. Bateman is likely to ruin Willy's married life and make it impossible for me to overlook his conduct; and then she is quite capable of chucking him, that is why I cabled I wished to wait a year before consenting to any final measure. In that time, he ought to find her out, and I feel from him what I am told, I am simply playing into her hands by vacating my place here. . . . I certainly told no one but Willy that I was willing to stay with you until he

> wanted me again, and I would remain in America if he wished. The game of trying to keep a husband doesn't seem worth the candle, nothing would ever put us back on the same footing of respect and love, but what I feel is, that he is absolutely cutting his own throat socially and morally and when I face the gossip etc., I feel as if my life was a nice clean garment which was being dragged through the mud.[46]

Friends knew. Family knew. Willy's three sisters sympathized with Daisy, and their public support told the world that she was not at fault for the failure of her marriage. Daisy agonized about the ignominy of being pushed aside for another woman and about besmirching the Gordon name. Willie and Nellie worried about how Daisy would be able to live, and fixated early on the necessity of her securing a financial maintenance in that era when women of her class did not earn their own living. Friends stepped in to host her so she would need no funds and so she would have a socially acceptable reason to be away from Willy.

Daisy returned to close up Wellesbourne on February 3, 1902. She had grown to love it, and Nellie agreed it had turned into a wonderful home. "Oh how dear and nice the house was on our arrival," she had written in November 1900. "I was never more impressed with its solid comfort as well as its luxury. Warm coal fires everywhere. Crowds of exquisite flowers, orchids, roses, and chrysanthemums everywhere. Everything in apple-pie order," Nellie had approved—without complaint of any sort for once.[47]

After her sad farewell to Wellesbourne, Daisy went to Mabel's "for some time." Staying away from Willy in that determined but informal way meant her situation had changed. Arthur was concerned lest she be noticed in a hotel restaurant with General Hunter. Daisy agreed not to see any male friend unaccompanied in a hotel again but made clear she was not going to give the impression that she was to blame: "I must go on and lead my life exactly as I have always done. It would be perfectly impossible for anyone to pick a flaw in it as far as proprieties go. . . ."[48]

Soon Daisy was back in Savannah, holding her head up, keeping her mouth shut, and looking for a diversion. Work had saved Mary Low after her fiancé died. It was a sign of Daisy's desperation that she asked her astonished father to let her run Belmont plantation. "I think," her father wrote in mock horror, "I had also better turn over the cotton business of W. W. Gordon and Co. to her and retire at once to the poor house." In fact, Daisy's plans were too uncertain for a steady occupation, even though her bred-in-the-bone impetus was to do something useful.[49]

The women of the family were divided as to how Daisy really felt about Willy. Eleanor believed everything her little sister did was "with a view to winning or coercing him back." Ridiculous, Mabel claimed; Daisy didn't—couldn't—love Willy any longer. Either way, Nellie was unabashedly ready to murder her errant son-in-law. Only Daisy knew whether she still cared for her husband, and that she kept to herself.[50]

CHAPTER 9

A Parting of the Ways

Daisy's immediate problem was deciding how to conduct herself in this new world with the unwelcome presence of Anna Bateman. There were too many questions. How long would this affair last? Daisy heard rumors of Mrs. Bateman's "violent tantrums" and her greed. Would Willy tire of her? Should she wait and see? Was it wise of Daisy to leave the country, or should she stay and fight? Which course of action cast the least public suspicion on her own character? How could they minimize the possible scandal? Was a legal separation best for Daisy? Was divorce better? Which did Willy want? Everything was murky and confused. Willy seemed to desire living with Mrs. Bateman while remaining married to and friendly with Daisy for decency's sake. That Daisy could not tolerate.[1]

There were cases of separation, particularly among the British upper class, in which couples remained married but lived independent lives. For honor's sake, this modern situation usually included monetary support for the wife. A contemporary observer maintained that marital infidelity in the past would have brought "elopements, duels, the breaking up of homes, and Heaven only knows what else. That sort of thing is sneered at by society to-day as obsolete, melodramatic, childish." Separation was unpalatable to Daisy. She had married in the Episcopal Church and considered her marriage a sacrament as well as a legal bond. Daisy personally believed that divorce was morally wrong. In society, the greater stigma applied to the partner who was divorced (and hence did the sinning), not the one who did the divorcing (the one sinned against), but it was a matter of degree. Divorce was publicly embarrassing.[2]

Nevertheless, Daisy decided on divorce rather than separation, a hard choice, as it would be an open declaration of her failure as a wife. English divorce law was deliberately complicated to reduce the possibility of divorce. Daisy would have to prove desertion, adultery, or cruelty. None of these courses of action were ideal. Desertion required a two-year waiting period, during which she would live in limbo—not quite married, not quite divorced—and yet depend on Willy for her financial upkeep. (Receiving such monies while attempting to prove desertion was acceptable under English law.) But Willy was financially unreliable, emotional, and forgetful, and his funds rose and fell depending on his luck at the racetrack and the gaming table. Daisy knew she would need an enforceable legal agreement for those two years to guarantee support.

Proving adultery entailed naming the other woman. This would mean announcing—beyond the circle of friends who already knew—that her husband had taken a lover. It would force a court-regulated alimony, but it would bring the worst sort of publicity. Anna Bateman's name would be tarnished and her family dishonored, which would complicate matters if Willy intended to marry her at some future date. Daisy, who could not be vindictive, preferred to wait two years rather than drag Mrs. Bateman's name through the courts.[3]

Divorce based on cruelty was both the most difficult to prove and the least likely alternative. There were many types of cruelty, but Reginald Poole, Daisy's attorney, thought that "if Mr. Low took a woman with whom he had had illicit relations in his wife's house against his wife's wish and while his wife was in the house and publicly flaunted his relationship with her before the servants I think this might amount to cruelty but I hardly see the necessity of treating it as cruelty when the question implies that there has been adultery."[4]

Poole did agree that any divorce had to originate with Daisy, because "Her loyalty and devotion and blameless life make it impossible for him to divorce her in England, which fact he is well aware of." The two-year period for desertion began on February 1, 1902 (when she closed Wellesbourne House), and would end on February 1, 1904.[5]

That is where things stood in the summer of 1902, as Daisy became an aunt to Mabel and Rowley's second child, Rowland Leigh. Nellie was with them in Great Britain for the baby's arrival. She enjoyed seeing friends Douglas and Corinne Roosevelt Robinson and Archie Hunter, but she had her hands full: Mabel giving birth; Daisy in the turmoil of separation; Arthur lovesick over the flirtatious, elusive Margaret McGuire; and Eleanor addicted to liquor-based "tonics." At that point Daisy's problems were best solved by waiting. Eleanor's situation, by contrast, was pressing.[6]

Daisy knew that her sister had been tossing back medicinal tonics by the bottle a year before the rest of the family learned about it. Displaying symptoms of addiction, Eleanor lied about how long she'd been without the tonics, hid her dependence on them from the family, and rationalized her need. Daisy insisted that Eleanor would shake her habit on her own, with loving support from the family. Her experience in this line came from the time she "cured" a butler from drinking alcohol by going cold turkey with him, and an instance wherein she helped wean a friend from opium. Nellie believed in tough love and fired off a stern sermon telling Eleanor that "she was going insane" and must cease all "spirits," including the ones in the tonics. Daisy despaired that their mother's tactlessness would do "irreparable harm." She preferred to wait to see if Eleanor was improving. If not, Daisy was prepared to persuade Eleanor "to go into an inebriate asylum." Wayne Parker agonized over it but preferred Daisy's plan. Eleanor remained a worry for everyone.[7]

Lacking productive work in the United States and afraid her absence from England was fomenting gossip—as though she had fled because she was guilty of misconduct—Daisy wanted to return. Willy wrote to say that he believed the two of them would never "be happy together again." He asked for her "consent to live apart." She trusted he would provide for her financially, despite her misgivings and his silence on the topic. Daisy made preparations to sail from New York and visited the Clarkes and Grace Carter. Other communiqués reached her: Wellesbourne remained closed, Meallmore rented, and Willy had deposited funds sufficient for her upkeep through September. Willie Gordon wanted his daughter to have something more stable than money cabled whenever Willy Low remembered to do so. He asked for a maintenance account for Daisy, with Willy's brothers-in-law George Robertson and Harry Grenfell as trustees. Daisy chose the men because Willy trusted them and they knew about his financial affairs. Before leaving Mary's home in Cooperstown, Daisy "wrote a short answer to Willy's letter [and] agreed to the request that we should part." This Cooperstown note would haunt her for the next three years.[8]

Reginald Poole told Daisy in September 1902, "In England, a divorce is only granted to a woman on the ground of her husband's adultery coupled with either desertion or with cruelty." Her note from Cooperstown meant that desertion was no longer an option, Poole asserted, because Daisy had written "consenting to separate from her husband, and desertion founded upon non-compliance with an order for restitution of conjugal rights is also out of the question as a woman can hardly ask for restitution when she has consented to a separation. The question therefore of divorce seems to me impossible in England." Poole believed, in other words, that by agreeing to live apart she could no longer claim to have been deserted. While fundamentally agreeing with Poole, Sir George Lewis, the senior solicitor in the firm, thought there was a chance, in a court battle, that Daisy's note would not necessarily be read as her acquiescing to the separation. He acknowledged her legal right to divorce based on Willy's adultery at Bad Nauheim in 1901 and at Meallmore a year later. Desertion was still Daisy's preference.[9]

Nothing moved quickly toward any sort of resolution. Misapprehensions, illness, dawdling attorneys, silences, backpedaling, and, if Eleanor was right, Daisy's reluctance to hurry measures, lest Willy ask her to return to him, all made for a slow process in which neither party's intentions were clear or consistent.

In between legal worries, Daisy tried to live her life. Buffering slightly the blow of Willy's rejection was an invitation from Archie Hunter to stay at his home in Edinburgh. Daisy explained to her watchdog brother that Archie was "such a stickler for never accepting invitations unless he can return the hospitality, that now that he has a house of his own I will accept." By late June 1902, Daisy and Grace Carter were en route to Europe together. More friends knew by then that Daisy had been exiled from Wellesbourne and extended themselves to take her in. Willy left England, decreasing her worries about running into him.[10]

Gossip remained a distressing concern, particularly for Daisy and the American Gordons. Mabel was more sanguine: "couples living apart are too common to cause much comment." She shrugged. Daisy told Willy's four sisters about his request for a separation—by letter to Jessie and Mary, but in person to Amy and Katie. The latter two were "sympathetic and loving." Amy insisted that Daisy come stay with them in September for as long as she could. She promised she would make it her business to see that her brother supported Daisy with a regular stipend. Katie was "very bitter against Willy." Daisy iterated that if they ever had to choose between her and Willy, she expected them to side with their brother, but both women promised they would never desert her. "This just shows me," Daisy wrote home, "I was morbidly sensitive when I imagined I would be ostracized as a woman separated from her husband."[11]

In her new, emancipated state, Daisy went to the one place Willy had prohibited her from going: the Newmarket races. Ota Wilton and Rowley Leigh accompanied her, and "most of the fashionable world was there," including some who suspected her relationship with Willy had fractured. Everyone was kind. One old friend remembered how Willy never let her attend Newmarket, and insisted on providing her lunch. Others shared betting tips. Their consideration made her less self-conscious. Daisy was saddened to hear that Willy was "very, very ill—perhaps dying." Mabel, who seemed to know all the rumors, learned he was at the spa in Nauheim again with Anna Bateman.[12]

When Alix Beech invited her to Meggernie for the fall, Daisy gladly accepted. This put her near Archie, and she and Mabel dined with him in Edinburgh. In August the women went to the home he rented in the suburb of Ratho Station. It was Mabel's opinion that Daisy, no longer living with an alcoholic, free-spending gambler, was "happier far than she has been for years." Friends assumed the fault was Willy's, and "her name is a synonym for goodness and purity," Mabel reassured their parents. Daisy was "a free, respected woman, whom all of Willy's friends and family regard as a heroine and delight to honor." Mabel remained certain that Daisy "despises and distrusts Willy as thoroughly as we do."[13]

For her part, Daisy had given up on happiness. Pray only, she told her mother, "that I will have enough money to be comfortable and contented." Finances were an unresolved source of concern. Willie and Arthur Gordon labored hard at transatlantic negotiations to force Willy to provide Daisy a steady income administered like clockwork through trustees. Mabel heard that Anna Bateman had an independent income of three thousand pounds a year. Willy had much more than that and could afford to be generous. In the early years of their marriage, he had showered Daisy with extravagant jewelry and made two large loans to the Gordons. She had written in 1890 that "Willy would give me anything on earth and never ask a question." But for any number of reasons—his absorption with Mrs. Bateman, his roller-coaster health, spite, annoyance—Willy did not offer a settlement, fueling Daisy's unhappiness.[14]

In September 1902, Poole sent Rowley and Mabel to Wellesbourne to retrieve Daisy's things. They only removed "a dressing case, a coat, and a tin box with Archie Hunter's journals." They made a list of Daisy's other possessions, including her furniture, books, and china. While they were thus engaged, neighbor Osbert Mordaunt arrived, "bursting with rage," he said, on behalf of all the people of Warwickshire. Then Basil Hanbury appeared, professing his anger toward Willy and promising to "come at any time from any where to serve

Daisy." Other friends found it painful to walk past Wellesbourne's tangible reminders of her: "The lions make me cry and the gates hurt worse," wrote one.[15]

Letters flew thick and fast among Gordon family members. To a person, they displayed uncharacteristic approbation of Daisy. "We know," testified Eleanor, "and so does the world in England, that for years Daisy has been Willy's saviour—keeping him in touch with decent people, making his house a rendezvous of people, who, but for Daisy, would scorn him. . . ." Their worries about Daisy's financial security were based on their knowledge that Willy "has always ignored difficult, or uncomfortable acts, even to being chased by bailiffs for trivial bills." Eleanor's husband, Representative Wayne Parker, commended Daisy for being so levelheaded. Wayne knew Willy's "desertion is willful, obstinate, and continuous, and leaves him without defense. . . . At present he decrees that she live apart from him. She does not consent, but she submits and asks a suitable support, leaving him to take the responsibility of his acts." Very prudent, Wayne concluded.[16]

When Mabel returned, she told her sister that Willy had lied again: Wellesbourne was actually open. Daisy's resolve stiffened. She rejected her parents' offer of support, because it was her husband's duty to provide for her. If he refused, she would divorce him. She must fight for that support, otherwise it would appear that she was at fault. Daisy insisted that she knew Willy best, and that he would not leave her truly destitute. He was unlikely to give her money consistently, she admitted, "and with a casual man like Willy such an arrangement is impossible." Still, she wrote Nellie, "English law gives a woman no option, between divorce or suing for restitution of conjugal rights. Both courses are revolting to me and even the course I have chosen of waiting without support for two years is very trying." If he took her to court, she would turn the tables and divorce him instead. "I shall prove him in the wrong and at least have the advantage of being free and quit of him forever—I have not the slightest desire to avenge myself and prevent him from marrying again. I don't in the least care what he does in future. I mean this but I will not appear before the world as a person who clings to a man who is kicking her aside. . . ." She promised she was "prepared for the worst." She would try to wait out the two years, avoid the courts, and force him to provide support on the grounds of desertion. If he refused, she would initiate divorce proceedings immediately.[17]

Then, in the midst of these painful decisions, she learned that Abby's good husband, Duncan Hunter, had died of diphtheria. He was thirty-nine and left her very little money, the result of "things busting up" in Montana. Their oldest daughter was only eight. A relative later acknowledged that "for the next six years she was held together by her children, her family on both sides of the Atlantic and by Daisy Low." Daisy could not help comparing her own misery to Abby's. "Death was easier than separation," Daisy mused. "At least she can look back and know she made him happy, but I can only look back on failure." Daisy tried to build a bridge of empathy: "I think I can understand . . . for I too have lost my husband, Abby, [for] . . . he has written to ask me to live apart from him." To Mary, Daisy confided, "I know that only God can help her, though if misery makes sympathy, I can and do feel for her."[18]

Daisy asked Mabel despairingly, "Isn't it strange, that Mary, Abby, and I, who all started life with such hopes and possibilities, should have each of us tasted such dregs of the bitterness of life." Mary Carter Clarke had inherited the depression that killed her father and her sister. She spent almost all of 1893 in Munich under the eyes of a doctor after she attempted suicide. Even before her wedding, while undergoing treatment in Dresden, Mary wondered whether she should enter into marriage and motherhood, because she was aware that she was not mentally stable. After the year in Germany, Mary was released to the tender but watchful care of her family. Her young sons were five and eight.[19]

Lacking the consolation of children, Daisy still knew, by the fall of 1902, that she was "far, far happier than I was tied to Willy." With savings, some money Willy sent in October, and his approval to take whatever she liked from Wellesbourne, Daisy rented "a dear little house" at 15 Portman Street in London. A stroll across Hyde Park brought her to Mabel and Rowley at 41 Montpelier Place. Mary's sister Grace would be Daisy's roommate and share the expenses fifty-fifty. After Mabel reassured her mother that Daisy really did manage her finances well, Nellie was thrilled because redecorating and the "menagerie" would distract her from her troubles. Daisy was never without her Georgia mockingbirds, her cats, and her dogs. But she also had guests—immediately. Old friends, family friends, and new friends arrived in force. Corinne Roosevelt Robinson, Romaine Turnure, Eva and Frank Dugdale, and the Murray Guthries came. The latter were "leaders of the most select London set in society," so Daisy was not ostracized from even the best circles.[20]

During the holiday season friends continued to sustain her. Daisy worked hard decorating a Christmas tree for the amusement of impoverished children, probably at Talbot settlement house. Still, beginnings are hard. In the joy of being once again in her own home, she genially proffered invitations heedless of the head count. One night she found herself with nine guests—but lacked dinnerware for everyone. She was ill at ease, and dinner was disordered. "I shan't ever ask so many again," Daisy vowed, and explained to her mother, "I get a little homesick for dear Wellesbourne where everything was so pretty and nobody could ask too many people [for dinner]," before adding contumaciously, "I would not go back for a kingdom."[21]

Through the grapevine she heard that Willy was "drinking himself to death." He must be miserable, Daisy sympathized, cut off from most of his friends and without even the consolation of being married to Anna Bateman. Daisy felt sorry for him. Unaware that her Cooperstown note had negated the two-year waiting period, she decided to truncate it and divorce him. That was "more moral," she believed, "than to let a man chuck away his life because he can't be quit of me." Better divorce than remorse, as Mabel put it to Arthur, even as she was praying for Willy's rapid demise. "No matter how right a woman is, publicity never helps her," Mabel emphasized. But Daisy could never forgive herself if she felt she had contributed to his death. She wrote Willy on January 27, 1903, to tell him so. Despite her promise to his sisters that she'd never divorce him and regardless of her belief that divorce was wicked, she wished, because of his ill health, "to set him free."[22]

Eleanor swore Willy deserved whatever he got for "leaving his wife without a roof over her head or a pound in her pocket." She warned her family that Willy's sisters had changed; they were now defending him: "Daisy seems to have lost the moral perspective of all this in her terror at being held responsible for Willy Low's death . . . and Mabel and Rowley . . . have had their sympathies played upon so long [by Willy's sisters], that this new anguish, seems to them far-fetched, compared to the Lows 'losing their only brother.'" Since Willy was too ill to oversee his own affairs, General Gordon believed that Willy's avaricious financial adviser at the firm of Chalmers, Guthrie would not authorize money for Daisy's upkeep until he had first "squeezed all of WML's assets out of him."[23]

In September 1903, Daisy met Willy face-to-face, alone, at her London home. It was her attorney's idea. "You know that there has never been anything that you wanted in the past that I have not tried to give you," she told her husband. If divorce was unacceptable to him because Anna Bateman's name would come out, then he must provide for her upkeep. Daisy believed he wanted to do so and asked why he was loath to put it in writing. Willy, perhaps not fully compos mentis, was fixated only on how much less he would pay should she remarry.[24]

Stunned and sick, she traveled to Wales. In Aberpergwm with her black cat and her niece Peggy and nephew Rowland, reveling in being out of "stale, dirty London," she felt her "spirits rise." The brisk Welsh air whipped Daisy into fighting form. She instructed her attorney to "break off all negotiations unless that clause about my remarrying is struck out altogether." She was indignant about "the injustice of Mr. Low having the power to dictate anything whatever about my future." She was ready to compel him to do right. "Most men when they desert their wives," she wrote angrily, "are prepared to support them without any stipulations whatever. It has been somewhat of a shock to have him haggle over the sum he is to give me. Considering he proposed to install another woman in the house that I have called my home and has enough money himself to gratify his every whim, one might have supposed that he would wish, as far as possible, to make up to me in the future, for the injury he has done me in the past." She was revolted by his stinginess.[25]

Her firmness worked. Sir George Lewis wrote with the good news that Willy had committed to a deed of support to provide her with twenty-five hundred pounds a year for life whether she remarried, and promised her the Low home in Savannah, plus stocks and securities. Mr. Gasquet was named trustee and charged to see that Chalmers, Guthrie provided the annual allowance.[26]

While outwardly things were falling into place, Daisy's heart was broken by Willy's perfidy. Adding insult to injury, it turned out Eleanor was right: she saw Katie and Amy, and they were, for the first time, frosty and withdrawn. Nellie reminded her daughter on her birthday that all of her family loved her, but she wished they could give her the kind of love she really wanted. "Indeed," Daisy replied sadly, "I have had to live to realize that it's the only love that endures and I crave for it." She hated the trouble and pain she caused her family but soothed them by reminding them that the "worst part for all of you will soon be over." The financial settlement would lift the worry of the Gordons having to support their daughter, then "the shame and loneliness will be softened by degrees and there is so much still to be proud of in your other children that you will be compensated for the disgrace Willy has brought on me."[27]

With the details of her upkeep satisfactorily settled, Daisy purchased her own home in November 1903. Her new address was 40 Grosvenor Street, still in the Hyde Park area of London, near Mabel and Rowley. She lived in 40 Grosvenor and later bought 39 next door, for the rental income. This was usually straightforward, except for the time she sent her sister a cable reading "MOVE ALL FURNITURE INTO 40 AND LET 39 FURNISHED." Remaining in England on Sir George's orders, Daisy stayed with friends over the Christmas holiday. Letters from Archie about his life in India cheered her. She began reading again—books about how to groom horses. With echoes of her plan to run Belmont, she told Arthur of her wish to "combine stables and work over our horses together." Christmas also brought news from Katie Low that Willy was again too ill to drink or smoke. Daisy hypothesized "softening of the brain" or the consequence of years of overindulgence. He was not able to speak for days on end. He was morose, moody, and occasionally violent.[28]

Another meeting between them at Sir George's instigation drove home Willy's declining health. "He broke down and wept [and was] incoherent and agitated when he told me 'he had to be shut up,'" Daisy wrote. She knew her lawyer had been attempting for eight weeks to get them back together again and had been showing Willy letters Daisy had written so he could learn her side of things in her words. As neither husband nor wife wished to be reconciled, Sir George's aggravating plan was doomed to failure. Wayne Parker took to calling him a "serpent" bent on his own course, regardless of his client's opinion.[29]

Arthur came to London on business and got the latest news of the divorce saga. Willy said he could not provide any evidence of past infidelity ("which of course is a lie," Arthur huffed), nor would he be seen purposefully at a hotel with another woman—because he did not want to cheat on Anna Bateman. This indignity was almost too much for Daisy. Then, without explanation, Willy provided proof of his stay at a Bournemouth hotel with a woman he registered as Mrs. Low. This was the information she needed. She would also reveal how "she had been compelled to leave Meallmore because W.M.L. had brought a woman there." Daisy signed a divorce petition. A hearing would occur in October, according to Sir George.[30]

With her mind at ease, Daisy left in August 1904 for a lengthy stay at Franzenbad, accompanied by Nellie. The spa was no more perfect than Daisy's German, but it was a useful rest and a reminder of her mother's love for her. The "vegetable baths" produced sneezing, coughing, and a runny nose that made her hearing infinitely worse. Nellie heard her sobbing at night and saying, "I cannot stand this deafness and being so helpless." Daisy irrepressibly managed a good story out of her hearing loss. "I was glad I was deaf," she joshed to Arthur after Nellie's anger flared once, "because Mamma's language was like brimstone and sulfur." Luckily, both Nellie's temper and Daisy's deafness improved once away from the vegetable baths.[31]

At her mother's orders, Daisy went to Glasgow, where Abby and her bairns were staying with her mother-in-law. Willy took a turn for the worse. On September 20, back at 40 Grosvenor Street, Daisy received a note from his doctor stating that "he might rally, but couldn't recover." Unable to speak and suffering the aftereffects of a possible stroke, even Willy's sisters took to praying for the release of death. Daisy absorbed the news that she might have to act on his behalf if he were found insane. She called off the divorce. "The world would think it very wrong to divorce him when incapable of defending himself," Daisy believed, and when he "could not profit from his freedom."[32]

Yet seven weeks later he rallied, and Willy's physicians told how their patient "host[ed] a large luncheon during the Warwick races." Jack Maxwell added that Willy "asked Katie to chaperone Mrs. Bateman at Wellesbourne, and Katie and all of [the sisters] refused." Willy then angrily barred them from the house. Appreciating the Low sisters' actions but suspicious about Willy's health, Daisy determined to wait a little while to ascertain whether he would be well enough for her to resume divorce proceedings, for "I would not undergo any more of this Hell upon earth . . . ; if I can get free I will do so." Despite paralysis, Willy steadily improved into December, and was seeing Mrs. Bateman.[33]

Daisy wanted to divorce him while he was with his lover and while his mind was clear, but his sisters told Mabel a divorce would give Anna Bateman control of his fortune. The Lows had hurt Daisy. She felt they had treated her unkindly and now were interested only in their brother's money. "I have decided that if Willy pays for the divorce and wants it again and returns to Mrs. Bateman then not only am I bound by my word of honor to divorce him, but I wish to do so," Daisy cried. "All I want is freedom."[34]

Further problems with Willy's trust manager, Mr. Gasquet, made her even more suspicious and more impatient to be done. The funds that were to ensure her yearly allowance had been mysteriously withdrawn, and Daisy blamed the Low sisters. But she confronted Chalmers, Guthrie and played them off against Mr. Gasquet in a stroke of genius and got her finances straightened out. It exhausted her. "I hope," she wrote, not entirely in jest, "if God thinks it best for Willy to live, that He will in his infinite mercy let me die."[35]

Willy's paralysis spread to his throat in January 1905. What physicians referred to as softening of the brain was possibly a stroke. Daisy believed his brain had been softening for years. What else could account for his actions? He insisted the divorce proceedings continue. She returned to Sir George Lewis—who by now felt like a second father to her—and began again.[36]

Distraction was hard to find. Daisy turned intermittently to her art, sketching more than painting, but in May she begged Mabel and Rowley to decorate their drawing rooms a light green and let her "paint in each corner life size cherry trees." Her brother teased her about this plan, suggesting it would only be complete when she included "life sized George Washingtons with life sized hatchets."[37]

Daisy moved quickly to take advantage of a brief trip with some friends to Kolhapur, India. This was the complete change of scene she needed, and she adored every minute. With members of the British military as guides, and the maharajah of Kolhapur as her host, Daisy relished one of the best holidays of her life. The principal activity was tiger hunting in a jungle region she described as "thick, and rough, [and] volcanic . . . [with] huge cliffs, [and] impenetrable undergrowth." The maharajah did no shooting but provided "capacious and well furnished tents . . . motors, carriages, horses, a cordial and abundant hospitality," and hundreds of beaters to drive the game out from under cover. Her description turned to poetry: "the chance at grand sport, the actual beauty and wildness of these hill forests, the champagne air, the bright sunshine of the day, the drifting clouds racing past the moon at nightfall."

Big-game hunting was not a woman's sport. It was popular with the British stationed in India, and there was no limit to the tigers a hunter could kill. Photographs of the time show the British with their Indian beaters posing next to ten and twenty tiger carcasses lined up in a row. The photographs seldom included female hunters, but Daisy shot a tiger. "I am so glad I saw him myself and fired in my own time and way without advice of native shikari," or guide. She proudly took seven different measurements of the tiger, and was thrilled to record that it was very large—more than nine feet from nose to tail. There is an unmistakable note of triumph in her account of how she had rid the local people of a nefarious and unpredictable beast they called Liar because he was never where he ought to be.[38]

From India she traveled to the United States. Her first stop was the Parkers', to find that Eleanor was faring better in her battle with the tonics. Wayne got an earful about Daisy's impending divorce. As an attorney he found the differences between the British and American legal systems engrossing. He willingly gave advice, and the Gordons readily consulted him. By 1905, Wayne's opinion of Willy as "an incubus . . . of no use to himself or the world" was shared by the rest of the family. Wayne provided a glimpse of Daisy's hearing at this stage in her life, as he had not seen her for many months: "How she does manage her deafness. It is real genius the interest that she can keep in life and excite in others."[39]

Wayne remained "invincibly opposed to divorce proceedings," because he believed Daisy was protected under the maintenance deed Willy had signed. Therefore, she should engage in "masterly inactivity" and make no real movement toward the divorce court—to avoid scandal and because he believed she might lose the case altogether. "Masterly inactivity" Daisy could not do, because she had promised Willy to reinstate the divorce case. Yet the courts themselves moved at a snail's pace, unlike the rapid rate of Willy's decline.[40]

Ignoring the physician's warning that he could not stand the trip from Wellesbourne to Wales, Anna Bateman took Willy to Ruthven Castle, where, Nellie noted impertinently, it took only one week "to finish him up." In the wee hours of the morning on June 8, 1905, Willy Low suffered another seizure and died without regaining consciousness. The saddest thing, Daisy thought, was that "he did not die before he had altered the opinion of the many friends who loved him." Anna Bateman, at Willy's request, supervised the funeral arrangements. Daisy attended. "[A]lthough I am glad he is dead, yet for the sake of those years long ago when I loved him," she explained to her mother, "I would like to see his poor suffering body laid at rest, and if I who am so full of human faults can forgive him, does not God also pity and love him?" Willy Low was buried, in a final affront, with Anna Bateman's love letters placed over his heart. He had chosen for his last resting place the graveyard at the Church of Saint Peter and Saint Paul in Widmerpool, near the grave of his sister Hattie Coke-Robertson. Eleanor was in the UK at the time, and she and Mabel supported Daisy, who was dignified, calm, and composed throughout.[41]

The funeral did not end Daisy's troubles concerning Willy. His 1896 will had been very generous, leaving her Wellesbourne for use during her life, the Savannah home, Willy's London flat, "and $25,000 a year . . . which seems almost too good to be true," Arthur opined. It was. Unbeknownst to them all, after he met Anna Bateman, Willy had altered the will. He left nearly everything to his mistress, revoking even Daisy's twenty-five-hundred-pound annual maintenance.[42]

Daisy insisted it would be more seemly if the sisters contested the will, and they led the charge. His estate was worth two hundred thousand pounds, according to Willy's lawyer. The attorneys negotiated a settlement on the following terms: "Mrs. Low to be paid the sum of £40,000 in discharge of her annuity of £2,500 a year, to be paid as follows: £20,000 within three months with interest at 3.5% from the 1st January 1906. £10,000 within six months with interest at 3.5% from 1st January 1906. £10,000 within three years with interest at 4% from 1st January 1906." In addition, she was to receive "[t]he land at Savannah Lafayette Ward near the house," along with fifty thousand shares in Chalmers, Guthrie. Daisy's father still sent her an allowance, and she owned stock in railroads and other American industries. The Gordon men oversaw her finances, and while she worried mightily about teetering on the edge of poverty, she was in fact very well off. Willy Low's lover also received a sizable legacy. All four of his sisters were awarded smaller sums, and Amy Low Grenfell kept Wellesbourne, after trying unsuccessfully to sell it in 1906.[43]

Willy's death left numerous questions unanswered, not the least of which was why he strayed. He might have been an incorrigible rake like the prince of Wales, unable or uninterested in resisting women who found his good looks and money alluring. He might have been weak and followed the smart set's fashion of free and easy infidelity. Perhaps Anna Bateman was a money-seeking, predatory woman who set her sights on him. He could have been repulsed by Daisy's deafness. She was, after all, not hard of hearing when they fell in love. The limited time they spent together worked against their establishing a real friendship. Perhaps Willy married the Savannahian because he wanted in some oblique way to recover the mother he barely remembered. The cachet of an American wife might have played a role in Willy's decision to propose to Daisy. Daisy probably felt like a great prize to Willy, since he stood up to his father and fought for her. Most likely, it was a mixture of all these. Willy had not been taught how to manage his money, or schooled to behave as a responsible adult. He could be sensitive and kind, but his inheritance, coupled with the flattering attention of the prince of Wales, turned his head. Willy fought for and won Daisy, but her hearing problems made life with her difficult. He decided to adopt the morals of the Marlborough set, including the acceptance of adultery. In short, he chose those friends and that lifestyle over his wife.

The countess of Warwick alleged that Willy "loved children dearly." No letters between the couple exist to provide a full understanding, and ultimately, no outsiders ever know what occurs in a marriage. Maybe the absence of an heir drove a wedge between them. Daisy remained for years a silent and optimistic wife. Mabel believed her sister had "a hard life, and has had no one to love her best, which is what every woman craves." And since her husband was supposed to love her unreservedly, completely, and exclusively, Daisy—with the model of her parents' marriage before her—clung stubbornly to hope. Willy's death released her to a future she would have to define for herself.[44]

CHAPTER 10

Journeys

Willy Low's death left Daisy feeling simultaneously liberated and sad. Her monetary worries were considerably smaller as 1906 began. She had her faith, her family, and a large circle of friends. But what would she do with her life? The twentieth century was in its infancy, and women with careers were anomalies. Painting was socially acceptable but hardly remunerative, and it was a difficult profession for women to enter. Daisy expressed a desire to sculpt, "to do some work in life," and to avoid being "just an idle woman of the world," but art would not be her calling.[1]

She could marry again, as her good friend Lady Grey Egerton did upon her 1905 divorce. But Daisy, when given the chance, chose not to. Archie Hunter had proposed, by letter, one year into her widowhood. "I am glad to know he cares for me," she told Arthur, but to Mary she elaborated: "I am too old and too deaf to 'try try again,' especially as I am not 'in love' though I think I love the man as a dear friend." Perhaps if Archie had a better sense of timing, or had gone down on one knee before her, he might have received a happier answer. He could have reassured her that her age and hearing troubles did not matter in the completeness of his love. But he was career military, a no-nonsense sort who had loved Daisy for two decades. His logical outcome to their long friendship was marriage. Apparently, it was not hers.[2]

Deep within and still calling out to her was the Gordon imperative to duty. It was muffled by Daisy's heartache, but all around her in England and in the United States, women such as Maude Stanley and Lillian Wald were contributing to social reform in the face of the new century's undeniable poverty and want. Nellie continued her contributions as a benefactor of the Kinzie Elementary School and guarded the literary legacy of her mother and grandmother. A plague of physical troubles, including gout and an enlarged colon, hardly slowed her involvement in civic institutions. Mabel was busy with Peggy and Rowland, and Eleanor's health precluded greater engagement. Daisy suffered from recurrent malaria, from gout, bursitis, and general tiredness linked probably to profound melancholy. But with status, time, money, and health enough to contribute to society, she continued to volunteer with the working girls' club in what Kipling called the "unholy spot" of Camberwell.[3]

In the absence of a career, a second marriage, or full-time charitable work, Daisy Low, then in her midforties, could travel or be a kind of spinster aunt to younger relatives. She did both. She also kept up her rounds of visiting friends at their castles and country homes, where she hiked and hunted. She thought nothing of a "ripping good shoot" where "they got 1024 head the first day and 665 the second day" and one man "killed 74 pheasants in 15 minutes."[4] When Abby brought her four daughters to Europe, Daisy made sure to meet up with them. Daisy loved Scotland so she rented Lochs, an old estate in Glen Lyon, on the grounds of Meggernie. Situated between Loch Giorra and Loch an Daimh, the house sat in the shadow of the stark Grampian Mountains. Ian Bullough owned Meggernie Castle, where his mother, Alix Beech, often stayed. Daisy stalked regal red deer through the twenty-five-mile-long glen. She fished in the River Lyon, which twisted, as one contemporary observed, like "a half-strangled serpent wriggling along, wounded but menacing," making a "coarse murmuring" as it passed over "honey-combed rocks."[5]

Daisy assisted young people on their European tours. She had an especially good time when her goddaughter, Anne Hyde Clarke, and Arthur Osgood Choate came to visit. "Reddy" Choate booked passage with Anne to England because of his theory that the best way to learn about someone was to spend a week together on a ship. Meeting him in London, Daisy glowingly endorsed Reddy and placated Anne's understandably worried parents: "His worldly prospects are good, he is well born, and he is passionately in love with her." All of Daisy's friends concurred. Furthermore, he was an American, she pointed out, which meant no ocean would separate mother and daughter. When Mary and Hyde wondered how the two young people could possibly know their hearts, Daisy joked, "I always have such an *engaging* effect on the young people around me." But she had to backtrack when Mary accused Daisy of abetting the relationship by being a permissive chaperone. Grace assured her sister that while Daisy was mercurial, she was never improper. All went well thereafter, and in the fall of 1911 Anne Hyde Clarke and Arthur Choate were married in Cooperstown, with Daisy in attendance.[6]

As her goddaughter was falling in love, Daisy's parents celebrated their golden anniversary. In December 1907 family and friends converged on Savannah to toast Nellie and Willie Gordon's fifty years of marriage. Gold gifts piled up, like the coffee set from Daisy and her siblings and an enormous gold loving cup from the Georgia Hussars. Daisy gilded the wreath that Nellie had worn as a bride so she could reprise it for the anniversary. Local newspapers covered the festivity, concerning as it did two of Savannah's most important citizens. Of course, it was Daisy's wedding anniversary, too—it would have been her twenty-first. Her emotional turmoil took the form of three hours of vomiting and diarrhea, and she spent the conclusion of the party behind closed doors.[7]

The next day, she took herself off to India. Daisy loved the tiger hunting she had done on her brief visit nearly three years earlier and had heard about the rest of the subcontinent from her military friends. Sojourns in India by Western women in the early twentieth century were rare. The majority of white women in India were wives of men with careers there. Daisy planned to travel via her network of British Army officers, but such a trip—lacking in amenities, dangerous, and far too adventurous—was unthinkable for most of her friends. Accompanying Daisy was her niece Beth Parker and Grace Carter, for whom India was a long-imagined, romantic "land of dreams." Daisy's friends suggested archly that she, too, had a romantic interest in India, and that the trip was much "more than a simple sightseeing expedition." Archie Hunter was still stationed there. Either they didn't know Daisy had already received a proposal from him or they sensed she had second thoughts about her refusal.[8]

They sailed on the S.S. *Majestic* on Christmas Eve 1907, leaving New York for Plymouth, Cherbourg, Paris, Marseilles, and Naples before stopping on January 5, 1908, for a remarkable day in Pompeii. The site of the eruption of Mount Vesuvius in the year 79 had been first excavated in the eighteenth century. Pompeii reawakened the artist in Daisy. She described in her diary "perfectly exquisitely gracefully drawn" cupids, walls of lemon yellow and "Pompeiian red," a "Cerulean blue" ceiling, and "the serpent-shaped ring" on the petrified hand of a woman dead for centuries. Daisy marveled at the fruits left abandoned on tables and visible ruts in the road made by chariot wheels as ancient inhabitants fled before the threatening volcano. The sense of immediacy touched her, and she "realized how little human habits have changed."

By January 9 they had reached Port Said, Egypt. Daisy's only mail contained the disappointing news that Archie had gone to inspect troops in Burma. He provided a servant for them—a thoughtful gesture that could not compensate for his absence. Had Archie been called away on military business, or was he nursing the broken heart of a spurned suitor?

Daisy had charge of the trip's arrangements. She sent the telegrams to secure hotel rooms, meals, and first-class train carriages, and negotiated in person with hotel proprietors and railway porters. They crossed the Indian Ocean into the "vivid color and brilliant sun" of Ceylon (now Sri Lanka), reaching Tuticorin, the seaport city in the south of India, on January 24, and entered Madurai that afternoon. Wasting no time, they found a guide to show them the towering, eight-gated, highly decorated Meenakshi Amman temple. The three women returned the next day because it was too much to take in: the carvings in the sixteenth-century thousand-pillar hall, the jewels of the deities, the vibrant shrines. They traveled through Madras and Calcutta and Benares. "Nothing can express the charm and beauty and interest of this place," Daisy enthused. She, Grace, and Beth laughed at a wedding procession in which the bride was seven years old and the groom twice her age. Daisy noticed how the groom "resented" their laughter, writing later that "these people are very sensitive to ridicule, even the servants are dignified and dislike anything approaching chaff. Life is serious, solemn and hard for them. In their own minds they suffer the English or any white man as the Bible says 'Suffer fools gladly, seeing they themselves are wise.' They fly to wait on you. They show servile respect outwardly, but in their own minds they feel superior to you."

Benares is known for its ghats, or stairways, leading down to the sacred Ganges. Daisy witnessed the Mahashivratri festival, dedicated to Shiva, with its ritual cleansing, procession, singing, and chanting. She appreciated the caste-collapsing experience of bathing in the Ganges and compared it to Savannahians, black and white, "coming down the steps of the bluff and plunging into the river." Daisy, Beth, and Grace made sure to look for brass items at the bazaar, "the real native shops," not the ones with fixed prices in English. "Aunt Daisy can beat the natives down beautifully, as far as a European could ever get them," Beth wrote appreciatively.[9]

Daisy's admiration for Indians receded as they reached Lucknow, a center of the bloody uprising against the English in 1857. Angry Sepoys, or Indian soldiers in the British East India Company's army, slaughtered their English officers and other Britons (including women and children) in and around the town. A variety of grievances, including the alleged use of pig and cow fat for greasing a new type of rifle—thus enraging both Muslim and Hindu soldiers—anger at the limitations on promotion for Indians in the army, and nascent Indian nationalism, brought about the Sepoy Rebellion. "The impression made on me," Daisy penned, as she gazed gravely at the place "where the Bravest of the Brave defended themselves in the mutiny of 1857, was too painful to be written up in this diary."[10]

By the second week of February, they were in Lahore, calling on Princess Bamba Jindan Singh, a most unusual woman. Her father, Maharaja Dalip Singh, was removed from India and raised in England after the British forcibly ended his family's rule over the Punjab. In 1864 he married a German, Bamba Muller. Princess Bamba was one of their six children.

Grace stayed with the princess, while Daisy and Beth, after eight solid weeks of travel, reached the home of General Bryan Thomas Mahon. Daisy felt that Mahon, who had served with Archie Hunter in the relief of Baden-Powell at Mafeking, welcomed their presence in his otherwise "lonely life." They accompanied him when he inspected troops and practiced polo. They also met Sir Francis Younghusband, whom Daisy described as the "power behind the throne" of the maharajah of Kashmir. Celebrated in England for having opened Tibet to British trade in 1904, Younghusband and his wife and sister shared a lovely home with "a view of surpassing beauty of the range of Himalayan mountains." Daisy, who loved luxury, compared herself to Cinderella as she was driven through the town with two servants wearing livery. "I grinned," she gloated, "until I nearly caught cold in my teeth." She went to bed that night remembering the most transcendent sight she had ever seen: the setting sun emblazoning the Himalayas in dazzling amber.[11]

Two days later she was perched atop an elephant in a velvet-lined canopied seat, making her way to Bahu Fort. Monkeys capered overhead, parrots swooped past, and bands serenaded Daisy as she sipped tea and pondered the sacred bo trees. Retiring that evening in Jammu, she watched delightedly when wild birds flitted into her room to admire themselves in her mirror. "It was worth coming all the way to India just to pay this one visit," Daisy wrote with gratitude to the Younghusbands for their hospitality.

Letters from Archie Hunter reached her there, "very cheeky letters," she related to her father, "of the extravagance of Americans in India and he went so far in his last letter as to accuse us of not only spoiling India but of spoiling Egypt also." He might have had a point, for Daisy ended her letter home with a postscript asking for one hundred pounds more.[12]

Returning to Lahore on February 24, they rejoined Grace and Princess Bamba for a tour of the Shalimar Gardens built by Shah Jahan, whose love of magnificent architecture culminated in the Taj Mahal. The next day, the princess treated them to a seven-course, two-hour breakfast. Shortly after, Grace ventured north to Kashmir while Beth and Daisy left to experience one of the highlights of their trip: Sri Harmandir Sahib, the most important place of worship for Sikhs. Known as the Golden Temple of Amritsar, it is surrounded by a reflective pool of holy water. Daisy pronounced the "whole effect simply gorgeous." The serenity they carried with them from the Golden Temple shattered that night when their train caught fire. No one was injured as they hastily gathered their belongings only to wait for hours at the station in Phillaur for the next coach. Their solicitous conductor served up impromptu tea at one a.m., but the women, *en deshabille,* found it all a bit ludicrous.[13]

Arriving in Delhi tired but game, they met up with some friends of General Mahon's, who took them to Humayon's Tomb, resting place for members of the Mughal dynasty, and to Shah Jahan's magnificent Red Fort on the Yamuna River. On March 2 they toured the ancient city of Meerut, where the Sepoy Rebellion actually began. Happily, Nevill Smyth, Bryan Mahon, and—finally—Archie Hunter appeared. Daisy did not mention the reunion with her former suitor in her diary, so the warmth or coolness of it can only be imagined.

She did not lack for military heroes, as Meerut social life largely involved the officers and men stationed there. One memorable evening, though, she was thrilled to find herself flanked by two Victoria Cross winners, Smyth and Francis Maxwell. In such vaunted company, the women watched horse shows and polo matches. They rode outside town to see the men participate in the blood sport of pigsticking.[14] The Delhi sightseeing continued: the tallest minaret in India, Qutub Minar; the fourteenth-century ruins of Tughlaqabad Fort; and a series of notable tombs.

A brief trip to Jaipur to ogle an eighteenth-century model town preceded their visit to Agra. The Taj Majal, built as a memorial to Shah Jahan's wife, was "beyond any words of praise." Daisy filled her diary with the history of the architectural masterpiece and the depth of Shah Jahan's love. "We consider Indian women downtrodden," she mused, "but in no other country in the world, has any wife been honored by such an exquisite monument." Throughout her time abroad, Daisy's diary shows a traveler intensely interested in the country and its people. She seldom judged or criticized, and she avoided the temptation to assume that if she didn't understand something, it was wrong or inferior. A sense of wonder pervades the entire journey.

It was less wonder and more good, old-fashioned Gordon pragmatism that helped her cope with the onset of chicken pox. All three women were quarantined by a physician, and that unfortunate turn of events meant Daisy, with real regret, was forced to cancel her plans to stay with Archie in western India, where she was to meet "the only woman who reigns in her own right in India," the reformer Kaikhusrau Jahan, called the begum of Bhopal.

The chivalrous Major Smyth came to their rescue in the chicken-pox crisis. He sent them to his own luxurious quarters in Mhow, in central India. They arrived—appropriately, Daisy thought—on April Fools' Day, and gratefully settled in. How Smyth overcame his excessive shyness and found "the courage to ask three women to stay with him," Beth couldn't imagine.[15] The quarantine was lifted from Daisy and Beth in short order, but Grace's case was acute. She languished in her room while Smyth showed the others nearby historic sites.

Three and a half months of truly thrilling travel thus ended with the kindness of their friends, particularly Nevill Smyth and Bryan Mahon. Daisy, Grace, and Beth dined with Archie Hunter on their last night in India, an ideal conclusion, Daisy thought. From Bombay on April 11, 1908, they sailed for London.

After the India trip, Daisy entered a difficult period. Mabel prescribed a trip to Savannah "to be petted and loved and made much of." Daisy certainly craved that, but she returned home most winters to parents who treated her like a child and assumed—wrongly—that she could not manage her money. Her friends expected her to, as she put it, "join the treadmill of life in the Season." The rewards of a committed social existence were meeting new and interesting people and seeing those she loved. But as Daisy knew thirty years earlier, such a giddy whirl felt hollow after a short time. It was frequently hard for her to trust the affection of friends, and the feeling that only her parents really loved her—and only because they had to—increased when Daisy was tired or sick. She felt herself "too deaf to ever be of real use to any one in illness," so caring for invalids—a perfectly acceptable role for widows—was not an option. Yet homilies from the pulpit and her own Bible reading urgently reinforced her inclination to do good in the world. What she lacked was a catalyst.[16]

While she continued to assist in Camberwell, she did not find her catalyst there. As her mother attested, Daisy took "an immense interest in these overworked creatures" and was glad to show off the "operetta given by the shopgirls," whom she "trained and drilled." Still, the Talbot settlement house work did not become the cause near to her heart, even though it sensitized her to the needs of those in grinding poverty.[17]

Nor did the suffrage movement rouse her to a lifelong commitment. She attended a "Suffragette meeting" with her feminist friend Agnes Anstruther. Before they went, she told her sister, "You know I do sympathize with their desire to make laws for women workers which will protect the women against unjust employers." Like many women of her class, Daisy believed the vote was necessary for working women but less so for elites. She drew a cartoon once of herself as a suffragist, pouring salt on the tail of a refractory, birdlike legislator to hasten along the franchise, suggesting that she saw its ultimate arrival as inevitable. In England, female landowners had been granted voting privileges two years earlier, and the movement for full women's suffrage was gathering steam. In the United States, suffrage activists put their case before the nation, but race complicated the issue. The plight of working women, as she had witnessed it in Camberwell, also incited Daisy to engage in political discussions with everyone from lords to architects. But even though she was evolving opinions on the income tax and tariff laws, politics was still a male bastion.[18]

Her forty-ninth birthday pricked her conscience as she contemplated what she could do to make a difference. She did not want to be with her family, and spent her birthday instead at Agnes Anstruther's home in Fife. From her stone room, she could see the Firth of Forth with its "isles that shine like opals glimmer[ing] on the misty bay." With the fresh Scottish air blowing in the window, she began a regimen to "develop [her] abdomen to such an extent that an iron wheelbarrow carrying a ton of coal can be wheeled over it."[19]

Her hearing was more disheartening than her abdominal muscles—though some days the worst part was her mother's insistence that she seek medical help. Driven to impatience, Daisy penned a letter to Eleanor using humor, her best defense: "As you have a typewriter, will you please write out the following bulletin to be pasted on [Mama's] bedroom door next to the telephone as she most frequently sees that—February 1st: Heard a fog horn. March 1st: Hearing improved, heard a camel when it rose. April 1st: Hearing decidedly improved—heard the pantomime rehearsal also the grass grow. . . . Have great hopes of hearing Gabriel blow his trumpet on the day of judgment." Then, turning serious, Daisy affirmed that her hearing was as variable as it had been for decades. And she had seen physicians—everywhere she traveled, she sought professional advice.[20]

She looked for better hearing through technological innovations, too. Daisy tried the violet ray machine, a contraption that utilized inert argon gas to send out a purple electrical pulse its adherents claimed could cure everything from the effects of aging to impaired auditory functions by "stimulat[ing] nerve endings." Daisy hoped the violet ray machine would ameliorate many of her chronic sources of pain, including gout and bursitis, and decrease her deafness, too.[21]

Another new device amplified sound when worn (rather than held up to the ear). She learned of the Acousticon Company's hearing aid when she assisted her brother Bill and his family in their search for treatment for eighteen-year-old B. His hearing was much worse than hers, although he was adept at lipreading. Dr. Fritz Hirschland, an otologist in Essen, Germany, found that B could speak and understand what others said, "yet [was] unable to recognize the sound of the simplest words." Physical examination proved him capable of discerning only a very narrow range of sounds. Hirschland prescribed a homeopathic remedy to vitiate the scar tissue and daily exercises with an electric hearing machine called an Akouphone to try "to learn words by ear."[22]

B could not hear music, but Daisy could. She cherished her modern Victrola gramophone. This early precursor to the CD player was remarkable because it allowed people to listen to a symphony or opera aria in their own home, over and over. Before Victrolas, there was only live music, which could be heard once and never replicated. Nellie bought a Victrola for herself and another for Daisy. She believed it would help her daughter's hearing. The two women kept up a lively commentary on and exchange of their favorite records.[23]

Restless and lacking the family that served as centerpiece for most women then, Daisy continued to search for something useful to do, despite her age and hearing impairment. Travel, which she enjoyed, was at least enlightening and thus more productive than the endless social whirl. She set off for Canada, where her friend, the 4th Earl Grey, governor general of Canada, helped Daisy explore Ottawa. Fifty couples on skates ice dancing in intricate maneuvers reminded her of the old germans she learned as a girl. Grey took her to her first professional ice hockey match. She loved the speed and the "skill and grace and rush of the game [which] simply carries one away."[24]

She decided to visit Egypt with Lady Maxwell and two young women from Savannah, Gwendolen and Eleanor Nash. During their crossing, Daisy spent hours sculpting Eleanor's head. Critical of the result, she tossed the bust into the sea. On Valentine's Day they reached Cairo, where George Hunter, then director general of the Egyptian Coastguard Service, sent one of his vessels to meet them. Also traveling on their ship was wealthy American financier J. Pierpont Morgan, who assumed the coast-guard launch was for him. "The sailors in charge informed him it had been 'sent for Mrs. Low and party.' So he stood aside, and I swept down the gangway" with all the passengers craning their necks to see which of the aristocracy was among them, Daisy chortled.[25]

By steam train, the women reached the luxurious Mena House hotel and marveled as the moon outside their window glowed on the Sphinx. The girls went off on a twenty-mile camel ride across the desert while Daisy shook off her headache and climbed the Great Pyramid. The next day, they rested in the heat of the afternoon, backs against the feet of the Colossi of Memnon after a sumptuous picnic there, basking in a deep, still silence.[26]

Restive on her return to England, Daisy drove her car across France and Spain with her friend and relative Minnie Davis. Next came the fruition of plans set a year earlier: with Laurie Harris, the daughter of the Savannah doctor who had treated her ears, Daisy rented a *petite maison* in Paris in which to sculpt. Travel was exciting, but she longed to create something tangible. She enrolled in a modeling class, as sculpting was called at that time. Her teacher immediately put her to work on copying the head of Dante, which she found dispiriting. "I longed for the tongue not of a poet, but of my Mother, to express how fervently I hoped that Dante was in the Inferno he so graphically described." She told her father that she wanted to learn enough "to work at home in my leisure hours, [so] my life will gain more serious interests."[27]

Daisy Low, nearing fifty, was a vivid personality. She journeyed to India on a trip few people—English or American, male or female—ever even contemplated. She created the itinerary and made the arrangements for friends, trekking nearly four months in a rugged land, devoid of many creature comforts. Returning to Egypt, wintering in America, spending the autumns in Scotland—such travel took bravery, a spirit of adventure, organizational skills, flexibility, a willingness to endure potential physical discomforts, and a sense of humor, all of which Daisy possessed. She was a devout Christian, a loyal friend, kind, and generous. But she did not feel bound to Edwardian rules of decorum for women, which excluded this sort of travel. And most Edwardians would have looked askance at the peregrinations of unchaperoned women halfway around the globe.

Daisy Gordon Low had become her own person, unbothered by actions others considered quirky. She loved the automobile she'd owned since at least 1906. She never turned away an animal in need and doted on her parrot, her mockingbirds, her turtle with the wagging head, and her dogs. She seldom rejected humans in need, either, and Nellie berated her more than once for befriending people who were "common, common, common." It was her daughter's "kind impulses and blindness as to all sorts of evil (for which I thank God!) that has made you always take up with people who, to say the least, were off color. . . ." Daisy's liberality was legendary, but it often got her in trouble. "You are so generous my dear and so anxious to help those you love out of difficulties that you don't bring enough practical sense to bear on your plans," Nellie told her. Faithful to a fault, she had the accompanying trait of being easily wounded. Class and her Southern upbringing meant Daisy could be imperious when rules of etiquette or hierarchy were breeched. Her first response to most situations, however, was compassion.[28]

Friends and family made her happiest. She managed to maneuver the shoals of her relationship with Archie Hunter and keep him in her inner circle, even after he finally married in 1910. She sometimes complained of loneliness, yet constantly filled her homes with guests—whom she occasionally forgot. Rowland Leigh attested to a party at Daisy's where she was glaringly absent. He ran upstairs to his aunt's room, only to discover her in bed, having put the gathering out of her mind. She hadn't even heard them arrive, and why her maid did not alert her is anyone's guess—perhaps it was her day off. Regardless, in five short minutes she had joined them. Events like these gave Daisy a reputation as a woman who was capricious but charming, antipodal but alluring, unpredictable but never unpleasant. Planning with her could be a nightmare. She reached decisions quickly and seldom decided as one expected. Those around her did not always follow her logic. She was, as a result, never boring. Some friends found this appealing, and others exasperating. Daisy was aware of and at least a little worried about it. In response to her warning, Nevill Smyth teased her gently: "I did not realize you were erratic, but I will observe in future and then decide whether it shocks my military instincts."[29]

What Daisy yearned for was a sense of purpose—some way to channel her energy and marshal her urge to do good. She needed a push to locate a project or to tap into the latent skills and experience she had in abundance. To suit her ideally, such an undertaking should keep her in touch with people, permit her to innovate, and provide wiggle room for her "erratic" nature. Ironically, General Sir Robert Baden-Powell provided the nudge.

CHAPTER 11

General Sir Robert Baden-Powell

Daisy was grumpy. On a mild day in May 1911, she discovered the man seated next to her at lunch was General Sir Robert Baden-Powell. She knew all about him. Who didn't? He was famous, the darling of the British press. He numbered her good friends Archie Hunter and Bryan Mahon among his military colleagues. Nevill Smyth, the shy and gallant officer who took her in when she had chicken pox, was his first cousin. She knew she was supposed to be impressed, but Daisy, who was nothing if not loyal, was determined to dislike him. She was convinced that he had received an unjustly large portion of glory for his leadership during the siege of Mafeking, and equally certain that her friends had been insufficiently praised. Thus she set her face against him utterly. That worked until just after the soup was served.

"[N]ow that I know him," Daisy gushed, "I think he is a remarkable man, a genius as a soldier. He draws, paints, models well." She came to consider even his vanity justifiable because of all he had accomplished. And Baden-Powell's program fascinated her. She explained to her father: "He left the Army against King Edward's wishes (but afterwards the King saw he was right) to organize the Boy Scouts. Now he has 40,000 boys all over Great Britain and branches in the U.S.A., France, and Germany." She marveled at how "little guttersnipes" so idle that they "became a danger to the public . . . now are growing up healthy, clean, orderly citizens." Daisy's admiration for Robert Baden-Powell was nearly instantaneous and utterly life changing.[1]

The object of her regard was the son of Henrietta Grace Smyth and Professor Baden Powell. Professor Powell was twenty-eight years older than his wife, had been widowed twice, and was a father. Although they met when Henrietta was fifteen, their courtship did not begin for another six years. Once under way, it moved swiftly, and the second time they were alone together Powell proposed. She accepted, and they wed in 1846. Not long after, Henrietta Powell gave birth to the first of ten children, seven of whom would survive infancy. Robert Stephenson, who went by Stephe in the family, was born on February 22, 1857, in Paddington, the fifth surviving child.

Professor Baden Powell was a Fellow of the Royal Society and served as a clergyman before taking up an endowed chair in geography at Oxford. He was a prolific author, with books on subjects ranging from theology to physics. He bequeathed his artistic talent and his love of the outdoors to his children. Stephe's maternal grandfather, William Henry Smyth, had been a career naval officer, president of the Royal Astronomical Society, and a founder of the Royal Geographical Society. An author himself, he cultivated friendships with many literary figures of the day, including William Thackeray, John Ruskin, Harriet Martineau, and T. H. Huxley.

The large Powell family was headed by the strong-willed Henrietta, who pushed all her sons to succeed. She oversaw her children's earliest education and allowed them to absorb what they could from their father's equipment and books. She placed a premium on a close family, and taught them all that they must assist one another to achieve great things. One by one, the boys left for boarding school—but they left as Baden-Powells, for Henrietta changed the family name from Powell to Baden-Powell, with the hyphen, in tribute to her husband, who died when Stephe was three.[2]

At age eleven, Stephe Baden-Powell matriculated at his father's alma mater, nearby Rose Hill School. Two years later, he became a "Gownboy" at London's ancient Charterhouse School. In 1870, thirteen-year-old Stephe fitted in easily and well. He took tremendous pleasure in anything connected with theater, sports, and the outdoors. He spent summers at home or with his brother Warington, a boating fanatic. When Stephe failed his entrance exam to Oxford, he turned instead to the military. He aced the grueling, twelve-day-long army examination consisting of math, geography, drawing with perspective, foreign languages, sciences, and English composition. In 1876, "Sub-Lieutenant R.S.S.B. Powell" received his commission in the Cavalry and joined the 13th Hussars.[3]

His military career took him around the world. For recreation, he hunted large game, becoming a published expert in pigsticking. In 1884 his *Reconnaissance and Scouting* was released. The book, an outgrowth of his teaching those essential military tasks to army officers, was used in classrooms in and out of the military. It emphasized the importance of individual self-reliance rather than "the slavishly obedient soldier" who followed rules despite what his own senses told him. A reconnaissance specialist, in 1890 Baden-Powell became aide-de-camp to his uncle, an intelligence officer. His creativity as a spy knew no bounds. He masqueraded as a butterfly collector and, when challenged, showed his brilliant sketches to enemy officers, who could not see that the designs in the wings were really maps of their forts that included coded information on the number and types of weapons Baden-Powell had observed.[4]

The tiniest details fascinated Baden-Powell. In the military, scouting information about the enemy was critical. Understanding the elusive tales told by bent blades of grass, the unaccountable presence of a leaf out of place, or the size of a footprint could mean the difference between battlefield success and failure. Throughout the 1890s, Arthur Conan Doyle had tantalized countless readers with his suspenseful tales of the uncanny abilities of his fictional detective Sherlock Holmes. American scouts figured largely in "cowboy and Indian" stories, and they walked off the page when Buffalo Bill's Wild West Show toured the United States and Europe. Baden-Powell had seen Buffalo

Bill's show in 1887 and adopted the trademark cowboy neckerchief and Stetson hat for use in Africa.[5]

Enamored with American culture, Baden-Powell subscribed to *Harper's Magazine* so he could read about the West and see it through Frederic Remington's drawings. Baden-Powell imbibed this ethos firsthand while working with Frederick Russell Burnham. That legendary American tracker served as military scout in the U.S. Indian wars but was also a cowboy, a buffalo hunter, and a gold prospector. Seeking further challenges, in 1893 he took his family halfway around the world to the new frontier of Africa, where he scouted for the British South Africa Company during its ill-fated attempt to build a railway across a hostile continent.

Baden-Powell met Burnham during the Second Matabele War in 1896. Combined African forces were trying to oust white settlers. By then Burnham was chief scout for the British Army, and Lieutenant-Colonel Baden-Powell was chief of staff to Commanding General Frederick Carrington. With South African tracker Jan Grootboom, the three men shared techniques while tracking through the cave-riddled Matapo Hills. Carrington called Burnham the greatest scout he encountered in South Africa, and Baden-Powell was impressed, too. Burnham taught the Englishman about American "wood-craft," a term Baden-Powell borrowed and later used in his book *The Matabele Campaign*. He defined wood-craft as "the art of noticing smallest details and connecting their meaning, and thus gaining a knowledge of the ways and doings of your quarry." Not long after, Baden-Powell published his second book on scouting, called *Aids to Scouting for N.-C.O.'s and Men*.[6]

Robert Baden-Powell rose to international fame during the second Boer War. In October 1899, the Boers—descendants of the Dutch who settled South Africa—trapped approximately twelve hundred British troops under his leadership in Mafeking. There are controversial aspects to Baden-Powell's management, but journalists then concentrated on British pluck. They filed nearly daily reports, raising concern in the nation to a fever pitch. Patriotic English men and women sent prayers heavenward for the safe rescue of the fearless forces cut off and outnumbered there. Baden-Powell had to administer the town—including hospital services, dwindling food stocks, police, and economic activity—while resisting the Boers. Besides provisions, his biggest challenge was keeping up the necessary morale. He put together scouting teams, led reconnaissance efforts, and was resourceful in his ability to strike back at the encircling Boers.

Field Marshall Frederick Roberts put General Archie Hunter in charge of devising a plan to end the siege at Mafeking before the food stores ran out. Hunter was keenly disappointed when Roberts denied him the chance to lead the relief column. Instead, Archie organized the preparations and put Bryan Mahon in charge of the one thousand men who marched to Mafeking. Hunter led his 10th Division toward the capital city, Pretoria, to tempt the Boers to fight him instead of Mahon. Mahon trekked a punishing 230 miles in less than a fortnight and reached Mafeking in mid-May 1900. Britain rejoiced euphorically as Baden-Powell won promotion to major general and a warm spot in the hearts of his countrymen.[7]

He next organized the South African Constabulary, or police force, until called to England in 1903 to become inspector general of the cavalry in Britain. He found, to his astonishment, that all across England, boys were emulating him by adapting information from his books. They wore homemade uniforms and played tracking games. Some groups of boys named themselves in his honor: "The B-P Boys of Greenock," "The B-P Brigade," or "the B-P Anti-Cigarette League." One boys' group patron published *Hints from Baden-Powell: A Book for Boys Brigades*. Baden-Powell's own *Aids to Scouting* appeared as a series of articles in the magazine *Boys of the Empire* in 1900, and the first installment was titled "The Boy Scout." The understandable flattery coincided with Baden-Powell's fears about national military preparedness and worries that British youths were too urban, too intellectual, and too lacking in self-reliance. These beliefs were widespread in the wake of the Boer Wars, and thus, when Baden-Powell began to tout the services rendered by young men during the siege of Makefing, he encountered receptive audiences.[8]

After 1904 several influential leaders were discussing ideas that Baden-Powell had expressed in an Eton College lecture titled "Soldiering." In that address and a subsequent letter published in the Eton College *Chronicle*, Baden-Powell suggested that boys form themselves into groups, model themselves on the Japanese samurai and the English knights of the Middle Ages, learn about chivalry, and teach themselves how to shoot, scout, and drill. Baden-Powell wrote that uniforms were not necessary, but financial self-sufficiency for each "clump" of boys was. Each boy should promise "to fear God, honour the King, help the weak and distressed, reverence women and be kind to children, train themselves to the use of arms for defence of their country, [and] sacrifice themselves, their amusements, their property, and, if necessary, their lives for the good of their fellow-countrymen." He dangled the promise of his presence as inspector to the largest such group formed that winter.[9]

In 1907, at Brownsea Island, Baden-Powell famously gave in to the relentless push from educators, social commentators, and reformers to formalize what he had inadvertently started. He called together twenty-two boys to test out his ideas near Bournemouth off the southern coast of England. He wove together his scouting practices and thoughts about the future of the nation with what he had learned from Burnham, what he had observed in talking to boys' organizations, the responses he had received from lecturing about teaching scouting to young men, and the concrete practicalities he found in *The Birch-bark Roll of the Woodcraft Indians* by American Ernest Thompson Seton.

The Birch-bark Roll laid out Seton's method of instructing boys in woodcraft, which Seton, a wildlife conservationist, author, and artist, defined as "nature-study, certain kinds of hunting, and the art of camping." For the outdoorsman it also meant "star-craft, finding one's way, telling direction, [and] sign language." Baden-Powell recognized the similarity between Seton's Woodcraft Indians, begun in 1902, and his own agenda. At Brownsea Island, the twenty-two boys camped, swam, prayed, played, sweated through calisthenics, and learned the rudiments of tracking. Baden-Powell told tales of scouting the empire's enemies in the Matapo Hills and mesmerized the boys with his Zulu war chant.[10]

For three years Baden-Powell deliberated about leaving the army to embark on what turned out to be his greatest career: the Boy Scouts. In the spring of 1910, at age fifty-three, Baden-Powell took in hand a flourishing—if unorganized—movement. It was not a straight line from the Brownsea experiment to Scouting. But the trajectory was set once his *Scouting for Boys* appeared in 1908. Groups of Boy Scouts grew up organically, as friends encouraged friends to join, and adult leaders stepped forward. By the time Daisy met Baden-Powell in May of 1911, Boy Scouting seemed an inexorable force.

His later formulation of the Boy Scouts would deemphasize the martial aspects of the organization, as he knew they would not play well to the parents of working- and middle-class boys. Baden-Powell's experiences in the Boer War taught him that nationwide preparation for armed conflict was critically important, and training Britain's boys for defense in case of invasion was, to him, an excellent start. Daisy shared an appreciation for the importance of military preparedness. But what really drew Daisy in was Baden-Powell's emphasis on fun. He spoke specifically about how "'children should be brought up as cheerfully and as happily as possible,' and . . . [how] 'in this life one ought to take as much pleasure as one possibly can . . . because if one is happy, one has it in one's power to make all those around happy.'"[11]

The joy that Baden-Powell brought into Daisy Low's life was evident from the time they spent together. The coronation of King George V in June 1911 brought millions of people crowding into London—pickpockets, royal watchers, friends of the aristocracy, friends of the friends of the aristocracy, and Daisy and Robert Baden-Powell. In the flag-draped West End, revelers sang and tooted tin horns in an "indescribable discord." The royal procession wound its way through seven miles of London, including neighborhoods near the Camberwell girls' club. Daisy's own home at 40 Grosvenor Street was a hive of activity. Her former traveling companion Minnie Davis was a houseguest, and the pair took advantage of every possible event, folding in family members and friends. Minnie and Daisy observed the great naval review at Spithead from seats provided by the Beeches. Meandering back to London, they went sightseeing on the Isle of Wight, paid homage to Jane Austen at her home, Chawton, and called briefly on Carrie and Rudyard Kipling in East Sussex. The Kiplings declined Daisy's invitation to London, because the coronation "brought friends from the end of the earth" and they had their own houseful.[12]

But the coronation highlights for Daisy were spent with Baden-Powell. One evening, Daisy and Baden-Powell swelled the crowd at the Shakespeare Ball in the Royal Albert Hall. The big day began as he breakfasted with Daisy and Minnie at 40 Grosvenor, then drove her car to Mercers' Hall for parade viewing and lunch as his special guests. Baden-Powell was resplendent in full dress uniform, and drew every eye as they walked a short one hundred yards to the door. Daisy couldn't wait to describe it to her parents. Baden-Powell was instantly recognizable. A great cheer went up. The crowd parted for the hero of Mafeking, and he, Minnie, and Daisy found themselves "in the middle of a perfectly empty space in the street—Soldiers, two deep, lining each side and thousands of people on sidewalks cheering B-P to the echo. I <u>liked</u> it!" Daisy conceded unabashedly. After the meal they motored to Saint Paul's Cathedral for the "touching and solemn and very beautiful" coronation. Baden-Powell's presence intensified her coronation memories.[13]

Back home, Daisy reflected on her newest friend. Robert Baden-Powell was difficult to resist. His slight frame contained an alluring mix of all the qualities Daisy loved: real military heroism, a contagious enthusiasm for life, a flair for acting, a slightly naughty enjoyment of pranks, a strong moral core, and an ability to get things done. Daisy and Baden-Powell shared three important commonalities: art as a hobby, a love of travel, and controlling mothers. One difference between them was Baden-Powell's lifelong chariness of organized religion. Baden-Powell considered nature sacred and thought that camping outdoors was the one certain way that "men may know their God."[14]

Nevertheless, the stern Victorian commitment to duty, honor, and fidelity drove them both. For Baden-Powell, that meant continuing the family name. After Mafeking, he determined it was time to begin a family, ideally with a woman of means who could assist his social and professional aspirations. Heretofore he had had no success in this arena. Past proposals had been rejected, even by Rose Kerr, a good friend whom he had quite wanted to wed.[15]

Were either of them contemplating marriage? Daisy clearly idealized him. One week after their first meeting, she made a two-hundred-mile pilgrimage, by car, alone, north to Louth, to see his sculpted bust of John Smith, which she found "a rare good thing." At the end of May she mused on the paradox of Baden-Powell as "essentially a Man of War" who gave her an unprecedented "feeling of Peace." She noted how he "rushes from one engagement to another yet he does not strike me as restless or fussy or 'driven.'" This "innate sense of repose" she attributed to her perception that "His activities are for mankind. . . ."[16]

The next day she found her thoughts "irresistibly" drawn to the "selfless unselfish" Baden-Powell. She ascribed her daydreaming to "a force outside myself [that] seems to compel me to think of him." This mystical impetus led her to a profoundly important conclusion, an answer to her long-sought desire: "a sort of intuition comes over me that he believes I might make more out of my life and that he has ideas which, if I followed them, a more useful sphere of work might open up before me in future."[17]

Yet Daisy was mortified at her response to him. She knew, or assumed, that other women had felt as she did. They had "forced a sort of hero worship upon him." She did not want to be counted as one of them. She felt a "dread lest he may possess some unexplained magnetism which might make me too, feel inclined to idealize him." She did not want to look foolish in front of him or to have him dismiss her as an idle celebrity hunter. But she was simply overwhelmed. "No doubt about his magnetism," she wrote bleakly the next time she saw him. After the opera one night, they returned to her home and he lingered after her other guest left. They discussed his effect on her:

"I told him a little about my futile efforts to be of use, and the shame I feel when I think of how much I could do yet how little I accomplish and when thrown with a man who has made a success of everything, by contrast I feel that my life brings forth 'nothing but leaves!'—a wasted life."[18]

The 1858 poem by Lucy E. Akerman, familiar to Daisy as a hymn, castigated those who squandered their lives in selfish pursuits:

> The Spirit grieves
> O'er years of wasted life;
> O'er sins indulged
> while conscience slept,
> O'er vows and promises unkept,
> And reap, from years of strife—
> Nothing but leaves!

The poem concluded with the fearsome thought that on judgment day such a soul would bring not "golden sheaves" to lay "at the Savior's feet" but instead, "nothing but leaves."[19]

Baden-Powell understood this trepidation, felt her deep sorrow, and responded in a way that spread "a golden warmth" through her and moved her to gratitude. In her diary she recalled, "He looked so kindly when he said 'There are little stars that guide us on—although they do not realize it.'" This phrase has been rendered "although we do not realize it." It is very clear from her diary, however, that the pronoun is "they." In the sentence, "they" would seem to refer to "little stars." In the larger context, the "star" guiding Daisy was Baden-Powell. She wrote repeatedly that he was—forgivably, to her—conceited, but it seems unlikely that Baden-Powell meant to refer to himself as "little stars." It is more likely that Daisy—with stars in her eyes—by then infatuated with Baden-Powell, miswrote the pronoun in a sort of Freudian slip. It is grammatically correct for the pronoun to read "we," but at that moment in Daisy's life the guiding star was Baden-Powell.

Daisy and Sir Robert found many occasions to enjoy each other's company in the summer of 1911, despite their hectic schedules. They were together during the London season, and, momentously, Baden-Powell even took Daisy home to meet his mother. Daisy gave him *Wau-bun,* which he thought marvelous, admiring her grandmother's "adventurous and plucky spirit." For their part, the Gordons liked Baden-Powell. Bill and Ellen were in Europe with B in July 1911. Baden-Powell joined the family for dinner and then a show at the Palace Theatre, complete with a reprise of the coronation in the new technology of moving pictures. Studying Baden-Powell, Bill noted his slight build, his baldness, and his average looks. He found Sir Robert a good conversationalist, and reported he "was quite shocked later to find how freely I had aired my views" as they drove back to Daisy's home together.[20]

In August, Baden-Powell visited her—along with other friends, as Daisy always had a houseful—at Lochs. She and Baden-Powell walked and talked and fished together. A keen angler, he suggested she could fatten the fish by adding clumps of ferns to the lake so the fish would eat the insects infesting the plants. In the evenings they listened to the Victrola, and Sir Robert pantomimed a love scene with Alix Beech that had them all in gales of laughter. He even acted as the head of the house by protecting Daisy from a drunken and potentially violent servant.[21]

They shared their art with each other. Both painted—he drew a watercolor sketch in her diary, a particularly intimate act—but at the time they met, sculpting engrossed both. Lacking a teacher since Paris, Daisy took advantage of Baden-Powell's encouragement to study with his sculpting instructor Edouard Lanteri, "the most respected teacher of sculpture and modeling of his generation," according to *Mercure de France.* His well-noted dedication to teaching at the Royal Academy of Art meant he left behind many talented students but few finished pieces. Strangely enough, though, Daisy had seen one of them: the memorial bust of her sister-in-law Harriet Coke-Robertson in Widmerpool, where Willy Low was buried.[22]

Lanteri believed that students should learn from the Greek masters by duplicating them in plaster. He set his pupils—male and female—to studying the muscles and skeleton of the human body. He insisted on their understanding and sculpting nudes before the figures could be draped. This "vigorous naturalism" helped to create the New Sculpture movement. Daisy worked on a bust of Peggy Leigh, her niece, and at least two other pieces during this time.[23]

By the end of September, Mabel described Daisy as looking uncommonly happy and healthy. She and Baden-Powell could be seen on the town, but Daisy also appreciated another side of him: the hunter. She knew her beloved Georgia offered game the expert pig-sticker had never pursued. Baden-Powell was embarking shortly on a speaking tour of the United States, and Daisy wanted him to see her hometown. She asked her mother to invite him and to entice him with "wild bird shooting" and "roughing it."[24]

Tim Jeal, Baden-Powell's biographer, concluded that after August, Sir Robert had made up his mind that Daisy could not be the wife of his dreams, even though he realized "the immense advantages that would accrue to his whole family if he chose to make her his bride. Her letters to him plainly intimated that she would have assented if asked. But in the end, as he tried to explain to his mother, he had felt unable to 'take a rich widow . . . A good comrade even without a fortune is what I should like. . . .'"[25]

But Baden-Powell proposed to Daisy, according to her niece. When and where that happened, Daisy did not record. Her papers leave one provocative possibility for the cessation of their courtship. A letter fragment in Daisy's handwriting from this period, missing the name of the addressee, contains this: "I must stop now, I am writing early in the morning and thinking of you, and longing for you, I love you so truly—I wish I could make myself over again, on a pattern that would be more acceptable to you. I look back on those . . ." And there the letter breaks off. Did making herself over include being younger, less deaf, and perhaps without the baggage of her first marriage? Jeal holds that Baden-Powell needed a woman with financial resources and the potential to carry on the family name. While Daisy had money, she appears to have been incapable of bearing children. She was, as her brother knew, "eager to enjoy everything to the utmost," which makes it much more difficult to credit the notion that she was not a "good comrade." It is far easier to believe that Baden-Powell simply used that as an excuse for Henrietta Baden-Powell, whose overriding concern was adding to the family's coffers.[26]

Meeting Robert Baden-Powell put Daisy's life on an ultimately fulfilling and joyful trajectory. The ideas he espoused attracted her, because she had already walked down that path of service. Daisy's was not a life dedicated to benevolent work, but then elite, white, Southern women of her era were not the driving force of civic charity—a message Willy Low reinforced. Still, Daisy listened to the teachings of her church and watched the example of her parents. From the Helpful Hands Club to ailing Spanish-American War soldiers, from her efforts among the villagers in Wellesbourne to helping poor girls in Camberwell, Daisy was no stranger to philanthropy. The work of substance for which she yearned was not fated to be coupled with a husband—Daisy always swore that she would never remarry—but it was made all the sweeter by her infatuation with Baden-Powell.

Being Daisy, she sought supernatural sanction. She turned to a horoscope reader who provided her with a thorough report; thirty-one typed pages of prognostication. Daisy analyzed it, hand marking what resonated for her, such as "The planet Neptune afflicted you through your affections, and indicates that you are in danger of suffering through scandal, loss of money through false friends, and much unhappiness through love affairs generally." Mars influenced her birth, bringing "opposition and strife" in all forms of partnership and especially in marriage, causing "discord" and "separation." Mars "usually causes one to marry either a very forceful man, or a military one, and who will be subject to accidents and sudden death." It eerily fit her marriage to Willy Low. "Your mother . . . was not in perfect sympathy with your nature," the psychic found—and that was spot on.

By the following point, Daisy wrote "BP Feb 22nd": "You will find people born along about the 26th of February . . . will have a very powerful and steadying influence upon your life and will bring to the front many of your latent possibilities and strongest characteristics and those of a very practical nature." This, in fact, is exactly what General Sir Robert Baden-Powell did. The most specific and brilliant example of this ability occurred during her long walks with Baden-Powell at Lochs in August 1911. It was then that Daisy first thought of combining two of her interests, one old—the Camberwell girls' club—and one new, Girl Guiding.[27]

Motivated most immediately by Baden-Powell, but also by a lifetime of reverence for duty, her sustaining and nurturing female friendships, and her impatience with her own lack of purpose, Daisy took what was, in hindsight, an enormous step: she called together the local girls from around Glen Lyon and created her own troop of Girl Guides.

The Girl Guides, she told her father earnestly, are "a sort of outcome of Boy Scouts. When Baden-Powell first formed the Boy Scouts, 6,000 girls registered as Scouts! And as he could not have girls traipsing about the country after his Boy Scouts, he got his sister to form a society of Girl Guides and the first law was that they must not even speak to a Boy Scout if they saw him in uniform." The public had first seen a massed group of girls dressed as Scouts in September 1909 at a London rally. Without invitation or leader, girls spontaneously took up the fun of Scouting. They cobbled together uniforms that looked like their brothers' and set out to have adventures as "Girl Scouts." Chief Scout Baden-Powell believed that parts of his program would be good for girls, and "by the summer of 1909, he had started planning for a girls' version of Scouting." They could not call themselves Girl Scouts, however, but must instead be Girl Guides, with an emphasis on being, in his words, "partners and comrades rather than dolls." Just as Boy Scouting would save young men from indolent and ineffectual lives, Guiding should lead girls "to take up useful woman's work with zeal." Of course, "useful woman's work," is precisely what Daisy had been searching for since Willy's death.[28]

Girl Guides were controversial. The appearance of girls in Scouting uniforms in England caused a protest on both sides of the Atlantic. British educational reformer and antisuffragist Violet Markham feared the perilous consequences of boys and girls on "glorified larking expeditions." Not only was it inappropriate for the two genders to be together, but boys' culture might rub off and create masculine girls. By far the loudest and longest resistance to girls being involved in Scouting came from James E. West of the Boy Scouts of America. He believed the taint would go the other way, and that "Girl Scouts 'sissified' the name," which should be forbidden for them to use. Other people decried the potential military ramifications of Scouting for girls. As Markham wrote, it was a menace to "the qualities which are essential to the nation [of] the wives and mothers of tomorrow."[29]

Nevertheless, Baden-Powell believed that a separate unit for girls could be fashioned to address adults' concerns and males' apprehensions. To distance the girls from the boys and to assist with the burgeoning bureaucratic operation of Scouting, Baden-Powell asked his multitalented, fifty-one-year-old sister, Agnes Baden-Powell, to take charge of Girl Guiding. Agnes was fully supportive of her brother's work. She led a Boy Scout troop in 1908, and authored a pamphlet explaining the benefits of Scouting for girls to dispel parental fears. Under her aegis, Guiding would teach girls appropriate domestic skills, inculcate feminine habits of "friendliness, propriety, helpfulness, obedience, patriotism," and provide the right sort of adventure to help girls be of service to their country in times of need. In 1910, Agnes Baden-Powell created an executive board to aid in converting unofficial and so-called Girl Scouts into official, registered Girl Guides. She capitalized effectively on the urgent desire of girls to be involved. Within a very short time, across the British Empire and beyond, Girl Guide troops appeared, sporting their own natty uniforms but working to master almost all the same skills as their brothers.[30]

Daisy asked seven local Glen Lyon girls to come to Lochs and become Girl Guides. Even though one girl made a six-mile hike to and from every meeting, the troop flourished. They applied themselves to acquiring new skills: knot tying, map reading, "the history of the flag, and the Guide laws. Then they went on to knitting and cooking and first aid." Daisy's officer friends showed the Guides how to drill and signal across the Grampians. Nevill Smyth prepared them for camping. Daisy conveyed subtle lessons in personal hygiene to these very rural girls, who were unfamiliar with a toothbrush. Hoping to make a concrete difference in their lives, she helped them raise chickens to sell eggs to the many Perthshire hunting lodges filling with autumn's guests. To guarantee the girls' financial independence the rest of the year, she taught her Guides how to spin wool (after she first learned how to do it from the village postmistress) and sell it to a weaving shop in London. The fun escalated when Daisy's nieces and friends were there to play with the Girl Guides.[31]

Hers was not the first Girl Guide group in Scotland. In 1908, girls joined the Cuckoo Patrol of the 1st Glasgow Scout troop. In 1910, girls of the Sheltie Patrol were attached to the 33rd Edinburgh Scouts. In March of 1910, Baden-Powell had visited Fife, where he had found fifteen Girl Guides, and after that more and more girls joined in across Scotland. Learning of another patrol in Perthshire, at Castle Menzies, led by Lady Marjorie Dalrymple, Daisy hurried over to meet her. Their girls met together and separately.[32]

Guiding agreed with Daisy. She had never looked "so well and so happy," Mabel thought. Leaving the Glen Lyon Girl Guides in the capable hands of local women, including the postmistress, Daisy returned to London for the 1911 winter season. But that year, in addition to teas and operas, she established and underwrote two patrols of Guides. The one dearest to Daisy's heart met in Fitzroy Square, and for half a dozen years she worked closely with those girls when she was in the city. The second group was begun in Lambeth, near Camberwell, where Daisy assembled twenty working-class girls eager to be Guides. She brought her marvelous Victrola to meetings and served full teas. Then she persuaded Baden-Powell's friend Rose Kerr, who was two decades younger, to be the leader of the Lambeth Girl Guides. Rose remembered protesting mightily: "'I have no time. I do not live in London. I am no good with girls.' 'Then that is settled,' [Daisy] said serenely, turning her deaf ear to me. 'The next meeting is on Thursday and I have told them you will take it.'" Daisy learned a great deal from working with three such very different Girl Guide groups: rural and poor, urban and wealthier, and urban and poor. In every case, the girls' lives improved. Fun, friendships, new skills, broader ideas, good role models, adventures, and, in the case of the Scottish girls, a way to earn a living accrued from Girl Guiding. Daisy's enthusiasm was contagious. "I like girls," she told her father. "I like this organization and the rules and pastimes, so if you find that I get very deeply interested you must not be surprised."[33]

In December, Daisy, by then an experienced patrol leader, wrote to all the Guide leaders in London to invite them to a tea where they could share ideas and meet one another. Daisy's eagerness spilled over to a plan for Mabel's daughter, Peggy Leigh, to "form a patrol of Girl Guides . . . for the Guide laws are good for rich or poor." In 1911, the Girl Guides, under Agnes Baden-Powell, were working out their fundamentals, which were only slightly different from those of the Boy Scouts. These were printed in the first Girl Guide handbook in May 1912, *How Girls Can Help to Build Up the Empire.* According to the Girl Guide laws, Guides were to be trustworthy, loyal, dutiful, helpful, courteous, obedient, thrifty, kind to animals, cheerful, "pure in thought, word, and deeds," "a friend to all, and a Sister to every other Guide, no matter to what Social Class the other belongs." The motto for all Scouts and Guides was "Be Prepared." The Girl Guide promise read:

> I Promise, on my Honour
> To be loyal to God and the King;
> To try and do daily good turns to other people;
> To obey the Law of the Guides.[34]

The Girl Guide promise and laws echoed exactly the Gordon family ethos. It was entirely natural for Daisy to support the Girl Guides wholeheartedly. The organization emphasized domestic training and citizenship, and sought to prepare girls for a useful place in the world. Daisy knew firsthand the uncertainties inherent in making one's entire identity "wife." Guides had fun learning "fitness training, handicraft, first aid . . . hiking, and camping" as well as "homemaking skills." Scouting and Guiding promised to equip young people with pride in their abilities, a broad array of skills, a social network beyond their immediate circle, excellent role models, and an increased sense of patriotism.[35]

And besides, there were uniforms. From her earliest memories, Daisy had revered uniforms and the men who wore them. Now she had one of her own. Scouting uniforms served many purposes. They made Scouts and Guides immediately recognizable. They helped smooth away class lines. They looked good, and in their military overtones suggested that Scouts and Guides were no strangers to discipline and order. Boy Scouts dressed in khaki. As Agnes Baden-Powell consolidated the girls into Guiding, a standard uniform of "dark blue serge blouse and skirt, wide-brimmed hat, black stockings and shoes" emerged. A light blue tie around the neck "would have a knot at the loose ends, to be undone only when the daily good turn had been performed." Uniforms were contentious in the early years. Some girls could not afford them, meaning the leveling effect was reversed entirely, as poorer girls stood out during large gatherings. Some adults decried the notion of young people aping the look of trained soldiers. Young people liked the uniforms, however, and doing away with them was never considered.[36]

Daisy might have fallen a little in love with all of the military men she knew. But Baden-Powell was different. Initially she measured her own life against his—but not against the others. She could not compare with them, because a military career was closed to her. Baden-Powell, alone of all her officer friends, headed a program to which she could contribute. Daisy's father was undeniably a respected pillar of Savannah society, but she had married a bad boy. Baden-Powell combined her father's drive, ambition, and dutifulness with just enough of Willy's iconoclastic, independent spirit. They could not have children together, but they could influence untold youth through his nascent Scouting program.

A poem Daisy wrote during this time of her life demonstrates her absorption of the two different roles of men and women in society along with her lack of a clear path:

If woman stands on a level with man
If she's convinced of the good of her cause
If she believes she must do what she can
To have equal rights in framing the laws
Sacrifice self for the good of the whole
Fill idle moments in trying to please
Workers not shirkers should have the control
The world is not governed by women of ease
Don't cry for votes, don't reform men
Simply begin with the child at your knees
Teach him the spirit of justice and then
You will find your vocation, oh woman of ease.

Daisy, a "woman of ease," had no son or daughter at her knee, but through Girl Guiding, she could teach myriad children. Baden-Powell and Daisy Low were kindred spirits. Daisy had many sides: the hero-worshipper, the woman seeking worthwhile employment, the extrovert who enjoyed people, the introverted artist, the enthusiast who sought adventures, the tenderhearted and compassionate altruist. All these might have been enriched by an intimate, lifelong relationship with Robert Baden-Powell.[37]

The heady mix of successfully establishing three Girl Guide troops and her feelings for Baden-Powell must have made for tremendous anticipation as she and Sir Robert both set sail on the *Arcadian* from England to America. Before he laid plans, he had written Daisy to coordinate their departure dates. He was looking forward to a lengthy shipboard rest, and the *Arcadian* put in at Barbados, Trinidad, Panama, Cuba, and Jamaica before heading north. She disembarked with Baden-Powell at New York City on January 31, 1912. The precise status of the relationship between the two cannot be known. Perhaps they had the expectation of a long and rich friendship. Maybe one or the other hoped for marriage. It seems likely that Daisy, at the very least, desired to continue as a special friend of his and counted on many years of sharing their avocation for art, and Scouting—which was rapidly becoming a vocation. Her hopes were cruelly dashed when suddenly and unexpectedly, she discovered that Robert Baden-Powell had fallen in love with another passenger, a wealthy woman thirty-two years his junior, Olave St. Clair Soames, who later claimed that she had stolen Baden-Powell away from Daisy. Before they reached Jamaica, Olave Soames and Baden-Powell were secretly engaged. Baden-Powell did not tell Daisy.[38]

CHAPTER 12

The Savannah Girl Guides

A metamorphosis came over Robert Baden-Powell during the voyage aboard the *Arcadian*. As he woke up early to exchange secret, predawn kisses with Olave Soames and hid clandestine love notes for her around the ship, Daisy must have noticed his distracted air. Yet when his attentions shifted to the younger woman, he failed to tell Daisy. Was he trying to spare her feelings? Did he experience guilt about falling in love with Olave while he was courting Daisy? Perhaps he did tell her in some fashion left unrecorded. If Daisy declined Baden-Powell's marriage proposal before they left England, then his instant infatuation with Olave was at least honorable. If she rejected him and selflessly suggested he find a wife who could bear children, then he took her advice. At age twenty-three, Olave Soames was admirably suited for motherhood. Still, he transferred his love with brutal and surprising speed.[1]

Daisy's own sense of worth—battered because of Willy's betrayal and her self-condemnation as a parasitic "woman of ease"—was just starting to rise with her Girl Guide successes. Doubtless it climbed higher as she and the Chief Scout (as Baden-Powell became known) together hatched grand plans to spread Girl Guiding across the United States. Daisy's response to the burgeoning Baden-Powell–Soames relationship has not been preserved. The absence of Sir

Robert's endearments could have removed a certain frisson from Girl Guiding. But if Daisy learned about the engagement only when it was publicly announced in September 1912, then it was too late to affect her eagerness and participation. By then Juliette Low's efforts on behalf of American girls—and her personal identification with the movement—were unstoppable.[2]

Upon reaching Savannah in February, Daisy wasted no time. Ablaze with the full support of Baden-Powell and knowledge of the tremendous difference Guiding made in the lives of British girls, she picked up the phone and called a friend. "Come right over . . . I've got something for the girls of Savannah and all America," she told her distant cousin Nina Anderson Pape, "and we're going to start it tonight!" A pioneer educator in Savannah, Nina Pape was the perfect choice. She believed in "body building, marching drills, folk dances, waltzing . . . basketball," and nature walks for her pupils. Daisy so truly wanted Girl Guiding to succeed in her hometown that she sought to handpick the first initiates. ". . . I want girls for my first patrol who have had some training together," Daisy explained, and who "are alert and can follow instructions. . . ."[3]

The enthusiastic description of Girl Guiding that followed made Pape think of naturalist Walter J. Hoxie. He assisted with the curriculum for her younger students and took a group of older girls on weekly nature walks that culminated with dinner around a campfire. One of his pupils thought Hoxie's "love and knowledge of human nature" exceeded even his understanding of the environment. Page Anderson, the twelve-year-old daughter of another of Daisy's cousins, was among those who hiked with Hoxie. This bit of good luck enabled Daisy to pursue her Girl Guides idea over the dinner invitation she finagled from the Andersons.[4]

She staged her arrival. Purposefully late, Daisy entered the dining room bent over "a large strip of leather," with which she was absorbedly practicing knot tying. When they queried her—as she knew they must—she had her opening. Page couldn't hear enough about Girl Guides and the remarkable things they did. Soon after, on February 18, 1912, Juliette Low recalled how she "first introduced" Girl

Guides "into America" and "the first patrol . . . was enrolled in Savannah on that date."[5]

Daisy's promotion of Guiding knew no bounds. She proselytized by letter and to anyone she met: girls, their parents, her own parents. She stopped acquaintances on the street, cajoled relatives, convinced clubwomen and church leaders. Even her maid became interested. Daisy fed girls endless finger sandwiches and glowing tales about Guiding adventures they would all have. Nina Pape admired her ability to make them "wild to become Girl Guides." As soon as she detected curiosity, Daisy gave them specific Tenderfoot tasks to do, then found leaders for would-be Guides and Guides for would-be leaders. She cornered Page's mother after church one Sunday, and Mrs. Anderson felt she could not decline Daisy's "imperious" request to lead a Girl Guide patrol.[6]

Meanwhile, Baden-Powell was writing to Daisy of the widespread fascination in Girl Guiding he encountered. Even though his trip across America aimed to "amalgamate the boy scouts of America into an international union," as the *New York Times* announced, he had many inquiries about Guiding. Baden-Powell concluded heartily, "the field is all ready to be sown in this country." He promised to forward the names of any who might help her, beginning with Louise Carnegie, wife of wealthy philanthropist Andrew Carnegie. On a more personal level, Sir Robert decried the "fuss" people were making over him and complained about newspapers linking his name romantically with women he'd never even met. Yet he did not use that as an opening to tell Daisy about Olave. Instead, in letters shorn of salutation—as though he didn't quite know how to address her now—he nattered on about books he was reading and the comfort of his accommodations.[7]

On March 12, 1912, Daisy was "deep in Girl Guides." With the assistance of Hoxie (to whom she paid one hundred dollars), and perhaps "a committee of women," she worked hurriedly to prepare a manual for the impatient girls who otherwise had to wait until they found her so she could personally teach them new activities. She explained to Mabel how she labored to Americanize the British sources, especially Robert Baden-Powell's 1908 *Scouting for Boys* and Agnes Baden-Powell's pamphlet "Baden-Powell Girl Guides, a Suggestion for Character Training for Girls." When Daisy received Agnes's *How Girls Can Help to Build Up the Empire* in the summer of 1912, she bolstered the section on domestic training. Daisy's first manual, to be titled *How Girls Can Help Their Country,* was being written even as girls in Savannah were earnestly muddling along.[8]

With the model of the Girl Guides she had organized in Great Britain, Daisy explained how to begin. Eight girls (between the ages of ten and seventeen) made up a patrol, led by a patrol leader elected from among the girls. A captain (age twenty-one or older), assisted by her lieutenant, supervised the patrol. Three patrols made up a company (or a troop). Companies in a region were a council. A new Guide was called a Tenderfoot. She moved up in rank by successfully demonstrating required knowledge and skills. The adult leadership at the local level began with an executive secretary. Daisy's title was commissioner. A board of councilors advised her. Patrol meetings were held once a week, and girls memorized the Girl Guide Promise and Laws, salute, and duties. They learned the rudiments of camping, the basics of home care and hospital work, and the importance of patriotism. Always Mrs. Low stressed having fun.[9]

Meanwhile, Daisy churned out publicity for national distribution (as the news of Girl Guides was naturally spreading to America from England) and located members for her local board of councilors. From her experience with the Savannah Kindergarten Association, Daisy tapped Sallie Margaret McAlpin to be the first executive secretary of the Savannah Girl Guides.[10]

The precise identification of the very first patrol—and indeed even the exact date of its formation—fell victim to the happy chaos of creation. Record keeping was not Daisy's strength; neither was prolonged, unwavering focus. But she did have four extraordinary leadership traits that helped Girl Guiding grow so rapidly. First, her rare and transcendent ability to inspire those around her. Second, her trust in the innate abilities of girls and women to create productive learning experiences based on the fundamentals of Guiding. Third, a corresponding willingness to give local leaders freedom to act: she was seldom tempted to micromanage. And finally, her profound conviction was that Girl Guiding was enriching and fun.

"The First Girl Guide Register" is a log of Savannah troops that lists girls, captains, councilors, and officers. There are no dates noted until October 1912. Appearing before the dated section in the register is the patrol from the Savannah Female Orphan Asylum, where Nina Pape's friend, Hortense Orcutt, supervised the Kindergarten Association. The seventeen girls of the Orphan Asylum troop led by Margaret Charlton might have been the first Girl Guide patrol formed in the United States. Because they were a captive—thus easily corralled—group, and because Daisy was adamant at every turn that Girl Guiding be a positive in the lives of poor girls, this is quite possible. The asylum matron probably needed little convincing from Pape and Orcutt to introduce her charges to the uplifting program of Girl Guiding.[11]

Elite girls, rather than orphans, more famously claim the honor of becoming America's first Girl Guides. Daisy held several meetings with Page Anderson and the daughters of other socially prominent Savannahians, and all was in readiness for their initiation except one thing—they discovered that Florence Crane wasn't old enough. Only ten, she wouldn't turn the requisite eleven until March 12. Mrs. Low couldn't bear to begin without her, so she delayed the ceremony until young Florence's birthday. Thus it was that on Tuesday, March 12, 1912, in the Louisa Porter Home, Daisy inducted eighteen Girl Guides. Florence and sixteen other girls gravely recited the Promise. When it was time for them to record their names in the register—this version continues—Daisy began with "Daisy 'Doots' Gordon," her niece, who wasn't even present. Doots lived out of town, but Juliette wanted her to go down in history as the first official Girl Guide. The others affixed their signatures. Daisy divided them into the White Rose Patrol led by Mrs. Page Anderson and the Carnation Patrol led by Miss Marjorie Van Diviere. Then they lifted mugs of hot chocolate to toast their new status as the nation's original Girl Guides.[12]

Except that the register does not contain "Daisy 'Doots' Gordon" in Daisy Low's handwriting. Nor are the girls' names all listed together. While Mrs. Anderson was recorded first among patrol leaders, nine other names separate hers from Miss Van Diviere's, which appears last. Adding to the uncertainty is the fact that in 1926, the city of Savannah, honoring Juliette Low for "distinguished service to her native city, to the State of Georgia, [and] to the country at large," claimed March 9, 1912, as the date of the founding.[13]

Regardless of who was first or when it began, Girl Guiding blossomed. Daisy urged Eleanor Nash to assist with a patrol of Savannah "factory girls." In the beginning, the social classes were kept separate out of fear that privileged girls would be forbidden to associate with working-class girls. Also, of course, Daisy depended on her wealthy friends to contribute their time and money. Discomfiting them risked losing their support at the critical start-up time, so Daisy's friends led patrols of working girls while their daughters joined troops of their own.

Guiding promised to cultivate "character and intelligence, skill and technical knowledge, physical health and development, and service to others," qualities necessary for girls of all backgrounds, and the social separation might have been more honored in the breech. The register provides an astonishing assortment of surnames on patrol rosters. For example, one troop included Fitzpatrick, McKindliss, Jackson, Sutton, Lasky, Lipsitz, Kronstadt, Helury, and Itzhovitz. Juliette Low utterly resisted her mother's urging to establish a completely separate charter and designation for African American girls. While the segregated South could not legally abide integrated Guiding units, the earliest Girl Guides remembered African American patrols existing from the beginning, including one headed by Daisy's maid, Mamie.[14]

Each patrol had to choose a flower for its name. Flowers were a noncontroversial nomenclature that nodded to both the importance of nature and the natural order of things. Once girls had a group identity, coming together in patrol meetings started the fun. Daisy turned the carriage house attached to the Low home into the Girl Guide headquarters. Patrols met at different days and times, commandeering the space to plan, to play, and to learn. Local experts often taught classes to provide the framework of knowledge on which the girls built. Members of the Lily of the Valley Patrol recalled their Thursdays at headquarters practicing "cooking, sewing, first aid and household duties." On the lot outside, they worked on marching drills, signaling skills, "basketball, volleyball and tennis."[15]

Basketball was a colossal draw. The public was so unaccustomed to seeing girls dash about after a bouncing ball that Daisy strung up a canvas curtain to stave off cries of indelicacy from adult passersby. Children could not resist peeking! Though the curtains soon frayed with the weather, their unintentional result was to pique other girls' interest in the mysterious activities they shielded. Basketball had been invented by a YMCA employee just two decades earlier but had found ready acceptance in eastern women's colleges. Savannah's Girl Guides eagerly embraced the sport, and an intertroop league soon formed. "Girl Guides in Thrilling Games," and "Fast Basketball by Girls' Teams in Girl Guides' League" read the local headlines. Everyone wanted to play. Factory girls complained until lighted courts were provided, because their patrols met in the evenings. The city of Savannah demonstrated early support for the endeavor by paying the electric bill.[16]

Even more publicity came to Girl Guides as a result of their uniforms, created to resemble those worn by Daisy's British Girl Guides. The blouse and skirt were dark blue serge, with light blue cuffs and collar. Sallie McAlpin and Henrietta Falk devised the patterns, cut them out, and distributed them among the girls, who then stitched together their own uniforms. So garbed, Girl Guides made quite a splash in public. The uniforms stated wordlessly but very, very clearly that these girls were set apart and special. They knew things that others didn't. Since usually only males wore uniforms, Girl Guides must have had access to arcane masculine knowledge, hitherto forbidden to girls. They looked patriotic, bringing to mind the sacrifices made by men in the U.S. armed forces. Some American parents looked askance at such attire for their daughters, decrying both the mannish and the military overtones. But the girls themselves thought otherwise. Uniforms were a point of pride for those who wore them, and a cause of jealousy for those who did not.[17]

From the substantial teas she had provided her British Girl Guides, Daisy understood the importance of food to growing girls. The centerpiece of most of the early gatherings was sharing a snack. Teas at headquarters could also reinforce etiquette, while picnics in the countryside could teach the girls about conduct in the outdoors. Sallie McAlpin remembered that their regular picnic menu was "bread, butter, bacon sandwiches, peanut butter, raw tomatoes, peaches, cookies or cake of some kind." Other times, campfire skills took precedence. Girls fried eggs and bacon, toasted marshmallows, and cooked up candy over fires they built themselves.

Guide patrols could meet at Lowlands, a shelter built by Hoxie on some wooded land Daisy owned, or in a barn she had sweet-talked the county commissioners into letting her use because it was accessible by streetcar. They hiked, rowed, practiced knot tying, studied animal tracks, and augmented what came their way with ideas from the British Guide book and the fertile mind and invaluable experience of Mr. Hoxie. "Though well on in years," Sallie McAlpin wrote, "he retained the spirit of youth to a wonderful degree, and though very poor in this world's goods, he was very rich in all the worthwhile things. Well educated . . . a great lover of nature; there was not a leaf or stick, or flower in the woods that he did not know its name, and where it belonged and all about it. It was the same with birds and fishes. . . ." Girls found woodcraft compelling, as such knowledge was usually taught only to their brothers.[18]

By the end of May there were several patrols, busily engaged in all manner of activities. Willie Gordon drove past headquarters one day to see it "packed with [Girl Guides] like a swarm of bees. I don't know what they were doing but apparently they were enjoying themselves. You are certainly giving a great deal of pleasure to a large number of individuals who would be very unlikely to get it otherwise and no doubt they will be improved in many ways," he told Daisy kindly, and then delivered a father's warning against exhausting herself.[19]

The first handbook for Girl Guides written by Robert Baden-Powell and his sister Agnes Baden-Powell. *How Girls Can Help to Build Up the Empire* is what Daisy Gordon Low used to launch the Girl Guides in Savannah.

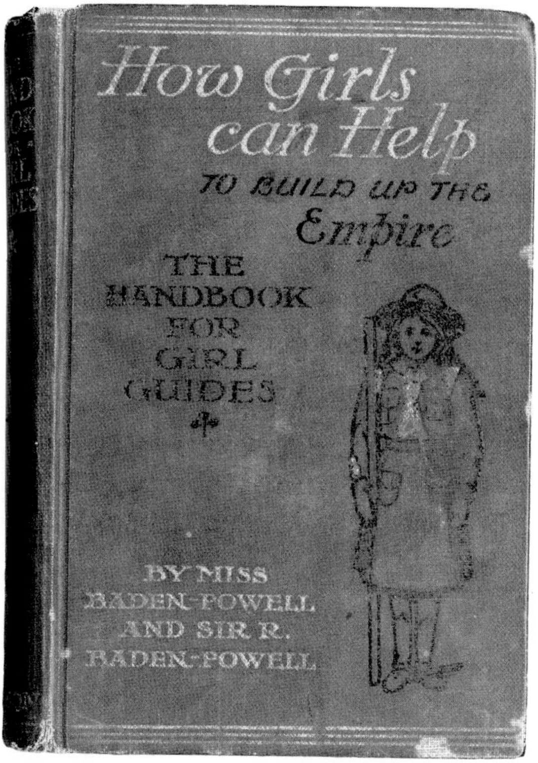

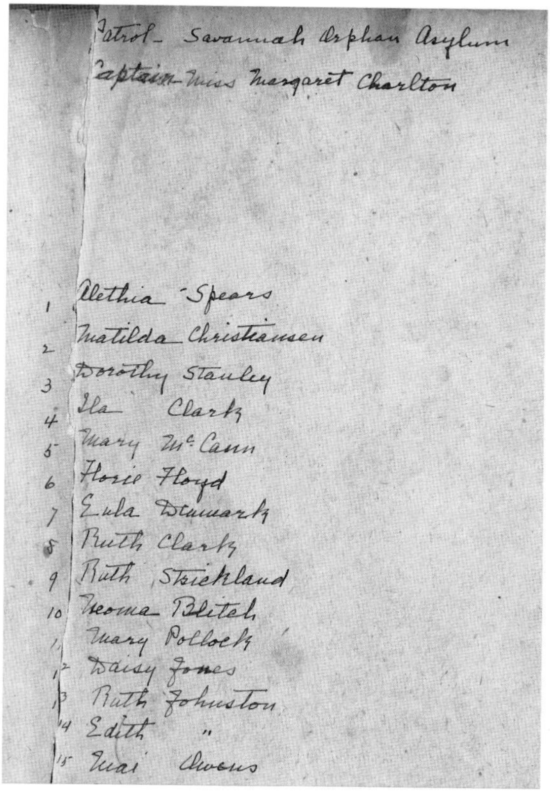
Patrol – Savannah Orphan Asylum
Captain – Miss Margaret Charlton

1 Alethia Spears
2 Matilda Christiansen
3 Dorothy Stanley
4 Ila Clark
5 Mary McCann
6 Florie Floyd
7 Eula Denmark
8 Ruth Clark
9 Ruth Strickland
10 Leoma Blitch
11 Mary Pollock
12 Daisy Jones
13 Ruth Johnston
14 Edith "
15 Mai Owens

A page from the Savannah Girl Guide Register, showing the first troop listed—from the Savannah Orphan Asylum.

Margaret "Daisy Doots" Gordon, Daisy's niece, considered the first Savannah Girl Guide.

Athletics provided healthy competition, exercise, fresh air, and fun.

The White Rose Patrol in front of Walter J. Hoxie's cabin at Camp Lowlands in the summer of 1912.

Daisy was an avid hunter and believed Girl Scouts ought to know how to handle a gun.

Camp Lowlands, the first Girl Guide camp, outside Savannah, c. 1914.

Archery was an important part of Girl Scouting from the earliest years.

Fun like this at Camp Edith Macy drew all manner of girls to Girl Scouting.

Daisy's first employee, Edith Johnston, served as the first national director of the Girl Guides.

Daisy surrounded by her national leaders. Helen Storrow is standing on the far left.

The Girl Scouts demonstrating their patriotism during a 1916 wartime preparedness parade.

Girl Scouts sewing to meet wartime needs.

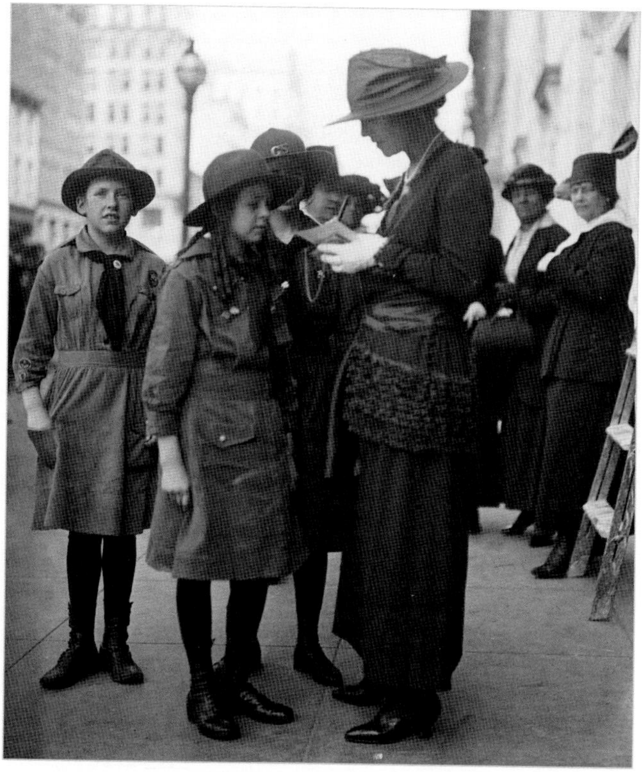

Alice Roosevelt Longworth buying Liberty bonds from Washington, D.C., Girl Scouts.

Girl Scouts working on their Victory Garden during World War I.

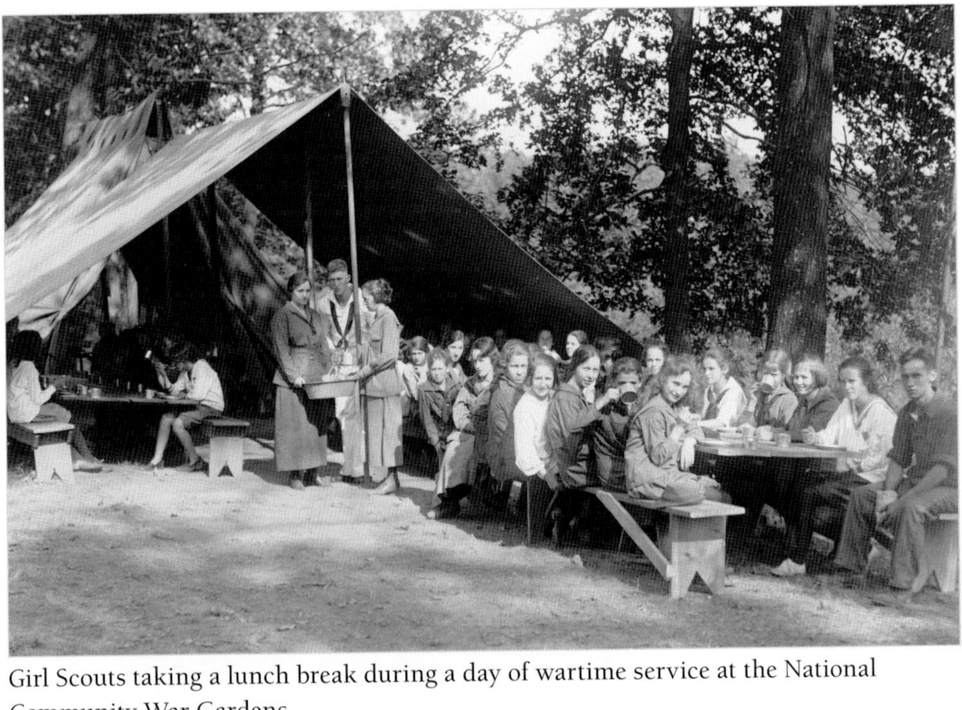

Girl Scouts taking a lunch break during a day of wartime service at the National Community War Gardens.

Daisy giving the Girl Scout salute with members of Troop #1.

An elegantly dressed Daisy pinning an award on a deserving Girl Scout in Washington, D.C.

Cooking over a campfire, 1920.

Wigwag signaling, 1920.

Daisy's goddaughter, Anne Hyde Choate, who became the second president of the Girl Scouts.

Lester Scott of the Camp Fire Girls; national director of the Girl Scouts, Jane Deeter Rippin; and chief Scout executive James West of the Boy Scouts of America.

Daisy holding one end of the founder's banner in 1922 on the tenth anniversary of Girl Scouting.

First Lady Grace Coolidge sampling a Girl Scout cookie in 1923.

A happy Lou Henry Hoover, president of the Girl Scouts, in 1924.

Daisy observing as Grace Coolidge hands out awards to Girl Scouts in 1925.

Three seminal figures in the Scouting movement: Robert Baden-Powell, Olave Baden-Powell, and Daisy Gordon Low.

Blue Boy, the African macaw, sitting on the arm of a relaxed and happy Daisy in Scotland in the 1920s.

Anne Hyde Choate and Daisy wearing their Silver Fish, with other members of the Girl Scout sisterhood.

The Gordons supported their daughter's new enterprise but could not help being skeptical. Perhaps they remembered the Helpless Hands Club of her youth. Nellie, though on the board of councilors, thought Daisy unlikely to stay with the project for long, and did not hesitate to ask her to continue in her filial duties. In early March, Nellie left for Chicago, pursuing the publication of more family history narratives. In her absence, Willie noted wryly, Daisy was taking excellent care of him but she was also browbeating the house painters and readying for a return visit of family friend President William H. Taft while bullying the city's health officer into locating a proper home for a woman forced to vacate her YWCA lodgings when she contracted smallpox.[20]

Leaving the Girl Guides in the hands of Sallie McAlpin and the patrol leaders, Daisy represented the family at the marriage of her niece Alice Gordon Parker to artist Henry Hoyt in mid-April. She stopped off to see Anne Hyde Choate's new baby and to tell her all about the Girl Guides before spreading the gospel of Girl Guiding along the East Coast. If she also saw Mary Carter Clarke, her old Venus, she did not mention it. Time began to take its toll on her friendship with Mary. "We live so far apart," she wrote her, "that to tell news it takes first a description of the people whose news I tell of."[21]

Daisy returned home in time for President Taft's brief stop at the Gordon home. She had a mission: to convince him that his daughter, Helen, should become a Girl Guide patron. This was an early instance of Daisy's making use of the benefactor model, familiar to her from British charity bazaars. Patrons lent the prestige of their name and sometimes their funds or volunteer hours. Securing such support from prominent people rapidly became a pressing business, because Mrs. Low was besieged almost immediately by competing organizations for girls claiming to be the closest model to Boy Scouting. In Daisy's mind, they competed wastefully for resources—patrons, leaders, and girls, as well as the nation's imagination.

These organizations met a growing demand to save America's children. Crowded, rapidly industrializing cities were hotbeds, reformers believed, of juvenile delinquency. Any number of bad influences could exert an unwholesome pressure, robbing young people of their childhood. Child labor, prostitution, homelessness, malnutrition, and accidents troubled many adults. Nickelodeons, dance halls, and easy access to alcohol and gambling worried others. Solutions ranged from federal legislation to holidays in the countryside. The Playground Association hoped to create safe places for children to play. In Chicago's model Hull House settlement, Jane Addams presided over a battery of programs to assist immigrant youth. Boy Scouts and similar organizations were part of this larger desire to provide children with healthful activities and the skills necessary to lead useful, moral lives. The Camberwell working-girls' club exhibited comparable goals, and her time there placed Daisy among the ranks of these sincere social reformers.

Girl Guides and Boy Scouts took inspiration from many sources. The playground movement in America began in the 1870s, drawing attention to the importance of amusement for young people. Vacation schools, which ran during school breaks; nature studies; and outdoor recreation leagues grew from this, and in the northeastern part of the country in particular, social reformers urged politicians to consider the palliative effects of nature on the human body and spirit. Influential thinkers such as Liberty Hyde Bailey told Americans that "nature is the norm," and immersion in the outdoors corrected the excesses of industrial society. The YMCA created some of the first campgrounds in the country in the 1870s and 1880s, and by 1910, the first camping association was founded. Camping for girls was under way in the first decade of the twentieth century, and in a very short time, faith-based organizations of all kinds hosted camps for their girls and young women. When Boy Scouting and Girl Guiding took children outdoors to learn to pitch a tent and start a campfire, they were incorporating ideas already pervasive in the culture. Parents were not stunned to discover their children clamoring to join in.[22]

Baden-Powell knew of the work of the Beard family, trailblazers in the field of children and nature study. Back in 1887, when Daisy was a newlywed, Mary Caroline (Lina) and her sister Adelia Beard had written and illustrated *How to Amuse Yourself and Others: The American Girls' Handy Book*. They had published five similar books by 1912, based on their brother Daniel Carter Beard's *American Boys' Handy Book*. In 1910 his organization, the Boy Pioneers, merged amicably enough with the Boy Scouts.[23]

Lina Beard began what she called the "sister organization of the Boy Scouts of America" in early 1912, about the same time Daisy Low started her Savannah Girl Guides. The Girl Pioneers, as Beard named them, had a uniform, a motto ("Brave, Honest, Resourceful"), and the goal of developing "brave, upright, noble, healthy womanly women." Camping and field sports Beard "adapted to girls and carried on under rules for girls." Given the friendly relationship her brother had with the Boy Scouts, Beard expected to be linked in the public mind with them, too. According to Daisy, there could be only one "sister" to Baden-Powell's Boy Scouts. It was a point of honor. Whichever female organization could prove its proximity to Boy Scouting would share the Boy Scouts of America's stellar reputation and favorable publicity. Daisy counted on her Girl Guide work in Great Britain and her indisputable friendship with Robert Baden-Powell to prove that her Girl Guides were the one and only sister organization with a manual and program absolutely patterned on Boy Scouting. What was clear to her, however, was not recognized by others. Defending her claim turned into an ongoing and often bitter battle.[24]

That is why she fought so hard to fold in pretenders, such as the Des Moines, Iowa, group called the Girl Scouts of America, begun by Clara A. Lisetor-Lane, or the Reverend David Ferry's Girl Guides in Spokane, Washington. Both organizations began in 1910 and remained local, although for the next twelve years Lisetor-Lane disputed Daisy for the title of "founder of the Girl Scouts."[25]

The more serious challenge to Daisy's Girl Guides came from the Camp Fire Girls. Luther Gulick, a physician and physical-recreation director, called a meeting of interested parties in March 1911. Gulick's wife, Charlotte; Lina Beard; and Anna Brown of the YWCA joined Ernest Thompson Seton and James E. West of the Boy Scouts and others connected with the Playground Association and the nascent camping movement. The Camp Fire Girls resulted. West, the chief executive of the Boy Scouts, believed in strict gender roles and segregation. His ardent expectation was that Camp Fire Girls would replace Girl Guides, so there would be no confusion in the public mind about Girl Guides and Boy Scouts. The purpose of the Camp Fire Girls was "to develop womanly qualities in the girls." It cost them six months of internecine wrangling and the desertion of Anna Brown and Lina Beard before the Camp Fire Girls could agree on a workable program.[26]

Camp Fire Girls also played up their connection with Boy Scouting, noting the "very interesting fact that some years ago, when the Boy Scout movement was first started, it began with the camp fire." While they accentuated the similarities, James West and the Gulicks stressed the gender distinction between Camp Fire Girls and Boy Scouts to relieve worried parents about unfeminine girls, and to protect the barrier around the masculine activities of Boy Scouts. Camp Fire Girls emphasized "a strictly home-based domesticity" stressing the "primitive hearth," which they considered "the center of family life, and the symbol of all the homely, wholesome activities." Camp Fire Girls had a creed ("Work, Health, Love"), three degrees of membership, "honors" to accomplish, and a ceremonial uniform that was supposed to call to mind traditional Native American female dress, since Camp Fire Girls were wedded to Native American rather than Anglo-American pioneer imagery. Their message attracted Northern white middle-class girls and leaders.[27]

On March 15, 1912, Daisy wrote assertively to Charlotte Gulick, inviting the Camp Fire Girls to disband and become Girl Guides. She laid out her prior claim: "Here in Savannah I had begun a movement similar to the Boy Scouts following the lines of training of the Girl Guides in England. We already have a headquarters, a play ground and a camping ground—a council of ten for examining work for efficiency badges (or elective honors) a membership of 108 girls and twelve patrol leaders—or Guide Mistresses taken from young society girls." She applied the honey, however lacking in candor. Daisy allowed that Camp Fire Girls' "training is so full of splendid ideas" and "interesting and beautiful and attractive ideals." "I therefore write at once," she trilled, "to find out if there is any possibility of these Guides affiliating with the Camp Fire Girls?"

The rest of her missive sweetly explained why the Girl Guides couldn't possibly take on the Camp Fire Girls' principles and practices. The Southern climate was too hot for every ceremony to center on a campfire. Some Camp Fire Girls' tests were impossible for the poor. "How can a factory girl or a slum girl who occupies a room with many of her family sleep with open windows or out of doors?" Daisy queried artlessly; how could "she keep account of money given her for a month when she don't receive money?" Certain Camp Fire Girls' honors were "not all useful" for everyone, and she warned, "I don't want to have honors or positions which are not attainable by every girl."

A merger could work, she said, and concluded, "[I]f you can allow me to keep the Girl Guide Law, which I enclose, as a basis of training, and the tests for the three classes about the same, I would very much like to add your Wood Gatherers, Fire Makers, and Torchbearers to my Girl Guides, omitting the requirements that are unsuitable." The Gulicks did not see this as an equal proposition, and perhaps read as a threat Daisy's promise to consult with her friend Agnes Baden-Powell about it all. They politely declined the merger.[28]

Seeing the likelihood of further resistance, Daisy played her trump card. Robert Baden-Powell himself came to her aid. He wrote man-to-man to Luther Gulick, tackling the unstated concerns that Daisy Low was simply power mad, wanting to take over the Camp Fire Girls or bent on glorifying herself in this public struggle over whose organization was best. On the contrary, Baden-Powell assured Gulick that Daisy's was a selfless and laudable mission for the good of the girls involved. Then Baden-Powell lectured Gulick on the benefits of one sisterhood united under the Girl Guide Law and suggested he reconsider Daisy's proposal.

She was grateful for the stalwart support of Sir Robert, but Daisy could not stop her suspicions about a sinister alliance between the

Camp Fire Girls and the Boy Scouts of America. She worried that "the Boy Scout headquarters in New York are influencing Boy Scout masters . . . to back up Camp Fires," and she cautioned her leaders to be friendly but stay alert. She knew that James West had stated matter-of-factly "that he meant to thwart us and oppose us as much as possible." That was true. Gulick and West collaborated against their shared menace, Mrs. Low. Girl Guides competed against Camp Fire Girls for members and for the honorary status of being the female equivalent of Boy Scouting. And with the comprehensive backing of Agnes and Robert Baden-Powell, Daisy's version of Guiding would not compromise woodcraft, pathfinding, camping, sports, and feats of physical endurance for perfecting "gender-appropriate" domestic accomplishments. West fretted endlessly that the public would question the masculinity of his boys, should Girl Guides and Boy Scouts do similar activities.[29]

West, Gulick, and Baden-Powell all knew one another. West was the Chief Scout's unofficial escort on his 1912 tour. Baden-Powell's itinerary included a meeting with the Tafts at the White House, which West attended. First Lady Helen Taft hosted four hundred of Lina Beard's Girl Pioneers, called by the *New York Times* "an organization akin to the Boy Scouts, lately organized here to extend throughout the world." William H. Taft, the honorary president of the Boy Scouts of America, reviewed four hundred uniformed boys parading before the executive mansion. Later that month, Baden-Powell, with West, lunched at Sagamore Hill with former president Theodore Roosevelt. Former chief forester Gifford Pinchot and three wealthy industrialists with Scouting interests joined them. Roosevelt was the honorary vice president of the Boy Scouts of America and a herald of the Boy Scouting emphasis on the strenuous life. The annual Boy Scouts of America dinner brought together Baden-Powell, West, Ernest Thompson Seton, Daniel Carter Beard, Gifford Pinchot, and Luther Gulick, among others. Thus, when Baden-Powell backed up Daisy Low's call for a single, national girls' organization, he already had the measure of the men who were opposing his friend.[30]

Girl Guide patrols continued to increase in number and size in

Savannah, and beyond Georgia's borders as well. Daisy's sister Eleanor marveled: "No one but Mamma (when she was Daisy's age) could have accomplished so much in so short a time." Still, Camp Fire Girls membership outpaced that of the Girl Guides. Daisy couldn't persuade Helen Taft to be a patron, because the first daughter led a Camp Fire group. Seeking tips and commiseration from the Girl Guide leadership, Daisy returned to England in May. En route, she spent at least one entire day "collecting, adapting, and writing the Girl Guide Manual" so that it was ready to be printed after her respite in England.[31]

From London she directed her mother in the quest to locate a suitable publisher for Agnes Baden-Powell's English Girl Guide handbook. Nellie was working with printers for her own work, the second edition of *Narrative of the Massacre at Chicago,* her family's version of events that were, by the early twentieth century, being challenged by historians. Daisy gathered up "twenty dozen gross of badges from Sir Robert, patrol badges, 2nd class and merit badges" exactly like the British Boy Scouts wore, to take home for her Guides. This forestalled for a year having to figure out how to manufacture them in the United States.[32]

Between Girl Guide errands, Daisy exclaimed over the bright blue-and-gold macaw that Sol Dungarvan (the earl of Cork) carried all the way from South America for her. "When the telephone rings," she told her parents excitedly, "it shouts out 'Coming!' It says after a shriek: 'I cannot bear it' in deep intense tones. It cries like a baby and sings passionate airs in a coarse Spanish voice." Thus it serenaded her that summer while she sculpted a bust of Peggy Leigh, which she deemed "a success."[33]

Agnes and her officers at the Girl Guide headquarters organized a Rally that brought together large numbers of all the London-area Girl Guides. They converged on Hyde Park to make new friends and to demonstrate their skills for onlookers. The journey downtown caused Daisy some merriment, so she wrote her family about it: "the Guide Mistress (a young society girl like Eleanor Nash) took the girls from the slums to Hyde Park by bus. Changed bus twice. In the first bus she made them get up and give their places to an old poor woman. In the next bus they saw a very fine young gentleman standing so they instantly offered him their places much to his embarrassment!"[34]

Nellie seemed proud that newspapers were "quite worked up over the Girl Guides." She had entertained a Savannah reporter and told him everything before turning him over to Sallie McAlpin for an explanation of the rules. The reporter asked for Daisy's photograph. Nellie put him off until she could consult with Willie, who said yes. This suggests a considerable level of parental support, for the names of well-bred women of that generation were supposed to appear in the newspapers only at their marriage and death—and their photos, never. Daisy reiterated to her mother and father her "double interest in Savannah since I have the enthralling work of Girl Guides."[35]

She knew, even if they didn't yet, that her prayers had been answered. She had found a worthy cause. Girl Guiding replaced the guilt of being an idle "woman of ease." What Daisy Low did not know is what she had set in motion, nor how successfully. She had no formal leadership or managerial training, no business experience or understanding of entrepreneurial enterprises. Daisy thus had no idea how much thought and energy launching the Girl Guides in the United States would involve. She took the next logical or available step as it came, thinking it through with her family and her advisory board. At this early stage, it never dawned on her that it could take up all her time.

It was good she had friends to distract her and Girl Guiding work to absorb her, because just as her horoscope predicted, "the last half of 1912, and first half of 1913 . . . will prove rather disappointing or sad years in a social or personal way." Three difficult blows fell. The first, and by far the worst, was the death of her beloved father. William Washington Gordon II was the bulwark of the family, the role model for all his children, and the center around which his wife pirouetted.[36]

Not quite eighty years old, Willie passed away at White Sulphur Springs resort on September 11, 1912. His stomach had been troubling him and his overall health declining, thus his obituary could report that his "death was not entirely unexpected." Daisy had returned from England to be with her parents. She and all her siblings but Mabel were present with Nellie at the end of his life, which came without pain.

Individual testimonials poured in to mark the loss of the "soldier, statesman, and loyal Georgian." They praised Willie's service to the Confederacy and the United States, the Central of Georgia Railway, Yale University, the Savannah Benevolent Society, the Savannah Cotton Exchange, and the Georgia Hussars. The public did not know of his support of far-flung members of his family, nor of his many private acts of benevolence. An editorial in Savannah's African American newspaper described Willie as "a man loved by all classes . . . [who] was especially kind to those occupying positions under him. His charity was unbounded, never turning away an appeal to a worthy cause. He was a very conservative man, and while he made no show of his magnanimity, he was especially kind to the Negro, and his attitude toward him was always that of justice and sympathy. . . ."[37]

Aunt Eliza encouraged his sons and daughters to take comfort in the "glorious heritage" Willie bequeathed to his family, in "his unspotted name and splendid fame." But they wondered, as Mabel cried, "how can we live without him[?]" Daisy had grown closer to her father after her husband's death. She had proved her mettle to him during the divorce proceedings, and the void left by Willy Low was filled in part by her father's extra letters and trips to see her in Great Britain, despite his abhorrence of travel. She had, she put it, "lost, in Papa, the only human being who was indulgent to my faults, and took my part in all ways and always." His death left her bereft. Mabel acknowledged Daisy's grief, suggesting she look to Scotland, sculpting, or the Girl Guides. But she cautioned her to take care of herself, for the time would soon arrive when Daisy would have to be strong enough to tend to their mother.[38]

Mabel was right. As she had when Alice died so many years ago, Nellie fell apart. In shock, she could neither focus nor quite grasp that Willie was not coming back. "This is God's merciful anodyne," Daisy believed, for soon enough her mother would realize the truth of her situation. Nellie had always put her husband before her children, as they well knew. Life without him would be an uphill climb. Daisy hoped the distraction of an ocean voyage would help, so she and Eleanor's daughter Lalla Parker took Nellie to see Mabel. At the Leighs', Nellie began the long grieving process. Her sister's presence allowed Daisy to flee, to endure the loss in her own solitary way.[39]

The second blow was the departure of her experienced executive secretary from the Savannah Girl Guide headquarters. Mrs. Lloyd Taylor replaced Sallie McAlpin, but she lasted only two months. In October, Edith N. Johnston took over. These transitions made Daisy's frequent absences from Savannah more discombobulating for the Girl Guides in those early days.[40]

Third came the late-September announcement of the engagement between Robert Baden-Powell and Olave Soames. The *New York Times* trumpeted "Baden-Powell's Fiancée 22." He was fifty-six and she was "about 22," the newspaper erroneously reported. The very small wedding took place on October 30, at the bride's church, Saint Peter's, Parkstone, Poole, a stone's throw away from Brownsea Island. Daisy sent a gift but did not attend. She could have read about it on the front page of the *New York Times* as she awoke the next day—her fifty-second birthday. Daisy left no record of whether it compounded her misery or made her glad that the Baden-Powells spent Christmas with Archie and Mazie Hunter and George and Hylda Hunter.[41]

After her father's death, Daisy sank into "a stupor of indifference," and a "cowardice which has made me long, not only to die but to be annihilated." In her usual fashion, Daisy worked through her grief by scanning for omens and studying God's words. Her horoscope suggested that "an attitude of nonresistance, and a feeling of resignation to whatever Fate may seem to have in store for you will assist you very much in getting over this period." But that was not her way. She had once admonished a grieving Mary to avoid "the luxury of woe" and heal instead by working to make others happy. In the bitter experiences of the Book of Job, Daisy found another sort of comfort. Her Old Testament showed her that "God restored Job's fortunes because he had prayed for his friends. More than that, God gave him double what he had before." Learning from Job, Daisy determined to take her own advice. She turned her labor and her thoughts outward, dedicating herself to Girl Guiding. And she, like Job, gained double what she had before.[42]

CHAPTER 13

The Excitement of Girl Scouting

Now Daisy was thinking big. Reconnecting with the British Girl Guides had inspired her, and bringing badges from England and making progress on the handbook increased her optimism. Resolving to move past her father's death and to live out his example of the dutiful public servant, she recrossed the Atlantic in the spring of 1913 in an expansive frame of mind.

The Savannah organization was in excellent shape, thanks to the dedicated people Daisy had installed to manage it. Foremost among these was Executive Secretary Edith Johnston, who moved seamlessly into her new role. Edith was an inveterate record keeper. She compiled data on the numbers of girls in the organization, the meetings held, and letters sent in response to queries about Girl Guiding. She created colorful charts to record games in the intertroop basketball league. Edith made tidy lists and graphs because it was totally foreign to her boss's nature to do so. Daisy was the visionary and the motivator. Edith was the administrator with the attention to operational details. A task made easier, she thought, with statistics. Together, they made an effective team.

Edith also possessed an aptitude for publicity. Articles about receptions, teas, even new grass near the tennis court rolled off her typewriter and into the city's newspapers. When the great day came for the first American Girl Guide (Elizabeth Purse) to earn a proficiency badge (Child Nurse), Savannahians read all about it. No topic was too insignificant for Edith to keep Guiding before the public.[1]

Her more difficult task was locating teachers for Girl Guide captains. Before they could help girls work toward merit badges, leaders had to be trained. Local physicians taught first aid. Arthur Chairsell of the YMCA provided gym lessons, and Walter Hoxie continued with nature study. Edith found a succession of drilling and marching instructors. Inside headquarters, captains learned the basics of cooking, sewing, and nursing to pass on to the girls. Savannahians glimpsed the scouting skills of the proud Girl Guides at a May festival planned by Edith, Chairsell, and Hortense Orcutt.[2]

Pleased that the Savannah organization was working so well, Daisy turned her attention to cultivating a broader field. Girl Guiding must go nationwide, just as Boy Scouting had done. Already there were Girl Guide patrols springing up elsewhere. Daisy wanted them to copy the British-based organizational ideal in Savannah: eight girls made up a patrol; three patrols made up a troop or company; companies formed a council. Local oversight fell to the executive secretary. Daisy's two-part vision was to establish Girl Guiding across the country and to bring the girls of America into the Baden-Powell program. She wanted girls everywhere to share in the unique and transnational Girl Guiding sisterhood and to enjoy its combination of fun, learning, service, and patriotism. To bring this about, three steps were necessary: a name change from Girl Guides to Girl Scouts, a national headquarters, and patrons from beyond Georgia. None of these objectives were easily achieved, but all were crucial to the organization's continued vitality.

The name change was not as inevitable as it seems now. In England, Baden-Powell insisted on a separate name for girls and boys from the start. He was a military scout. Scouting involved skills that girls could learn, such as tracking, map reading, and stalking, but the term itself must be reserved for boys. Baden-Powell said girls should model themselves on "the famous corps of Guides in India, who are 'distinguished for their general handiness and resourcefulness under difficulties, and their keenness and courage.'" He forbade British girls to call themselves Scouts to avoid angering those who believed boys and girls should not pursue the same activities—chiefly, Boy Scouts themselves.[3]

The national leaders of the Boy Scouts of America jealously guarded the name, suggesting, sometimes vehemently, that copying boys would produce hoydenish girls unfit for marriage and motherhood. Furthermore, according to James West, executive director and inveterate foe of Daisy Gordon Low, Girl Scouts "'trivialized' and 'sissified' the name of 'scout.'" He blamed Girl Scouts for creating such an acute dishonor among older Boy Scouts that they quit altogether.[4]

Yet for American girls, the word "guide" meant losing the excitement boys enjoyed. Daisy recognized this, but she also understood the culture's separation between the worlds of women and men. In her first U.S. Girl Guide manual, *How Girls Can Help Their Country,* she included Baden-Powell's sentiment that "Scouts are sent out to track or do other work in pairs, and never go scouting or marching with boys, and are forbidden while on duty to speak without leave to boys." Treading a fine line, she also suggested, "Some reference to the Boy Scouts book may be of service to the instructors but should not be followed too closely. Good womanly common-sense will be a sure guide as to how far to go with it."[5]

Daisy wanted to respond to the wishes of her girls. Aware that they favored the name Scouts, she did not fuss when she learned the Savannah Girl Guides had renamed themselves while she was abroad in early 1913. Perhaps she, too, preferred Girl Scouts for the independence it connoted and its military overtones. "Scouts" recalled the pioneer days of the United States when her own family—men *and* women—had acted so heroically and whose tales she told around campfires.[6]

The issue of the name was thorny, as Baden-Powell had written and lectured so extensively on the importance of Boy Scouting for rebuilding a robust masculinity that Britons understood Boy Scouts as a training corps for virile, wholesome men. The entire Boy Scout program was developed to cultivate "true manliness." Since parents wanted feminine daughters, once Daisy authorized the change to Girl Scouts, she also took on the task of separating out, in the public mind, the masculinity of "Scouts" from her girls while maintaining the exciting things that boys got to do that drew so many young women into the program. Daisy was not the sort of leader to sit down and write out white papers. Instead, she trusted herself, her leaders, and her girls to make it come out all right. She herself was ambivalent. She was close to Girl Guide leaders, and they wanted all girls to fly under that banner. Yet Daisy had never let society's rules stop her from doing what she wanted—she hunted, fished, learned to drive a car and sculpt with metal—and she understood when girls suggested that Guiding sounded insipid and dull compared to Scouting. When she adapted the British handbook, she had a chance to remove badges such as Electrician, Farmer, Flyer, Horsemanship, Path-finder, Pioneer, Rifle-shot, Signaling, and Telegraphist—but she did not.[7]

Interestingly, Robert Baden-Powell never insisted that his friend Mrs. Low conform to the British system. Instead, despite misgivings, he supported her use of the term "scout." Thus armed with his official blessing, and despite West's noxious offensive, Daisy considered the battle to have been won and "Girl Scouts" to be the official name.

In the midst of those important deliberations, Daisy boldly opened a national headquarters in Washington, D.C. Such a location would proclaim the nationwide destiny of the Girl Scouts while reinforcing the message of their civic goals. The Washington office would be the central information dispenser, assisting new councils to form, putting leaders in touch with patrols, fielding media questions, and overseeing the coast-to-coast growth of Girl Scouting. Girls could purchase the handbook and their badges from Washington. Daisy funded it all herself, including an executive secretary to run the office. Because she was abroad for months at a time, Daisy needed someone she could trust. Overriding every objection Edith Johnston could muster—and there were many—Daisy relocated her. When Edith left Savannah in May 1913, the city had "165 Scouts, and 8 Captains, and 10 patrols." In Washington she worked hard on a shoestring budget, bringing her proven secretarial and communication skills to the task of growing the organization. To tackle the ever-growing number of mail inquiries, Edith had an assistant, Miss McKeever. Daisy paid both their salaries. Office rental was another fifteen dollars monthly, and furniture and typewriter costs were extra. The proud new sign on the door announcing their presence set Daisy back two dollars.[8]

The Washington posting disclosed Edith's limitations. She preferred to execute the orders of others rather than make important decisions herself. She wanted constant communication and clarity, neither of which she got from Mrs. Low. To live the peripatetic life she pleased, Daisy depended on reliable friends and the belief—sometimes illusory—that everyone understood her wishes and knew how she wanted them to be carried out. She always thought she made herself clear, but frequent misunderstandings arose between the two women.[9]

Unwilling to overstep her position, Edith eventually reached out to Daisy's family. A two-and-a-half-page single-spaced typed letter to Eleanor contained six tactfully worded criticisms of Daisy Low. With Eleanor's encouragement, Edith wrote along the same lines to Daisy, and added her angst about her boss's stinginess. "You know you can't run a business office without some monthly expense," she reminded Daisy crisply. The relationship between Girl Scout Commissioner Low and National Executive Secretary Johnston remained fraught with irresolvable tension.[10]

The 1913 move to Washington was the right one. Edith's genius for publicity, her diligence in responding to an ever-increasing number of inquiries, and her willingness to reach out to schools, YWCAs, churches, and charitable organizations in the capital paid off in increased visibility and the formation of new patrols. Daisy, too, was hard at work. Edith recalled her style: "Mrs. Low called upon her Washington friends, informing all of them that they were now to help the Girl Scouts movement, and designating some of them to become leaders of the troops which were shortly to be organized!" As was the case with Rose Kerr in London, Daisy did not hear the word "no." Her charismatic dream carried everything along with her. She gave recruiting talks in Georgia, Virginia, New York, Rhode Island, New Jersey—anywhere, to any group that would listen. Edith and Daisy once struggled through hip-deep snow to inspire a few girls who wanted to start a patrol, and they didn't leave until the girls had established their next meeting time and place.[11]

How Girls Can Help Their Country, the American handbook, came out in the summer of 1913. It helped recruiting by explaining Girl Scout ideas to girls and parents, and membership rose as a result. Daisy designed the trefoil badge that every Tenderfoot wore, and patented it after fighting off a challenge by James West, who insisted that Girl Scouts had no right to use the trefoil, as it belonged to Boy Scouts. He told her she should find a way to "Americanize" the shamrock instead! An executive board member marveled at how Daisy Low "met every demand, writing the Girl Scout literature, acting as its publicity agent, as the one who trained the first captains, as the organizer of its first local councils, as the establisher of the first shop and headquarters and offices. . . . Mrs. Low saw the vision. . . ."[12]

The whole Gordon family pitched in. Dubious at first, they called her organization "Girl Scoots," as though expecting Crazy Daisy to scoot off to some new endeavor at any moment. Once convinced of Daisy's earnestness, their efforts made an incalculable difference in the national launch. In Washington, Eleanor visited potential patrons, handled Edith's questions, and allowed the third floor of her house to be turned into a basketball court for the girls. Wayne gave the first donation of any size. Arthur looked after the Girl Scout finances. As a member of the board of councilors, Nellie opened her Savannah home to the girls' activities, helped secure patrons, donated items for fund-raisers, accompanied Daisy on some of her speaking trips, and offered advice.[13]

While Edith wrestled with printers' errors, definitions of badge requirements, a lack of patrol leaders, and other important issues, Daisy went reluctantly to England in the summer of 1913. Financial matters, including the rental of 39 Grosvenor Street, always called her to London, and there was ongoing Girl Guide work. That June she also sought radium treatments to ameliorate her gout, which she described as crippling. Because they were recently popularized, the new therapy captured Daisy's interest. Radium depleted the gout-causing uric acid in blood. At the time, physicians were unaware that radium is also a highly dangerous, radioactive, cancer-causing element. Daisy's "cure" consisted of inhaling twenty-four doses of the carcinogen. She missed the Ascot races because of a "gouty rash" that drove her "to sit in a Radium room instead."[14]

Daisy's enduring interest in inventions prompted her infatuation with flying, and, as usual for her, there was a personal connection to this futuristic new hobby—her old friend Colonel Nevill Smyth. Smyth reappeared not long after his cousin Baden-Powell married Olave Soames, as though he knew Daisy would have need of comforting. Their friendship was affectionate and easy, full of confidences. "SHE IS JEALOUS," he concluded emphatically, after having seen a letter from Olave Baden-Powell to Daisy. It was his opinion that Olave would not write similarly to anyone else, suggesting that Daisy was the only other woman for whom Baden-Powell cared. "Can I do anything for you instead of Sir Robert?" he offered considerately.[15]

After his military campaigns ended, Smyth vowed to avoid "comfortable self complacency" by learning how to fly. The Wright Brothers in America had achieved manned flight in 1903. A decade later, Smyth's passion was the Deperdussin monoplane, the fastest plane in the world. He took up temporary residence at London's Hendon Aerodrome to take advantage of the predawn stillness. Daisy wanted to fly. Smyth advised her to skip the monoplanes and try a slower biplane. He specifically warned her against ever stepping into a second seat with the daredevil Norman Spratt but that is precisely what Daisy did. "It was a delicious experience," she exulted—unladylike, exhilarating, and so audacious she meant to keep it a secret.[16]

A sense of derring-do, a desire to know more about what inflamed her friend, or the desire to earn the Girl Guides Flyer merit badge—any of these might have fueled this exploit more than two hundred feet up in the air. Since Daisy would not discuss her own flight, she coaxed Smyth—who had just earned his pilot's license—to lecture to Girl Guides about aeronautics. Nevill's interest in her Girl Guides was only one point of contact for them. That summer they were together a fair amount. He dropped in for tea at 40 Grosvenor, they attended various amusements of the London season, and he invited her to visit his home in Cornwall. This old friendship sustained her.[17]

In the 1913 London season, Daisy returned to Buckingham Palace. This time she actually met the monarchs. With only a hired footman, she joined a long queue of carriages disgorging their passengers, all as gorgeously arrayed as she was. She passed through the cloakroom and a long mirrored hallway, the feather she wore black in memory of her father. King George and Queen Mary first received the diplomats, and then she, as Daisy described, "salaamed with dignity before the sovereigns." She thought the queen unimpressive, with her dowdy hairstyle and graceless deportment. A few steps past the thrones and everyone was released to seek out friends, which Daisy did, gladly.[18]

More royalty crossed her path when Princess Louise, duchess of Argyle, presided over a display of Girl Guide accomplishments. A sculptor and an advocate for children's causes in Great Britain, she awarded Daisy a Girl Guide Thanks Badge for promoting Guiding. It was nice, Daisy felt, to have her endeavors "thoroughly appreciated," but she was very proud that her "girls were the best in London and were chosen from among over 3000. . . ." Agnes Baden-Powell still headed up the Girl Guides, but her leadership was troubled, and the long, uncomfortable dissolution of her presidency was already under way.[19]

Those summer months were hard on everyone. Daisy wanted to recruit along the East Coast, yet Eleanor needed her in Washington. Even though she hadn't finished letting her London home, Daisy readied to leave. Then Nellie expressed a desire to go to Lochs, so Daisy said she would stay for her mother. Plans changed and changed again. Her relatives blamed her for a series of confused arrangements and reverted to the childhood Crazy Daisy image to explain her actions. She joked about needing a husband firm enough to stick to the schedule but one "who loves Girl Scouts."[20]

He would have had to really love the Girl Scouts, because innumerable troubles popped up that year. There was never enough money in the bank—more precisely, Daisy wanted both to finance the Girl Scouts and to keep enough back to live on for the rest of her life. She never expected to draw a salary from the Girl Scouts, but she did hope that once the handbook appeared, the office could be self-supporting. That did not happen overnight. Edith was glad to fill the mail-order requests for the manuals but worried that she did not have "the Captains' badges, medals, All-Round Cords, Silver Fish, the 'Nursing Sister Red Cross,'" and other things she knew girls and leaders would want having read about them in *How Girls Can Help Their Country.* She begged Daisy to send samples of all of them from England so she could get them made and avoid disappointing the troops.[21]

Uniforms caused everyone fits. The homemade models in Savannah ran the gamut from stylish and attractive to what Edith termed "an abomination." The blue dye faded unevenly and looked awful. When Savannah girls complained about the light blue tie, Daisy told them they could choose any color tie. Red became the instant favorite. It might have been true that the blue uniforms were incompatible with Georgia's red soil and hot summers, but Daisy seems to have advocated a permanent switch to khaki to strengthen the connection to Baden-Powell's Boy Scouts. Once she settled on khaki, clothing manufacturers wanted rights to be the official uniform makers, so Edith requested samples and the search began for a standardized uniform.[22]

When she allowed the conversion from Girl Guides to Girl Scouts, Daisy trusted it would assist her goal of consolidating all the girls' organizations in the country. Emulating a successful tactic of the Camp Fire Girls, Daisy created an "honorary committee of Girl Scouts." The Camp Fire Girls boasted patrons including the Carnegies and the Rockefellers, but she began modestly with Nellie, Eleanor, Mary Carter Clarke, Nina Pape, and Hortense Orcutt. She utilized family connections to secure Susan Ludlow Parish, wife of a prominent New York banker and Eleanor Roosevelt's godmother. Others followed, including Mina Miller Edison, wife of the inventor, and Bertha Woodward, wife of the U.S. House of Representatives majority leader. Such patrons allowed Daisy to argue that hers was the premier girls' organization in the United States.[23]

One important person who declined to be a patron was fellow Savannahian Ellen Axson Wilson. Like Taft before him, Woodrow Wilson became the honorary president of the Boy Scouts once he entered the White House. Daisy and Nellie attempted to line up First Lady Ellen Wilson on behalf of the Girl Scouts. They hoped the prestige of sponsorship would draw in the Girl Pioneers and Camp Fire Girls. Nellie began with Ellen's aunt, suggesting she tell her niece that all of the major girls organizations "will unite if they think Mrs. Wilson . . . will head the combination." The first lady could not be persuaded, but she did host a White House meeting, chaired by Daisy, on the topic of amalgamation.[24]

Mrs. Low also tried an end run around Luther Gulick and James West. She made a direct appeal to one of the Camp Fire Girls' largest underwriters, Baltimore businessman Robert Garrett. His reputation for aloofness did not stop Daisy, who sought an introduction from a mutual friend. She soon had Garrett laughing at a humorous anecdote about a Camp Fire Girls meeting she attended. She asked him to lend his name to her project of unifying all organizations for girls from kindergarten to age fourteen, when they were old enough to enter the Camp Fire Girls. She urged him to promote her idea to Gulick and West. To stop the wasteful competition, she concluded, everyone joining this "universal association" would only have to abide by the ten Girl Scout laws—a requirement that left no doubt as to the primacy of her own organization in the larger scheme.[25]

Although she had acquired national patrons, money remained tight because Daisy continued to pay for salaries, office space, furniture rentals, stationery, badges, printing of the manual, mailings—in short, everything. She relieved Arthur from the burden of financial oversight and hired a professional accountant. Before he started, she tended the Girl Scout accounts, which were in such dire straits that she sold her dazzling pearl necklace. Not long after, she received a

Chalmers, Guthrie dividend that, as she related sadly, "made it quite unnecessary for me to have sold the pearls."[26]

Recruiting new Girl Scout patrols became almost a full-time occupation for Daisy in 1914. In April she visited Chicago to meet with Jane Addams at Hull House and to persuade "juvenile leaders" to start Girl Scouting in the Windy City. Winning over Addams, a Camp Fire Girls supporter, was her unspoken goal. She did not expect to have to ward off a dual offensive from the heads of the Chicago Camp Fire Girls and the local Boy Scouts. The latter demanded she use the name Girl Guides and threatened to "resign from Scouts if a Girl Scout organization came here." Uncharacteristically cowed, Daisy wrote Nellie that she would "let the girls here register as Girl Guides if I find that will be more acceptable." Nellie warned her not to be "bullied." Who cares if a Boy Scout leader quits? she asked. Do not make the "serious mistake" of compromising, for "it is not fair to the Scouts elsewhere, to allow the girls in Chicago to join under a different name." Daisy took this sage advice.[27]

All her recruiting efforts paid off, and growth continued. In May 1914 the nation's capital had ten registered patrols, and by November Chicago boasted eight. The travel took its toll on Daisy, however. Her sister Mabel, with "wondering admiration," thought she was "working herself to death for philanthropy," and Nellie warned her, "Perhaps you won't believe me, but you looked 5 years older when you left here, than you did 3 months ago! Nothing but the wear and tear of all your rushing about on behalf of these scouts. For God's sake, take a rest!" She couldn't.

In June 1914, after one overwhelming year as national executive secretary, Edith Johnston resigned. Cora Neal took her place, and headquarters became her domain.[28] That same month Europe tumbled into war. The assassination of the heir to the Austro-Hungarian Empire triggered a series of events that launched World War I. The United States remained neutral; however, when German submarines sank passenger ships, President Wilson had a difficult time keeping Americans from taking sides. Many Americans shared Abby Lippitt Hunter's sentiment that the war was so terrible, "one can't grasp it, and the slaughter is so fearful with these modern implements of warfare. Is there anything bad enough for the race of men who brought it on and can there be any question as to the guilt of Germany."[29]

Mary was unable to share her friend's patriotic response. She had just fought, and lost, her own long and grueling battle with her husband's stomach cancer. Busily involved in running a school she had begun in 1908 at Hyde Hall, she was shattered by the devastating diagnosis of Hyde's cancer, which changed everything. She nursed him through the agonizing illness until his death in August 1914. These traumatic events caused a return of her mental instability. Mary's son George had her declared incompetent in 1916 for her own protection. The family turned the chapel on the first floor of Hyde Hall into a suite of rooms for her where they could more easily keep watch over her. The life she had known—the school, her involvement in Cooperstown society and civic affairs—vanished.[30]

While the war was very remote to poor Venus, Daisy could see its effects everywhere after she and Nellie braved the submarines and sailed for a grimly patriotic England. Men she thought had retired from service returned for one last hurrah. Nevill Smyth, Archie Hunter, and Bryan Mahon stepped back into uniform. Prices in London doubled in a day, fuel for cars was scarce, and the government requisitioned horses. Daisy rented Castle Menzies, in Aberfeldy, fifteen miles south of Glen Lyon. She started hoarding oil and coal. They would not lack wood to burn or food to eat, surrounded as they were by the glades and teeming brooks of Perthshire. She urged Mabel to bring her family and stay with her and Nellie in Scotland, where it was safe.[31]

Instead, Mabel joined the Lady Lugard Hospitality Committee, volunteering to assist Belgian refugees made homeless by the German invasion. Daisy offered rooms at Castle Menzies, and soon a Belgian family temporarily moved in. Nellie reminded Daisy that she complained about being broke and queried, "If you can't keep up the salaries of your very important [Girl Scout] heads . . . why 'monkey' with the Belgians?"[32]

British Girl Guide leadership saw an opportunity to serve, and

Girl Guides responded marvelously to the crisis. By taking over traditional female, domestic functions like child care, elder care, food preservation, and efficient housekeeping, they freed adults to leave the home and take war-related jobs. Girl Guides knew nursing and first aid as part of home front preparedness, and they also trained in "men's work," such as signaling, map reading, and stretcher bearing. Daisy Low sent letters to Cora Neal at the Washington headquarters and to other leaders and patrons alerting Girl Scouts in the United States to their sisters' war work "helping to run lunchrooms and soup kitchens for the families of soldiers, getting up packages of food and raiment for the sufferers and even helping to harvest the crops." Cora turned the letters into stirring newspaper columns.

American girls looked for ways to assist the Girl Guides and were glad when Red Cross executive Mabel Boardman invited Girl Scouts to participate in "Flag Day." The Red Cross sold white flags (for peace) on October 12, 1914, to support war relief in Europe. The list of cities where patrols offered flags gives an idea of how far Girl Scouting had spread in just two years: Boston, Washington, New York, Chicago, Baltimore, Philadelphia, Savannah, Newark, Cleveland, Richmond, Cincinnati, Saint Louis, Atlanta, Detroit, San Francisco, Saint Paul, and New Orleans. Every uniformed girl helping the Red Cross increased the visibility and reputation of the Girl Scouts.[33]

Girl Scouts knitted "belts and socks for soldiers and scarves and gloves for the sailors in the North Sea." Daisy spun yarn and knitted twelve belts and eight pairs of socks but fumed, "I simply yearn and long and pant to get back to America." She was revising the handbook and wrote the executive board about a manual to organize girls younger than ten. It was frustrating to be so far from Girl Scouting when she could envision a new mission for the organization.[34]

Nellie Gordon returned safely to Georgia in the fall of 1914. Daisy remained in Great Britain, enmeshed in Girl Guiding and war work, which by then overlapped. She continued to direct the Girl Scouts by communicating with the national office and her hometown headquarters. When the local director in Savannah left to marry, Edith Johnston stepped into the breach, offering to work without pay.

Despite the hypochondria Nellie charged her with, Edith's dedication to Girl Scouting—particularly in Georgia—could not be denied. Daisy's praise was effusive. Edith had lots of ideas and the skills to implement them, including a leaders' manual she wrote that drew praise from the Chief Guide himself.[35]

In Washington, Cora Neal learned to lean on the board of councilors because of Daisy's extended time overseas. Evelyn Wainwright was the most persuasive voice. Over Daisy's initial hesitation, the board members accepted her idea to raise funds through twenty-five-cent annual dues from each girl. An exciting project from the capital was the establishment of *The Rally,* the monthly Girl Scouting magazine that aimed to "arouse the spirit of goodfellowship among the members and strengthen the active cooperation of the scouts of the North, South, East and West." Baden-Powell thought the idea of this news magazine so impressive that he gave the Girl Scouts permission to publish his articles when they went to press—but *The Rally* was more idea than reality until 1917.[36]

The bankruptcy of Lady Menzies forced Daisy to leave Castle Menzies in January 1915. She resettled the Belgians in a London flat and continued to provide their maintenance while making plans to return to the States. "If a torpedo finishes our ship," she wrote matter-of-factly to headquarters, "you will I hope go on with Girl Scouts all the same." She sailed on February 13, aboard the *Lusitania.*[37]

Crossing without incident, Daisy set to work on behalf of Girl Scouts. She fired off press releases countering the charges that Girl Scouts and Camp Fire Girls were identical and that her organization was in financial trouble. More important, she spent what Wayne Parker called "a strenuous day" with him, hashing out the legalities of a national constitution, which he drew up and duly sent to her in April. Daisy accurately calculated that the time was right to professionalize her relatively informal organization. She had assembled 73 patrons, more than 2,400 registered Girl Scouts, and patrols in several states. The need for a stronger central organization was clear to her.[38]

The new constitution placed the governance of the Girl Scouts in the hands of an executive committee consisting of a president, an executive secretary (Cora Neal), a treasurer, a vice president, a chief commissioner, and a minimum of six members of the National Council. The National Council was "composed of delegates from the cities or communities where more than one hundred Girl Scouts were enrolled." The executive committee had the following responsibilities: "(1) To grant charters to the Local Councils of Girl Scouts. (2) To manufacture and copyright the badges. (3) To select uniforms and other equipment." Daisy called a meeting of the National Council on June 10, 1915, and placed the document she and her brother-in-law had created before them. The members not only enacted the new constitution but elected her president. She followed this rapidly with articles of incorporation in Washington for the organization officially called Girl Scouts, Inc.[39]

Just in time, as it turned out, as war fever in the United States escalated in May after a German submarine killed almost twelve hundred people when it sank the British passenger ship *Lusitania*—the same ship that had brought Daisy to America just three months earlier. She longed for President Wilson to act on Theodore Roosevelt's call to assist Britain militarily. Roosevelt may be "playing to the gallery as usual," she thought, but "he does voice the feeling of the true bred Americans." Not declaring war after sinking the *Lusitania* would convince Germany that the country was weak, Daisy believed, but Wilson would not be swayed.[40]

The European conflict encouraged some cooperation between the Girl Scouts and their male counterparts. British Boy Scouts on patrol along the North Sea wore scarves knit for them by Girl Scouts of Tacoma Park, Maryland. The Boy Scouts of America asked Cora Neal and Girl Scout captains in Washington, D.C., to attend its national convention there. Savannah Boy Scouts invited local Girl Scouts to take "part with them in the Semaphore and Virginia Reel during May Week." This consisted of a raucous drive to the river for rowing and swimming, dining by campfire, playing games, and a reflective return under a moonlit sky.[41]

Nellie Kinzie Gordon turned eighty in June 1915. Daisy was at her side, and the celebration was heartfelt, as Nellie beamed on friends and family gathered in Savannah to toast her. Birthday congratulations came from the Goshen men she rescued on the train during the Spanish-American War and from relatives and friends in Chicago. She confessed to feeling no more than twenty-one years old most days, but the years since Willie died had been hard on her. She had suffered two heart attacks, various other ailments, and wore an electric Acousticon hearing aid, just like Daisy sometimes did.[42]

The birthday party was only a pause in Daisy's work. She swung north to Pleasantville, New York, to seek out Anne Hyde Choate, her goddaughter. A Girl Scout troop had been started in the area, Daisy told her, and needed a little boost. Anne was suspicious. What would her duties be? "'Oh,' said Mrs. Low very causally, 'just pin on badges once a year.'" Anne agreed. It was not long before she learned the full extent of her godmother's expectations, and in less than a year she became national vice president, in line for the presidency.[43]

That trip also entailed a brief visit with Abby Lippitt Hunter. Abby spent many months in Europe, raising her daughters after Duncan's death. Some of her time was in Scotland with her in-laws, but much of it was in France, where the living was inexpensive and the girls could learn the language. Abby and Daisy were glad to be together. Daisy always kept a consoling note Abby had written to her during the Anna Bateman ordeal, and their friendship withstood time and distance. In 1915, Abby, Mary, and Daisy were widows. Hyde had been gone just about one year, and Mary's was a bleak and desolate existence. If Daisy was cognizant of this, it was not reflected in the letter she sent, explaining to Mary why she could not call. Her Belgian family, Mabel's war work, the Girl Scouts, a friend's wedding—these were the topics of which she wrote, and Daisy guiltily swore to her that she "saw Abby only because she was in the direct line of travel."[44]

Even though the seas were studded with U-boats, Americans went about their lives. Financial concerns and family drew Daisy back across the Atlantic to Britain in June 1916. It was a harrowing trip. Women slept on deck in case of a torpedo attack. The ship's telegraph was disengaged two full days before reaching Liverpool so no spy aboard "with a pocket Marconi" wireless could alert the enemy of their position. German submarines continued to target the ships of nonbelligerents, including passenger liners. Just after the *Lusitania* went down, the *Nebraska* was hit even though its name—clearly American—was written on its side in letters six feet high.[45]

Mabel was gratified to see her sister so "full of bounding energy." Daisy visited her Belgian refugees and attended a Belgian Relief Fund tea with Ota Wilton. She mourned with families when reports of soldiers' deaths came in. Alix Beech lost her son. Two of Rowley and Mabel's nephews were killed in action. Daisy communicated with officials in the American Consular Service in Berlin on behalf of the Kiplings when their boy went missing in action. Later, they discovered that he, too, had been killed. From the front, Nevill Smyth's many letters attested to the attrition among his soldiers. As the death toll climbed, more men had to leave civilian life for soldiering. Women took their places, and Girl Guides assisted.[46]

In a speech to gain support for Guiding, Daisy told of a girl whose parents forbade her to leave the house without her governess. But when she joined the Girl Guides she was able, after training, to stay up all night on airship watch. When a threat appeared, she and her fellow Guides—sans governess—marched through the streets and blew whistles to warn citizens. Every time a Girl Guide saved a life, newspapers celebrated. Girl Guides knew how to signal when the telegraph was down and found satisfaction in household tasks that earned merit badges and the gratitude of the nation.[47]

The war wrought other changes for the Girl Guides. Robert Baden-Powell's wife edged his sister out of decision-making roles in the organization. In 1918 Olave Baden-Powell became Chief Guide. She put a positive spin on her youth, stating in her memoir that Agnes Baden-Powell, who governed Guiding with her acquaintances much as Daisy led Girl Scouts with her friends, was "clever but thoroughly Victorian in outlook." The social transformations produced by war called for a younger perspective; in fact, Olave decided—with her husband's sanction—that an entirely new group of leaders was necessary. They cleaned house and reformed the Guides. A Charter of Incorporation was followed by an annual report; publication of *Policy, Organisation and Rules*; a new headquarters; and a mushrooming of personnel. This methodical institutionalization resulted in rapid membership increases.[48]

Neuritis slowed Daisy down for a month, as her "right arm was useless," she reported to a worried Edith, who had not heard from her. The Parkers arrived en masse at Grosvenor Street, ostensibly so Wayne could "study the present war" but really to provide a change of scenery and remove him from the spotlight after his recent incarceration in an insane asylum. The congressman had been irritable in the extreme, insistent on getting his own way, and never stopped talking. An eight-mile barefoot horseback ride across Newark had pushed the family into extreme action. In the wake of the publicity, Eleanor thought the risk of the Atlantic crossing was worth removing Wayne from New Jersey for a rest. As it turned out, she need not have been anxious. His constituents were unbothered and reelected him to Congress two more times.[49]

The war in Europe continued to attract girls to the Guides. Daisy worked so hard on their behalf that she caused concern among her friends. Baden-Powell, for example, warned her to "go on with your great ideas for the Girl Guides, but [do] not overstrain yourself in doing so, and make others responsible for carrying out the detail." The Girl Scouts also grew, to five thousand by the middle of September 1915, with troops in more than 150 cities. Cora Neal was an excellent national executive secretary, efficient and loyal. She hired a publicity staff, and the good that Girl Guides and Girl Scouts did received an even wider hearing. When Daisy was home, she crisscrossed the South and East, explaining how the motto, rules, and training of Girl Scouting encouraged girls to help the effort overseas and "be prepared" at home. First aid lessons, Red Cross courses, cartography, and Morse code rested easily beside invalid care, nursing, dietetics, sanitation, and similar domestic chores as the war made nontraditional work acceptable—even necessary—to the larger public. As Girl Scouts mastered these skills and earned badges for their uniforms, they literally wore their competence on their sleeves. Further expansion occurred with the creation of Senior Girl Scouts for young women over the age of eighteen and for married women. Daisy liked to tell about a married Senior Girl Scout whose "baby is the mascot of the troop."[50]

Continued growth and visibility—evident in the announcement of a Girl Scout scholarship in Atlanta and a campground donated by the Navy League—convinced Daisy that 1916 was the time to move the national headquarters from Washington to New York City, home of the Boy Scouts and the Camp Fire Girls. Girl Scouting was growing faster in New York than anywhere else, thanks in part to the work of now-zealous Anne Hyde Choate. Around the time of the move, Cora Neal fell ill and resigned, leading to the appointment of Montague Gammon as the third national executive secretary of the Girl Scouts.[51]

National preparedness was the main topic of the second conference of the Girl Scouts in June 1916. With growth came the need for more leaders, and in that month Daisy announced the creation of a Boston summer camp to train them. Many "society women" wanted to volunteer as troop leaders, but because they had maids and cooks and nannies, they did not know how to make a campfire or sew. They would have to be taught how to roll bandages and use Morse code. Most of all, their training would stress making these vital tasks enjoyable for the girls. Close on the heels of the national conference was the publication of a new version of *How Girls Can Help Their Country.* Agnes Baden-Powell assisted Daisy with some additions. This second edition was announced in August 1916 and sold nearly 4,500 copies in the first sixty days, meaning another step toward financial independence for the Girl Scouts. Daisy was very pleased.[52]

As Montague Gammon took up his job, he began to pelt her with long letters requesting confirmation of details and specifics: What color of chevrons? (Red.) Is a straight bar for patrol doctors and nurses only? (Yes.) What color cover should the new edition of the handbook have? (Blue, or khaki if blue is not possible.) How often should the financial statement be issued? (Once monthly.) What are the gold cords for? (Captain's hats, to be worn crossed in the front.) She told him how to manage—without stooping to blackmail—their uniform manufacturer, Eisner's, who had, she suspected, reneged on an exclusivity clause.[53]

Daisy was tireless. Returning to England in the early autumn of 1916, she helped secure donations and open "a house for relatives of wounded soldiers. . . . They are met at the train—are fed and housed and forwarded to their destination free of expense." She worked there three nights a week. Mabel administered seven homes for Belgian refugees and supervised those whom she had placed with English families. For one evening, Daisy rested: her fifty-sixth birthday. She was with Abby that night, reminiscing, having a marvelous evening "without any real Girl Scout work, taking it easy."[54]

November saw Daisy back in Savannah. Nellie, her usual equal parts support and disparagement, called her Girl Scout work "doing stunts" but kept her mouth shut as her daughter made calls in several cities in Georgia before setting off like a "cyclone" for Boston and Washington. "I do not know how she lives through it all—losing things every hour—telephoning every moment—changing her plans every hour!" After she left, her octogenarian mother confessed to feeling "like a rag doll with all the sawdust run out," but at least, she told Mabel, Daisy "looks well" and "has been very successful in all directions."[55]

In January 1917 Germany announced a policy of unrestricted submarine warfare, making travel on any ship anywhere near Europe extremely dangerous. President Wilson, reelected in 1916 with a promise to keep the country out of the war, found himself pushed to reconsider by the Zimmerman Telegram, a German effort to tempt Mexico to join the conflict in return for Texas, New Mexico, and parts of Arizona. Cleverly, Girl Scout headquarters aimed specific newspaper articles titled "What Girl Scouts Can Do in Case of War" to those three states. When Wilson broke off diplomatic relations with Germany, the ranks of Girl Scouts multiplied. Montague Gammon circulated a record two thousand letters in one month. Daisy Low contacted the leaders of the Red Cross and put the Girl Scouts at their service. War would follow the discontinuance of diplomatic relations, but first Daisy faced the terrible personal tragedy of her mother's death.[56]

Nellie had an iron constitution and had rallied despite Willie's absence. Nevertheless, old age was taking its toll. She enjoyed visitors but liked solitude more. Her hearing was nearly gone, and her distance vision impaired. She described herself as a woman of "strong likes and dislikes." In the "likes" column she put music, reading, sewing, embroidery, warmth, and "everything witty and clever." She disliked sermons, eating, flowers, and all children except her own. The secret of her longevity was "a strict avoidance of exercise and fresh air." "There is nothing," she wrote in November 1916, "I so sincerely desire in this world than to get out of it."

Within the year, she had her wish. As all of her children gathered in the library, talking quietly about her, she suddenly emerged from her bed, where she had been for days. She stared at them, a smile barely breaking through. "I just want you to know," Nellie said testily, "you can stop talking about my funeral! I'm not dead yet!" They stood, stunned, until one of them chided her for risking a fall by walking downstairs. "I didn't walk down the stairs," she retorted. "I slid down the banister!" Not long after, on February 22, 1917, Nellie succumbed to a series of heart attacks. Daisy was numb with grief. Eight days later, the United States declared war on Germany, and the Girl Scouts—who had been preparing for nearly five years—stepped to the center of the national stage.[57]

CHAPTER 14

Good Deeds

"I have had a sort of break down but I am now better," Daisy wrote two weeks after her mother died. She and her siblings faced the awful task of deconstructing the detritus of a long life, dividing up the things that were dear to Nellie. Decisions had to be made about the house itself. None of them could bear to live there. Daisy fled to Lowlands for the "woodland air and the quiet surroundings," which were "like a sanctuary" for her. Selling the Gordon house appeared to be the best idea, until Bill spoke up. To keep their childhood home from passing out of the family, they configured the equitable plan of allowing Bill to purchase it from his sisters and brother. This was a boon for Daisy, because when the United States declared war against Germany and its allies in 1917, transatlantic travel stopped. She counted on receiving rental income from the Low house, and Girl Scouts often needed Lowlands. Bill allowed her to stay in the Gordon home.[1]

Even so, she was not there much. She was on the go, canvassing the eastern half of the country as a field worker for the Girl Scouts. American entry into the First World War provided Daisy Low with an occupation to fill every single minute of every single day. She could create a schedule that left no time to dwell on her mother's death. Nellie could disparage, dictate, boss, and belittle, but she had become her daughter's biggest backer. As Nellie once observed, Girl Scouting made Daisy happy and gave her a purpose, and so she was supportive. When she died, Daisy lost her last parent, the one who would "brag for" her.[2]

Escaping her grief set Daisy moving at the same time the war was making significant demands on the Girl Scouts' resources. As more girls and women understood that they could be of use in the national crisis through Girl Scouting, the calls for assistance in establishing troops, or clarification of Girl Scout procedures, or help with local administrative matters made Daisy redouble her efforts. She and the executive committee responded to questions from regional leaders during the enormous growth spurt. Mrs. Low stayed in contact with Montague Gammon at the national headquarters. She was a stickler for details. She scrutinized every word in the rerelease of *How Girls Can Help Their Country,* and made sure the new edition was affordable. Daisy closely edited the leader's manual and worked out the pricing. The design for each new badge had to be perfect. Placing the right people in district offices entailed consideration of qualities from typing to tactfulness. Plans for the Brownies (the younger version of Girl Scouts) had to move forward. All these topics and more flew back and forth in their correspondence. Daisy was acutely aware that the Girl Scouts had to respond patriotically and publicly to the war effort even as it was preparing for postwar activities. She did not want to lose members because of snafus from headquarters, such as unanswered concerns from leaders, or handbooks that girls could not afford or an inconsistent message from the top.[3]

To that end, President Low carefully mentored Gammon. He considered his ideas the best ideas and offended some of the office personnel. She urged them to work together and to concentrate on his assets. But she pushed back at him in ways she had not done with Edith Johnston or Cora Neal. Much ink was spilled as she drummed into him that he was not allowed to change the Girl Scout salute by altering the illustration that had been used for pamphlets from the beginning. And, she insisted, even if the Boy Scouts had switched to oxidized metal and he thought it looked better, she did not want oxidized Tenderfoot pins for her girls. Once Gammon and his wife started their own patrol, Daisy hoped his appreciation of Girl Scouting traditions would deepen.[4]

Montague Gammon asked Daisy to do battle with Eisner's manufacturing company during the sticky contractual negotiations concerning Girl Scout uniforms. She did so. He eventually agreed that she should also "take the responsibility of the details of the writing and all matter with reference to" the reissuing of the handbook. Uniforms, fabric, and handbooks constituted the largest items in the national budget. Daisy directed the disbursement of funds and was responsible for paying the bills, even after she hired an accountant. She watched the pennies at headquarters just as she did in her own home.[5]

Edith had taught Daisy the usefulness of publicity, and now she zealously sought coverage in newspapers, magazines, and the new medium of film. A member of Gammon's staff organized all clippings. Daisy spurred local leaders to think of ways to promote Girl Scouting. Some days Daisy fired off fifty letters, to troop leaders, regional secretaries, the Savannah headquarters. She wrote to clarify, to encourage, and to entice friends to start patrols. She worked with legal counsel to patent the uniform and cap. Daisy designed a distinctive cape she wanted all Girl Scouts to wear. One side was to be khaki and the other the Stars and Stripes, so when on parade, Girl Scouts would literally be "draped in the U.S. flag."[6]

Because the national headquarters received hundreds of letters a day asking about Girl Scouting, Daisy authored an information pamphlet to be sent in response to queries or handed out after any officer's public appearance. The pamphlet listed the Girl Scout Promise and Laws, and included brief descriptions of the history, purpose, goals, and hierarchy of the organization.[7]

All the hard work paid off. "We are doing wonderfully well," Gammon enthused in April. "Business is growing and improving constantly. This morning's mail had over $150.00." They hoped that the sales of registrations, uniforms, books, and badges would help make Girl Scouting self-funding, so that Daisy, whose income had decreased because of the war, could cut back on her subsidies. One Monday in June, $412 came into the office. Two weeks later, Gammon opened $601.65 worth of mail-order requests, some for badges and some for registrations. Significant financial help arrived in the spring of 1917, when some well-heeled New Yorkers, impressed by the earnest usefulness of Girl Scouts in the war effort, promised a donation of $5,000 to $10,000 annually for three years "to assist in the promotion of [Girl Scout] work." Robert Baden-Powell sent his congratulations on this stroke of good fortune, which saved his friend from financial worries for the short term. Then auditors turned their magnifying glasses on the books in June 1917, and found not the deficit that Daisy and Montague expected but a surplus of $1,047.02. This stunner, Gammon admitted, gave him "renewed vigor," and certainly the president felt the same way.[8]

Daisy consulted with Gammon and others to locate new members for the board of councilors, people with prior experience in nationwide organizations, including John E. Russell, dean of the Teachers College at Columbia University, and New York University economist Jeremiah W. Jenks. Jenks had helped the Boy Scouts of America "formulat[e] the Boy Scout Oath and Law." This management decision gave her national leaders access to the expertise of those with experience in the administration and funding of large organizations.[9]

The Girl Scouts were in good shape. In their trim uniforms the girls were recognizable and esteemed by the American public because of their useful war service. The organization was financially sound and backed by a number of prominent patrons and board members. The obvious success of Daisy's leadership persuaded other girls' groups to join with them, while her lectures and appearances brought in even greater numbers. "The Camp Fire Guardians of Montclair [New Jersey] had a meeting yesterday which I had Miss Towner attend," Gammon wrote Daisy. "They wish to organize as Scouts." At the same time, the YWCA in Newark wanted "to start Troops in their association at once." Daisy was most persuasive. She rejoiced when, after giving a talk in Mount Kisco, New York, seventy new girls became Girl Scouts. These pieces of good news reached headquarters at an astonishing rate.[10]

Great publicity followed when the Chief Scout wrote from England that two Girl Guides were serving as orderlies in U.S. general John Pershing's London command. The British War Office assigned the girls to Pershing, just as other Guides had been sent before them to do similar war work. One of the Guides, Ivy Rudd, was a member of Daisy's Fourth Westminster Company. Daisy broadcast this information everywhere with the promise that "America will soon come to realize, as England has already done, that these girls are of real value to the country in any emergency." She seized the spotlight shone on Pershing to explain the plans under way "for the Girl Scouts to work directly under the guidance of the National Council for Defense" and to prove the popularity of the organization, which was "adding two thousand or more members to its list of registered Scouts each month. . . ."[11]

United States Secretary of War Newton Baker called on women to assist with National Registration Day, during which American men would register for the military under the newly passed Selective Service law. Daisy was less enthusiastic about this than about other plans put forth by the multitalented Dr. Anna Howard Shaw, chair of the women's committee of the National Council for Defense. Suffragist, temperance activist, Methodist minister, and physician, Anna Shaw declared that the purpose of the women's committee was "to coordinate women's wartime activities, to mobilize the woman-power of the Nation; and the task before us is to show women what war really means, to make them think and serve in terms of the Nation as a whole, to make them, in fact, soldiers in the service of their country." Their first concern was "the thrift program." Under the aegis of Herbert Hoover, recently appointed head of the U.S. Food Administration, the thrift program aimed to teach women how to conserve food. Daisy Low's honorary membership on the woman's committee of the National Council for Defense "linked up Girl Scouts with Government war work."[12]

Before they could become involved, however, Daisy announced

that Montague Gammon would "devote himself exclusively to special field work," suggesting that the differences between Low and Gammon were irreconcilable. Dr. Abby Porter Leland replaced him, becoming the fourth executive secretary. Her title was national director, and her job was to carry out the vision of President Low and the executive board. Leland had been a teacher and a principal, and earned her doctoral degree from Columbia University. Leland's immediate charge, Daisy told her, was "to bring about a closer unity" between local leadership and headquarters. Her first tasks were those left on Gammon's desk: thrift, training scholarships, and *The Rally*. Leland followed Daisy's letter of introduction to the captains with one of her own containing the good news that three five-hundred-dollar scholarships were available to train leaders, one each at the Teachers College at Columbia University, Johns Hopkins, and Boston University. Further, Gertrude Hill Springer had been hired to publish a newsletter in September, prefatory to the full-blown *Rally* magazine. The "closer unity" Daisy called for would be facilitated through *The Rally*.[13]

Leland almost immediately sent another missive to the captains, part lecture and part cheerleading. Hoover's Food Administration proclaimed "Food Will Win the War." The larger idea was that if families grew and conserved their own food, more would be available to send overseas to soldiers. A centerpiece of the program was the pledge card given to housewives who would promise to use all leftovers; adhere to voluntary rationing plans, such as wheatless Mondays and porkless Saturdays; plant a kitchen garden; and preserve their garden's excess. Children could sign a pledge card not to eat between meals. "The Scout laws and promise are of no value unless translated into deeds of real service," Leland sermonized. Therefore, all Girl Scouts were to inscribe special pledge cards committing them to give up "candy and soda-water."[14]

"Girl Scouts of Washington have made a record in war service," Leland broadcast. "They have formed a demonstration team composed of scouts from all troops. They have harvested their garden crops and are canning all perishable farm products." The Washington

Girl Scouts drew the attention of Herbert Hoover himself. He wrote Daisy to thank her for their contributions and to say he hoped that all other Girl Scouts "will follow the splendid example set by these girls in our Capital City." The gauntlet had been thrown down. Abby Leland and Daisy Low were certain all ten thousand Girl Scouts would rise to the challenge. The national director's parting words to the captains would have made Edith Johnston proud: "secure all the local publicity possible."[15]

It was not long in coming. Daisy was eager to have the Girl Scouts work with the Red Cross again. Soon the *New York Times* carried the news that the New York Girl Scout Council had added fourteen hundred Girl Scouts to that cause. "Red Cross Auxiliary No. 271 of the New York Chapter" opened on Park Avenue. Girls between the ages of ten and fifteen staffed the room three days a week to "make surgical dressings, cut flannel shirts for infants, and knit sweaters, wristlets, mufflers, and socks for our soldiers in cantonments and overseas." On the very first day, the Girl Scouts made two hundred bandages.[16]

According to an illustrated article in *The Outlook*, Girl Scouts "picked oakum and swept out workrooms from one end of the United States to the other." Picking oakum entailed unraveling rope that could then be used for bandages. It was a tedious job commonly done by asylum inmates and prisoners. Girl Scouts applied their artistic talents to creating scrapbooks and "puzzle cards" for wounded soldiers. They also fabricated "thousands upon thousands" of smokeless trench candles, which soldiers used to heat their dinner rations by boiling tightly rolled newspapers in paraffin. Philadelphia Girl Scouts held a bazaar, raised eight hundred dollars, and bought wool for knitting into scarves for servicemen. In Washington, D.C., nearly thirty girls studied hard to become home demonstrators, giving up their Saturdays to teach groups of church- and clubwomen "canning methods and war cookery." The U.S. Department of Agriculture trained the Girl Scouts, who worked with Canning Club girls.[17]

Endeavors like these paid rich dividends. Lou Henry Hoover, wife of Food Administration head Herbert Hoover, became Girl Scout commissioner for Washington, D.C. Instantly divining her worth,

Daisy coaxed her to take on the national vice presidency by the end of 1917.[18] First Lady Ellen Wilson had declined Daisy's offer to become honorary president of the Girl Scouts, but President Wilson's second wife, Edith Bolling Galt Wilson, declared in mid-October 1917 that she would be "very glad indeed" to take up the position.[19]

This began a long and fruitful line of first ladies serving as honorary Girl Scout presidents. Most were only titular, but some, like Edith Wilson, were more involved. She made a habit of presenting the organization's highest honor, the Golden Eaglet, to Girl Scouts who had earned it, beginning, to Daisy's intense delight, with the "first Golden Eaglet ever won." Daisy described to Mabel how the Golden Eaglet "required 25 different proficiency badges" to be earned. It took dedication and hard work, and every time a Girl Scout achieved the honor, it was a milestone.[20]

It was a tremendous coup to have the public support of America's first lady, but in June 1918, when Edith Wilson traveled to Philadelphia to present a flag to Troop #57 for their war work, her kind actions unintentionally brought up the difficult topic of race relations. Daisy Low introduced her to the audience, saying, "This is a day for Girl Scouts to remember. You have done your bit and through Mrs. Wilson you will be assured the country is grateful." She conferred a Thanks Badge on the first lady, who, after the closing ceremony, asked all Girl Scouts to the stage so she could shake their hands. The *Philadelphia Inquirer* added that "a little troop of colored girls, recently organized and as yet without uniforms, was called forward for the same purpose."[21]

Daisy Low had proclaimed in 1912 that she had "something important for the girls of Savannah and all America," and the constitution verified such inclusiveness: "We affirm that the Girl Scout movement shall be open to all girls and adults who accept the Girl Scout Promise and Law." As far back as 1912, and despite nationwide discrimination against non-Protestants, Catholic, Jewish, and Protestant girls had been members of the same Girl Guide patrols in Savannah. The first exclusively Catholic Girl Guides troop was founded in Savannah while Edith Johnston had been the local secretary. In 1917 two patrols of Hawaiian girls existed. There were Girl Scout troops "in institutions for deaf and blind and for tubercular children" by 1918. The Onondaga Reservation patrol would form in New York in 1921, the earliest Native American troop in the Girl Scouts, although it was almost certainly not the first troop to have Native American girls as members, and in 1922 Mexican American girls would create a patrol in Houston. But it is safe to say that in 1912, a time of virulent racism, neither Daisy Low nor those who authorized the constitution considered African American girls to be part of the "all." The United States was so strictly divided by race that including black girls would not have even entered their minds.[22]

In early 1917, the question of admitting troops of African American girls arose. Responding to a query from Gammon, Daisy told him that she could not make a decision for the entire organization, and the board of councilors would have to be consulted. Georgia was a states' rights bastion, and Daisy echoed what she had heard growing up by suggesting that every state decide for itself whether to register African American troops. She knew that New York might vote for registration, "but they should not make a precedent of starting negro troops, until our June [executive board] meeting."[23]

Registration as official Girl Scouts was the sticking point. No one could stop a group of girls from getting together, purchasing a handbook, and abiding by Girl Scouting principles. This is what happened in the earliest days in Savannah. But the Girl Scouts had become an institution by 1917. Daisy feared that "most of the girls [of the] South would resign, if negroes were admitted." She recognized that white parents would object to gatherings like Rallies, being integrated, because black youngsters "can and do corrupt other children." She knew that Baden-Powell had "vetoed all blacks in South Africa" in Scouting and Guiding. The key to continued growth, Daisy concluded, was to allow "our entire organization" to have a say "in deciding this question."[24]

No mainstream organization was integrated in the 1910s. Even the considerable prestige Daisy Low enjoyed would not have been sufficient to overcome pervasive and entrenched racism or to prevent a backlash, had the Girl Scouts integrated in 1917. She needed to look no further than her own mother for a personification of the virulent and ugly bigotry all around her. Though Daisy believed "[w]e are bound in the end to admit them," to have done so immediately would have resulted in rapid and widespread resignations or defections to the Camp Fire Girls. So when First Lady Edith Wilson shook the hands of the African American Girl Scouts in June 1918, she drew attention to a thorny issue that Daisy much preferred to have remain unexamined.[25]

The rapid wartime expansion brought other growing pains. Backlogs in uniform orders were difficult to solve. There had to be enough cash on hand to order the cloth—but there seldom was before late 1917. Even then, Eisner's was not routinely paid until three months after delivery, which, before he left, Montague Gammon had sworn was fine with the clothing merchant. Eisner's took longer than the Girl Scouts wished to create the uniforms, and then, lacking a dedicated shipping clerk in the national headquarters, the actual mailing had to wait until Gammon or one of his small handful of assistants had finished opening, sorting, and responding to the mail. The delays made troop captains peevish. When the Philadelphia council requested permission to establish its own city headquarters empowered to do what the national did, Daisy and Montague were in agreement that it was a bad idea. Hire a part-time, in-house shipper, she told him.[26]

Eisner's created the first uniform Daisy had not made for herself. She ordered a "size 36 inch bust, as I am exactly stock size. I want a Norfolk [single-breasted, belted] jacket, not the ordinary Girl Scout blouse, and I also want a hat both cloth and felt." Just as the girls did, Daisy loved her uniform. It was not Confederate blue, nor did it resemble the Red Cross representative uniform Arthur currently wore in France. Neither was it the British Army khaki of Archie Hunter and Nevill Smyth, but it was the Boy Scout khaki of Robert Baden-Powell. Newspaper photographs from this point on feature her proudly garbed in her Girl Scout uniform, and usually smiling.[27]

Her commitment to the uniform might have helped Eisner's pitch a new selling scheme to the Girl Scouts. To overcome the reluctance of mothers who preferred to have their daughters try on clothing before purchasing it sight unseen, Eisner's wanted to place Girl Scout uniforms in department stores nationwide. Abby Leland was all for it. Department store clerks would bar non-Girl Scouts from purchasing uniforms by requiring a note from the girl's captain. In short order, fine stores like Gimbel Brothers were advertising their status as "official agents." The incentive for Daisy was the steady income promised by Eisner's. She was having only middling success selling the khaki fabric for girls who wanted to sew their own in the new era of standardization.[28]

What was selling were Liberty bonds and war saving stamps, and, more specifically, Girl Scouts were doing the selling. They went door-to-door to secure pledges, or they asked citizens to sign the pledge card during bond rallies and patriotic parades. The money went to the federal government to underwrite war costs and would be returned with interest to purchasers when the war ended. The government sponsored four Liberty bond drives. Girl Scouts began their involvement during the second drive, when they sold almost $500,000 worth of bonds. They broke their previous record in the third Liberty bond drive in 1918, selling an astonishing $3,151,000 worth and nearly doubling that figure in the fourth bond drive with $6,023,550 worth of bonds. The federal government awarded Girl Scout diligence by minting a medal in recognition. One young woman sold $24,000 worth by herself.[29]

The war work was so absorbing for girls that the U.S. commissioner of education worried that young people would fail to return to school in the fall. He called on Mrs. Low to exercise her influence over the more than seventeen thousand Girl Scouts and encourage school attendance. She did so with a letter in *The Rally*, launched that autumn. The education commissioner's request acknowledged Daisy's status in America. As a national figure, other organizations sought her for honorary membership and active participation, including the Plymouth Tercentenary Commission and the America's Gift to France Committee. She was most interested in expert British aviator Laurence La

Tourette Driggs's idea to start an association to memorialize American pilots who fought in the air war behind enemy lines.[30]

While the recognition was nice, Daisy confessed, "The only thing I really do know thoroughly is field work." For most of her time in the United States during the war years, she traveled from city to city, speaking to girls and to women, leaving new Girl Scout troops and committed volunteers in her wake. She attended camps and Rallies all over, where she spoke to and inspired large groups of Girl Scouts. American composer Mabel Wheeler Daniels dedicated her song "On the Trail" to Daisy, who modestly replied it was too big a reward," since, she told Daniels, Girl Scouting would have thrived "no matter who founded it."[31]

Daisy was overly self-effacing. Girl Scouting would not have succeeded as it did without the many valuable qualities she brought to it, and she did know fieldwork, but that was not all she knew. Her extensive travels gave her priceless knowledge of Girl Scout leaders across the country. She met them, learned their strengths and weaknesses, and was able to fit them together into a highly productive team in part because above all, she was extremely good at pinpointing the right person for the job. Having spent whole days at the national office, she knew the workings and the personnel there, including leaders who came in to discuss business with her. Catching Daisy, however, was as difficult as grasping a will-o'-the-wisp. Her disregard for established schedules did not decrease. She was either irreplaceable or irresponsible, depending upon one's viewpoint.

"The simplest method of fixing criticism is to get the critic to suggest improvement" was Daisy's own technique and one she applied when criticism arose from within the organization. She received a crushing letter from one of her leaders, ostensibly about the revision of the handbook, which Daisy had completed on August 29, 1918. In October, Daisy met with the executive board in New York, but apparently the topic of the handbook did not go well. Helen Storrow, a wealthy Bostonian who had been working with the Girl Scouts since 1915, wrote to Daisy with the tone of someone utterly at the end of her rope. Storrow helped design the training program for leaders and was the "commandant" of the training camp she donated for that purpose. She was well versed in the ethos of Scouting, and both she and her husband were committed to it.[32]

In her letter, Storrow professed her wish for "an efficient organization." To get the task of revising the handbook done quickly and well, she wanted the board members to assist Daisy. Yet it was impossible. "You cannot realize," Storrow wrote, "the nervous strain under which the ordinary mortal labors in trying to work with you. Your mind is brilliant and you are full of imagination, but you make it absolutely impossible to concentrate on any subject and get anywhere." Helen accused the president of being suspicious of their motives and of seeing their revisions as a personal attack, so much so that "the plain truth is we could not work with you present."

Daisy resisted the council's attempt to take the book's copyright away from her. Helen Storrow tried to explain to her that should something untoward happen, the national headquarters would be unable to protect the handbook. And the book as Daisy envisioned it must have included what Helen called unauthorized expenses. Who would pay for them? she demanded of the president. "Dear Mrs. Low," she concluded:

> I must tell you how I long to get out of this whole hateful mess. . . . It should be an easy matter [in] even so huge an association as the Girl Scouts is bound to become if we only make of it a team, instead of having personal feelings. It is too important for one person to block things, or to run off and do things in their own way without consultations or authority. Your child is grown up and has a will of its own. . . .

Helen concluded with a warning: "You want to see it choose the right associates but you must be careful not to try personal control, it has outgrown it."

This extraordinary letter marked a turning point. Helen Storrow was used to getting her own way. So was Daisy Low. Helen was right that the Girl Scouts had grown up. There were nearly forty thousand members when she wrote that letter, and the institutional bureaucracy—which Daisy had built—had increased proportionally. Daisy no longer had to teach everyone everything. Helen was only one of many experienced leaders who felt themselves quite capable of leading the national organization as well as they led their patrols.[33]

Daisy's creative genius gave birth to American Girl Scouting, but Helen wanted to follow a rational plan of business. Daisy was used to paying bills on the fly, from her own purse. Helen entered an organization that was self-supporting. No wonder she questioned paying for "unauthorized" debts. Daisy worried about copyright because Agnes Baden-Powell had lost hers, to their shared consternation. Ever since Daisy Low had brought Girl Guiding to Savannah, she had been under attack from James West of the national Boy Scout leadership and from the Camp Fire Girls. She'd fought long and hard to establish the Girl Scouts as the sister of Baden-Powell's Boy Scouts. Helen suggested that her siege mentality had no place in the new reality of Girl Scouting.

But the biggest conflict concerned ownership. Girl Scouts would always be personal for Daisy Low. She was linked with it forever in the public mind. Helen Storrow's veiled threats—of quitting, of the doom that would befall the organization should Daisy continue with her "personal control"—must have cut very deeply, and quite possibly been confusing for Daisy. Everything had been going so well. No response to Storrow's letter exists in the files, but Daisy became ill not long after receiving it. This occurred when the influenza pandemic followed like a foul souvenir of the war just ended.

Once the fighting stopped on November 11, 1918, the world's attention turned to the difficult problem of a lasting peace in Europe. The flu interrupted, striking young and old, veterans and civilians, across Europe and America. It was a terrifying time, for the flu strain was virulent, infecting one-third of the world's population and killing an estimated fifty million people. One stoic Girl Scout leader revealed how the sickness "has interfered with all Scout work, which is to be deplored but made the best of." In Washington, D.C., Edna Mary Colman and her Girl Scouts assisted the city's director of playgrounds to cook and distribute soup "to the little anemic poor children on the playgrounds during December. This is an emergency measure to help guard against the Influenza which is creeping up again here. . . ." Colman turned a "Diet Kitchen" that had been feeding as many as 2,180 a fortnight into the playground soup kitchen. Most Girl Scout troops found it wiser to curtail activities while the flu raged.[34]

The Girl Scouts could be very proud of their war work. Helping the Red Cross, the Food Administration, the War Garden Commission, and the Liberty Loan raised the profile of Girl Scouting among the nation's leaders. In movie theaters in 1918, everyone could see what Girl Scouts were capable of as they watched *The Golden Eaglet* and thrilled to the story of two bored girls whose lives were changed for the better after joining the Girl Scouts. Girls themselves felt the usefulness so graphically illustrated on-screen, and they knew that few other avenues were open to teenagers that combined fun with practical assistance to a nation in crisis. Their efforts relieved the suffering of soldiers, convalescents, and veterans. They freed up adults for other sorts of war work. Girl Scouts also learned new skills and broadened their understanding of their own potential. The khaki-clad girl providing directions, knitting for the troops, making surgical dressings, reading to children, planting a garden, or doing messenger work for the government went about her jobs surrounded by approving smiles. The country's esteem, national publicity, and the satisfaction and joy of the labor prompted thousands of girls to join. Girl Scout membership climbed from 9,000 in October 1917 to an astounding 41,225 on March 1, 1919, and the latter figure does not count Brownies who were younger than ten. By the time the 1920 handbook, *Scouting for Girls,* was published, there were 82,000 girls registered.[35]

Ready to put some distance between herself and national headquarters, and desperate to know how things were faring in England, Daisy took the first ship that crossed the ocean following the armistice. She wanted to see how the war had changed Great Britain and her friends. She resumed her duties as a London Girl Guide commissioner and went to meet her Girl Guides—offering personal congratulations to Ivy Rudd for her service on General Pershing's staff. The war had interrupted the exchange between Girl Scouts and Guides, and Daisy was eager to tell and hear of their many accomplishments. She begged the Chief Scout and the Chief Guide to return with her in the spring to congratulate the girls. The Baden-Powells agreed, because, like Daisy, one of their main goals was to strengthen the ties between Girl Scouts and Girl Guides.[36]

The project that Daisy found most exciting was Olave Baden-Powell's plan to create an International Council of Girl Guides and Girl Scouts. World War I had united the world in many ways. The United States was one of more than a dozen countries fighting as allies, and there was a concerted effort by many Americans to learn about these other nations. But ultimately driving international programs in the 1920s was the fervid desire to put an end to all war. When the Chief Guide held the first meeting of the International Council in February 1919 in London, Daisy became a "corresponding member" for the United States. Rose Kerr observed that it "was one of Mrs. Low's most cherished children. She never missed a meeting when she was in Europe and often came over especially for it." Daisy assisted others to attend as well, opening her home to foreign delegates and underwriting their travel. "We all remember her so well," Kerr wrote, "sitting at the table with her hearing instrument in her hand, concentrating the whole of her attention. . . ."[37]

Rose Kerr's recollections provide more information about the behaviors that drove Helen Storrow to distraction. Daisy was "not an easy member of any committee," Kerr admitted. Her deafness created misunderstandings, and when she thought she had heard something, no one could convince her that she had misapprehended. At other times, Daisy's "thoughts would go off down a track of their own," causing her to interrupt "with some very emphatic remark" after the committee members had moved to a different topic. This caused discomfort, delay, and embarrassment. Kerr was more forgiving than

Storrow, finding it "well worth while" listening to Daisy. "Her remarks were always illuminating; she was that rarest of human beings, an original thinker; she had a fresh and unbiased approach to any problem. And as . . . she had unbounded courage, she was a most valuable member of the International Council and helped greatly in all its decisions."[38]

Sometimes all one could do was laugh. At the very first meeting of the International Council, Daisy demonstrated four characteristics uniquely hers: her comfort with leading, her warmhearted concern for others, her hearing loss, and her sense of humor. When a good friend's speech seemed to be falling flat, Daisy thought to inspire listeners to greater support by applauding during the pauses. The fact that she could hear nothing of what was being said did not stop her from clapping and shouting, "Hear, hear!" "It was only afterward," Daisy related, "that I found her speech had been all about me and must have sounded like this: 'Mrs. Low is a very remarkable woman.' (Hear, Hear! from [me]) 'It is a marvelous piece of work to have founded the Girl Scouts of the United States.' Loud applause from me, while the audience remained in stony silence!"[39]

In London again, friends and family joyfully welcomed her back into her old social life. With her niece Peggy she attended a charity costume ball at the Royal Albert Hall to benefit "blind soldiers and their families," and thrilled as thousands of people sang "Rule Britannia." Peggy brought her friends to 40 Grosvenor Street to meet her famous aunt. They rolled up the rugs and danced for hours. "Everyone dances," Daisy noted. "It is a reaction from the awful four years." She next had a series of American officers over for tea, hoping to lighten their homesickness as they waited for transport back to the States.[40] The "March Past" of the British Guards stirred her to heights of patriotism. This was the symbolic return of the troops, "very different" she noted, "were our feelings to the former Guards March, when they were going <u>to</u> the front." Eight young men whom Daisy knew well died in the war. Heartfelt cheers and fluttering handkerchiefs met the veterans in the streets of London, silence falling only when "the colors passed, a laurel wreath on each flag, a tribute to the lads who never came back." She found animals memorable in all the parades of that heady time. One horse earned a commendation for serving through the entire war, and two cows accompanied a regiment for having faithfully provided milk for the duration.[41]

Lord and Lady Cork, Lord and Lady Askwith, Ronald Parker, Lady Muriel Worthington, Frank Dugdale, Sibyl Graham, Rudyard, Carrie, and Elsie Kipling, and other old friends met up with Daisy between her lecturing on behalf of Girl Guides. She was preparing the way for the message she would bring to America with the Baden-Powells. It had been a satisfying reunion with acquaintances and with Mabel and her family. The warmth of their greeting and the obvious desire of the Baden-Powells to work with her on behalf of worldwide Guiding and Girl Scouting lessened the sting from Helen Storrow's letter. But distance allowed Daisy to see that it was time to turn in a different direction. It was impossible to deny that Girl Scouting had "grown up." Daisy was innovative, imaginative, adaptable, and comfortable with chaos. But the early days of hand-to-mouth existence for the Girl Scouts were over. To manage a national association took discipline and restraint. The leaders had to be predictable and dependable. That described women such as Anne Hyde Choate, Lou Henry Hoover, and Helen Storrow.

The conclusion led Daisy to relinquish the reins. She asked that her name not be placed on the 1920 ballot for president. "I have always felt strongly," she told the nominating committee, "that it is unwise in a democratic organization such as G.S. for any officer to remain in office permanently and I think it is a privilege that I possess as the president to set the example of retiring at a moment when the organization is flourishing and thus make room for other workers who deserve the chance of attaining this highest office as a reward for hard work and devotion to the cause of Girl Scouts." No doubt she really felt that way, but it was partly a tactful and realistic response to the truths in Storrow's note. Voluntarily relinquishing the presidency, Daisy turned her talents back home to Georgia and outward, to the new project of internationalizing the Girl Guides and Girl Scouts. In these endeavors, she would again find her niche.[42]

CHAPTER 15

Girl Scouting in the Roaring Twenties

The challenge for the Girl Scouts at war's end was to maintain the momentum. Success had crowned nearly every one of its efforts since Daisy Low began Girl Scouting in 1912 with a handful of eager Savannahians. The organization had proven its usefulness to the country during World War I. It had a tremendous appeal for girls who loved the combination of fun and service. Girl Scouts were pleased with their new wartime skills and the nation's approval, and their friends clamored to join. At the national headquarters in New York City, managing the phenomenal growth called for wise decision making. The 1920s ushered in a complex set of issues. Above all, the Girl Scouts operated in defiance of the prevailing isolationism preferred by most Americans made bitter by the "European war" and the toll of the "Spanish flu." While the Senate debated and ultimately rejected U.S. entry into the League of Nations, Daisy Low and the Girl Scouts reached out to an international sisterhood of Girl Scouts and Guides.

It was a time of both expansion and retrenchment in the United States. The wake of World War I brought the prohibition of alcohol, the return of the Ku Klux Klan, jazz music, suspicion toward socialists, increased consumerism, and organized crime. Apprehension about an immigrant invasion gave rise to nativist calls for immigration restriction or mandatory Americanization programs. Conservative Americans returned to religious fundamentals. Many women capitalized on doors opened by their war work to enjoy remunerative jobs, college educations, and their newly won right to vote.

Girl Scouting had been as mum as possible on that controversial subject, even though Daisy Low was in favor of women's suffrage—for white women. "I believe the theory of the justice of women having votes," she wrote in 1915, but she was unable to throw off beliefs endemic to her class and background. Carrie Chapman Catt, leader of the National American Woman Suffrage Association, would have agreed with Low's sentiment that "the negroes and the immigrants in this country are a serious obstacle to votes being given to women. . . ." The argument was that uneducated women—often code for African Americans and recent immigrants—were not sufficiently schooled in democracy to vote thoughtfully. Newspapers played up fears of a flood of foreigners, and for many Americans in the virulently racist and xenophobic 1920s, the antisuffrage campaign turned on ethnicity. For others, such as Nellie Gordon, who had identified herself as an antisuffragist before her death, gender expectations played an additional role. "I am not anxious to hear a hen attempt to crow," she had stated firmly.[1]

After seventy-two years of agitation, the Nineteenth Amendment passed in the summer of 1920, giving all female citizens the franchise. Girl Scouts could be seen minding babies as mothers rushed to exercise their constitutional right. Voting, higher education, and career options told of a new world unfolding for American women. Another sort of evidence could be seen in women's freedom of action, personified by the flapper. Her bobbed hair, short skirts, makeup, and trademark slouch consigned self-denial and drudgery to the past. Dancing, drinking illegal liquor, and talking about sports with young men were daring and attractive enterprises. It was a form of liberation that untold women embraced while simultaneously repelling most middle-aged Americans who defined a proper life as modest, selfless, and service driven. The end of World War I splintered the shared understanding of a woman's role. Against such shifting sands, Girl Scouting had to redefine itself.

In Kalamazoo, Michigan, patrol leader Isabel Twist intoned, "The more Girl Scouts we have this winter, the fewer flappers next summer." Robert Baden-Powell "deplored" the appearance of chewing gum, "jazz, cocktails, high heels, nail varnish and, particularly, lipstick." Daisy was more charitable. Flappers, she said, were women "who make themselves conspicuous in public and love light and noise!" Those urban party girls of the 1920s were not drawn to Girl Scouting. Girl Scouts had been cutting edge as they pushed past traditional, domestic boundaries for women, but the terrible costs from the European battlefields made some Americans reconsider the worth of earnest, self-sacrificing, duty-driven lives. The fads of the Roaring Twenties helped wartime horrors recede. Young people especially looked toward a brighter future. Other Americans could not understand why youth—flappers and their raccoon-coat-wearing escorts—seemed suddenly disrespectful, lazy, irreligious, selfish, and immoral.[2]

Girl Scouting was the antidote to flappers. In 1920, newly elected President Warren G. Harding broadcast his "entire approval and support" of "the triple aim of the Girl Scout movement, home making, health getting, and citizenship, [as] an ideal of womanhood." His fellow citizens agreed. Girl Scouting grew dramatically in the 1920s, contradicting the stereotype of every girl's aspiration to be a flapper. A record 304 Girl Scout camps were held in 1924 alone. Girl Scout leader education drew in young women seeking the kind of adventure that had little to do with petting or the Charleston. Senior Scouts multiplied; so did Brownies. World War I had temporarily resolved the dilemma at the heart of Girl Scouting—the simultaneous promotion of traditional female domestic training *and* traditional masculine outdoor activities. But sound national leadership in the new decade located a middle ground between reactionary forces that would have Girl Scouting concentrate only on marriage and motherhood training, and their opposite, calling for full emancipation. Daisy Low, who personified many of the social contradictions of the time, believed Girl Scouting should be adaptable and was willing always to be guided by the girls. "The girls will decide whether the plan is good or not, and reject it if it isn't," she preached. "You can trust them to know."[3]

The postwar vision of British Scouting and Guiding was delivered personally in 1919, when the Chief Scout and the Chief Guide made a triumphal visit to the United States. Their message was clear: international Scouting would help bring about lasting peace. In Europe, where the war had been fought and the scars were so harrowing, the desire to make World War I "the war that would end all wars" was urgent. Daisy accompanied the Baden-Powells, reconstructing their message for Americans where necessary by explaining how intentionally expanding Girl Scouting would strengthen the nation. "It is only through their children that many of our foreign-born mothers in America can be influenced," she asserted. The three leaders shared the hope of a strong postbellum partnership between the United States and the Great Britain.[4]

They had nothing but praise for war work done by girls in all organizations. But in every speech, Robert Baden-Powell turned to the future. Unswerving in his belief that international understanding could make war obsolete, Baden-Powell spoke of how Scouting fostered tolerance. "The boy and girl scout organizations stimulate interest in the . . . ideas of other peoples, and we have boys in England and this country writing letters to boys in China, Japan and other countries, and in that way, becoming acquainted with them, their customs and ideals." England joined the League of Nations, and the Baden-Powells saw in that international cooperative agency a model for Scouting and Guiding. At smaller gatherings they spoke of how "to get all girls in all countries into the Girl Guide organization."[5]

This was the purpose of Lady Baden-Powell's International Council of Girl Guides and Girl Scouts (IC) established in February 1919. Daisy was a sincere supporter. The Girl Scouts had registered troops in Alaska, Hawaii (not then states), and Puerto Rico, but like the Baden-Powells', Daisy's sights were on the limitless possibilities inherent in universal Girl Scouting for the girls and for the world. Her earlier travels to India and Egypt led her to embrace the idea of international cooperation. Girl Scouting was a way to assimilate immigrants to America, but she did not preach Girl Scouting as a method to Americanize the globe. On Olave's International Council, Daisy represented the United States as a corresponding member at the first meetings in 1919, 1920, and every two years thereafter. The initial gathering was composed of "about 5 foreign women who happened to be in London" and English women who promised to become experts to represent other nations. Very soon the IC became more diverse, and Daisy felt that "the International job is now the one I am responsible for and I feel it is of the greatest importance."[6]

The Baden-Powells' American tour raised the profile of Girl Scouting, and Daisy's nearness to the couple underscored her status in the pantheon of leaders. So did meriting the Silver Fish, Girl Guiding's highest award. Lady Baden-Powell presented it to Daisy, who today remains one of only three Americans to have earned it. More glory followed as she was given a diamond-rimmed Thanks Badge from American Girl Scouts who had saved their pennies to show their appreciation to their founder. Her travels to troops and leaders in the eastern half of the United States continued after the Baden-Powells returned to Great Britain.[7]

It was not long until Daisy joined them there. She visited friends, checked her British finances, promoted Girl Guiding, and met with her London patrol, all the while funneling ideas to headquarters in New York. When the Scottish hunting season came around, Daisy rented the luxurious Dalclathic Lodge on the estate of the earl of Ancaster in Perthshire. The Kiplings stayed with her for a fortnight. Rudyard fell in love with the "mountains and the moors . . . [the] grouse, blackgame, pheasants and partridges and rabbits and snipe . . . simply jostling each other all around the landscape," and the "breathless, burning blue weather" of that September. Those conditions drew Daisy outside for the fresh air and restorative walks she craved every day.[8]

One morning her hike brought her to a stream barely crossable because of high waters. A log was the only bridge. A man drew near as she contemplated the precarious passage. She instantly conscripted him. Her equilibrium was hampered by her deafness, she said, thus she required his aid. He protested, but she cut him off. She explained again with the same result. Daisy won their dispute, of course, so he cautiously crossed the turgid stream as she clutched his shoulder for balance, squeezed her eyes shut, and leaned close to him. The perilous journey over, she then "beamed upon him and said, 'Now, my good man, what was it you wished to say?' 'I wanted to tell you I am blind, madam,' he replied." It was a story she told on herself often, in a humorous recognition of her tendency to peremptoriness.[9]

The autumn Girl Scouts Council meeting drew her back to the United States, and she was present also for the momentous January 1920 meeting when Anne Hyde Choate's presidency began and her own ended. She assumed the title of founder. National headquarters hung Daisy Gordon Low's portrait in a place of honor. "Nothing that she ever did was a greater, a finer thing than when she stepped back and let other people take charge of Girl Scouting in the United States," Rose Kerr acknowledged. "It was not easy for her with her ardent temperament, her strong likes and dislikes, her passionate belief in the righteousness of her own convictions, to work with other people, to give in to other people, but she did it with a completeness, with a generosity, with a magnanimity which proved of what stuff she was made."[10]

"Founder" entailed only a slightly smaller time commitment. One of her lieutenants wrote that "hers was often the controlling voice." Even after she was no longer the only person who knew how to do something, Daisy Low still possessed "the clearest vision, the soundest judgment as to whether the matter . . . was wise for the organization." For recruiting purposes, she answered every call for publicity, handed out her photo, and gave countless interviews. When Florence Harding became America's first lady, Daisy traveled to Washington to bestow on her the rank of honorary president. Her attention to detail never floundered. She made sure her name, as founder, appeared on Girl Scout membership cards. Her criticisms of the Brownie manual draft were specific and thoughtful. Daisy held firm ideas about internal policy and forwarded them to the appropriate governing bodies. When the notion of raising membership dues came up in the spring of 1921, Daisy argued robustly against it on the grounds that the most impecunious girls—with parents tempted by socialism—could not afford to join, and lacking the instruction to American values and political ideals included in the Girl Scouts program, such girls were doomed. Raising dues for leaders was similarly counterproductive because the organization lacked sufficient captains as it was. Her colleagues on the executive board counted on their founder to remind them that "every part of the organization [must remain] flexible" because "Girl Scouting was a game." This she demonstrated at one meeting by standing on her head and wiggling her feet—shod in the new shoes under consideration for adoption as part of the uniform.[11]

Daisy did not lose touch with countrywide issues, because she and the new national director, Jane Deeter Rippin, were regular correspondents. Rippin held the post for eleven important years. She was richly qualified: her background in social work included the post of Philadelphia's chief probation officer with a starting salary in 1914 of five thousand dollars and a staff of 365. Her interest in innovative probationary centers, particularly to meet the needs of females, brought her to the attention of the U.S. War Department's Commission on Training Camp Activities during World War I. Rippin became an expert on delinquency, and her research suggested that Girl Scouting could deter young women from poor life choices.

Jane Deeter Rippin was highly motivated and very committed. Her tenure brought to reality what Helen Storrow longed to see: the transition from a local, one-woman organization to a modern, national nonprofit. The administrative model she instituted remained in use for more than thirty years. According to her obituary, Rippin "developed standard scouting procedures for the whole country, established close coordination between local units and national headquarters, and provided special training of Girl Scout leaders."[12]

Just as important, Daisy trusted her. To Jane Deeter Rippin she could vent her frustrations about Clara Lisetor-Lane's continued attacks and other aggravating topics. To the national director Daisy communicated her personnel preferences and her financial concerns. Eventually, they reached a first-name basis and familiarity that allowed Jane to complain to Daisy. Rippin forwarded the field captains' reports and, as an experienced field organizer, Daisy read them avidly. She also made sure Daisy received her copy of *The American Girl*—the postwar name for *The Rally*. They made a good team, because they generally thought alike. Jane was tactful and solicitous, and understood how to mollify Daisy when she was feeling out of the loop and sounding querulous and cranky. Daisy knew what a prize Jane was, and told her so regularly. Jane enjoyed the founder's backing for her projects, and Daisy had the support of the director when she wanted to effect changes. "I can't tell you how much I appreciate your attitude towards me—it is so loyal and it makes me so thankful to feel I have a clearheaded calm friend at Headquarters," Daisy wrote gratefully.[13]

They became closer that fall, after Jane confided she had just resigned because of "sufficient unpleasantnesses with Mrs. Storrow." Helen Storrow's expertise was in training camps for leaders, and these had proliferated during the war. She and her husband donated Long Pond, in Massachusetts, where she "ran an almost military-style" leadership training camp. Girl Scouts utilized her experience as other training camps appeared in Michigan, New York, South Carolina, and Pennsylvania. Regardless, Jane swore that Mrs. Storrow was a bit of a puzzle. She "seems . . . to suggest things which are definitely harmful to the organization," Rippin cried. "I am sure she does not do it intentionally," but it was confusing. Despite a letter that sounded as though her resignation was final, Jane Deeter Rippin continued in her position. The wariness with which both Daisy and Jane approached Storrow remained a bond.[14]

In May 1920 the Girl Scouts published their new handbook, called *Scouting for Girls*. It was dedicated to their founder and included a foreword by Robert Baden-Powell, reiterating the importance of the transatlantic bond between Guides and Girl Scouts. Josephine Daskam Bacon, chairman of publications, consulted a host of experts in everything from "the use of leftovers for breakfast" to the sheepshank knot to create a handbook four times longer than the 1913 manual. The desire for national standardization was clear by the inclusion of "Forms for Girl Scout Ceremonies." The duties of a Girl Scout ("Be Womanly," "Be Strong") were excised. The first handbook contained photographs of the Savannah Girl Scouts, but in 1920, nature photos (for identification purposes) abounded. *Scouting for Girls* integrated patriotism, nature study, camping, gardening, exercise, first aid, drilling, scouting, and household skills. Bacon's handbook remained a close cousin to the original British editions.[15]

Daisy carried *Scouting for Girls* to England to distribute to the Baden-Powells, Rose Kerr, and others at a big London Rally and Girl Guide inspection by Princess Mary. The highlight of the summer was the second International Conference in Oxford. Other Girl Scout leaders accompanied Daisy so they could provide an alternative perspective to national headquarters. Daisy thought an American living full time in England should be found to represent Girl Scouting and "have a constant supervision of our interests" in the council's work, which did not stop during the two years between meetings. After two years of looking, she convinced Katie Low—barely an American!—but someone whom Daisy could trust in this capacity. She described Katie as "a very rich woman, with no duties except the Camberwell settlement, of which she is Treasurer. She has attended all the International [Girl Guide and Girl Scout] functions and knows the work. She has been loath to accept this responsibility but she feels that we must keep United States in touch with Guides and she will have influence in a social way as her relations . . . are of the ruling class here. . . ."[16]

Daisy's International Council business introduced her to people from around the world. She worried about the Polish delegate, Janina Tworkowska, whose trip home necessitated a brave breaching of the Russian troop lines. Daisy could not persuade her to wait out the skirmish, but at least she "sent her off well provided." A young Danish woman, Estrid Ott, sought an entrée to the Girl Scouts in New York, which Daisy provided, to facilitate her project of gathering information about Girl Scouting and Guiding around the world. Receiving Ott at headquarters "will help the international work which I have so much at heart," Daisy wrote in her letter of introduction. There were Russian Girl Scouts visiting when Ott arrived, providing, Jane Deeter Rippin commented happily, "quite an international breeze!" Another friend Daisy made through the council was Matilde Van Wyngaarder, the representative from the Netherlands. She hoped to host an IC meeting but needed Daisy to urge women from the former Allied countries to allow a German delegate to attend. Daisy and the Girl Scouts' International Committee in New York drafted this tactful response: the United States stands "ready to receive German Representatives at the International Congress when the Allies are ready to invite them."[17]

Back in the United States, Daisy resumed her fieldwork. A particularly deadly flu hit Savannah, and Daisy unhesitatingly sewed "pneumonia jackets" for the Red Cross and joined the Ambulance Corps to ferry nurses about. Once the flu was controlled, Girl Scouting was top priority again. She rented a hall in Savannah to show the Golden Eaglet film "and work up a good Council, present badges, do a semaphore alphabet, and a flag drill." Trying out new schemes in Savannah did not always sit well with Girl Scout leaders there who had their own plans, but it was difficult to dismiss the founder. Daisy meant to reprise the Savannah program in Atlanta where the *Atlanta Constitution* and the city's "prominent women" expected her. However, when the executive board invited the ever-insistent Lisetor-Lane to its Chicago meeting to hear her explanation of why she was the true founder of Girl Scouting, Arthur Gordon advised his sister to attend, with an attorney for protection.[18]

Frustrated but never idle, Daisy fired off a note to Jane Addams, who was a friend of a Gordon-family friend, asking to use Hull House as a base while she visited Girl Scout troops, starting with "some of the patrols . . . among the Hull House girls." While Daisy was in Chicago, Jane Deeter Rippin went to Savannah, not to rest, Daisy emphasized, but for the luncheon with the Savannah executive board and a troop review. They laughed at the bolstering effect of "an inspecting general," because Girl Scouts were seen cramming for "examinations to bring them up to standards" before the national director's arrival.[19]

In Chicago, the diversion by Lisetor-Lane was just that. In the end, she had no case to be made and no lawsuit that could succeed. Daisy was much more interested in the local council's idea "to encourage the older high school girls to take up aviation." Always keen to offer Girl Scouts the same advantages Boy Scouts had, Daisy fully supported pilot Edwin Paul Richter's training for the young women. Later that year, female aviator and Girl Scout captain Laura Bromwell taught Chicago Girl Scouts about "the theory of flying." It was easy for Daisy to promote aeronautics, because it had become one of her favorite activities. Flying was still a very new and dangerous sport. Adherents routinely broke records for height, speed, and distance as the technology evolved. Crashes could be spectacular and lethal. Women pilots and passengers were rare but not unheard of. "It is the most thrilling sensation," she confided to Doots, but swore her to secrecy until she could tell her siblings herself. "I go across country for a two hour flight tomorrow. I went 1,000 feet in my first flight in a Deperdussin monoplane but the slow flying on biplanes is better because you can take in the views of the Earth." Nevill Smyth had been right all along when he suggested the biplane! "[T]he monoplane goes 120 miles an hour, too quick for pleasure," she admitted to her niece.[20]

The national leadership wanted to capitalize on the popularity and growth of Girl Scouting. By the fall of 1920, the Girl Scouts boasted 82,000 members in 1,343 towns nationwide, but with more funds they could train the leaders so desperately needed for the "thousands of girls who wish to join [but] are turned away each month." An advisory committee on business and finance formed. "The men's committee," as Jane called it, "is really active and most helpful." They decided that the target sum for the big fund-raising drive was $1,033,400. "Please don't gasp!" Jane cautioned Daisy. Between good friends and good publicity, they expected to raise all of it. The Girl Scouts angled for cover spots on magazines such as *The Saturday Evening Post*, *Collier's*, and the *Woman's Home Companion*.

The *New York Evening Post* offered them a column and a half, just what the Boy Scouts had. One supporter, Cleveland Dodge, promised to donate one thousand dollars for three years if nineteen other people could be persuaded to follow his example. Daisy was among the nineteen who did so.[21]

The sixty-year-old founder kicked off the fund-raising campaign with a spectacular flourish—from an airplane. Her friend Laurence Driggs flew the old-fashioned Farman biplane while she leaned out from three thousand feet and dropped Girl Scout pamphlets on the crowds below. She circled right above Central Park, flew down Fifth Avenue, and buzzed Girl Scout headquarters on Thirty-ninth Street as spectators looked on delightedly from below. The airplane stunt opened Girl Scout Week, which included a parade with "six thousand girls of ten different nationalities" (including thirty Chinese American Girl Scouts) and seven floats that made their way through New York City. Daisy Low, Anne Hyde Choate, Jane Deeter Rippin, and the New York Scout commissioner walked at the front of the parade. A pageant and celebration in Central Park followed. Before leaving, one troop gathered all the fruit and flowers that had decorated the floats and set off to deliver them to city hospitals. The largest gift of the campaign was from the family of former senator William Andrews Clark. Clark donated the "first Girl Scout National Camp," 135 acres in Briarcliff, New York, in memory of his daughter, Andree, who had been a Girl Scout.[22]

A delightful part of that fall drive was the establishment of Founder's Day, October 31. Do not make a fuss, Daisy urged Jane, who was behind the idea, and "please let the function be purely one of pleasure for the children, such as Rallies, competitive games, sports and amusements that will interest them. All Hallow's Eve ceremonies will help the program." Her nephew described her at this time in her life as "a compact little woman with iron-gray hair, warm brown eyes, a strong nose, firm mouth, and a very determined chin." She "was always either roaring with laughter . . . or foaming with indignation about some injustice." She and Jane decided she would deliver an annual birthday message in *The American Girl*. It usually dispensed good advice. For Founder's Day in 1923, for example, she suggested to girls that "the deliberate cultivation of the gift of putting yourself in another's place is the beginning of wisdom in human relations," which no doubt was a lesson she tried to remember in her own work with Girl Scouting. But that particular night, Daisy hoped to usher in her seventh decade by quietly reminiscing with Abby Lippitt Hunter—after, that is, she completed her inspection tour of Girl Scouts in Providence, Abby's hometown.[23]

The 1921 national Girl Scout convention would be in the Midwest, in Cincinnati, Ohio. Jane Deeter Rippin scheduled the founder to speak about "Qualities of Leadership" and "Scouting: An International Program." She had not consulted Daisy Low on these topics, and Daisy was amused at the first one. "I could not give a talk on that subject to save my life," she said and laughed. "I only know that those who believe sincerely in any plan or scheme of life, can usually influence people to believe also in that plan." She conceded that she knew "a lot about the international work," and agreed to speak on that topic. Her friend Rose Kerr—now chief Girl Guide commissioner in London—attended the Ohio meeting as part of the promise to maintain close ties between the United States and Great Britain. Kerr stayed on after the convention to take part in several Girl Scout activities, including a meeting at national headquarters with nearly "three hundred council members and captains from greater New York" who were "most enthusiastic" to see a leading light of British Scouting. Rose Kerr wended her way south, and on reaching Savannah, Daisy promptly put her to work. Savannah had been chosen as the site of the 1922 Girl Scouts national convention, and Daisy was already buttering up local dignitaries.[24]

Cora Neal was in Europe about the same time, working in Paris with the American Woman's Club of the YWCA. When that position expired, she wrote fondly to Daisy Low, asking whether there was a remunerative job to be had. Glad to have experienced help, Daisy labored industriously with headquarters to locate the necessary salary to hire Cora as an assistant for the January 1922 Savannah convention, and then as a field worker, a three-month position.[25]

A sense of déjà vu must have enveloped Cora Neal as she stepped right back into a Crazy Daisy fund-raising scheme: a wrestling match. Daisy rented an auditorium and worked with a sports promoter to bring professional athletes to Savannah. She induced the mayor, the school superintendent, her brother Bill (who was president of the Kiwanis Club), the Catholic clergy, and the head of Rotary to sign on. Cora conscientiously churned out newspaper articles to convince locals that "high class wrestling matches are equally enjoyable to ladies and gentlemen," because wrestling nowadays was "robbed of all the brutalities that formerly surrounded prize fights, and they are, therefore, becoming popular social events." Cora was wrong about the "brutalities" but correct concerning the social events. Boxing and wrestling, like most spectator sports, would be all the rage in the 1920s. Savannahians were not quite that appreciative of the trendy and the new, and the project lost money.[26]

The conference occurred in early January 1922 regardless. The executive board, including Edith Macy, Lou Henry Hoover, Anne Hyde Choate, Helen Storrow, and Jane Deeter Rippin, took the train south. All the leaders stayed comfortably in the homes of Savannahians, while other visitors lodged at the DeSoto Hotel or one of the city's boardinghouses. Following lunch at the Savannah Golf Club, Daisy scheduled a lengthy demonstration of camping techniques. "I know Northerners are familiar with such out door activities, but way down South no one has any idea of them," Daisy wrote, a little disingenuously. Her elaboration was full of bathos: "I saw, last week, 15 men <u>Volunteer</u> <u>artillery</u> <u>men</u> try to pitch a tent they took ½ hour to do it, our girls could have done it in 5 minutes. They tried to tie all pegs after the pole was hoisted! All wrong, of course." This opportunity to immortalize Girl Scouting returning to its roots sent Daisy, flushed with hometown pride, to hire an Atlanta film company. Josephine Daskam Bacon remembered Daisy's soaring happiness during the conference. "The endless discussions, the reports, the voting, the singing, the crowds in the hotel, the great banquet with speeches and toasts, all thrilled her. She had seen her little clubs grow into a vast national organization—international, even. . . . Boards of trade and chambers of commerce and rotary clubs listened to our speakers and supported us; three religious faiths were represented on our National Board, the wife of the president of the United States wore our uniform."[27]

At the Savannah convention the main speaker was Colin H. Livingstone, president of the Boy Scouts of America. He watched as Lou Henry Hoover (whose husband had recently been appointed U.S. secretary of commerce) was duly elected the new president of the Girl Scouts. Livingstone learned that national membership stood at more than 112,000; larger regional districts had replaced states that made the fieldwork more difficult but saved money; nearly a dozen universities were "experimenting and observing a training course for leaders"; New York City's board of education was giving credit for the Girl Scout leadership course for public school teachers (lending tremendous prestige to the organization); and a study was under way on the West Coast to analyze and remedy dietary deficiencies in Girl Scouts there. As Josephine Daskam Bacon noted, all these successes were a dream come true for their founder.[28]

Lou Hoover's presidency continued the changes under way in Girl Scouting since Daisy resigned from that position. Mrs. Hoover increased the number of paid staff—believing, as did Daisy—that salaried professionals would solidify wartime gains and draw more women to Girl Scouting. As a generational shift occurred, younger women such as Jane Deeter Rippin moved into positions of authority, while older women, like Helen Storrow, retreated when faced with unpalatable changes (in her case, paid trainers). Girl Scouting across the nation provided an excellent avenue for women to gain leadership experience at every level. Lou Hoover, highly educated and experienced herself, worked avidly to professionalize Girl Scouting and streamline and rationalize its operations.[29]

Once the Savannah conference ended, Daisy turned to another dream of hers: a camping facility for Georgia girls who, because of "the risk of sun stroke and malaria and fever," had to abandon Girl Scouting in the summer. She secured donations of lumber and ten acres of land on Lookout Mountain, Georgia, for the purpose.

"Imagine yourself," she urged Jane, "on a shelf 2000 feet above the level of the sea, a sheer drop of 2000 feet, you could sit with your feet dangling over the tops of the tallest trees and see for miles a most amazing view and at your back rugged rocks and virgin forests." That was the lure of Cloudlands—that and the clear well water, the swimming pool just for Girl Scouts, and the clubhouse they would build.[30]

Daisy came up with a new idea—to train leaders side by side with girls in a more "realistic" and practical experience—and she thought Cloudlands was the place to test it. Overcome with enthusiasm, Daisy summoned tents, marshaled publicity to reach all Girl Scout leaders in the South, and "commandeered" Dorris Hough and Inez Oliveros to run things. "Then, she went to England!" Hough recalled. While she was "nonplussed," her colleague Oliveros was "resentful." But they had fourteen girls to train and fourteen more to entertain. Hough admitted "that two weeks training camp was a complete success. Once again Mrs. Low's vision led the way," especially her brainchild of training leaders with girls present.[31]

Cloudlands came to be called Camp Juliette Low. "Every detail of the camp was of intense interest to her," Hough knew. She determined the layout of the buildings and their rooms, stood her ground for the location of the swimming pool, and chased down—on foot, in a skirt, up a cliff, and with a Pekingese under her arm—the officials whose signatures were necessary for the dream to begin. She tried valiantly to employ Jane Deeter Rippin's husband as an architect, as he had aided the building of the Bear Mountain campsite in New York, but to no avail. When "another [bank] failure in Savannah" wiped out "$20,000 of [her] capital," Daisy acted as her own contractor. Loyally, Jane promised to raise $1,000.[32]

On the other side of the Atlantic, Olave Baden-Powell and the Girl Guides were lucky enough to be given a campsite—a gorgeous, ideally placed sixty-five acres of land in Hampshire called Foxlease, the gift of American socialite Anne Archbold. Her 1922 divorce from Armar Dayrolles Saunderson of Castle Saunderson, Ireland, coincided with the donation. Olave described to Daisy how Foxlease came with "a lovely big house with 24 bedrooms, nine bath-rooms (!), electric light, central heating, lovely garden, camping grounds, etc. Too perfect for description." Of course, the cost of upkeep was a concern. Olave hoped various groups might sponsor a room or one of the outlying buildings. The idea entranced Daisy. Straightaway a donation came in from Helen Storrow. With it, Daisy herself chose the furniture for a "quaint little bungalow" near the main house. She insisted on installing a bathroom, for which later campers blessed her. Daisy named the cabin the Link to signify the ties between Girl Guiding and Girl Scouting. The Link was always open to Americans, and she found it all "too 'cunning' for words."[33]

International Council business for the summer of 1922 resolved three issues: the reelection of Olave Baden-Powell as international chairman, the admission of Germans to the next meeting along lines already determined by the United States, and that there was room for interpretation in the Girl Guide Oath concerning the "promise of loyalty to God." Japanese leaders had broached the latter topic. Daisy networked with other delegates, and instructed Jane to send *Scouting for Girls* off to her counterparts in France, Sweden, Denmark, Belgium, Latvia, and China.[34]

Since 1919, Daisy Low's life had focused on international Girl Scouting, but her service to American Girl Scouts never ceased, nor did her interest in Georgia Girl Scouts waver. It was a great day when Camp Juliette Low opened—but it was, by the 1920s, just one of many camps dotting the landscape. The focus of Girl Scouting always had to be fun, and at camp even exertion was fun. Girls practiced their woodcraft skills; learned lifesaving, swimming, and boating; made progress toward badges difficult to achieve in the city; bonded with fellow campers; and deepened their devotion to Girl Scouting. If they were lucky, the founder might turn up. She hiked and swam and took part in every outdoor activity. She read their palms and imparted wisdom. Then, when darkness fell, she gathered them around the fire to tell stories of Scottish ghosts, Civil War heroes, and brave Illinois pioneer women. Girls clamored to hear the exciting tale of how, in the eighteenth century, Daisy's intrepid great grandmother Eleanor Lytle McKillip Kinzie had been kidnapped by the Senecas when she was nine and given the name Little Ship Under Full Sail. That made Daisy Low happiest—camping with the girls and sharing their sense of wonder.[35]

CHAPTER 16

Making New Friends Internationally

In her sixties, Daisy Low could take pride in many accomplishments. She was a generous member of a loving family, always ready to assist or sympathize. She counted true and dear lifelong friends on both sides of the Atlantic. She had earned the respect of vibrant, dedicated women who shared her vision for the uplift of girls in the Girl Scouts, and the affection of those who struggled with her to bring about global understanding in the International Council. Through sculpture, sketching, painting, and metalwork, she created items of lasting beauty. Her remarkable experiences included meeting royalty, hunting tigers, flying in airplanes, climbing the Pyramid, nursing soldiers, living on two continents, and traveling to Africa and India. She went up the Eiffel Tower when it was new. She drove through Europe when automobiles were in their infancy, and made one of the earliest films. She invented and patented a liner for garbage cans. She knew, a scant decade into its life, that the Girl Scouts would be her legacy. Yet Daisy Low never rested on her laurels. The challenge she relished at sixty-two was both the simplest and the most difficult of her life: to foster global peace by bringing together Girl Scouts and Girl Guides from around the world, despite American isolationism. To accomplish this would take determination, devotion, tenacity, money, and the assistance of those very good women friends in the Girl Scouts.[1]

From the International Council reports in the mid-1920s she learned how Girl Guiding progressed in India, South Africa, New Zealand, Australia, the West Indies, and elsewhere. Shanghai, for example, boasted half a dozen companies of extremely active Girl Guides—Chinese and English—who had been meeting since the end of the war. They all struggled with the Girl Guide handbook, because so much of it did not harmonize with Chinese culture. Regardless, "One picks up a paper and reads [about] a company of Chinese Guides in some remote and unknown places in the interior . . . ," the Chinese delegate reported with awe. Daisy made sure that the translation of *Scouting for Girls* done by the Chinese American Girl Scout troop from New York was sent to Shanghai.[2]

In Hungary, the Catholic bishop banned Girl Scouting as too mannish, while the Protestant clergy supported it. The Hungarian Girl Scouts president pleaded with her International Council sisters for public letters of support and ideas to combat the opposition. She knew it would raise eyebrows with American Girl Scouts, but Daisy suggested the "politic move" of a name change to Girl Guides in Hungary. With the entire Catholic Church against them, she believed firmer gender distinction would soften the resistance. Luckily, in the United States, Roman Catholic clergy supported the Girl Scouts.[3]

Daisy's positions as corresponding delegate to the International Council and chair of the Girl Scouts international committee made her the liaison between Olave Baden-Powell's London group and the leaders and staff in New York. Daisy became a thoughtful international policy director but found raising interest among her American colleagues extremely difficult. She did not consider herself truly effective until the beginning of 1926—seven years after the International Council formed. It took that long for her to establish a clear chain of command, and to implement her trio of ideas: quarterly Girl Scout international committee meetings; reports consistently published in *Leaders Monthly*; and an effective deputy.[4]

In between her International Council duties, Daisy remained busy with variations of the Girl Scouting work she had been doing since 1912: gathering with girls and leaders, writing hundreds of letters, publicizing, fund-raising, speech making, camping, and recruiting. Her creativity just flowed. Daisy discovered that the members of one rural troop earned a laudable 170 badges. She designed a silver shield as an award meant to encourage "inter-troop competition" to keep the girls from going "stale." When the girls of another troop conceived a celebratory program and asked her to award all their badges, she enthusiastically participated.[5]

The expansion and professionalization of the Girl Scouts released Daisy from several jobs. She no longer had to train leaders, oversee publicity, write literature, organize councils, hire personnel, locate items to sell in the headquarters shop, or supervise legal and financial matters. Jane Deeter Rippin made her aware of the largest decisions and of the debates behind them. With rare exceptions, her letters were jovial and downplayed disharmony among the leadership. Jane continued to channel Daisy's ideas and votes to the executive committee, dissuade her gently when necessary, keep straight Daisy's expenditures (preauthorized or not), and run occasional interference between Daisy and the board.[6]

In the spring of 1923, the board members sought Daisy's view as to whether disabled girls could receive the Golden Eaglet, Girl Scouting's highest award. To be eligible, one had to be a First Class Scout and earn twenty-one merit badges, among them Athlete, Child Nurse, First Aide, Home Nurse, and Pioneer. Daisy's views were to run side by side with Anne Hyde Choate's in *Field News* to solicit opinion from captains and lieutenants. Daisy submitted her article in May, but the publications office misplaced it. There was a mix-up, and Anne's article ran by itself in September. Daisy was furious. It wasn't "a fair way to put the whole question before the field," she stormed. She demanded of an executive board member that her column run, as "a matter of principle," not just in *Field News* but also in *The American Girl*. Perhaps it was the founder's wrath that persuaded the executive board to appease her by voting to send *Field News* gratis to all captains as she thought best to do.[7]

Anne Hyde Choate opposed awarding the Golden Eaglet to disabled Girl Scouts. Daisy was very much for it. ". . . I am certain that our organization will suffer . . . and thus lose the finest examples of Scout spirit which our crippled scouts give to their sister Scouts" if they were denied, she wrote firmly. She believed that prudent, fair, and humane adjustments would maintain the integrity of the Golden Eaglet. From Michigan, Kalamazoo's executive director, Agnes M. Shier, responded thoughtfully. She felt all Golden Eaglet Girl Scouts "should represent perfect examples of the 'Spirit of Scouting.'" A girl physically capable of earning the honor might be morally unworthy of it, Shier pointed out, and this seemed unjust to her. Lillian Plotkin remembered how she "longed and hoped to reach the heights of the Golden Eaglet" when she entered Girl Scouting, and declared she would never want any Girl Scout to be denied that goal. Over Robert Baden-Powell's objections, Daisy's sentiments carried the day, and disabled Girl Scouts would go on to earn the Golden Eaglet. This ideological disagreement drove a wedge between Daisy and her goddaughter.[8]

Her nephew B's lifelong struggle with deafness colored Daisy's views on this subject. He was shamed by not qualifying for enlistment in the First World War. After it ended, so many men, Daisy observed, had been "knocked out, crippled, made deaf and blind" that everyone lost the "impulse to cherish and help out any disabled one." Unlike Anne, Daisy saw those veterans in England and in France. And unlike Baden-Powell, she could not easily accept their physical traumas as collateral damage. Her own difficult hearing often frustrated her, but she never complained of discrimination. It would have been natural for Daisy Low to empathize with disabled Girl Scouts and their yearning for the Golden Eaglet. Perhaps it was a sign of how lightly she wore her deafness that her goddaughter did not make the same connection.

When Girl Scouts first raised the issue in May, Daisy was in a very different place in her life from where she was when her article came out in November. As she worked to put her thoughts on paper about the nature of physical disabilities and the bravery of Girl Scouts who managed somehow to push past them, her recurring physical problems drove her to a doctor. Daisy had taken "desperately ill." "A slight operation," she wrote Jane Deeter Rippin, was followed by the flu, which kept her confined to bed through early February 1924. Daisy did not go into detail nor confide the extent of the pain and worry that had been hers since the middle of 1923. The operation was to remove malignant lumps in her breast, and the diagnosis, although it is not clear when or if Daisy ever heard these words, was breast cancer.[9]

Physical illness frustrated her. Many plans needed her attention as the next International Council convention—by then called World Camp—loomed. It would be at Foxlease, in England, and Daisy was imagining a large number of American delegates and girls whom she hoped afterward to show around London. Then she wanted to bring foreign delegates to the United States so they would understand American Girl Scouting. By March she had recovered enough from the surgery to visit Foxlease as a member of the IC's British Entertainment Committee tasked with providing amusements for visitors. Though she would be staying in the Link, she also had to claim a campsite for the American Girl Scouts. Her correspondence swelled with details of ship embarkation tables, passport information, consulate questions, and lodging and meal possibilities.[10]

And it was time for the 1924 national convention in Chicago, where four hundred leaders and two thousand girls were expected. The Chicago Historical Society requested a lecture on "why 'the girl Scouts of today are the pioneers of tomorrow,'" which Daisy squeezed in before the opening ceremonies. The election returned Lou Henry Hoover to the presidency of the national Girl Scouts. Despite her obvious dedication, Hoover was not Daisy's choice. She preferred former dean of Simmons College Sarah Louise Arnold, who, she thought, "does far more at present for Scouts than even the President." Nevertheless, Hoover applied her formidable organizational skills to the 91,994 Girl Scouts in her care and to the regional restructuring plan in progress. Under her watch, the Girl Scouts bought and remodeled a building at 670 Lexington Avenue in New York City to accommodate their growth.[11]

President Lou Henry Hoover also encouraged what turned out to be a brilliant fund-raising idea—the baking and selling of cookies. The Mistletoe Troop from Oklahoma sold cookies at Muskogee High School in 1917. Five years later, a Chicago leader wrote about the successful homemade cookie endeavor by two thousand Illinois Girl Scouts. Once her story was published in *The American Girl,* the idea caught on. In 1923, Manhattan Girl Scouts presented First Lady Grace Coolidge with a five-foot-long bag of cookies to garner publicity for their fund-raising drive. The *New York Times* noted that during Girl Scout Week, in late October, "more than 1,000,000 Girl Scout cookies will be put on sale in this city," baked by the girls of New York's Troop #24, to raise money for "a new home and the 1924 budget." Daisy was in England then, and reported that "[t]hey were thrilled at Girl Guides Headquarters at the idea of the cookie sale." Daisy supported it also, because she believed in what she called decentralization, that is, of "forcing localities to pay for themselves."[12]

By May, Daisy knew she needed help if she was to rouse the Girl Scouts to the importance of a global understanding of the problems of youth and the solutions Girl Scouting could supply. She asked to be provided with a deputy chairman to assist her with building the bridge between the International Council and the Girl Scouts. Daisy's choice, executive board member Leila B. Delano, stepped into the job and was immediately hit with a tornado of details concerning the travel to England for the July World Camp.[13]

It went more smoothly than expected. At Foxlease, spirits were undaunted, even in the face of a drenching rain that flushed sodden campers from their tents to the Link for hot baths and temporary beds. Daisy entertained delegates with that very American dish, ice cream, between lectures, "displays of dancing, singing, games, and national 'stunts' in costumes [that] really are stunning!" The Girl Scouts summed up their nation's heritage through a series of tableaux that included Indians, Pilgrims, the covered wagon, and—of course—the Girl Scouts. Reports of Guiding and Scouting around the world kept adults busy, but the chance to "make new friends and keep the old" was the true reason twenty-six Girl Scouts and eight leaders traveled so far. Daisy appreciated the "masterful way" the camp was organized. Bubbling with enthusiasm, she and Anne Hyde Choate invited everyone to the United States for the next World Camp.[14]

These ideas percolated on the journey home, to emerge in a full-blown scheme that terrified Jane Deeter Rippin. Daisy was immovable. "We are bound to lead in Scouting," she asserted, "it is up to us now to show what we can do. The world has learned about all that England can teach, and though I do not lack full gratitude and appreciation of our debt to England, we now also can teach things of infinite value to other nations." And, she persevered, "the deeper and solider things can only be taught by having the members of the International come to [the] U.S.A." The only barrier, as Daisy saw it, was the State Department, which placed too many obstacles before foreign visitors. Jane was pretty sure there would be other difficulties—starting with the breathtakingly enormous job of planning an itinerary intended to show off both Girl Scouting and the United States, while simultaneously organizing a meeting for hundreds of international guests. Leaving Jane and the national staff staggered, Daisy left on her usual autumnal trip to England.[15]

She was in poor health, so much so that she sought out her niece Peggy Leigh, Mabel and Rowley's daughter, who was by then a trained nurse. Daisy asked Peggy to locate a doctor for her and to keep it a secret. Peggy did so. She found a physician, coincidentally also named Low, who performed a two-hour surgery on her aunt. Ten days of recovery brought her home to Grosvenor Street. She settled in her bedroom, with her Scottish maid Bella MacDonald, to look after her. Peggy assisted during a house call from Dr. Bruce Williamson. She recalled having to clear a space on Daisy's nightstand. They removed her Bible and "a most fanciful array of paraphernalia for making tea during the small hours of the night." Her aunt's "airy badinage" entertained them both, and the champagne that followed helped Peggy regain the optimism that had withered when she saw Daisy's condition.[16]

Mabel wrote to Arthur at the end of December 1924 to bemoan the terrible year with a grisly checklist. Her son Rowland had been in an auto accident. Her husband had cataract surgery. Arthur's baby had been very sick, like Arthur himself. Their brother Bill had financial setbacks and was ill. Eleanor's husband, Representative Wayne Parker, had died in April. And Daisy could not shake off her mystery illness. Except for "dear old Wayne, everything has worked itself out," Mabel concluded, "but I feel 1000 years older than" a year ago.[17]

The unexpected death of Edith Macy on February 1, 1925, brought changes to the Girl Scouts. She had served as chairman of the executive board for six years, and Daisy and Jane mourned the tactful, considerate woman who "really was the pivot that kept our whole organization in harmony." Lou Henry Hoover replaced Mrs. Macy, and Daisy's close friend Sarah L. Arnold won election to the presidency that Hoover vacated. Daisy rejoiced. "There is only one evenly balanced woman who could at all keep up Mrs. Macy's standard," she wrote Jane, "and that woman is Sarah Louise Arnold."[18]

Jane wrote confidentially to Daisy with the news of V. Everit Macy's wonderful memorial to his wife. He donated "a permanent training center for Leaders," which would sit on two hundred acres of land he purchased in New York, next to the already successful Camp Andree for Girl Scouts. Daisy was delighted—with the gift and with the national director's confidences. "I feel so often, that I am drifting away from the heart of the organization," she wrote plaintively. Macy promised "$50,000 for the building and another $50,000 as an endowment for its upkeep." The organization immediately set to work, with the goal of readiness by June 1926 for rudimentary camping.[19]

Camp Edith Macy, Daisy decided, would be perfect for the 1926 World Camp. National Director Jane Deeter Rippin felt a little faint as she "thought of the blue prints, of the roads to be constructed, of the wells to be dug, the water to be piped before Camp Edith Macy could be a camp at all. I thought of the hundreds of our own leaders who would wish to be there with our guests. I thought of the tents that must be bought and pitched, of the meals that must be served . . . from every side there seemed to leap out at me some new detail to be considered." Jane tried to talk her out of it. She marshaled a hundred arguments. Daisy prevailed and, a week later, convinced the executive board. "No greater tribute was ever paid Juliette Low," Jane affirmed. Girl Scout headquarters hoped soon to have the responses from all the International Council delegates to the plan proposed by Daisy Low in July, when she traveled to England for the IC meeting. In the meantime, Jane and the national staff bent their every effort to making Camp Edith Macy a reality.[20]

Daisy, too, increased the pace of her international work. Everything was complicated by the fact that most European countries had joined the League of Nations. This prototype for the United Nations was sponsored by the United States to provide a place to resolve international disagreements. The isolationist United States, however, did not join the league. Therefore, the internationalism that Daisy Low advocated—the cooperation with Girl Guides and Girl Scouts from around the globe—was both countercultural and worrisome to politicians in that decade. To preserve the good reputation of the Girl Scouts, Daisy had to walk a fine line. Robert Baden-Powell extolled the League of Nations and spoke of how Boy Scouts and Girl Scouts and Guides could assist its work. The labor Daisy did to bring the World Camp to America was neither uncontroversial nor risk-free.[21]

As she monitored communications from abroad, approved the issuance of a charter to a new patrol in Puerto Rico, and worried about a leniency toward communism in the IC, her health faltered again. Unaccustomed lethargy forced her to confer with a doctor in March 1925, and as she was in Richmond, Virginia, helping to establish a training camp, she briefly consulted Stuart McGuire at Saint Luke's Hospital. She returned to Richmond four weeks later. In between she handwrote fifty letters to Girl Scouts, encouraging them to subscribe to *The American Girl;* had a visit from a national leader, for whom Daisy hosted a dinner; and accepted thirty-five hundred dollars from Savannah's Community Chest for the local Girl Scouts.[22]

The purpose of the second trip to Richmond was another

operation, after which Daisy was under doctor's orders to rest. But the Girl Scouts regional conference was under way in the city, and Daisy just had to go. Having asked permission and been refused it, she slipped out anyway. She made a speech, returned, got in bed, and made her confession to Dr. McGuire. His wife, Ruth, believed Daisy asked him then to tell her how long she had to live, and that he replied "approximately six months." Peggy's recollection, however, was that he told Daisy she needed no more treatment and should "go on leading [her] everyday life." Privately, downstairs, McGuire told Peggy that Daisy had six months. Peggy marched back to her aunt, purposefully cheerful. "Isn't that good news? Aren't you pleased?" she asked. But Daisy held her gaze levelly and said only that she was glad to know. There was a certain fatalism to her acceptance of Dr. McGuire's verdict. She had never forgotten the horoscope done in her youth that told her she would die in her fifty-fifth or her sixty-fifth year. Peggy thought it "obvious" that they both grasped the truth—but that Daisy "could only guess at the actual time limit."[23]

Getting the Richmond training camp up and running took many visits, many more letters, and diplomacy worth a Nobel laureate. And while this was under way, she had an airtight reason for being near Dr. McGuire. Following a late June check-in, she, the McGuires, and several of their friends sailed together for Europe. Everyone enjoyed Daisy's companionship but could not help but be distressed by her obvious poor health. Seeing this, she put on a long face, too. When they asked kindly what troubled her, Daisy said straight-facedly that it was her birthday, and she was sad that no one remembered. Everyone threw themselves into a party, with presents, songs, and an enormous cake. Not until it was all over did the McGuires recall that her birthday was on Halloween. When they called her bluff, she laughed merrily and told them the party was to cheer them all up. Daisy would not show self-pity. When no one would attend the ship's costume ball with her, she was untroubled. Daisy covered herself completely in white sheets, tied a rope about her middle, threaded empty whiskey bottles on it, and went as "Departed Spirits."[24]

In the UK, she made a point of seeing as many old friends as possible. Rudyard Kipling painted an intimate word picture of Daisy, an evocative view of the alienating effects of her diagnosis:

> . . . Daisy has been staying with us for a few days—as quaintly funny and as sadly lonely as ever. . . .[H]er joy during all her stay was to fish. I was duly in attendance each evening but no luck till the last when she got a fish of over half a pound, after the dressing-bell had gone, on the Black Bridge by the cess-pit. After ten hectic minutes, during which the rod fouled itself with *all* the tree-tops, I managed, by lying on my tummy on the cess-pit wall, *just* to reach and net it. Never was any one more simply and childishly rejoiced than Daisy, and I think she went away quite happy. I am most awfully sorry for her, but she has the pluck of a whole "pride of Lions." She has no vestige of a notion of time, or, indeed, of anything else, and she drifts along locked up in her infirmity, like a balloon that can't signal, to the earth.[25]

Kipling, of course, meant by her "infirmity" her deafness, as he knew nothing of her cancer. Few people did. Daisy maintained what Peggy called an endless network of deception about it. Daisy said it was because she preferred "not to be an object of worry to anyone." But those who loved her read her actions and worried all the more. Mabel wrote privately to Arthur that she understood that their sister's health scare was significant. Mabel knew that Daisy had confided in Peggy and also in an old friend to whom she'd given letters for the family in case she died as a result of one of the operations. "Personally, I will lie to [Daisy]," Mabel vowed, "or to anyone if it makes things easier for her." Still, it did not set well with Mabel. "It makes me sick, to think of that brave little thing gallantly struggling in this devilish fear and anxiety. She is worthy of Papa," Mabel believed. It was only a few weeks after Daisy caught the fish with Kipling that "violent spasms of nausea" forced her to stop in the middle of a story she was trying to tell Ruth McGuire about the Brownies.[26]

The professional reason for the trip to England was the International Council committee meeting. Jane cabled her to say that 1928 would be much better for the Girl Scouts to host the World Camp, but "I have $5,000 assured and we will do our best for 1926 if International Council so desires." It wasn't the International Council's desire. It was Daisy Low's. At some point, Daisy confided solemnly to Jane that "if we don't have it next summer, I won't be here," and then swore her to secrecy, too. Less than forty-eight hours after receiving Jane's cable, she eagerly read aloud the official invitation to the delegates assembled in London. She hoped, as she told Girl Guide leader Dame Katherine Furse, that "we should cultivate friendships and arouse interest in foreigners" to combat the isolationist sentiment in the United States. By October, when the positive responses came in, it looked as though a start had been made. The IC delegates wanted to invent "a badge for International tests," and design a "form of introduction" when a Guide or a Girl Scout travels abroad, while Girl Scout headquarters drew up a Folk Dancer's badge that would require knowledge of dances around the world.[27]

Thanksgiving found Daisy in Richmond, Virginia, again grateful for what a "fair and square friend" Jane Deeter Rippin was to her—and amused that Jane was thankful for the same thing. "How good it was of God," Daisy wrote, "to have let you come into Scouting." And there was more to be appreciative for when the national director wrote confidentially of Everit Macy doubling his endowment, from fifty thousand dollars to one hundred thousand dollars.[28]

Perhaps it was her own mortality, or the visit she made to Duncan Hunter's sister in Scotland, or working so closely with Anne Hyde Choate, but Daisy visited Mary Clarke with increasing frequency. The terrible reach of mental illness in her old Venus was staggering. The 1924 winter was a difficult spell for her mother, Anne related, but she went "every 2 or 3 weeks" to the apartment Mary shared with her canary—a gift from Daisy. Periods of violence gripped Mary, but Daisy knew her dear friend could never hurt her. A ruby ring caught Mary's eye during a stopover, so Daisy let her wear it. When she would not relinquish it, "the attendants got all frantic and said if [I] tried to take it away from her it might make [Mary] ill, but if I left it with her she was liable to throw it in the pond . . . never [to] be found again," Daisy recounted for Anne. Daisy did leave it, but purchased a similar ring and sent it to her superstitious friend with a note requesting hers back because "Willy . . . knows that I'm not wearing his ruby ring." Mary returned it. Too much stimulation seemed to trigger Mary's "loss of control." She moved between an asylum and her apartment, depending on her mental state. Daisy spent a week at a time with her in 1925 and 1926. There was no cure. Those who loved her hoped for the best.[29]

Daisy stayed in Richmond before heading home for Christmas. Her brothers met her anxiously. With them, she could give vent to her anger about her increasing weakness. But she enjoyed every minute when, on Georgia Day in February 1926, Savannahians spread roses and hyacinths before her to honor their internationally famous daughter. In a Forsyth Park ceremony, the mayor presented her with an ornate scroll of appreciation as the Eighth Infantry Band played and Brownies, Girl Scouts, Boy Scouts, officers of the U.S. Army, and "throngs of people" celebrated her life and work. It was the sugar she craved but never sought, and it was sweet to be honored in her hometown.[30]

Conquering the fatigue that followed the ceremony, Daisy concentrated her energies on a debutante ball the *Savannah News* called "a gem of originality and interest," given for her niece, Mary Stuart Gordon. Like all good Southern parties, the festivities would spill outside, but it was a chilly February. Even with Japanese lanterns dancing overhead and "four gas stoves brightly burning in the supper tent, it was cold." The party would have been incomplete without that quintessential Southern flower, the camellia—but hers had not fully bloomed. This did not stop Daisy. She asked her neighbors for any camellias that had opened. When they arrived, Daisy didn't put them in vases. She tied them to her camellia trees! It was an inimitably Daisy-like triumph.[31]

The diversion of the ball quickly disappeared under the avalanche of World Camp demands. Every aspect of the visitors' time had to be considered, from passports to ship reservations to travel itinerary to American escorts, to sleeping arrangements, food, and more. Planning meetings took arranging and time. Tempers needed soothing. At least the ever-resourceful Jane Deeter Rippin had procured travel funding. Daisy promised to pay any cost overruns incurred in getting the delegates from a port in England or France to New York.

The end of February included another bout of "influenza" with her brain, she claimed, "as stuffy as a London fog." Jane sent bracing notes about the progress at Camp Edith Macy, and updates of Daisy's arrangements for the "big Board of Director's meeting" in Saint Louis, a critical planning session for the World Camp and important because it was the first time the national conference had been held that far west. Daisy hoped to convince the other board members that unlike Foxlease, where the programming emphasized basic Girl Scouting and Guiding information, at Camp Edith Macy, it was American organizational and camping skills that should be taught. Daisy needed to divulge the problems she was having maintaining control of the decision making—because the Girl Guide executives were used to running everything. President Arnold had to make crystal clear that the Girl Scouts were "the dispenser of hospitality and the arbiter of who decides on who is to come [so] we will achieve a big step towards independent action. . . . I want the nations to feel that we each stand along and with equal rights in this big sisterhood." Daisy was more than ready to "end the dictatorship of England."[32]

Worsening cancer felled her again in April, and this attack was so severe it kept her from the Saint Louis convention. She wrote from her bed in Richmond, where Dr. McGuire forbade her to travel. She sent a cable to be read at the opening ceremony, telling of her irritation with her illness, which she still called influenza. She quoted "the advice of our old colored cook," who stated often that "manners and behavior will carry you though." The impatient founder was "trying to cultivate both."[33]

All the national leaders feared Daisy would be too ill for the World Camp. Leila Delano, her right-hand woman in the IC, sent an SOS or perhaps a plea: "Just remember the work I have done has been entirely for you because I care for you so much. If you can get here please do for my sake." She made it. Anne, Leila, Jane, Daisy, and others met the arriving delegates in New York City. With great fanfare, a motorcade with a police escort squired them to City Hall to greet the mayor. Lunch at the prestigious Colony Club followed, and they boarded the boat for Cedar Hill Girl Scout Camp outside Boston. A day of sightseeing; presentation to the governor, the Speaker of the House, and the entire Massachusetts Senate; tea at Harvard University; and a tour of Girl Scout sites concluded their second day. The international delegation next traveled to Washington, D.C., where, at the White House, they met President Calvin Coolidge and First Lady Grace Coolidge, who was both an honorary Girl Scout president and a Tenderfoot Girl Scout. Lou Henry Hoover hosted dinner that evening. Somehow they fit in visits to the national monuments. The agenda was calculated to impress. The delegates spent one day at the New York headquarters and then proceeded to Camp Edith Macy.[34]

This was the culmination of her fondest hopes, and Daisy Low welcomed everyone gladly. Then delegates ritualistically came "one by one, each bearing a small bundle of twigs, which she cast on the [Council] Fire, saying as she did so what her country had given to the world." The week was packed full of events. Casual discussions fostered friendships, and formal meetings provided information. The arrival of the Chief Scout and the Chief Guide was the highlight. By popular acclaim, the delegates agreed to an international Thinking Day, on which Girl Guides and Girl Scouts around the world "should remember each other, and send messages of friendship and goodwill flashing across the world by the wireless of thought." They decided on February 22, the shared birthday of the Baden-Powells. The final camp day was dubbed Juliette Low Day, and the founder herself presented the badges, including the Golden Eaglet to Olave Baden-Powell.[35]

Leaving Camp Macy, the delegates saw Buffalo, New York, and Niagara Falls before crossing the international border to be received by the Canadian Girl Guides and eventually put on ships bound for home. Their time in North America was punctuated by Girl Scout Rallies and overtures of friendship, and the response was tremendously positive. The organizers were justifiably proud of their work. When it was all over, Daisy's good friend Jane sent the best summary: "It is not given to most of us mortals to see the success of our achievements. And no doubt this is because it usually takes so long for success to come. But success has come to Girl Scouting through the vision of its founder and her perseverance in the face of discouragement."[36]

But Daisy did not stop. She worried about having a patriotic program in place to celebrate the sesquicentennial of the nation's birth on July 4, 1926. She planned to be in Philadelphia on that day, hoping to participate in whatever was happening. When Jane cautioned her to slow down, Daisy reported that Dr. McGuire was "awfully pleased with the little operation" and promised her friend that she was "fit as a flea." "I do hope," she wrote candidly, "that I shall not live to feel old. . . . When I see a sunset or a glorious view, or hear of a fine action, worthy of heaven, I always pray that I may go soon, into that country before I get old and worn out."[37]

Knowing she had a brief time left, Daisy wanted to create a memorial for her parents. Near the Savannah Country Club was land owned by the Gordons that the siblings wanted to develop as a streetcar suburb to be called Gordonston. Daisy was "the emotional and financial force behind the creation of the park" that would be both a "'public playground' for the residents" and a memorial for her parents. In July 1926 they broke ground, and the centerpiece was the Wellesbourne House gates she had brought to Georgia from Warwickshire. Arthur, the practical one, asked how she came up with the idea. Daisy replied, "[W]hen I get depressed, or doubtful about what I should do, I shut my eyes, open the bible, and put my finger on a verse. I often get excellent counsel. I tried this one day, and found my finger on the last words in the Book of Proverbs. 'And let her own works praise her in the gates.' Of course I knew at once this meant I must place my gates, the work of my hands, in the Memorial Park at Gordonston."[38]

Shortly after this feat was accomplished, Daisy returned to England to put her affairs there in order. She saw the Kiplings again, this time with five American friends in tow. Peggy came to visit. She took a quiet walk with her aunt Daisy. The older woman broke the silence. "I know that medical research is going on all the time. I wonder if there are any hopes for finding a cure for what is incurable now?" Peggy desperately wanted to fudge the truth but couldn't. Without blinking, Daisy trotted out an amusing story to comfort her niece.[39]

Nevertheless, when a new treatment did present itself, Daisy agreed to it. She took Peggy—still sworn to secrecy—to Liverpool on Dr. Williamson's advice, there to consult with Dr. William Blair-Bell, a gynecological surgeon and professor at the University of Liverpool who had spent two decades researching cancer cures. The treatment for which he was famous was an intravenous injection of "a solution of colloidal lead." Fewer than 50 of his 250 patients showed even marginal improvement. Daisy was not one of them. As another physician commented later, "[T]he best that can be said of this research is that a less-opinionated man would have abandoned the treatment long before Blair-Bell did."[40]

She spent her sixty-sixth birthday in the convalescent ward, fighting heavy lead poisoning as well as the cancer, with her maid Bella, a full-time nurse, and a visit from her sister-in-law Jessie Low Graham. Daisy lied to Mabel and wrote that Blair-Bell saw "no internal trouble, no growth nor inflammation."[41]

Mail came regularly from the steadfast Jane Deeter Rippin to keep the founder informed. There was a move afoot to change the color of the Girl Scout uniform. Khaki had come to connote World War I for Americans, who wished by then to forget about their involvement in the costly conflict. The executive board felt it was "illogical, when we are all striving for world peace, to wear a color which . . . brings to mind memories of death and destruction." Three other pieces of news were very welcome. An International Merit Badge and a World Citizenship Badge were under consideration, and Camp Juliette Low had been paid for in full.[42]

Reunited with Mabel in London, Daisy completed an unfinished plaster bust of her grandfather that she wanted to have cast in bronze to present to the city of Savannah. Out of love for her nephew Rowland, she went to a musical review that featured songs he had written. She took ten friends with her—each one hearing impaired and sprouting various apparatus. They all appropriated the front row and enjoyed themselves hugely, to Rowlands's great delight. Somehow she found the strength to board the ship for New York. Eleanor met her and cared for her until she could travel to Richmond and Dr. McGuire. Peggy believed this was the point at which Daisy asked him point-blank to tell her how long she had left to live. "Not long" was all he could truthfully say.[43]

She made her way to Savannah, to the Low home on Lafayette Square, where the carriage house echoed with the laughter of so many happy Girl Scouts. On December 7, 1926, Daisy cabled to Girl Scout headquarters, "I have been very ill . . ." to explain her silence to those girls who had sent her birthday cards and holiday greetings. The executive committee hurried off a telegram, lovingly reminding her, "You are the best Girl Scout as well as the first in this country."[44]

The family gathered. Mabel came from England, Eleanor from New Jersey. Mary sent flowers and a telegram. On January 16, 1927, Daisy wrote her last letter, a note of thanks to her dear Venus: "How nice it is, to believe we may meet in the future, for Mary we have loved each other many years, and our love will always endure after death." The next afternoon, Monday, January 17, at peace with herself and the world, Juliette Gordon Low died.[45]

EPILOGUE

"Long Live the Girl Scouts!"

On Tuesday, January 18, 1927, Savannah's Girl Scouts were released from school at one o'clock to witness their founder's last journey. An honor guard stood at attention on the sidewalk leading from her front door and preceded the casket into Christ Church as the choir sang "Lead, Kindly Light." "There was the most wonderful sense of peace and all felt her spirit," Girl Scout executive Inez Oliveros recalled. After the candlelit service, 250 Girl Scouts lined the path as mourners started toward Laurel Grove Cemetery. Five young women wearing the Golden Eaglet arranged flowers around the grave as Daisy Gordon Low was laid to rest in her Girl Scout uniform. Her tombstone read, from 1 Corinthians 13, "Now abideth faith, hope, and love, but the greatest of these is love."[1]

Encomiums poured in, as friends and strangers tried to express their loss and admiration. "There was nobody like her," Rudyard Kipling wrote, summing up the sentiments of all who knew her. Daisy's "superb courage" lifted her past her struggles, especially the hearing impairment that was her constant companion. Only those very near to her could appreciate how maddening she found her inability to hear. Abby Lippitt Hunter, whose sister was profoundly deaf, did understood the struggle and the centrality of sacrifice for her friend: "Her life was so really wonderful, in the way she turned from her own suffering and put her heart and soul to something of lasting good for the rising generation whom she understood and loved."[2] The "Crazy Daisy" role from her youth was burnished until it helped her become a pied piper for girls seeking sprees. She had that quality of carrying others along with her own enthusiasm, that "gift," her nephew Rowland Leigh described, "of turning the most commonplace experience into an adventure."[3] As they explored Egypt together, Eleanor Nash came to see that for Daisy "life was really the Great Adventure." "She savored its flavor to the fullest, and through her keen enjoyment of it she enabled others to taste of it with her."[4]

Daisy Low led the girls of America to great deeds because she believed in them. She also had a clear vision and the purity of heart that comes from unreserved commitment to her mission. "There is something very fine in her devotion to her work and with the disadvantages under which she has worked it has taken not only brains but character to stick to it and make it a success," her sister Mabel Leigh acknowledged.[5]

Young women followed Daisy because of what her brother Arthur called her "craving to be of use to others" and her excellent sense of fun.[6] "No one was 'better company' than she," Rose Kerr attested, perhaps because of what Kipling called her utter disregard for convention when it interfered with fun.[7] That quality enabled her to launch the most important movement for girls in American history. "That is all I have done," she claimed modestly. "I took the first step, and we are all marching on now to great achievements."[8] Daisy credited her coworkers and cherished the "sterling and true friends" whom she "found in our Girl Scout's sisterhood," but it was her perspicacity that put them in place.[9] Arthur—the sibling most unlike her in his logical, precise thinking—provided a fitting eulogy: "And so she had the joy which comes to so few; a dream come true; a vision realized; a visible proof that the happiness she passionately desired for them was actually being brought, not only to American girls, but to those of the nations scattered to the four corners of the earth."[10]

From such small beginnings in Savannah, the Girl Scouts have grown to encompass 3.2 million girls and 880,000 adult volunteers on the eve of their one-hundred-year anniversary. Since Juliette Gordon Low first transplanted Girl Guiding across the Atlantic, 50 million American girls and women have been members of the Girl Scouts. The organization has endured because Daisy's vision—of fun, of duty, of service, and of sisterhood—was contagious. Remaining flexible but listening to what the girls wanted has helped Girl Scouting remain relevant to girls in every generation. The volunteer ethos of the Girl Scouts encouraged a positive response in times of national crisis. Troops provided relief to local communities during the Great Depression and collected scrap metal during World War II. The leaders of the organization publicly supported the quest for civil rights, proposed environmental programs to raise members' awareness of pollution, and, through membership in the World Association of Girl Guides and Girl Scouts, retained Daisy's internationalist vision.

While girls today can pursue "interest project awards" on child care, family life, and sewing, the majority of earned awards stress career preparation, environmental awareness, global understanding, money management, and political consciousness. Camping remains central to Girl Scouting. Working together to solve problems is a stated goal, but leadership opportunities have drawn extraordinary women to Girl Scouting over the years, including Hillary and Chelsea Clinton, Jackie Joyner-Kersee, Lucille Ball, Elizabeth Dole, Linda Chavez-Thompson, Mariah Carey, Joyce Brothers, Rosalynn Carter, Rachael Ray, Sandra Day O'Connor, Wynonna Judd, Nancy Lopez, Barbara Walters, Condoleezza Rice, Ann Landers, Sally Ride, and Gloria Steinem.

When Daisy Gordon was Girl Scout age, she had tried to do a good deed by making clothing for the immigrants in the Helpful Hands Club. She lacked a compassionate adult to act as a guide. In her early twenties, she had to plan and oversee a dinner for her father in her mother's absence. Daisy recalled that she didn't know whether shrimp and crab were bought by the dozen or by the pound, and had no idea how to calculate how much to purchase, anyway. About such domestic matters she was, she confessed, "terribly puzzled and frightened."[11] When her marriage fell apart, Daisy did not have a career to fall back on. She had sisters and friends and nieces, and by the time she was widowed, she knew that her experiences were not unique. Girl Scouting supplied the education and understanding necessary to provide useful information and more opportunities for young women, with an emphasis on fun and room for civic duty. Creating the Girl Scouts might not have been an easily predictable part of Daisy Gordon's future, but it was a goal she reached with the wisdom of middle age.

In a handwritten draft of a speech prepared only five years after Girl Scouting began, Daisy Low could have written her own farewell oration: "[W]hen I started I was for two years almost alone. I had to use the tools that were in my hand. . . . I am perfectly astonished at the result. . . . [E]ven with the handicap of having no good textbooks and no definitive fixed training . . . [and] in spite of my shortcomings we have grown and flourished. Thanks to the solid merits of Girl Scout laws and to the whole heartedness of the captains and leaders who have taken up this work and I say with all my heart, Long Live Girl Scouts!"[12]

Acknowledgments

Juliette Gordon Low initially captured my attention four decades ago when I was a Brownie in Michigan. Later, with my best friend, Helen Ann Holmes, I recall listening breathlessly as our Girl Scout leader—whose name I have, alas, long ago forgotten—told us in greater detail about Daisy Low and all she had accomplished. The riveting story of her deafness remained with me. I was struck that Daisy had created, seemingly from nothing, the very organization I cherished. From my mother's tenderly preserved uniform I knew that the Girl Scouts had a history stretching back far before I fell in love with my bright orange Brownie handbook. Many years after I had carefully packed away my own Girl Scout uniform, I sought, as a graduate student at the University of Texas, to write my dissertation about Daisy Low and the Girl Scouts. For various reasons that did not work out, but I never forgot the woman of indomitable spirit I first learned about in that Brownie circle when I was young. It is my great pleasure now to thank all those who helped me finally realize this biography of Juliette Low.

Historians depend on primary sources, and to access them we rely on archivists. I am particularly indebted to the phenomenal staff at the Georgia Historical Society, who work with Director Nora Lewis: Lynette Stoudt, Alison Bentley, Nancy Birkheimer, Elizabeth Delmage, John Dickinson, Rana Edgar, Jenna Schrengohst, and

Lindsay Sheldo. At Cornell University, a whole host of cheerful professionals made my experience there memorable: Ana Guimaraes, M. J. Eleanor Brown, David W. Corson, Evan Fay Earle, Elaine D. Engst, Eileen E. Keating, Laura M. Linke, Brenda J. Marston, Margaret F. Nichols, and Eisha Prather. My thanks go also to Tim West and the University of North Carolina's Wilson Library staff, who were similarly helpful. Tim Engels and Holly Snyder, Special Collections, John Hay Library, Brown University; and Karen Eberhart, Rhode Island Historical Society, answered questions about their holdings, which I appreciated very much. Pat Styles, in the Archives & Heritage Department, Gilwell Park, Chingford, London; and Lynda Leahy, at the Arthur and Elizabeth Schlesinger Library on the History of Women in America, Radcliffe Institute for Advanced Study, were nice enough to send me pertinent materials.

No biography of Juliette Low could be complete without consulting the papers held by the Girl Scouts themselves. Pamela Cruz, director, and archivist Yevgeniya Gribov, at the National Historic Preservation Center in New York City, were hospitable and solicitous. Just like Karen Taylor Stapley at Girlguiding UK in London, they threw open their archives and welcomed me warmly. Jami Brantley at the Girl Scouts of Historic Georgia, Inc., in Savannah allowed me to look at relevant papers there.

Fran Harold is the director of the Juliette Gordon Low Birthplace in Savannah, and Katherine Knapp Keena is the program director. I am greatly obliged to them both for allowing me access to their important documents. Katherine Keena granted me research space in her office, where her insights were the true treasures. Indeed, this book would not have been possible without Katherine's tactful, objective, and constant help. I am exceedingly grateful to Fran Harold, Katherine Keena, James Varnadoe, Jeb Bush, and all the staff in Savannah.

There are many experts to whom I owe a tremendous debt for the wisdom they shared with me on specific topics: Father John Horn, the Episcopal Church of the U.S.A.; Richard Sidell, Saint James Episcopal Church, Chicago; Virginia Krumholz, the Episcopal Diocese of Ohio; Cathy and Cecilia Fasano, Girl Scouting today; Nicky Pearson, the Jockey Club; Judith Potter, Meggernie Outdoor Centre; Jim Parish, the history of Morley, Derbyshire; Jonathan Tunnell, Lude House; photographer Colin Wilson, Perthshire; Mike Hanlon, World War I trench candles; Todd Howard, partridges in Georgia; Lynn Miller, art and Daisy Low; Lieutenant Rebecca A. Rickey, USN, and Dr. Edward Marolda, U.S. naval yards; Gail Parnell, Georgia National Guard uniforms; Professor Lisa Gitelman, shorthand; Tim Trager, grand orchestrions; Ann Robbins, deaf culture; and Elizabeth E. Cogswell, the Governor Henry Lippitt House.

I am lucky to work with exceptionally competent faculty colleagues at Monmouth College, who gave munificently of their knowledge: classicist Thomas J. Sienkewicz, Latin translations; physicist Christopher Fasano, radium's effect on health; psychology professor Kristin Larson, why women choose unsuitable men; chemists Brad Sturgeon and Eric Todd, morphine dosages; English professors Rob Hale and Mark Willhardt, British literature; and art department members Brian Baugh on art history, Stacy Lotz on female metalworkers, Cheryl Meeker on pottery, and Mary Phillips on art history. Rick Sayre and Rose Dillard of the Hewes Library again provided matchless support while Lynn Daw and Lauren Jensen proved once more to be superlative sleuths. Thanks to Andrea Crum for logistical assistance of the highest level.

To my historian colleagues far and wide I owe a special debt for sharing their expertise. These generous people include Douglas Baynton, Peter and Rosalind Bolton, Stan Deaton, Lewis L. Gould, Brian Hosmer, Richard B. McCaslin, Susan Miller, Tammy Proctor, Steven Reschly, Nancy Beck Young, and especially Dan Weinbren, who, magicianlike, with his fellow British historian Simon Cordery, amassed quantities of information on the mysterious Anna Bateman. Ongoing thanks to my talented women's history group: Tina Brakebill, Kyle Ciani, Sandra Harmon, Debbi McGregor, Monica Noraian, Stacey Robertson, and April Schultz. I am likewise indebted to members of my department at Monmouth College, fellow historians Tom Best, Amy Caldwell de Farias, Simon Cordery, Tim Lacy, Bill Urban, and Fred Witzig.

I benefited from the research assistance of three able women: Hope Grebner and Anne Skilton, who wielded fast cameras, and Paige Halpin, who scoured a Savannah newspaper. Nelson Block; Captain Todd Creekman, USN (Ret.); Milly Hawk Daniel; Beryl Diamond, USA NGGA TAG; Karina Gee; Patricia Lyons; Leah Price; and Meghan Seki helped me connect with pertinent sources while Alisa Corsi, Jan Speer, and Nancy Beck Young provided valuable documents.

For ungrudging time to sprint to the finish, I would like to thank the amazing team at the Theodore Roosevelt Center at Dickinson State University, where I was welcomed as a visiting fellow: Clay Jenkinson, Sharon Kilzer, Krystal Thompson, Grant Carlson, Jennifer Berry, Amy Shroyer, and DSU president Richard McCallum. I am also grateful to them for their encouragement concerning this book, and to Pattie Carr, David Meier, Karen Nelson, Deb Dragseth, Jim McWilliams, Suzanne Russ, and Frank Varney, as well.

It would be difficult to overstate the salutary countereffect that readers of my blog, www.stacycordery.com, have had on the generally lonely process of writing. I sincerely appreciate those kind people who comment, cheer, and follow my blog.

Experts at the places connected with Daisy Low's life granted me invaluable information, particularly Susanna E. Prull at the Lippitt House, Larry Smith at Hyde Hall, and Stephen Bohlin at the Andrew Low House. Douglas Kent's friendship with Anne Hyde Clarke Choate gave him a unique understanding of Mary Gale Carter Clarke that was critical to my interpretation. The unselfish help from five people in Warwickshire, England, with an intimate acquaintance of Wellesbourne—Anne Eccles, Tony Hanson, Peter and Rosalind Bolton, and most especially Clive Hanley—brought a keen joy to this project.

Savannah has been like a second home to me because of the kindness of many people there, including Stan Deaton, Katherine Keena, Patti Lyons, and Preston and Barbara Russell. Roger Smith and Kevin Peek hosted me in their beautiful home on several research trips, and the extent of their warmth and generosity still leaves me humbled.

I continue to pinch myself in disbelief that Sterling Lord is my agent and Wendy Wolf is my editor. Their counsel and support have opened doors I did not know existed. I would like to express my gratitude also to Mary Krienke at Sterling Lord Literistic, and Margaret Riggs and Carolyn Coleburn, Sonya Cheuse and Maggie Payette at Viking for their vision.

All writers know the value of trusted associates who will be unsparing in their criticism of the book manuscript. Paige Halpin and Mary Lou Pease provided initial feedback. Karen Cates, Simon Cordery, Hope Grebner, Katherine Keena, and Roger Smith read each page, and their thoughtful comments made the book immeasurably better.

Friends and relatives exhibited tremendous patience throughout this process and in so doing bestowed on me the priceless gift of time. I am fortunate to have such people in my life as Paula Barnes, Karen Cates, Mary Cordery, Ned Cordery, Karen Gould, Lewis L. Gould, Robert T. Grimm, Paige Halpin, Clay Jenkinson, Krissi Jimroglou, Sharon Kilzer, Kristie Miller, Danielle Nierenberg, Paula Nuckles, Mary Lou Pease, Steve Reschly, Jim Rozek, Anne Sienkewicz, Tom Sienkewicz, Eloise Spurgeon, Nancy St. Ledger, Carolyn Suda, Bill Urban, Jackie Urban, and Kathy Wagoner.

My deepest debt of all is to my family, who made the biggest sacrifices, cheering me on all the while. It is an awe-filled adventure to have a son like Gareth Cordery. It is an extraordinary gift to share this life with a partner like Simon Cordery. I could not have done this book without their tender care.

Notes

Abbreviations

ALH—Abby Frances Lippitt Hunter
APL—Abby Porter Leland
EGP—Eleanor Gordon Parker
GHC—George Hyde Clarke
GAG—George Arthur Gordon
JRC—Jane Russell Carter
JGL—Juliette Gordon Low
JDR—Jane Deeter Rippin
MGC—Mary Gale Carter Clarke
MGL—Mabel Gordon Leigh
NKG—Nellie Kinzie Gordon
OBP—Olave Baden-Powell
RBP—Robert Baden-Powell
RWP—Richard Wayne Parker
SAG—S. Alice Gordon
WML—William Mackay Low
WWGII—William Washington Gordon II
WWGIII—William Washington Gordon III
CFP—Clarke Family Papers, Cornell University Special Collections, Ithaca, New York
GFP—Gordon Family Papers, Southern Historical Collection, Wilson Library, University of North Carolina at Chapel Hill
GGHUK—Girlguiding Headquarters, London, United Kingdom
GHS—Georgia Historical Society, Savannah, Georgia
JGLB—Juliette Gordon Low Birthplace, Savannah, Georgia
NHPC—National Historic Preservation Center, Girl Scouts of the U.S.A. National Headquarters, New York City

Chapter 1: Civil War and the Problem of Loyalties

1. Sherman to Ellen Sherman, June 12, 1864, in M. A. DeWolfe Howe, ed., *Home Letters of General Sherman* (New York: Charles Scribner's Sons, 1909), 298. Anne Hyde Choate and Helen Ferris, eds., *Juliette Low and the Girl Scouts* (New York: GSUSA, 1928), 4. A variant on this story comes from NKG, who wrote in 1914 that the men in her drawing room that day were General Howard and his chief of staff, William Strong—not Sherman, although Sherman did call at the Gordons' home. NKG to *Ladies Home Journal*, November 25, 1914, GHS MS318/7/81.
2. Gladys Denny Shultz and Daisy Gordon Lawrence, *Lady from Savannah: The Life of Juliette Low* (Philadelphia: J. B. Lippincott, 1958), 87. William W. Gordon quoted in Anne J. Bailey, *War and Ruin* (Wilmington, DE: Scholarly Resources, 2003), 113.
3. Information on the Gordon men comes from Charles J. Johnson, Jr., "William Washington Gordon," Savannah Portraits, and "Background Information: General William Washington Gordon II," both from GHS Bio File—Gordon; from *The Register of Graduates and Former Cadets of the United States Military Academy, West Point, New York* (West Point, NY: Association of Graduates, USMA, 2005): 91; and from Paul Pressly, "The Northern Roots of Savannah's Antebellum Elite, 1780s–1850s," *Georgia Historical Quarterly* 87, no. 2 (Summer 2003): 157–200. On the railroad, see Richard E. Prince, *Central of Georgia Railway and Connecting Lines* (Salt Lake City: Stanway-Wheelwright, 1976).
4. NKG Memoirs, GHS MS318/13/131.
5. NKG's quote: Shultz and Lawrence, 54; George L. Miller, "Bishop Clarkson," *Transactions and Reports*, Nebraska State Historical Society, 1885: http://digitalcommons.unl.edu/cgi/viewcontent.cgi?article=1054&context=nebhisttrans. The Reverend Robert H. Clarkson performed the marriage ceremony.
6. Shultz and Lawrence, 60, 61.
7. Shultz and Lawrence, 61.
8. Adelaide Wilson, *Historic and Picturesque Savannah* (Boston: Boston Photogravure Company, 1889), 190; Shultz and Lawrence, 63.
9. Shultz and Lawrence, 63, 65.
10. Shultz and Lawrence, 66.
11. Shultz and Lawrence, 67, 68.
12. Roger K. Warlick, *As Grain Once Scattered* (Columbia, SC: The State Printing Company, 1987), 85. Warlick stresses that Elliott was a "zealot." "Georgia expects every man to do his duty" may or may not have been from the homily Nellie and Willie heard that day, but Elliott's sermons and charitable works were strongly pro-Confederacy. Mary D. Robertson, ed., "Northern Rebel: The Journal of Nellie Kinzie Gordon, Savannah, 1862," *Georgia Historical Quarterly* 70, no. 3 (Fall 1986): 479.
13. Family finances, WWGII to NKG, June 11, 1861; diet, WWGII to NKG, June 6, 1861; "I love you," WWGII to NKG, June 17, 1861; "Kiss," June 18, 1861, all from GHS MS318/1/5. Gordon's unit was Company E, Sixth Virginia Regular Cavalry from October through December 1861. On December 13, they became Company F of the Jeff Davis Legion until the end of the war. A. McC. Duncan, *Roll of Officers and Members of the Georgia Hussars* (Savannah: The Morning News Printer [no date]), 35, 232.

14. To Manassas, WWGII to Sarah A. Gordon, October 15, 1861; "God bless you," WWGII to NKG, October 22, 1861, both GHS MS318/1/5.
15. NKG to WWGII, May 10 (1861), GHS MS318/1/5.
16. EKG Civil War Diary, January 16, 1862, GHS MS318/12/125 (hereafter cited as EKG CWD).
17. EKG CWD, April 6 [1862]; War Department Order in Edward A. Miller, Jr., *Lincoln's Abolitionist General* (Columbia: University of South Carolina Press, 1997), 96; "disgraceful," EKG CWD, May 4, 1862.
18. Miller, 98–102.
19. EKG CWD, [no date] [1862], GHS MS318/12/125. Most of EKG's Civil War Diary is undated, but she kept the journal between January and November 1862. Bishop Elliott, Warlick, 85.
20. EKG CWD, May 25 and June 1, 1862.
21. "Willie's open enemy," EKG CWD, May 25, 1862; "buckets of filth," EKG CWD, September 28, 1862. "Obituary: Henry Huntington Wolcott," *New York Times*, September 30, 1890.
22. EKG CWD, February 8 [1862]; WWGII to Sarah A. Gordon, April 2, 1862, GHS MS318/1/6.
23. "Violent fit of grief," EKG CWD, June 8, 1862; "The Southerners," EKG CWD, May 4, 1862.
24. WWGII to NKG, May 12, 1862, GHS MS318/1/6; for the retreat, see John Brown Gordon, *Reminiscences of the Civil War* (New York: Charles Scribner's Sons, 1903), chap. 4.
25. EKG CWD, July 6, 1862; Charles W. Stewart, ed., *Official Records of the Union and Confederate Navies in the War of the Rebellion,* ser. 1, vol. 23 (Washington, DC: U.S. Government Printing Office, 1910), 180; Edwin C. Bearss, "The White River Expedition, June 10–July 16, 1862," *Arkansas Historical Quarterly* 21, no. 4 (Winter 1962): 324–27.
26. EKG CWD, August 14, 1862, and September 21, 1862.
27. Assessment of Yankees, WWGII to NKG, October 2, 1862, GHS MS318/1/6; Daisy's speech, NKG to WWGII, October 12, 1862; money from father, WWGII to NKG, October 2, 1862; both GHS MS318/1/6.
28. NKG to WWGII, October 12, 1862, GHS MS318/1/6.
29. George A. Mercer to WWGII, January 9, 1863, GHS MS3181/7.
30. Meritorious service, Robertson, ed., 513; WWGII to NKG, September 4, 1864, GHS MS318/1/9; "Background Information on General William Washington Gordon II," from GHS BioFile: W. W. Gordon II; n.a., "Brigadier-General William Washington Gordon, U.S.V.," [no date] GHS MS318/11/121.
31. Juliette Kinzie to NKG, October 24, 1864, GHS MS318/1/9; William O. Bryant, *Cahaba Prison and the Sultana Disaster* (Tuscaloosa: University of Alabama Press, 2001).
32. Quotes from NKG's letters, WWGII to NKG, August 20, 1864, GHS MS318/1/9, and NKG to WWGII, March 5, 1863, GHS MS318/1/7; Eleanor Gordon Parker, "My Little Sister," in Choate and Ferris, 12; Joe A. Mobley, *Weary of War* (Westport, CT: Praeger Press, 2008), 134; Anya Jabour, *Topsy-Turvy* (Chicago: Ivan R. Dee, 2010), 90–95.
33. "Sad and strange," Juliette Kinzie to NKG, February 19, 1864, GHS MS318/1/8; "plenty of," NKG to WWGII, October 21, 1864, GHS MS318/1/9; "skirmishing," WWGII to NKG, June 22, 1864, GHS MS318/1/8.

34. Existence of a Union League, Bailey, 111; "whip," Brooks D. Simpson and Jean V. Berlin, eds., *Selected Correspondence of Sherman's Civil War* (Chapel Hill: University of North Carolina Press, 1999), 760; "sumptuously," Howe, 318.
35. "An Act to Authorize a Levy En Masse of the Population of Georgia for the Protection of Its Liberty and Independence," November 18, 1864, pp. 13–14; and Proclamation, November 19, 1864, p. 15, reprinted in Charles C. Jones, Jr., *The Siege of Savannah* (Albany, NY: Joel Munsell, 1874). P. T. Beauregard to the People of Georgia, November 18, 1864, in Lamont, et. al., *The War of the Rebellion*, ser. 1, vol. 44, 867.
36. Defense of Savannah: N. C. Hughes, "Hardee's Defense of Savannah," *Georgia Historical Quarterly* 47 (Spring 1963): 43–67; Charles C. Jones, Jr., *The Siege of Savannah* (Albany, NY: Joel Munsell, 1874), 75; Roger S. Durham, *Guardian of Savannah* (Columbia: University of South Carolina Press, 2008), xiv (for "guardian" quote) and chaps. 9 and 10; and Bailey 105–6.
37. NKG to WWGII, December 20, 1864, GHS MS318/1/9; Nathaniel C. Hughes, Jr., *General William J. Hardee* (Baton Rouge: Louisiana State University Press, 1965), 267; Report of W. T. Sherman, December 22, 1864, and W. T. Sherman to A. Lincoln, December 22, 1864, in Lamont, et al, *The War of the Rebellion*, ser. 1, vol. 44, 7, 783.
38. Gideon Welles, *Diary of Gideon Welles,* vol. 2 (Boston: Houghton Mifflin Company, 1909), 209, 220. N. C. Hughes, in "Hardee's Defense of Savannah," states that there were 35,000 bales of cotton, and that they were distributed throughout the city, and thus it was impossible for Hardee to gather them up and burn them before Sherman reached Savannah. (Hughes's article in *Georgia Historical Quarterly* 47 [Spring 1963]: 59.) The worth of the cotton was estimated by F. D. Lee and J. L. Agnew in *Historical Record of the City of Savannah* (Savannah: J. H. Estill, 1869), 101. For the Gordons' part, see Shultz and Lawrence, 95.
39. NKG to WWGII, December 20, 1864, GHS MS318/1/9.
40. Juliette Kinzie to NKG, December 7, 1864, GHS MS318/1/9.
41. For Green and Low, "From Savannah," *New York Times,* January 30, 1864; Howe, ed., 319–20. Stanton quote, *Diary of Gideon Welles,* vol. 2, 228. Entry dated January 21, 1865.
42. See the reminiscence of Mrs. Peter Meldrim in John P. Dyer, "Northern Relief for Savannah During Sherman's Occupation," *Journal of Southern History* 19, no. 4 (November 1953): 7. Sherman quote, William Tecumseh Sherman, *Memoirs of General W. T. Sherman* (New York: Penguin, 1990 [1875]), 716.
43. Lightest hand, Simpson and Berlin, 760; Arnold quoted in Dyer, 460.
44. NKG to WWGII, December 29, 1864, GHS MS318/1/9; Bailey, 114.
45. "I pray," WWGII to NKG, June 19, 1864, GHS MS318/1/8; conversion, WWGII to NKG, August 10, 1864, and August 13, 1864, GHS MS318/1/9. WWGII to SAG, August 17, 1864, GHS MS318/1/9. Willie continued to attend the Presbyterian church when Nellie was out of town.
46. "Annihiliating Sherman," WWGII to NKG, July 14, 1864, GHS MS318/1/8; "galls me," Robertson, ed., 514.
47. Shultz and Lawrence, 88. The best analysis of NKG during the war comes from Carolyn J. Stefanco, "Poor Loving Prisoners of War," in *Enemies of the Country*, John C. Inscoe and Robert C. Kenzer, eds. (Athens: University of Georgia Press, 2001), 148–71; "tearing my heart out," Bailey, 122–23.
48. Shultz and Lawrence, 88–89.

Chapter 2: A Savannah Childhood

1. Friend's quote and "delirium" from Juliette Low, "When I Was a Girl," in Anne Hyde Choate and Helen Ferris, eds., *Juliette Low and the Girl Scouts* (New York: Girl Scouts, 1928), 5; indulging Daisy from Gladys Denny Shultz and Daisy Gordon Lawrence, *Lady from Savannah: The Life of Juliette Low* (Philadelphia: J. B. Lippincott, 1958), 89; NKG to WWGII, March 16, 1865, GHS MS318/1/10. Mrs. John H. Kinzie, *Wau-bun: The "Early Day" in the Northwest* (Chicago: D. B. Cooke & Co., 1857). The book is now online in its entirety: http://www.gutenberg.org/etext/12183.
2. *History of Chicago* (Chicago: Chicago Historical Publishing Company, 1889), n.p. (4). According to Ulrich Danckers and Jane Meredith, *A Compendium of the Early History of Chicago* (River Forest, IL: Early Chicago, Inc., 2000), 219, the land itself belonged to the U.S. federal government, because of the 1795 Treaty of Greenville, which "the Chicago area Potawatomi did not recognize. They gave the land to Kinzie as a gift on November 4, 1806. Title to the land from the United States was not acquired until 1830." The cabin was built around 1785. However, according to Alfred Theodore Andreas, *History of Chicago*, vol. 1 (Chicago: A. T. Andreas, 1884), 72, Kinzie bought the cabin from the trader LeMai in 1804.
3. For his brief slave trading, see Bessie Louise Pierce, *A History of Chicago,* vol. 1 (New York: Alfred A. Knopf, 1937), 18–19. He apparently owned Jeffrey Nash. For the trade with Native Americans, see John D. Haeger, "The American Fur Company and the Chicago of 1812–1835," *Journal of the Illinois State Historical Society* 61, no. 2 (Summer 1968): 120; *History of Chicago,* n.p. (4).

   Milo M. Quaife, "Documents: The Chicago Treaty of 1833," *Wisconsin Magazine of History* 1, no. 1 (September 1917): 297, 300–302; *History of Chicago,* n.p. (5), states that Kinzie killed John Lalime, an Indian interpreter popular with soldiers and Native Americans, in self-defense. Indian friends of Kinzie's moved him to Milwaukee, where he stayed "until the facts were known." Then Kinzie returned to Chicago, and eventually Lalime's allies ceased their threats against Kinzie and the "officers of the fort," and handed down a verdict of "justifiable homicide" (n.p. [5]). The best source on John Kinzie is John F. Swenson's essay, "John H. Kinzie," in Danckers and Meredith, 220–25. See also Mentor L. Williams, "John Kinzie's Narrative of the Fort Dearborn Massacre," *Illinois State Historical Society Journal* 46 (Winter 1953): 343–62.
4. "Inexplicable," Eleanor Lytle Kinzie Gordon, *John Kinzie: "The Father of Chicago"* (Eleanor Kinzie Gordon, 1910), 28. At the Fort Dearborn massacre, friend of the family Black Partridge, a Potawatomi chief, personally saved Margaret Kinzie's life. He may have been acting on his own, out of respect for Kinzie. Four other houses, Haeger, 132, 136; "rich" in real estate, Gordon, *John Kinzie*, 29; "Father of Chicago," John Wentworth, "Lecture Before the Sunday Lecture Society," May 7, 1876, in Mabel McIlvaine, ed., *Reminiscences of Early Chicago* (Chicago: Lakeside Press/R. R. Donnelley & Sons, 1912), 70.
5. Language skills, Shultz and Lawrence, 29.
6. Shultz and Lawrence, 31–32, state that Juliette Magill graduated from Troy Seminary. *Mrs. Emma Willard and Her Pupils, or Fifty Years of Troy Female Seminary 1822–1872* (New York: Mrs. Russell Sage, 1898), does not list Juliette Magill among the institution's graduates. It is likely that Juliette Magill

attended earlier schools of Willard's, either the Middlebury Female Seminary (opened in 1814) or the Waterford Academy (opened in New York in 1819). For the Kinzie home in Wisconsin, see Bertha A. Holbrook, "The Old Indian Agency House at Portage," *Wisconsin Magazine of History* 29, no. 1 (September 1945), 32–42.

John Harris, Ellen Marion Wolcott, Maria Hunter, and Robert Allen Kinzie received $5,000 each, which would be worth approximately $130,000 in 2008 dollars. "Articles of a Treaty, Made at Chicago, . . . 26 September 1833," *Public Statutes at Large of the U.S.A.*, vol. 7 (Boston: Charles C. Little and James Brown, 1846), p. 438, http://memory.loc.gov/ammem/amlaw/lwsllink.html. Haeger, 136, states that the money probably went to pay debts. According to Andreas, the Potawatomi gave $3,500 to the widow Eleanor Kinzie "in consideration of the attachment of the Indians to her deceased husband, who was long an Indian trader, and who lost a large sum in the trade, by the credits given them, and also by the destruction of his property," Andreas, 76.

7. Jacob Houghton, Jr., and T. W. Bristol, *Reports of William A. Burt and Bela Hubbard, Esqs., on the Geography, Topology, and Geology of the . . . South Shore of Lake Superior for 1845* (Detroit: Charles Willcox, 1846), 94. Kinzie owned 2,000 shares in a Michigan copper mine. See also William L. Downard, "William Butler Ogden and the Growth of Chicago," *Journal of the Illinois State Historical Society* 75, no. 1 (Spring 1982), 50.
8. Bessie Louise Pierce, *A History of Chicago,* vol. 1 (New York: Alfred A. Knopf, 1937), 229. Background on J. H. Kinzie's affiliations from Pierce and Andreas. The quote of the Reverend William F. Walter (rector 1843–1844) is from Rima Lunin Schultz, *The Church and the City* (Chicago: The Cathedral of Saint James, 1986), 25; the Orphan Benevolent Society manager is from Schultz, 46.
9. "Republican Meeting," *Chicago Tribune*, October 24, 1857; "Our Cairo Letter," *Chicago Tribune,* July 24, 1861.
10. EGP, "My Little Sister," in Choate and Ferris, 15–16.
11. Harriet Martineau, *Society in America*, vol. 1 (London: Saunders and Otley, 1837), 353, 354.
12. Shultz and Lawrence, 64.
13. Shultz and Lawrence, 95. Nellie won her appeal to the federal government and was awarded $3,013.27 for the cotton. After the attorney's fees, she kept $1,456. 42. See Barlow, Larocque & MacFarland to WWGII, December 23, 1873, GHS MS318/2/27.
14. Mistrust, NKG to WWGII, June 21, 1865, GHS MS318/1/10; "Pardon me," Shultz and Lawrence, 100.
15. Willie quotes, Shultz and Lawrence, 93–94; "Daisy says," Sarah Gordon to WWGII, June 11, 1865, GHS MS318/1/10.
16. Tatnalls and "no money," WWGII to Sarah Gordon, June 21, 1865 and Sarah Gordon to WWGII in June 11, 1865; "poor indeed," WWGII to Sarah Gordon, June 23, 1865; China, David Oliphant to WWGII, June 16, 1865; and Sarah Gordon to WWGII, July 5, 1865, all from GHS MS318/1/10.
17. "Do not write cruelly" and "$60.00," NKG to WWGII, June 21, 1865; "money enough," WWGII to Sarah Gordon, June 21, 1865, both GHS MS318/1/10. For the pardon, see Jonathan T. Dorris, *Pardon and Amnesty Under Lincoln and Johnson* (Chapel Hill: University of North Carolina Press, 1953), 110–11.

18. George A. Gordon to WWGII, April 26, 1866; NKG to WWGII, July 13, 1886, both GHS MS318/1/11.
19. WWGII Diary, August 4, 1865, GHS MS 318/11; NKG to WWGII, July 13, 1866, both GHS MS318/1/11. JGL quoted in Shultz and Lawrence, 113.
20. Shultz and Lawrence, 107–8.
21. GAG, "As Her Family Knew Her," in Choate and Ferris, 39, 41–42; "extraordinary intuition," GAG, "Address by G. Arthur Gordon," April 30, 1955, NHPC, JGL Gen'l Info-Pubs.
22. Eleanor and the dolls, EGP, in Choate and Ferris, 14; GAG, "As Her Family Knew Her," in Choate and Ferris, 43–44.
23. "New Victor Record," GHS MS318, box 35, item 5636.
24. Sarah Josepha Hale to NKG, November 24, 1866, GHS MS318/1/11. Nellie's aunt Maria Indiana Kinzie (her father's sister) married General David Hunter. His brother, Dr. Hunter, married Sarah Josepha Hale's daughter.
25. "Excellent factors," Charles C. Jones, Jr., to Mary Jones, December 3, 1866, in Robert Manson Myers, ed., *The Children of Pride* (New Haven, CT: Yale University Press, 1972), 1364. Cotton production figures from the New Georgia Encyclopedia online, http://www.georgiaencyclopedia.org/nge/Article.jsp?id=h-2533. Tison and Mrs. Davis, Lizzie Cary Daniel, *A Confederate Scrapbook* (Richmond: J. L. Hill Printing Company, 1893), 49. NKG to WWGII, [no date] GHS MS318/42/11.
26. For NKG as go-between, see, for example, NKG to WWGII, July 21, 1866, GHS MS318/1/11. "I wish," NKG to WWGII, November 7, 1865, GHS MS318/42/10; "sleeping," NKG to WWGII, November 12, 1865, GHS MS318/1/10; "do not apologize," NKG to WWGII, [no date], GHS MS318/42/11.
27. "Financial ruin," GAG, in Choate and Ferris, 40; for pessimism, see WWGII to George Gordon, December 5, 1865, GHS MS318/1/10, and *Diary of Gideon Welles*, vol. 2, p. 313. For the diary, see WWGII Diary, 1865. The specific sums to the churches were found in 1872, but such donations run throughout the weeks and months of Gordon's diary.
28. Caroline Stiles Lovell, "Twenty Cousins," in Choate and Ferris, 20, 22. See also Eileen Sauer, "Setting the Record Straight," *GS Leader* (September 1976), 32, in NHPC Archives, box JGL—Bio Info to Correspondence 1920.
29. Lovell, "Twenty Cousins," 21; JGL to WWGII, [no date], GFP MS2235/SHC/318. See also EKG to WWGII and NKG, [no date] (1873), GHS MS318/2/27.
30. Lovell, "Twenty Cousins," 23–24; Indian missions, Shultz and Lawrence, 121; Reynard dinner and poetry, from Caroline Couper Lovell, *The Light of Other Days* (Macon, GA: Mercer University Press, 1995). In this remembrance, 87, Lovell called the play with the beheading *Anne of Austria*. Perhaps there was more than one play with that dramatic conclusion.
31. Lovell, *The Light of Other Days*, 30; "Miss L. Blois" was listed as "Teacher, High School," in the 1867 Savannah City Directory, but she probably taught the Gordon girls in her home at 24 Hull Street (Stan Deaton, e-mail to author, November 24, 2009); "weird spelling," Shultz and Lawrence, 118; "conscientious," EGP in Choate and Ferris, 14.
32. Rabbit, SAG to Gulie Stiles, May 24, 1871, GHS MS318/2/27; drowning, Shultz and Lawrence, 108; Lovell, *The Light of Other Days*, 137.
33. GAG, "Address by G. Arthur Gordon," April 30, 1955, NHPC, JGL Gen'l Info-Pubs.

Chapter 3: Schooling in the South and Beyond

1. Preston Russell and Barbara Hines, *Savannah* (Savannah, GA: Frederic C. Beil, 1992), 11–13, 38.
2. "Funereal lichen," Eyre Crowe, *With Thackeray in America* (New York: Charles Scribner's Sons, 1893), 166; Russell and Hines, 132.
3. Christopher Lee Harwell, "William Henry Stiles: Georgia Gentleman-Politician" (Ph.D. dissertation, Emory University, 1959), 339. For Eliza Hendry, see G. Arthur Gordon, "As Her Family Knew Her," in Anne Hyde Choate and Helen Ferris, eds., *Juliette Low* (New York: Girl Scouts, 1928), 46–48.
4. NKG to WWGII, June 23, 1867, GHS MS318/1/12. It is not exactly clear whether Daisy accompanied her mother and siblings to Chicago that year. This might have been the trip intended for fall 1866 to show off Arthur, delayed for some reason.
5. Juliette Kinzie to NKG, November 1 [1868], GHS MS318/2/18. Daisy was born on the eve of All Saints' Day, which is also known as Halloween. All Saints' Day is November 1, so Grandma Kinzie had the date of Daisy's birthday wrong by one day.
6. This mistake happened enough that at least some scientists suggested proposing a law requiring the addition of a mephitic substance to morphine so as to render it obviously different from quinine. See the proceedings of the Mississippi and the Massachusetts state pharmaceutical associations, in John Maisch, ed., *American Journal of Pharmacy*, vol. 57 (1885): 362.
7. Lee's endorsement: 1873–1874 Advertisement for VFI in *Virginia University Magazine* 11, no. 7 (April 1873), 409. In 1907, VFI was renamed Stuart Hall, in honor of principal Flora Stuart, the wife of WWGII's friend Confederate general J. E. B. Stuart.
8. GAG, "Address by G. Arthur Gordon," April 30, 1955, NHPC, JGL, Gen'l Info-Pubs.
9. DeRenne did gift his West Broad Street mansion and a building on East Broad Street to the Board of Education for the purpose of educating African American children. William Harris Bragg, *DeRenne: Three Generations of a Georgia Family* (Athens: University of Georgia Press, 1999), 125.
10. NKG to SAG, [no date] [c. 1876–1877], GHS MS318/2/28. Nellie was proudest of the brand-new dessert of orange sherbet, served in hollowed-out oranges and tied with a bow. Daisy sat next to DeRenne at this dinner. Hock was a German white wine.
11. JGL, "When I Was a Girl," in Choate and Ferris, 6–7. Daisy recalled founding this club in 1876.
12. JGL to NKG, November 8 [1876], GHS MS318/14/141/#2958.
13. James Johnston Waring, Supplement to the Mayor's Report, January 1, 1879, *The Epidemic at Savannah* (Savannah: Morning News Printing House, 1879), 23; NKG yellow fever diary, GHS MS318/13/132.
14. For the number of people who died, Waring, 23; NKG yellow fever diary; the clerks: Gladys Denny Shultz and Daisy Gordon Lawrence, *Lady from Savannah: The Life of Juliette Low* (Philadelphia: J. B. Lippincott, 1958), 132.
15. WWGII to NKG, October 11, 1876, GHS MS318/2/27.
16. NKG to SAG, May 13 [1876 or 1877], GHS MS318/2/27. Shultz and Lawrence have the Gordon girls back at boarding school in the fall of 1876. Other evi-

dence suggests they did not return until the fall of 1877, nearer to the time Tison died. JGL quote from Low, "When I Was a Girl," 7.

17. Jane Randolph, the granddaughter of Thomas and Martha Jefferson, and her two daughters, Sarah Nichols Randolph and Carrie Randolph, ran Edgehill. JGL to NKG [1874], GHS MS318/14/141 (#2946).
18. "Ladylike" from Winsor Wood, "Daisy's Life," July 2004, Stuart Hall School Web site, http://www.stuart-hall.org/content/view/35/196/. ALH Hunter's essay, "Daisy Goes to Boarding School," in Choate and Ferris, 32, states that at age fourteen Daisy left for Edgehill. After two years there, she studied at "Stewart" Hall for one year, and then went to the Charbonniers school in New York City. Anastasia Sims writes that thirteen-year-old Daisy "spent a few months at a boarding school in New Jersey" before she matriculated at the Virginia schools. See "Late-Blooming Daisy," in *Georgia Women*, Ann Short Chirhart and Betty Wood, eds. (Athens: University of Georgia Press, 2009), 373. Shultz and Lawrence, 121, state that Daisy began "the fall she became thirteen," at Stuart Hall. "I can't be good," JGL to NKG, January 25, 1878, GHS MS318/14/142.
19. JGL to NKG, January 25, 1878, GHS MS318/14/142.
20. JGL to Sarah Gordon, August 7 [no year], JGLB, folder (1868–1877).
21. JGL to NKG, [no date], JGLB.
22. "Guid to Knoledge," JGL to NKG, January 24, 1875: "disappointed in me," JGL to NKG, March 18, 1875, both from GHS MS318/14/141.
23. "Busts," NKG to JGL, December 9, 1877; Bible, JGL to NKG, October 2, 1874, GHS MS318/14/141; "scold me," JGL to NKG, [no date] (#2956), all from GHS MS318/14/141.
24. JGL to NKG, January 13, 1875, GHS MS318/14/141.
25. Miss Burn, JGL to NKG, January 13, 1875; skating, JGL to NKG, February 14, 1875, both from GHS MS318/14/141.
26. JGL to NKG, [no date], GHS MS318/14/141 (#2947) tells the story of the funeral.
27. JGL to NKG, March 11, 1878, GHS MS318/14/142. Theta Tau was a chapter of Alpha Phi founded at Syracuse University in 1871. It is likely that the girls at Daisy's boarding school were aping their elders and created their own—unrelated—version of the women's fraternities becoming more common then.
28. Valentines, JGL to NKG, February 14, 1875; "Lelia Gittings," JGL to NKG, October 2, 1874; "Ida Ewing," JGL to NKG, November 9 [1874], all from GHS MS318/14/141; poem, November 1, 1877, JGLB, box 1, 1868–1882.
29. John Thomas Scharf, *History of Baltimore City and County* (Philadelphia: Louis H. Everts, 1881), 128, 351. Physical description from "Death of Miss Belle Cross," *New York Times*, November 19, 1887. This newspaper article does not state how she died, but it does mention that at the time of her death she had been engaged to the son of Mayor Latrobe of Baltimore. "Shooting a pistol," JGL to Sarah Gordon, December 12, 1877, GHS MS318/14/141; "devoted to her," JGL to NKG, March 17, 1878, GHS MS318/14/142.
30. JGL to NKG, June 22 [1878], GHS MS318/14/142.
31. WWGII to NKG, December 21, 1875, GHS MS318/2/27.
32. Hesba Stretton (Sarah Smith), *Hester Morley's Promise*, vol. 2 (London: Henry S. King & Co., 1873), 2, 4. SAG to Sarah Gordon, January 13, 1878, GHS MS318/3/29.

33. ALH to MGC, March 14 [no year], CFP MS2800/21/8. "Chars" and "Charbs" were used interchangeably in the letters among Daisy and her friends and family.
34. JGL to NKG, September 27, 1878, GHS MS318/14/142.
35. JGL to MGC, October 31, 1905, CFP MS2800/11/15. Daisy was the oldest; Abby was one year younger; Mary, born in 1862, was one year younger than Abby and two years younger than Daisy.
36. Information on the history of the Lippitt family comes from Henry F. Lippitt, *The Lippitt Family* (Los Angeles: Henry F. Lippitt, 1959). For the mills, see Richard M. Bales, ed., *History of Providence County, Rhode Island,* vol. 2 (New York: W. W. Preston, 1891), 306, 307. "The Biographical Cyclopedia of Representative Men of Rhode Island," quoted in Lippitt, *The Lippitt Family*, 9A.
37. Joe died sometime between 1852 and 1855. Henry, George, and Fred died in 1856 of scarlet fever. Thus, the Lippitts endured the loss of four of their six children born before 1856. For Jeanie's life, see Henry F. Lippitt, *Jeanie Lippitt and the Mastery of Silence* (Los Angeles: Henry Lippitt, 1974).
38. Jeanie had the best bedroom in the Lippitt house. See Elizabeth W. A. Cogswell, "The Henry Lippitt House" (master's thesis, University of Delaware, 1981). "Indoor sport," Marian Almy Lippitt, *I Married a New Englander* (Los Angeles: Ward Ritchie Press, 1947), 24–25; tennis, ALH to MGC [August, no year], CFP MS2800/21/13; getting up early, ALH to MGC, letter fragment [no date], CFP MS2800/21/18.
39. Venus de Milo, JGL to MGC, [no date] ("The delay you made" [1880]), CFP MS2800/22/7. "Death of Rev. Lawson Carter," *New York Times*, July 16, 1868. Grace Church later became part of Trinity Cathedral. ALH to MGC, March 20 [no year], CFP MS2800/21/8.
40. *General Alumni Catalogue of New York University, 1833–1905* (New York: General Alumni Society, 1906), 24. *The Cooperstown Centennial Celebration, 1907* (Cooperstown, NY: *Otsego Republican*, 1907), 167–68. Jane Russell Averell was born on September 29, 1833, and died on January 31, 1888, the daughter of William Holt Averell (d. 1873) and Jane Augusta Maria Russell Averell, who married in 1829. There is some evidence that Jane's mother (Mary's grandmother) died two weeks after giving birth to Jane (Mary's mother). Jane's only other sibling did not live to adulthood. For the Ohio sojourn, see Mary Clark Brayton and Ellen F. Terry, *Our Acre and Its Harvest* (Cleveland: Fairbanks, Benedict & Co., 1869), 446. The Carters were married in October of 1857.

    For the death of MGC's father, see *General Alumni Catalogue of NYU,* 24, which states that he died in 1872 in Brooklyn. Depression and suicide, from author's interview with Douglas Kent, September 6, 2010.
41. JGL to Sarah Gordon and Aunt Eliza, November 9, 1878, GHS MS318/14/142; JGL to NKG, January 23, 1879, GHS MS318/14/143.
42. JGL to Sarah Gordon and Aunt Eliza, November 9, 1878, GHS MS318/14/142.
43. "Allen T. Dodworth Dead," *New York Times*, February 14, 1896; "swell," JGL to Sarah Gordon and Aunt Eliza, November 9, 1878, GHS MS318/14/142; Allen Dodworth, *Dancing and Its Relation to Education and Social Life* (New York: Harper and Brothers, 1885), 257.
44. "Whenever I see," JGL to NKG, October 27, 1878, GHS MS318/14/142. "Make love to her" in this era meant to court or woo. JGL to Sarah Gordon and Aunt

Eliza, November 9, 1878, GHS MS318/14/142. Meilhec and Halévy, *Frou Frou: A Play in Five Acts as Performed by Madame Helena Modjeska* (Indianapolis: Wasselman-Journal Company, 1883). "Modjeska's Farewell," *New York Times*, November 7, 1878, 4.

45. JGL to NKG, January 25, 1878, GHS MS318/14/141.
46. Dreading coming out: JGL to NKG, May 11, 1879, GHS MS318/14/143. For the location, see JGL to MGC, CFP March 1 [no year], MS2800/22/1.

Chapter 4: Emotional Upheaval

1. EGP to JGL, September 1, 1880, GHS MS318/3/33.
2. Maria Higginson was the daughter of Irish immigrant Charles Henry Higginson and Maria Potter Higginson. She was born in Trenton, New Jersey, and, like Daisy, grew up an Episcopalian. Maria married Wayland Manning in 1896 and moved to Beacon Street, Boston. Maria Manning maintained a lifelong interest in art. See John William Leonard, ed., *Woman's Who's Who of America* (New York: American Commonwealth Company, 1914), 537.
3. Exactly which Mr. Weir was Daisy's teacher is an educated guess. Robert Weir (1803–1889) had two sons, John Ferguson Weir (1841–1926) and Julian Alden Weir (1852–1919), both of whom were artists, the latter more famous. From 1869 on, the elder son was connected with the School of Fine Arts at Yale University in New Haven, Connecticut. In the 1880s, after his studies at the Ecole des Beaux-Arts, the handsome J. Alden Weir also lived and painted in Connecticut. On Robert Weir, see Susan G. Larkin, "A Delicious Day: Robert Weir's *Greenwich Boat Club*," *American Art Journal* 33, nos. 1 & 2 (2002): 20–33. For Daisy's schedule, see JGL to NKG [1881], GHS MS 318/14/145(#3036).
4. Irene Weir, *Robert W. Weir, Artist* (New York: House of Field-Doubleday, 1947), 124, 125 (Whistler), and 144–45 (studio). On Weir as a teacher, see Michael E. Moss, ed., *Robert W. Weir of West Point* (West Point, NY: United States Military Academy, 1976), chap. 2. "Doing splendidly," JGL to NKG, [no date], GHS MS318/14/145/3043. The Weir quote was given in a newspaper interview in 1877, and can be found in Moss, 53, and Weir, 144. "Never learned as much," JGL to NKG, November 20, 1881, GHS MS318/14/145.
5. Volkmar left a forty-one-page memoir, in German, which includes the story of how and why he left the United States in 1861. The memoir is located at the Smithsonian's Archives of American Art. See also John B. Clark, "The Volkmar Legacy to American Art Pottery" (Greenwich, CT: Bruce Museum, 1985), "American Pottery Exhibition," *New York Times*, December 5, 1899, 6.
6. Edwin Atlee Barber, *The Pottery and Porcelain of the United States* (New York: G. P. Putnam's Sons, 1901), 460–65; Edwin Atlee Barber, "The Pioneer of China Painting in America," *The New England Magazine* 19, no. 1 (September 1895), 37.
7. Barber, "The Pioneer of China Painting," 48. "Art Notes," *New York Times*, September 28, 1890, for example, mentions that First Lady Caroline Harrison had a plaque exhibited at the Western Decorating Work show in Chicago.
8. Debby DuBay, "Hand Painted Porcelain: Women Played a Major Role," *Journal of Antiques and Collectibles*, February 2003, http://www.journalofantiques.com/Feb03/featurefeb03.htm.

9. Bernhardt, JGL to NKG, [no date] (1880), GHS MS318/14/143; "all my energies," JGL to NKG, November 3 (1881), GHS MS318/14/145; galleries, JGL to NKG, October 5 [1881 (#3029)], GHS MS318/14/144.
10. "Surrendered," Gladys Denny Shultz and Daisy Gordon Lawrence, *Lady from Savannah* (New York: J. B. Lippincott Company, 1958), 153–54; "sad to think," EGP to JGL, April 24, 1881, GHS MS318/14/145; "favorite," JGL to MGC, February 6, 1881, CFP MS2800/5/1.
11. JGL to MGC, February 6, 1881, CFP MS2800/5/1.
12. JGL to NKG, [no date], GHS MS318/14/145(#3036).
13. Author interview with Douglas Kent, September 6, 2010. Kent, who knew Mary Gale Carter Clarke's daughter Anne Hyde Choate, speculated that the depression behind Marcia's suicide was bipolar disorder. JGL to MGC, February 6, 1881, CFP MS2800/5/1.
14. "A year," JGL to MGC, May 9, 1881, and "the only way," JGL to MGC, May 9, 1881, both from CFP MS2800/5/2; "family circle," JGL to MGC, June 8, 1881, CFP MS2800/5/2; "if it affords," JGL to MGC, February 6, 1881, CFP MS2800/5/1; "if we could not," JGL to MGC, May 9, 1881, CFP MS2800/5/2.
15. All the unattributed quotes in this chapter come from a letter written on October 30, 1882, from JGL to MGC. Mary (from London) and Daisy (from New York) both wrote each other letters at that time to be opened when they turned fifty. A xerox copy of the letter can be found in JGLB, box 1, 1868–1882. William Mackay Low and Juliette Gordon were distant cousins.
16. JGL to MGC, October 30, 1882, JGLB, box 1, 1868–1882.
17. Caroline Couper Lovell, *The Light of Other Days* (Macon, GA: Mercer University Press, 1995), 33; Christopher Lee Harwell, "William Henry Stiles: Georgia Gentleman-Politician" (Ph.D. dissertation, Emory University, 1959), 273.
18. Thackeray quote from James Grant Wilson and Frederick Stoever Dickson, *Thackeray in the United States*, vol. 1 (London: Smith, Elder and Company, 1904), 280; without financial reversals, "From Savannah," *New York Times*, January 30, 1865.
19. Eleanor returned home in May of 1881. "Happier than I ever," JGL to MGC, June 8, 1881; "sweet Venus," JGL to MGC, June 8, 1881, both from CFP MS2800/5/2.
20. MGC to GHC, March 17, 1885, CFP MS2800/6/18.
21. ALH to MGC, August 7 [1881], CFP MS2800/5/3.
22. Fred Habersham's love letters are in the Clarke Family Papers at Cornell University. For more on Fred, see Anna Habersham Wright Smith, *A Savannah Family, 1830–1901* (Milledgeville, GA: Boyd Publishing, 1999). Among the young people, his nickname was "the Yak."
23. "So unhappy," JGL to MGC, January 2, 1882, CFP MS28000/5/6.
24. Fred Habersham to MGC, June 20, 1882, and July 5, 1882, CFP MS2800/5/10.
25. ALH to MGC, July 21, 1882, CFP MS2800/5/10.
26. JGL to MGC, July 30, 1882, CFP MS2800/5/10.
27. Pakenham-Mahon was born on the Isle of Wight, where his family's home was Westbrook Manor, in Ryde, but his family owned extensive lands in County Roscommon, Ireland. Born in 1852, he was a captain in the Scottish Hussars. He was eight years older than Daisy. See Susan Hood, "The Famine in the Strokestown Park House Archive," *Irish Review* 17/18 (Winter 1995): 109–17.

28. Leah Price, "Diary," *London Review of Books*, 30, no. 23 (December 4, 2008): 43; *Shorthand: A Scientific and Literary Magazine* 3 (London: James Wade, 1889). On masculinity, see Leah Price, "Stenographic Masculinity," in *Literary Secretaries/Secretarial Culture* (Burlington, VT: Ashgate Publishing Company, 2005), 32–47.
29. Story of taking liberties, Shultz and Lawrence, 150–51.
30. JGL to MGC, August 19 [1881], CFP MS2800/5/3.
31. JGL, "Who Is a Gentleman?" May 1, 1879, JGLB, box 1, 1868–1882.

Chapter 5: Broken Hearts

1. ALH to MGC, August 29, 1882, CFP MS2800/5/12.
2. GHC to JRC, September 1, 1882, CFP MS2800/5/13; JRC to GHC, October 17, 1882, CFP MS2800/5/15. Mrs. Carter further stipulated that Hyde Clarke be able to prove his income sufficient to care for Mary, should they survive the year apart.
3. ALH to MGC, September 12, 1882, CFP MS2800/5/13.
4. JGL to MGC, November 6, 1882, CFP MS2800/5/15.
5. JGL to MGC, ("Here is the letter" and "I received very very sad news") both [no date] [1883], CFP MS2800/22/7.
6. JGL to MGC, March 9, 1883, CFP MS2800/6/2.
7. JGL to MGC, February 29, 1883, CFP MS2800/6/2. What Daisy called partridges might have been something else, as partridges were introduced to America with only moderate success before Daisy's birth. There were renewed efforts to stock the East Coast states in the late nineteenth century, after the hunting lessons Daisy described. Partridges live in the Midwest and West, but grouse and quail are hunted in Georgia. Todd Howard, Head Huntmaster, Pine Hill Plantation in Donalsonville, Georgia, believes Daisy and her cousin were hunting quail. Author interview with Howard, October 1, 2010.
8. JGL to MGC, February 18, 1883, CFP MS2800/6/2.
9. JGL to MGC, December 11 [no year], CFP MS2800/22/5.
10. Malicious pleasure, ALH to MGC, February 25, 1883, CFP MS2800/6/2; "I can't tell you," ALH to MGC, March 19 [no year], CFP MS2800/21/8; "how very wrong," JGL to MGC, March 29 [no year], CFP MS2800/22/1; "hates the south," ALH to MGC, March 14 [no year], CFP MS2800/21/8.
11. According to Anne Clarke Logan and Karen Lodinsky Nelson, Louisa Gregory was Hyde Clarke's cousin. See their *The Ladies of Hyde Hall* (Cooperstown, NY: Hyde Hall, Inc., 2009), 65. JRC to GHC, April 1, 1883; denied hiding, GHC to JRC, April 18, 1883, and GHC to MGC, April 22, 1883, all from CFP MS2800/6/3.
12. JGL to MGC, April 27, 1883, CFP MS2800/6/4.
13. "Champagne supper," JGL to MGC, August 8, 1883, CFP MS2800/6/5; "ancient admirer," JGL to MGC, August 24, 1883, and "we do not lack beaux," JGL to MGC, August 24, 1883, both from CFP MS2800/6/6. Fred Habersham would eventually marry Junie Hazelhurst.
14. JGL to MGC, November [no year], CFP MS2800/22/5. There is more than one navy yard, and it is not clear where she played.
15. List of horses, "Horses of Every Kind: Opening of the National Association Exhibition," October 23, 1883; "Preparing for the Horse Show," October 17,

1883; "Feature of the Horse Show," October 21, 1883; "Horses of Every Kind: Opening of the National Association Exhibition," October 23, 1883. All from the *New York Times*. Abby returned for three of the five days. ALH to MGC, October 29 [1883], CFP MS2800/6/8.

16. "Cast was splendid," JGL to MGC, October 27 (1883), CFP MS2800/22/4; "The New Opera House," October 23, 1883, *New York Times*; "instead of," JGL to MGC, November 5 [no year], CFP MS2800/22/5.
17. JGL to MGC, August 10 [no year], CFP MS2800/22/3.
18. JGL to MGC, November 5 [no year], CFP MS2800/22/5.
19. See JGL to MGC, August 16 [no year], where Daisy blames a sore throat on "too much disappation." She meant dissipation, CFP MS2800/22/3; "quinine and patience," JGL to EGP, November 31, 1883, GHS MS318/14/147.
20. Reni, JGL to MGC, November 30 [1883], CFP MS2800/6/8; recuperation and activities, JGL to MGC, December 9, 1883, CFP MS2800/6/8 and JGL to MGC, December 15, 1883, CFP MS2800/6/9.
21. ALH to MGC, January 2, 1884, CFP MS2800/6/10; "tied at home," JGL to MGC, October 27 [1883], CFP MS2800/22/4.
22. JGL to MGC, December 31 [1883], CFP MS2800/22/15. For biographical information, see William E. Sackette and John J. Scannell, *Scannell's New Jersey First Citizens*, vol. 1 (Paterson, NJ: J. J. Scannell, 1917), 386–88. Wayne's father was Cortlandt Parker.
23. JGL to MGC, February 10, 1884, CFP MS2800/6/11.
24. "Blue devils," JGL to MGC, August 8, 1883, CFP MS2800/6/5; JGL to MGC, February 10, 1884, CFP MS2800/6/11.
25. Dress, JGL to MGC, January 27 [no year]; JGL to MGC, March 1 [1884]; JGL to MGC, March 3 [no year], all CFP MS2800/22/1.
26. JGL to MGC, March 1 [1884], CFP MS2800/22/1.
27. JGL to MGC, May 24 [no year], CFP MS2800/22/2; JGL to MGC, [no date], CFP MS2800/22/6.
28. JGL to MGC, April 10, 1884, CFP MS2800/6/12.
29. "Dividing Derby Honors," *New York Times*, May 29, 1884; JGL to WWG III, June 2 [1884], GHS MS 318/14/148.
30. JGL to MGC, July 16 [no year], CFP MS2800/22/3.
31. The otherwise unattributed quotes in these pages come from the lengthy letter of JGL to MGC, dated October 30, 1882, and July 17, 1884, a copy of which can be found at JGLB, box 1, 1868–1882.
32. "If you have any," JGL to MGC, December 29 [no year], CFP MS2800/22/5.
33. "Mr. Low," JGL to NKG, June 18, 1884, GHS MS318/14/148.
34. JGL to EGP, July 12 [1884], GHS MS318/14/148; JGL to MGC, July 9 [no year], CFP MS2800/22/3; sketching, JGL to MGC, July 9 [no year], CFP MS2800/22/3.
35. Brussels, JGL to MGC, August 17, 1884, CFP MS2800/6/12. There Thackeray had the Gordon clan dance a Highland fling for the crowd on the eve of the Battle of Quatre Bras in the Napoleonic War. Antwerp, JGL to MGC, August 24 [1884], CFP MS2800/22/3; the "plucky" Dutch, JGL to MGC, August 31 [no year], CFP MS2800/22/3.
36. JGL to MGC, August 31 [1884], CFP MS2800/22/3.
37. JGL to MGC, August 24 [1884], CFP MS2800/22/3.
38. JGL to MGC, December 29 [no year], CFP MS2800/22/5; GHC to JRC, March 9, 1884, CFP MS2800/6/11.

Chapter 6: Omens and Weddings

1. In 1874, a well-known text suggested several uses for silver nitrate but warned against its extremely caustic nature. An article published less than twenty-four months before Daisy's treatment in the *Boston Medical Journal* by a Viennese doctor, H. L. Morse, included silver nitrate as one option for simple ear infections. Morse preferred powdered boric acid because of its decreased likelihood to burn the skin, but for "acute and chronic" problems in the middle ear, Dr. Morse recommended catheters soaked in "a ten per cent solution of nitrate of silver, and then dried before" insertion into the eustachian tube, where they stayed for no more than a minute, unless the patient complained of irritation. H. L. Morse, "Treatment of Diseases of the Ear," *Boston Medical and Surgical Journal* 110 (February 14, 1883), 164–65. The earlier text is Peter Allen, *Lectures on Aural Catarrh: The Commonest Forms of Deafness and Their Cure* (London: J. & A. Churchill, 1874). Physicians still treat certain types of perforated eardrums by applying a growth-stimulating chemical to the tympanic membrane—although today it can be applied more precisely.

   According to W. T. Harrison, ed., in *Webster's New International Dictionary* 2nd edition (Springfield, MA: G. & C. Merriam Company), 1958, silver nitrate is "a salt, obtained in the form of colorless crystals by dissolving silver in nitric acid, and evaporating. In contact with organic matter it turns black, owing to the separation of silver, staining skin, cloth, etc.; hence its use for indelible ink. When fused and molded it constitutes lunar caustic [sticks or rods of silver nitrate used for cauterization] or, when fused with twice the weight of saltpeter, mitigated caustic [usually for use on the eyelid]. It is also used internally in diseases of the stomach and the intestine, typhoid fever, epilepsy, and tabes [a wasting disease]."
2. WWGII to NKG, January 19, 1885, GHS MS318/3/42; JGL to NKG, January 21 [1885], GHS MS318/14/149. Dr. Read's office was on Liberty Street, Savannah. Dover's Powder was made of opium, ipecac, licorice, saltpeter, and tartar. "Invented Dover's Powder," *New York Times*, June 1, 1902.
3. "She insisted," WWGII to NKG, January 19, 1885, GHS MS318/3/42; JGL to NKG, January 21 [1885], GHS MS318/14/149; "burned a hole," JGL to MGC, January 22 [1885], CFP MS2800/22/1; "blew me up," JGL to MGC, February 8, 1885, CGP MS2800/6/15.
4. WWGII to NKG, January 20, 1885, GHS MS318/3/42.
5. "Her deafness is much," WWGII to NKG, January 22, 1885; "miserable muddle," WWGII to NKG, January 21, 1885, both from GHS MS318/3/42.
6. "Houston was right," WWGII to NKG, January 24, 1885, GHS MS318/3/42.
7. "Poor child," WWGII to NKG, January 24, 1885, GHS MS318/3/42; Gladys Denny Shultz and Daisy Gordon Lawrence, *Lady from Savannah: The Life of Juliette Low* (Philadelphia: J. B. Lippincott, 1958), 170–71.
8. "Highly sedated," WWGII to NKG, January 31, 1885, GHS MS318/3/42. WWGII to NKG, January 28, 1885, and WWGII to NKG, January 30, 1885, both from GHS MS318/3/42.
9. JGL to MGC, February 8, 1885, CGP MS2800/6/15.
10. For information about ear infections today, see "Perforated Eardrum," at the American Academy of Otolaryngology Web site, http://www.entnet.org/HealthInformation/perforatedEardrum.cfm.

11. Shultz and Lawrence, 167.
12. Shultz and Lawrence, 167–68; JGL to MGC, February 8, 1885, CGP MS2800/6/15.
13. MGC to GHC, March 14, 1885, CFP MS2800/6/17.
14. "Very little remains," MGC to GHC, March 21, 1885, CFP MS2800/6/18; Mary's portrait, MGC to GHC, April 2, 1885, CFP MS2800/7/2; "slept with Daisy," MGC to GJC, March 17, 1885, CFP MS2800/6/18.
15. Rhode Island, JGL to NKG, May 4, 1885, and JGL to NKG, June 16, 1885, both from GHS MS318/14/149. Engagement, EGP to MGC, September 18, 1885, CFP MS2800/7/13. JGL to EGP, October 18 [1885], GHS MS318/14/150; for "dread," see JGL to MGC, April 8 [no year], CFP MS2800/22/2. Ralph Birdsall, *The Story of Cooperstown* (Cooperstown, NY: A. H. Crist Co., 1920), 221. See also "George Hyde Clarke," *New York Times*, August 2, 1914.
16. "Dull," JGL to NKG, November 16, 1885, NHPC, box JGL Corresp. 1920 to Diary; Hyde Hall, Birdsall, 219–22; "tumbledown," ALH to MCG, February 18 [no year], CFP MS 2800/21/7.
17. First and last quotes from JGL to MGC, December 17, 1885, CFP MS2800/7/17; remodeling questions from JGL to MGC, July 4 [1886], CFP MS2800/22/3.
18. Jennifer Guthrie Ryan and Hugh Stiles Golson, *Andrew Low and the Sign of the Buck* (Savannah, GA: Frederic C. Beil, 2011), 298.
19. ALH to MGC, letter fragment, [no date], CFP MS2800/21/18.
20. Ryan and Golson, 298, 300.
21. JGL to MGC, January 24, 1886, CFP MS2800/8/1. Ryan and Golson, 298, quote Jessie Low for the annual worth of the Savannah property: £3000, or approximately $390,000 today.
22. Pious, pure, domestic, and submissive, from Barbara Welter, "The Cult of True Womanhood, 1820–1860," *American Quarterly*, vol. 18, no. 2 (Summer 1966), 151–74; "haven in a heartless world," from Christopher Lasch, *Haven in a Heartless World* (New York: W. W. Norton, 1995).
23. JGL to MGC, January 30, 1886, CFP MS2800/8/1.
24. William L. Wakelee to JGL, June 28, 1886, JGLB. See Ryan and Golson for the specifics of the will. It is impossible to know precisely how much any of the Low children inherited, in part because of the fluctuating value of stock prices. The £750,000 is in 1884 pounds and would be worth nearly $703 million in today's purchasing power.
25. WWGII to NKG, July 7, 1886; Jesse Tyson to JGL, July 7, 1886; Mary Lippitt to JGL, July 7, 1886, all JGLB.
26. MGL to EGP, [no date], 1886, JGLB. Gregor had been paying court to another American woman whose family became suspicious. They discovered the wife in Russia. NKG to WWGII, July 22, 1886 (rec'd.), GFP MS2235/SHC/105-107.
27. NKG to JGL, [no date], 1886, JGLB. They gave her $1000, which has a purchasing power of more than $20,000 today. For the accident, see JGL to MGC, March 19, 1886, CFP MS2800/8/3.
28. For WML, see Jessie Low to JGL, July 13 (1886); Katie M. Low to JGL, July 13, 1886; "show him off," NKG to JGL, July 31, 1886, all from JGLB.
29. For betting incident, see Shultz and Lawrence, 174; "one big wager," JGL to WWGII, August 30, 1886, GFP MS2235/SHC/105-107; WWGII's lecture, WWGII to JGL, September 4, 1886, postscript to September 3, 1886, JGLB. "3 August 1886 Notes from Fortune Teller," JGLB.
30. ALH to JGL, October 28 [1886], JGLB.

31. MGC to JGL, [no date] [1886], JGLB; on the house, see, for example, NKG to JGL, September 26, 1886, and October 14, 1886, both JGLB.
32. "Most important day," MGC to JGL, [no date] [1886], JGLB; "looked up in," Ryan and Golson, 311; Robertine K. McClendon to Mary Jo Shelly, December 30, 1964, NHPC, box JGL Gen'l Info-Pubs. Katie and Jessie wore "pure white" instead of black, even though they were in mourning for their father, because it was "not cricket to wear black at a wedding." Fred Habersham was Willy's best man.
33. NKG to Laura Magill, January 13, 1887 (ear), and February 25, 1887 (bronchitis and boil), both GFP MS2235/SHC/108.

Chapter 7: The Whirl of Married Life

1. Timing, Gladys Denny Shultz and Daisy Gordon Lawrence, *Lady from Savannah* (Philadelphia: J. B. Lippincott, 1958), 180. JGL's condition, NKG to WWGII, April 25, 1887 and WML to WWGII, April 27, 1887, JGLB; NKG wishing to be home, NKG to RWP, May 7, 1887 and NKG to EGP, May 8, 1877, both GHS MS318/14/151; "fading flower," JGL to MGC and ALH, July 12 [1887], CFP MS2800/8/10 [misdated at Cornell].
2. JGL to EGP, July 24, 1887, GHS MS318/14/151.
3. Mary King Waddington, *Letters of a Diplomat's Wife* (New York: Scribner's, 1903), 259–64.
4. "Four Miles of War Ships: The Jubilee Naval Review at Portsmouth," *New York Times*, July 24, 1887. For the size of the yacht, see "Testing His New Yacht," *New York Times*, March 24, 1887; Vanderbilt yacht, JGL to EGP, July 24, 1887, GHS MS318/14/151; suitcases story, JGL to ALH, August 5, 1887, CFP MS2800/8/11.
5. NKG to Laura Magill, May 22, 1887, GFP MS2235/SHC/108. St. Clair Thomson, "Great Medical Victorians," *British Medical Journal*, December 3, 1938, 1165. On Wilde, see Ashly H. Robins and Sean Sellars, "Oscar Wilde's Terminal Illness: Reappraisal After a Century," *Lancet*, vol. 356 (November 25, 2000): 1841–43.
6. William B. Dalby, "On the Management of Perforations of the Membrana Tympani," *British Medical Journal*, vol. 1, no. 1367 (March 12, 1887): 565.
7. William B. Dalby, *Lectures on Diseases and Injuries of the Ear* (Philadelphia: Lindsay & Blakiston, 1873), 28.
8. NKG to Laura Magill, May 22, 1887, GFP MS2235/SHC/108.
9. Alexandra, Christopher Hibbert, *The Royal Victorians* (New York: J. B. Lippincott Company, 1976), 86–87.
10. Douglas C. Baynton, e-mail to author, November 13, 2010. For background on deafness in Gilded Age America and the struggle between oralists and manualists, see Baynton's *Forbidden Signs: American Culture and the Campaign Against Sign Language* (Chicago: University of Chicago Press, 1996), especially chap. 1.
11. JGL to ALH, August 5, 1887, CFP MS2800/8/11. See Josephine K. Henry, "Lady Florence Douglas Dixie," *Liberal Review*, vol. 2, no. 6 (July 1905): 336–42. Florence Dixie published two books in 1882 about her time in Africa. She might have given either to JGL: *A Defence of Zululand* (London: Chatto and Windus, 1882) or *In the Land of Misfortune* (London: R. Bentley and Sons, 1882).

12. David Cannadine, *The Decline and Fall of the British Aristocracy* (New York: Doubleday/Anchor, 1992), 344. For a description of how London society worked at the time Daisy knew it, see "Mr. Smalley on English Society," *Review of Reviews*, Albert Shaw, ed. 15 (January–June 1897), 78–79.
13. "King," T.H.S. Escott ["A Foreign Resident"], *Society in London* (London: Chatto, Windus, Piccadilly, 1885), 87; Cannadine, 346.
14. Cannadine, 348. For the larger background, see Anita Leslie, *The Marlborough House Set* (New York: Doubleday, 1973).
15. Frances Evelyn Greville (Countess of Warwick), *Life's Ebb and Flow* (New York: W. W. Morrow, 1929), 183; Charles Mordaunt, *Annals of the Warwickshire Hunt, 1795–1895*, vol. 1 (London: Sampson, Low, Marston and Company, 1896).
16. Charles G. Dawes, *Journal as Ambassador to Great Britain* (New York: Macmillan, 1939), 56; Samuel Lewis, *A Topographical Dictionary of Scotland*, vol. 1 (London: S. Lewis and Company, 1851), 140; Adam and Charles Black, *Black's Picturesque Tourist of Scotland*, vol. 1, 13th ed. (Edinburgh: R. and R. Clark, 1857), 272–78.
17. "Looking better," NKG to WWGII, GHS MS318/3/43. For the invitation for the two Bs and the Bishop, see NKG to WWGII, October 6, 1887, GHS MS318/3/43.
18. "One of the most gifted," Escott, 90. Crown Prince Frederick would become Frederick III, emperor of Germany and king of Prussia, in March 1888. He died in June the same year. He was married to Victoria, who was the sister of the prince of Wales. Sir Morrell was known for his congeniality, his kindliness, and his "big banquets," which brought together "politicians, *litterateurs*, artists, actors, journalists, professional men of all grades." This, and his client list, would have made him acceptable to Willy Low (Escott, 90). See also Pierce A. Grace, "Doctors Differ over the German Crown Prince," *British Medical Journal*, vol. 305 (December 19–26, 1992), 1536.
19. JGL to MGC, November 30, 1887, CFP MS2800/8/11; "The Crown Prince's Throat," *New York Times*, July 8, 1887.
20. "Hunting ladies," Edward Chandos Leigh, *Bar, Bat and Bit* (London: John Murray, 1913), 207–8; JGL to MGC, November 30, 1887, CFP MS2800/8/11. And besides, the Master of the Hounds had located an especially gentle horse for Daisy.
21. "Exercise," JGL to Grace Carter, undated, CFP MS2800/22/7; JGL to MGC, October 16, 1887, CFP MS2800/8/11.
22. JGL to MGC, February 5, 1888, CFT MS2800/8/14; Elizabeth Hamilton, *The Warwickshire Scandal* (London: Pan Books, 1999).
23. JGL to MGC, January 3, 1888, CFP MS2800/8/12; Peter Bolton, *The Naples of the Midlands* (Wellesbourne: Local Time, 2007), 95; "they have laughed," JGL to MGC, February 5, 1888, CFT MS2800/8/14.
24. Engagement, JGL to EGP, September 20 (1887), GHS MS318/14/151; JGL to MGC, January 3, 1888, CFP MS2800/8/12.
25. ALH to MGC, February 18 [1888], CFP MS2800/21/7; "Fifty and Nineteen," *New York Times*, January 19, 1888.
26. JGL to MGC, February 14, 1888, CFP MS2800/8/14.
27. JGL to MGC, March 8 [1888], CFP MS2800/8/15; story of horse, GAG, "As Her Family Knew Her," in Anne Hyde Choate and Helen Ferris, *Juliette Low and the Girl Scouts* (New York: Girl Scouts of the USA, 1928), 48.

28. Lady Colin Campbell [Gertrude Elizabeth Campbell], *Etiquette of Good Society* (London: Cassel and Company, 1893), chap. 14.
29. JGL letter fragment, May 14, 1888, GHS MS318/14/151.
30. JGL to MGC, May 25, 1888, CFP MS2800/8/18.
31. JGL's hearing, Grace Carter to MGC, July 4, 1888, CFP MS2800/9/11. For JGL affirming Averill's depression, see JGL to MGC, July 6, 1888, CFP MS2800/9/1. See also Grace Carter to MGC, June 1, 1888, CFP MS2800/8/19. Averell's melancholia was suidical.
32. Smuggling, JGL to MGC, June 23 [1888], CFP MS2800/8/19; "only a tiny," JGL to Eliza Stiles, June 29, 1888, GHS MS318/14/151.
33. "Obituaries: William Gardner, M.D.," *Transactions of the American Gynecological Society*, vol. 52 (1927): 264; and William J. Mayo, "Radical Operations for the Cure of Cancer . . . ," *Transactions on the Sections on Obstetrics, Gynecology, and Abdominal Surgery* (Chicago: AMA Press, 1916), 163. Tait was also consulting surgeon to the West Bromwich Hospital, John A. Shepherd, *Lawson Tait: The Rebellious Surgeon, 1845–1899* (Lawrence, KS: Coronado Press, 1980), 46 (cysts); and W. J. McCardie, "Lawson Tait, A Pioneer in Certain Methods of Anaesthesia," *British Journal of Anaesthesia* 3, no. 2 (1925): 76–79.
34. JGL to MGC, CFP MS2800/9/2. The London doctor was probably Dr. Wells.
35. JGL to MGC, August 26, 1888, CFP MS2800/9/2; ALH to MGC, September 11 [no year], CFP MS2800/21/14.
36. Abscesses, NKG to JGL, August 7, 1890, GHS MS318/42/15. NKG to WWGII, July 25, 1904, GFP 2235/SHC/183. Daisy had consulted this unnamed physician before. He saw progress toward normal in the shape of her uterus the second time he saw her, in 1904. See also MGL, Memoir (MGL to Daisy Gordon Lawrence), October 1937, GHS MS318/15/172. Because no rumors have surfaced about Willy Low having fathered children with other women, it is possible that he was the source of the couple's inability to have children.
37. JGL to MGC, January 7, 1889, CFP MS2800/4/8.
38. NKG to GAG, April 18, 1889, GHS MS318/42/31.
39. JGL to NKG, June 9, 1889, GHS MS318/14/151.
40. JGL to MGC, June 16 [1889], CFP MS2800/22/2 for Daisy's description of the exposition. De Maupassant quote from Jill Jonnes, *Eiffel's Tower* (New York: Viking, 2009), 164. "Ascend into heaven," JGL to NKG, June 16, 1889, GHS MS318/14/151.
41. JGL to MGL, September 30, 1889, GHS 318/14/151; "devote my self," JGL to MGC, March 6 [1890], CFP MS2800/9/13.
42. "Jumped-up hunting box," Peter Bolton, *The Naples of the Midlands: Wellesbourne, 1800–1939* (Wellesbourne: Local Time, 2007), 293. For the electric lights, see JGL to NKG, October 29, 1892, JGLB and JGL to MGC, October 29, 1892, CFP MS2800/8/17. Nearby sites, Ann Eccles e-mail to author, October 31, 2010.
43. JGL to Grace Carter, January 8, 1890 [filed 1896 at Cornell], CFP MS2800/10/14.
44. See Bolton's chapter titled "Infidelity and the Girl Scouts," 290–99; Shultz and Lawrence, 203; Peter Higginbotham, *Workhouses of the Midlands* (Stroud: Tempus, 2007) and Higginbotham, "The Workhouse: Stratford-on-Avon, Warwickshire," http://www.workhouses.org.uk/index.html?StratfordOnAvon/StratfordOnAvon.shtml; Leprosy, GAG, "As Her Family Knew Her," in Choate and Ferris, 59; 1896 Grand Bazaar notice, GHS MS318/15/173.

45. Bolton, 294–95; Chris Upton, "Off to the Races—in Bromford Bridge in Birmingham," *Birmingham Post*, January 22, 2010. For the argument that the "aristocracy played a positive role in developing" their estates and assisting the surrounding area, see J. V. Beckett, *The Aristocracy in England* (Oxford: Basil Blackwell, 1986), 7.
46. For Valentine Eliot, see Bolton, 226–27. For JGL's other pieces, see Ralph Bagnall, "Girl Scouts Founder Was Also a Woodworker," *Woodworker's Journal*, June 2007: 22–24. With the exception of the mantel, the pieces listed are in Savannah, at the Juliette Gordon Low Birthplace. The location of the mantel is unknown.
47. George C. Williams and Charlotte Crabtree, "Women Metalworkers in the American South," *Women of Metal* (Washington, D.C.: The Thrift Shop, 2004), 136–41; Anthea Callen, *Angel in the Studio* (London: Astragal Books, 1979), 152–62.
48. "Women Metal Workers," *The Art Record: A Weekly Illustrated Review of the Arts and Crafts*, vol. 2, no. 27 (August 24, 1901), 787–98.
49. Bolton, 99; Chedham's Yard Web site: http://www.chedhamsyard.org.uk/family tree.html. The 1881 Great Britain census lists William Chedham as a wheelwright.
50. Peter Bolton, e-mail to author, December 10, 2010.
51. Sleeves, Dorris S. Hough, "Juliette Low, Craftsman," *Girl Scout Leader*, JGLB.
52. NKG European Diary, May 24, 1891, GHS MS2800/12/28. Grace was training as a musician and had been studying with various teachers in Europe since her mother's death—and after she had deposited Averell at boarding school. Doctor's warning, JGL to MGC, June 10, 1891, CFP MS2800/9/16. For the context of prescribed medicinal seaside rest, see Janet Oppenheim, *Shattered Nerves* (New York: Oxford University Press, 1991), 126–31.
53. "Baron Leigh's Son to Wed," *New York Times*, January 10, 1898. The information in "What Is Doing in Society," from the *New York Times*, October 23, 1898, is incorrect. Mabel did not meet Rowley Leigh in 1896 but rather in 1891. Leigh graduated from Cambridge and from 1892 to 1895 worked for the Right Honorable Henry Campbell-Bannerman, who went on to become prime minister in 1905. "A great blow," NKG European Diary, most entries undated, GHS MS2800/12/28. The marble bust is from "The Robertsons of Stanton," from the Web site of Stanton on the Wolds Parish Council, http://www.stantononthewoldsparishcouncil.gov.uk/the%20Robertsons%20of%20Stanton.htm.
54. Archie Hunter, *Kitchener's Sword-Arm: The Life and Campaigns of General Sir Archibald Hunter* (New York: Sarpedon, 1996), 2–3.
55. Joaquin Miller, *An Illustrated History of the State of Montana* (Chicago: The Lewis Company, 1894), 184–85; Patty Dean, "'Unique and Handsome': Cass Gilbert's Designs for the Montana Club," *Drumlummon Views*, vol. 1, nos. 1 & 2 (Spring/Summer 2006): 154–76. For the names of his partners, see Isabel F. Randall, *A Lady's Ranch Life in Montana* (Norman: University of Oklahoma Press, 2004), 169–70 (n. 24) and Phyllis Smith, *Bozeman and the Gallatin Valley* (Helena, MT: Twodot, 1996), 151–54. Smith lists the partner as Major Andrew Cracraft Amcott. The sale to Anaconda Copper is in Smith, 154. Smith is incorrect about the titles of some of the British immigrants, including the title she gives to Hunter. None of the British settlers stayed long. They don't appear in the nearly seven-hundred-page-long *Headwaters Heritage History* (Butte: Three Forks Area Historical Society, 1983).

56. ALH to MGC, October 29 [no year], CFP MS2800/21/15. Abby and Duncan were lodgers in the same hotel. "Rustling for our million," ALH to MGC, September 17 [no year], CFP MS2800/21/14.
57. JGL to NKG, March 18, 1892, JGLB.
58. JGL to NKG, [no date] [1890], GHS MS318/14/152.
59. "H.R.H. was very gracious," JGL to NKG, May 19, 1895, GHS MS318/14/152; Shultz and Lawrence, 183, 208.
60. Escott, 100; NKG Spanish-American War Diary I, p. 2. On Lady Randolph Churchill, see Anne Sebba, *American Jennie* (New York: W. W. Norton, 2007).
61. Bolton, 293–94.
62. Thomas Pinney, ed., *The Letters of Rudyard Kipling*, vol. 3 (Iowa City: University of Iowa Press, 1996), 38–39. Kipling wrote to James M. Conland on December 2, 1900. The families were shirttail relations through the Wolcott family.

Chapter 8: Wars, Colonial and Domestic

1. All the information concerning the Cairo trip is from JGL to MGC, March 12, 1891, CFP MS2800/9/16.
2. JGL to MGC, March 27, 1895, CFP MS2800/10/10.
3. JGL to NKG, March 22, 1895, GHS 319/14/152; "two ladies," JGL to MGC, CFP March 27, 1895, MS2800/10/10.
4. "We have seen," JGL to MGC, March 27, 1895, CFP MS2800/10/10; Abby called it a "mutual admiration society." See ALH to MGC, [no date] [1895], CFP MS2800/21/9. NKG's view, NKG 1895 Diary, August 5, 1895, GHS MS318/12/128.
5. "Tremendous fancy," ALH to MGC, November 24 [1895], CFP MS32800/10/12. Great-nephew's analysis, Hunter, 41, 90. A point of seeing her, Duncan H. Doolittle, *A Soldier's Hero: General Sir Archibald Hunter* (Narragansett: Anawan Publishing Company, 1991), 112.
6. Doolittle, 96, 112, 165.
7. JGL to Eliza Stiles, September 27, 1897, GHS MS318/14/152.
8. Nellie Gordon's 1898 diary asserts that her husband served as head of the Second Brigade, First Division, Fourth Army Corps, USV. Lucian Lamar Knight, in *A Standard History of Georgia and Georgians*, vol. 5 (Chicago: Lewis Publishing Company, 1917), 2772, states that he was head of the Second Brigade, Second Division, Seventh Army Corps.
9. "Background Information: General William Washington Gordon II," GHS, "Biographical File: Gordon."
10. WWGII to EGP, June 20, 1898, GHS 318/4/50; Gladys Denny Shultz and Daisy Gordon Lawrence, *Lady from Savannah: The Life of Juliette Low* (Philadelphia: J. B. Lippincott, 1958), 217.
11. Walter Reed, Victor C. Vaughan, and Edward Shakespeare, *Report on the Origin and Spread of Typhoid Fever in U.S. Military Camps During the Spanish War of 1898*, vol. 1 (Washington, D.C.: GPO, 1904), 507, 518–19.
12. Information for the convalescent ward comes from Nellie Gordon's 1898 Spanish-American War Diaries, GHS MS318/12/126; and Jacqueline E. Clancy, "Hell's Angel: Eleanor Kinzie Gordon's Wartime Summer of 1898," *Tequesta*, vol. 43 (2003): 37–61. Quote from the latter, 54. The church had not yet been consecrated. For the milking, see Shultz and Lawrence, 221.

13. NKG, Spanish-American War Diary, "Thursday, 28th."
14. Shultz and Lawrence, 222. Daisy and Nellie arrived in Pablo Beach on August 5; Willie received orders on August 16; Nellie left for Savannah on August 22. Clancy, 56–57.
15. NKG, "Account of the Death of Charles Perry," GHS MS318/4/51; Shultz and Lawrence, 227–28.
16. "Will Marry a Titled Englishman," January 10, 1898; "Will Be Wed in the Autumn," February 21, 1898; "Horse Will Soon Reign," October 30, 1898; "Marquise de Fontenoy's Letter," October 30, 1898; "Marries a Southern Girl," November 1, 1898; "Descendent of Kinzie Weds," November 2, 1898, all from *Chicago Tribune.*
17. Representative Wayne Parker served in the 54th through the 61st Congresses, the 63rd through the 65th, and the 67th.
18. WWGII to NKG, October 19, 1895. In 1905, Grace Carter, who had helped her brother Averell with his hearing impairment, sent Daisy two different sizes of "earpats" for her to try, JGL to MGC, October 31, 1905, CFP MS2800/ 11/15.
19. Knight, 2772–74.
20. The Huntingdon Club was a women's literary club. See William Harris Bragg, *DeRenne: Three Generations of a Georgia Family* (Athens: University of Georgia Press, 1999), 362; "Want the Girls Admitted," unidentified, undated clipping, NKG Scrapbook 5635, GHS MS318/35 and WWGII to NKG, October 28, 1897, GHS MS318/4/49. "Reprint a Kinzie Book," *Chicago Tribune,* January 26, 1902; "Schley Hostess a Chicagoan," *Chicago Tribune,* January 11, 1902. See also Mrs. Clarence Gordon Anderson, "Eleanor Kenzie Gordon," *Georgia Historical Quarterly* 42, no. 2 (January 1958): 163–69.
21. JGL to MGC, October 13, 1895, CFP MS2800/10/12.
22. "All nice men," MGL to NKG, August 26, 1910, GHS MS318/5/62. Making fun of, author interview with Stephen Bohlin, May 9, 2009. Willie "jeered and derided" Daisy and her women friends for returning before reaching a ball in Warwickshire. They found the fog far too thick for safe navigation, and the horses were impossible to see (JGL to NKG, [no date] JGLB).
23. "Society is very hollow," JGL to MGC, December 24 [no year], CFP MS2800/22/ 5; "My life," JGL to Grace Carter, January 8, 1890, CFP MS2800/10/14; "a very unsatisfactory mode," NKG 1895 Diary, August 5, 1895, GHS MS318/12/128.
24. Frances Evelyn Greville (Countess of Warwick), *Life's Ebb and Flow* (New York: W. W. Morrow, 1929), 172.
25. T.H.S. Escott ["A Foreign Resident"], *Society in London* (London: Chatto, Windus, Piccadilly, 1885), 103, 104.
26. Philippa Pullar, *Gilded Butterflies: The Rise and Fall of the London Season* (London: Hamish Hamilton, 1978), 149.
27. EGP to NKG, October 15, 1902, GFP 2235/SHC/175; ALH to MGC, November 16 [no year], CFP 2800/21/16.
28. "I did not half," JGL to MGC, May 17, 1894, CFP 2800/10/7; Greville, 276; ball, untitled 1896 clipping pasted to inside back cover of scrapbook 5635, GHS MS318/35.
29. "A very bad husband," JGL to GAG, October 23, 1900, GFP MS2235/SHC/158; JGL to NKG, January 5, 1901, GFP 2235/SHC/161. Anna Bateman did not sign

the Wellesbourne House guest book (Katherine Knapp Keena to author, November 20, 2010).

30. Anna was the daughter of Edward Bridges of Dorset, a member of the Shropshire Fusiliers. Sir Hugh's parents were Georgina Bannatyne and Thomas Keelinge Bateman. Anna Bateman married again in 1913, see Bernard Burke, *Burke's Peereage*, vol. 79 (New York: Putnam's 1914), 1096. Story of Sir Hugh's death from the Morley Parish Heritage Walk Brochure '08 from http://www.morleyparishcouncil.com. Morley Manor: Charles Kerry, *Smalley in the County of Derby* (London: Bemrose and Sons, 1905), 124–25. Two other people, Sir Peter Carlow Walker and Richard Stephens Taylor, were mentioned in the 1897 *England and Wales National Probate Calendar,* 138, and presumably had a claim on the estate. She would have inherited no less than one-third. From Ancestry.com.
31. Peter Bolton, *The Naples of the Midlands* (Wellesbourne: Local Time), 296; Jessie Low Graham to JGL, [no date], GFP 2235/SHC/176a. Whispering, MGL, Memoir (MGL to Daisy Gordon Lawrence), October 1937, GHS MS318/15/172, hereafter cited as MGL, Memoir.
32. NKG to WWGII, January 29, 1901, GFP 2235/SHC/161. It is possible that the Camberwell working girls' club met in the Talbot settlement house that opened in 1901, part of the Trinity University settlement house begun in Camberwell in 1895. Miss Goodenough might have been the matron to whom Nellie referred in the letter of January 29, 1901. The Camberwell settlement work seems to have been amalgamated with the Union for Girls' Schools for Social Service. See "A London Mission: Talbot Settlement," *Evening Post* (Wellington, New Zealand), July 18, 1931, http://paperspast.natlib.govt.nz/cgi-bin/paperspast?a=d&d=EP19310718.2.82&dliv=&l=mi&e=-------10--1----0--panojs); M. A. Douglas, "Union for Girls' Schools for Social Service," The Godolphin School Web site, www.godolphin.org; "Former places of worship in the diocese of Southwark," Diocese of Southwark Web site, http://www.southwark.anglican.org/downloads/lostchurches/ELT03.pdf; and Alice Stronach, "Women's Work in Social Settlements," *Windsor Magazine* 36 (June–November 1912): 403–14.
33. "Bringing peace" and "commanding," Doolittle, 167, 168. Doolittle, 176–77, states that it was a rectal abscess, and so while Daisy knew it was an abscess, she probably didn't know the particulars. Kilbride and London celebrations, Doolittle, 180–82.
34. "British Lose More Men," *New York Times*, December 13, 1899; JGL to GAG, October 23, 1900, GFP MS2235/SHC/158; WWGII to JGL, February 22, 1900, GFP MS2235/SHC/157. For Hunter's role, see Doolittle, 226, and "All Eyes Upon Gen. Hunter's March to Relieve Mafeking," *New York Times,* May 13, 1900.
35. Baden-Powell would be inspector general of the British Cavalry (1903), and Hunter would be general officer commanding the Scottish Command (1901), Doolittle, 234.
36. JKL to GAG, January 9, 1899, JGLB.
37. JGL to GAG, February 1, 1901, GFP 2235/SHC/161.
38. WWGII to GAG, February 26, 1901, GFP 2235/SHC/161; MGL to GAG, April 8, 1901, GFP 2235/SHC/162.

39. MGL to EGP, May 6, 1901, GFP 2235/SHC/162. The Low home was usually rented out when Daisy and Willy were abroad for great lengths of time, so they were probably staying at the Gordon home.
40. "I wish," JGL to GAG, August 6, 1901; "worth a fortune," JGL to GAG, August 11, 1901; "it was not," JGL to GAG, August 12, 1901, all from GFP 2235/SHC/164.
41. "No women here," JGL to MGL, August 21, 1901. Friday was the 23rd. Same hotel, MGL, Memoir; "I need you," JGL to MGL, August 29, 1901; Mabel will join, MGL to GAG, August 29, 1901, letters from GFP 2235/SHC/164.
42. "Looks pretty well," MGL to GAG, September 2, 1901; JGL to GAG, September 5, 1901, both from GFP 2235/SHC/165. Mrs. Bateman is the only female guest for whom Daisy did not use a first name.
43. MGL to GAG, September 5, 1901, GFP 2235/SHC/165.
44. JGL to "Dearest" (probably GAG), August 7, 1904, GFP 2235/SHC/184. Later it would be important to know whether JGL left willingly or whether WML asked her to leave. The truth is not clear.
45. MGL to GAG, September 11, 1901, GFP 2235/SHC/165; Lady Ota's offer, JGL to GAG, October 13, 1901, GFP 2235/SHC/166; NKG to WWGII, December 5, 1901, GFP 2235/SHC/167a.
46. JGL to WWGII, January 28, 1902, GHS MS318/14/153.
47. NKG to GAG, November 2, 1900, GFP MS2235/SHC/159. Rosa Lewis was there to do some of the cooking during the Gordons' stay.
48. "For some time," JGL to NKG, February 3, 1902; "I must go on," JGL to GAG, September 19, 1902, both from GHS MS318/14/135.
49. WWGII to MGL, March 10, 1902, GHS MS318/4/53.
50. EGP to GAG, February 18, 1902, GHS MS318/4/53.

Chapter 9: A Parting of the Ways

1. NKG to EGP, February 17, 1902, GHS MS318/4/53.
2. T.H.S. Escott ["A Foreign Resident"], *Society in London* (London: Chatto, Windus, Piccadilly, 1885), 57.
3. Complicate matters, MGL to GAG, September 23, 1902. Not dragging Bateman through the courts, GAG to Edward Rowland Pickering, September 14, 1902, and E. R. Pickering to GAG, September 16, 1902, all from GFP 2235/SHC/174.
4. Reginald Poole to MGL, September 18, 1902, GFP 2235/SHC/174.
5. Pickering to GAG, September 17, 1902, GHS MS318/4/53.
6. NKG to WWGII, June 3, 1902, GFP 2235/SHC/171.
7. JGL to WWGII, June 8, 1902, and "irreparable harm," JGL to GAG, June 13, 1902, both GFP 2235/SHC/171.
8. JGL to GAG, June 19, 1902, GFP 2235/SHC/171.
9. Reginald Poole to MGL, September 25, 1902; MGL to GAG, [no date] [September 1902], both from GFP 2235/SHC/174.
10. JGL to GAG, June 7, 1902, GFP 2235/SHC/171; JGL to GAG, July 4, 1902, GFP 2235/SHC/172.
11. MGL to WWGII, June 24, 1902, GFP 2235/SHC/171; JGL to GAG, July 4, 1902, GFP 2235/SHC/172.
12. JGL to GAG, July 4, 1902, GFP 2235/SHC/172; MGL to GAG, July 4 [1902], GFP 2235/SHC/315.

13. Beech invitation, JGL to GAG, July 4, 1902; dinner with Archie, MGL to WWGII, July 10, 1902, both from GFP 2235/SHC/172. Archie's home, MGL to GAG, August 10, 1902; "happier far," MGL to NKG, August 20, 1902; "despises," MGL to NKG, August 29, 1902, all from GFP 2235/SHC/173.
14. "Enough money," JGL to NKG, August 3, 1902; Bateman's income, MGL to NKG, August 29, 1902, both from GFP 2235/SHC/173. EGP to NKG, October 15, 1902, GFP 2235/SHC/175; undated letter fragment, probably MGL to NKG and WWGII, GFP 2235/SHC/318. One loan was to Willie; the other to Arthur; "would give me anything," JGL to MGC, November 4 [1890], CFP MS2800/22/5.
15. MGL to GAG, September 23, 1902, GFP 2235/SHC/174; Mrs. Mordaunt to JGL, October 6, 1902, GFP 2235/SHC/175.
16. EGP to NKG, October 15, 1902, GFP 2235/SHC/175; RWP to WWGII, September 6, 1902, GFP 2235/SHC/174.
17. Willy lied, GAG to Edward Rowland Pickering, September 14, 1902, and E. R. Pickering to GAG, September 16, 1902, GFP 2235/SHC/174. Rest of paragraph from JGL to NKG, September 15, 1902, GFP 2235/SHC/174.
18. Duncan died in the fall of 1902. "Busting up," Duncan H. Doolittle, *A Soldier's Hero* (Narragansett, RI: Anawan Publishing Co., 1991), 120; "held together," Doolittle, 242; "Death was easier," JGL to NKG, October 1, 1902, GFP 2235/SHC/175; "I think I can understand," Doolittle, 243–44; "I know that only God," JGL to MGL, October 6, 1902, GFP 2235/SHC/175.
19. "Isn't it strange," JGL to MGL, October 6, 1902, GFP 2235/SHC/175. Regarding Mary, author interviews with Douglas Kent, September 6, 2010, and December 15, 2010. Kent believes that Mary suffered from bipolar disorder, and that all letters regarding her mental difficulties were pulled from the correspondence and burned by a family member. See also Anne Clarke Logan and Karin Lodinsky Nelson, *The Ladies of Hyde Hall* (Cooperstown, NY: Hyde Hall, Inc., 2009), 71, for mention of 1893. Alfred had been born in 1898 and Averell in 1901.
20. "Far, far happier," MGL to WWGII, October 14, 1902, GFP 2235/SHC/175; location of house, JGL to GAG, November 21, 1902; MGL to NKG, November 28, 1902, GFP 2235/SHC/176a; "menagerie," NKG to JGL, December 20, 1902, GHS MS318/42/16; "leaders," JGL to WWGII, December 10, 1902, GFP 2235/SHC/176a. For the complicated and adulterous life of Romaine Turnure, see Archie Hunter, *Power and Passion in Egypt: A Life of Sir Eldon Gorst, 1861–1911* (London: I. B. Tauris, 2007), chap. 8.
21. MGL to NKG, December 23, 1902; JGL to NKG, December 15, 1902, both GFP 2235/SHC/176a.
22. JGL to WWGII, January 24, 1903; MGL to GAG, January 26, 1903, both from GFP 2235/SHC/177; JGL to MGL, December 23, 1903, GHS MS318/14/153; "to set him free," JGL to WML, January 27, 1903, GFP 2235/SHC/177.
23. EGP to GAG, February 18, 1903, GFP 2235/SHC/177; WWGII to GAG, July 18, 1903, GFP 2235/SHC/178.
24. JGL to WWGII, October 17, 1903, GHS MS318/14/153. It is not clear whether Daisy met with Willy on the advice of counsel or against his wishes, but probably the former.
25. "Stale, dirty," JGL to MGL, October 3, 1903, JGLB; JGL to George W. Lewis, [no date], GHS MS318/14/153.
26. George W. Lewis to JGL, October 15, 1903, GHS MS318/14/153.

27. WML's sisters, JGL to NKG, November 3, 1903; "Indeed, I have had," JGL to NKG, November 3, 1903, both from GFP 2235/SHC/179.
28. "Move all furniture," Margaret Leigh Graves, "In Proud Memory of My Aunt Juliette Gordon Low," NHPC, JGL Gen Info-Pubs; Letters from Archie, JGL to GAG, December 15, 1903, GFP 2235/SHC/179; "combine stables," JGL to GAG, November 24, 1903, GFP 2235/SHC/179; "softening of the brain," JGL to WWGII, December 23, 1903, GHS MS318/14/153; MGL, Memoir.
29. JGL to MGL, December 23, 1903, GHS MS318/14/153; RWP to GAG, November 18, 1903, GFP 2235/SHC/179.
30. Arthur in London, GAG to EGP, June 25, 1904; "a lie," GAG to WWGII, June 24, 1904, both from GFP 2235/182; "she had been compelled," JGL to WWGII, July 15, 1904, GFP 2235/SHC/183; Gladys Denny Shultz and Daisy Gordon Lawrence, *Lady from Savannah: The Life of Juliette Low* (Philadelphia: J. B. Lippincott, 1958), 246.
31. Mind at ease, JGL to "Dearest" (probably GAG), August 7, 1904, GFP 2235/SHC/184. Nellie found Daisy's German "astonishing" in its efficacy although "execrable as to grammar," NKG to WWGII, July 22, 1904, GFP 2235/SHC/183; NKG to WWGII, August 21, 1904, GFP 2235/SHC/184. The vegetable baths were at Karlsbad. "Brimstone and sulpher," JGL to GAG, July 31, 1904, GFP 2235/SHC/183.
32. "He might rally," NKG to WWGII, September 20, 1904; MGL to GAG, September 23, 1904, both from GFP 2235/SHC/185. Divorce is off, JGL to WWGII, September 24, 1904, JGLB; JGL to GAG, October 2, 1904; "the world would think," JGL to WWGII, October 14, 1904, both GFP 2235/SHC/186.
33. JGL to GAG, November 26, 1904, GFP 2235/SHC/187a.
34. JGL to GAG, December 4, 1904, GFP 2235/SHC/187a.
35. Confrontation with Guthrie, JGL to NKG, December 14, 1904; JGL to NKG and WWGII, December 23, 1904, both from GFP 2235/SHC/187a.
36. "Paralysis," JGK to WWGII, January 17, 1905, JGLB; JGL to WWGII, January 5, 1905, GFP 2235/SHC/188; second father, JGL to WWGII, January 17, 1905, JGLB.
37. For an example of sketching, see JGL to GAG, June 13, 1902, GFP 2235/SHC/171. Cherry trees, JGL to Rowley Leigh, May 7, 1905, JGLB.
38. All information from the May 1905 trip to India is from JGL, "Notes on the Field," May 10, 1905, GFP MS318/14/154. The tiger was 9 feet, 4.5 inches from nose to tip of tail.
39. RWP to GAG, May 26, 1905, GFP 2235/SHC/189.
40. RWP to GAG, May 29, 1905, GFP 2235/SHC/189.
41. Katie M. Low to MGL, June 8 [1905], GHS MS318/4/55; JGL to ALH, June 9, 1905, GFP 2235/SHC/11/15; "he did not die before," and funeral arrangements, JGL to MGC, June 10, 1905, CFP MS2800/11/15; JGL to NKG, June 9, 1905, JGLB. According to Peter Bolton, the death certificate read "epilepsy and general paralysis," which he suggested "could often be a thin and transparent cover for syphilis." Bolton, *Wellesbourne: The Naples of the Midlands* (Wellesbourne: Local Time 2007), 297. Letters, Bolton, 298.
42. GAG to WWGII, July 27, 1905, GHS MS318/4/56; George Lewis to JGL, July 14, 1905, JGLB; Clarke Rawlins & Company to Mr. Gasquet and Mr. Metcalfe, July 13, 1905, GHS MS318/16/175. The will itself and the codicil, GFP 2235/SHC/187a. See also Shultz and Lawrence, 252.

43. "Robertson v. Low and Bateman," *The Times* (London), July 25, 1905. This document suggests that it would have been very difficult to contest the will by claiming undue influence. "Robertson v. Low and Bateman," *The Times* (London), March 20, 1906, shows that the British courts concluded that Willy Low was British, not American. "Now Deceased Robertson v. Low and Another, Terms for a Settlement of This Action" (1906), GHS MS318/16/175. For the family members' awards, see Bolton, 298; for more details and a different interpretation, see Ryan and Golson, 339–41.
44. Frances Evelyn Greville (Countess of Warwick), *Life's Ebb and Flow* (New York: W. W. Morrow, 1929), 276; MGL to WWGII, [no date], GFP 2235/SHC/40/312.

Chapter 10: Journeys

1. Gladys Denny Shultz and Daisy Gordon Lawrence, *Lady from Savannah: The Life of Juliette Low* (Philadelphia: J. B. Lippincott, 1958), 260.
2. "I am glad," Shultz and Lawrence, 257; JGL to MGC, May 16, 1906, CFP MS2800/11/16.
3. Physical ailments, WWGII to MGL, June 14, 1906, GHS MS318/4/56. Nellie recovered enough at the Grand Hotel on Mackinaw Island to continue westward to see Yellowstone Park, Seattle, and Vancouver. Rudyard Kipling to Elise Kipling, July 19, 1922, in *The Letters of Rudyard Kipling*, vol. 5, Thomas Pinney, ed. (Iowa City: University of Iowa Press), 2004.
4. JGL to NKG, December 9, 1906, JGLB. It is not precisely clear whether all of the animals killed were pheasants or whether other birds were among the slaughtered.
5. Geography, Colin Wilson to author, November 29, 2010; Shultz and Lawrence, 261; River Lyon, Duncan Campbell, *The Lairds of Glenlyon* (Perth: S. Cowan, 1886), 1.
6. JGL to MGC, June 7, 1906, JGLB; Grace Carter to MGC, August 22, 1907, CFP MS2800/11/18; "Weddings of the Autumn: Miss Anne Hyde Clarke to Marry a Nephew of Joseph Choate," *New York Times*, October 11, 1907. The couple was married by the Reverend Phillip A. H. Brown at Christ Church in Cooperstown.
7. Diary of Juliette Low, 1907–1908, GFP 2235/SHC/210b.
8. Grace Carter to MGC, August 18, 1907, CFP MS2800/11/18. All quotes not otherwise cited concerning Daisy's trip to India come from her India diary, GFP 2235/SHC/210b.
9. Beth Parker to EGP, February 2, 1908, JGLB.
10. Lawrence James, *Raj: The Making and Unmaking of British India* (New York: St. Martin's, 1997), 233–53.
11. See "Mafeking Relief Head to Command in Serbia," *New York Times*, October 29, 1915. Younghusband "opened" Tibet using a force of British and Sikh soldiers whose superior rapid-fire machine guns annihilated the Tibetan force attempting to stand against them.
12. JGL to WWGII, February 18, 1908, JGLB.
13. Beth Parker to EGP, February 27, 1908, JGLB.
14. Robert Baden-Powell, *Pig-Sticking, or Hog Hunting: A Complete Account for Sportsmen or Others* (London: Harrison and Sons, 1889).
15. Beth Parker to RWP, March 3, 1908, JGLB.

16. "To be petted," MGL to NKG, August 26, 1910, GHS MS318/5/62; JGL to NKG, May 8, 1910, GHS MS318/14/156; JGL worse when ill, MGL to NKG, April 2, 1910, GHS MS318/5/61; "too deaf," JGL to Margaret Gordon, June 1, 1910, JGLB.
17. NKG 1908 Diary, GHS MS318/12/129.
18. "You know I do," JGL to MGL, November 8, 1908, JGLB; politics, JGL to MGL, January 19, 1910, GHS MS318/14/156, and JGL to GAG, November 24, 1909, GHS MS318/14/155; suffrage cartoon, JGLB.
19. JGL to MGL, October 27, 1909, JGLB.
20. JGL to EGP, [no date] [February 1911], GHS MS318/14/157. She had consulted doctors in Egypt and France most recently.
21. E. P. Cumberbatch, "Observations on Ultra-Violet Ray Therapy," *British Medical Journal* 2, no. 3523 (July 14, 1928): 43–46 (quote from p. 45); Jack W. Jones, "Ultra Violet Ray Therapy in Dermatology," *Southern Medical Journal*, vol. 16, no. 6 (June 1923): 423–27.
22. WWGIII to NKG, July 16, 1911, GHS MS318/6/66; William Boericke, *Materia Medica*, 9th ed. (Santa Rosa, CA: Boericke & Tafel, 1927), 515. The homeopathic remedy was thiosinaminum-rhodalin.
23. Victrola, NKG to JGL, May 22, 1911, GHS MS318/43/1; NKG to JGL, June 16, 1911, GHS MS318/42/22; JGL to WWGII, June 29, 1911, GHS MS318/14/157. Daisy seems to have heard about Victrolas in 1906. Her mother purchased one and had it shipped to her in 1911.
24. JGL to WWGII, GHS MS318/14/157; Lord Grey was Albert Henry Grey, the 4th Earl Grey. See J. Castell Hopkins, "Earl Grey's Last Months as Governor General," *Canadian Annual Review of Public Affairs 1911* (Toronto: The Annual Review Publishing Company, 1912), 618–20, for a brief summary of Lord Grey's years in Canada.
25. Off to Egypt, "Social Notes," *New York Times*, December 13, 1910; "Society at Home and Abroad," *New York Times*, December 18, 1910. Gwendolen was the daughter of family friends Mattie Chenault and Edmund S. Nash and the sister of poet Ogden Nash. Edmund Nash was in the shipping business. Bust into the sea, Eleanor Nash McWilliams, "Adventuring in Egypt with Daisy," in Anne Hyde Choate and Helen Ferris, eds., *Juliette Low and the Girl Scouts* (New York: Girl Scouts of the USA, 1928), 155. Valentine's Day, Archie Hunter, *Power and Passion in Egypt* (London: I. B. Tauris, 2007), 102. "The sailors in charge," JGL to WWGII, February 14, 1911, GHS MS318/14/157.
26. Mena House, JGL to WWGII, February 14, 1911, GHS MS318/14/157, Memnon, McWilliams, 156–57.
27. European car trip, Shultz and Lawrence, 290; rental of studio, JGL to NKG, October 22, 1910, JGLB, "I longed for," JGL to WWGII, April 12, 1911, GHS MS318/14/157.
28. "Common," NKG to JGL, November 9, 1908, GHS MS318/42/18. See also NKG to JGL, August 21, 1910, GHS MS318/42/21, for Daisy having been "a fairy godmother to the Savannah girls!" "You are so generous," NKG to JGL, November 7, 1908, GHS MS318/42/18.
29. JGL to NKG, April 27, 1908, JGLB. Archie Hunter continued to send her presents and letters. He married Mary Inverclyde on All Souls Day 1910. He had just been appointed governor of Gibraltar. See Archie Hunter, *Kitchener's Sword-Arm* (New York: Sarpedon, 1996), 202–4. Forgetting the guests, Shultz

and Lawrence, 264–65. "I did not realize," Nevill M. Smyth to JGL, July 5 [no year], GFP 2235/SHC/320.

Chapter 11: General Sir Robert Baden-Powell

1. Meeting in Lincoln, Tim Jael, *Baden-Powell* (New Haven, CT: Yale University Press, 2001), 426; the rest from JGL to WWGII, GHS MS318/14/157.
2. The information on Baden-Powell's family and youth comes from William Hillcourt and Olave Baden-Powell, *Baden-Powell* (New York: G. P. Putnam's Sons, 1964), chap. 1. Hereafter cited as Hillcourt.
3. Information on Baden-Powell's schooling is from Hillcourt, chap. 2.
4. "Slavishly obedient," Jeal, 72; butterfly code, Hillcourt, 96–98.
5. Arthur Conan-Doyle's Sherlock Holmes stories were published in the widely read magazine *The Strand* in the 1890s.
6. Meeting Burnham, Jeal, 177. Burnham worked for the British South Africa Company when he met Baden-Powell. Carrington's assessment from Richard Harding Davis, *Real Soldiers of Fortune* (New York: Charles Scribner's Sons, 1912), 217; Robert Baden-Powell, *The Matabele Campaign* (London: Methuen and Company, 1897), 120–21. The Matapo Hills are today called the Matobo Hills. *Aids to Scouting* was published in 1899.
7. Archie Hunter, *Kitchener's Sword-Arm* (New York: Sarpedon, 1996), 140–47. See also Filson Young, *The Relief of Mafeking: How It Was Accomplished by Mahon's Flying Column* (London: Methuen, 1900).
8. Jeal, 359–61 (quotes from pp. 364, 367). According to Jeal, RBP did not actually form troops of boys to do the scouting at Mafeking.
9. Baden-Powell's Eton College's *Chronicle* article reprinted in Michael Rosenthal, "Knights and Retainers," *Journal of Contemporary History* 15, no. 4 (October 1980): 606–7; see also Jeal, 369–70.
10. Jeal, 376–77; for Brownsea, see 384–86. For Seton, see David Witt, *Earnest Thompson Seton: The Life and Legacy of an Artist and Conservationist* (Layton, UT: Gibbs Smith, 2010), and H. Allen Anderson, *The Chief: Ernest Thompson Seton and the Changing West* (College Station: Texas A&M University Press, 2000).
11. Jeal, 365.
12. "Indescribable discord," "London Jammed for Coronation," *New York Times*, June 22, 1911; procession route, "Rain Mars Night Rejoicing," *New York Times*, June 24, 1911. Daisy's description of coronation week and of meeting RBP, JGL to WWGII, June 29, 1911, GHS MS318/14/157. Carrie Kipling to JGL, [no date] [1910], GHS MS318/14/156.
13. Shakespeare Ball, JGL to NKG, June 21, 1911; "in the middle of," JGL to NKG, [June 1911], both from GHS MS318/14/157.
14. Jeal, 203.
15. Jeal, 373.
16. JGL diary fragment [no date] 1911, JGLB.
17. JGL diary fragment, June 1, 1911, JGLB. "Selfless unselfish," from JGL diary fragment, [no date] 1911, JGLB.
18. "Dread lest he," June 1, 1911; "No doubt," both JGL diary fragment, June 17, 1911, JGLB.

19. *The Mission Hymnal* (New York: Bigelow & Main, 1885), 85. Akerman took as her text Mark 11:13.
20. "Adventurous," Gladys Denny Shultz and Daisy Gordon Lawrence, *Lady from Savannah: The Life of Juliette Low* (Philadelphia: J. B. Lippincott, 1958), 297; to meet Henrietta, Jeal, 352; WWGIII to WWGII, July 26, 1911, GHS MS318/6/66.
21. At Lochs, JGL to NKG, August 7, 1911; letter fragment (item #3090) [no date]; JGL to WWGII, August 11, 1911, all GHS MS318/14/158; servant, JGL to EGP, August 6, 1911, and JGL to MGL, August 7, 1911, GHS MS318/14/158.
22. Mathias Morhardt in *Mercure de France*, March 1898, quoted in Odile Ayral-Clause, *Camille Claudel: A Life* (New York: Harry N. Abrams, 2002), 45. Few pieces, Marion Harry Spielmann, *British Sculpture and Sculptors of Today* (London: Cassell and Company, 1902), 127. Harriet's bust, Stanton on the Wolds Parish Council Web site, http://www.stantononthewoldsparishcouncil.gov.uk/the%20Robertsons%20of%20Stanton.htm.
23. Stuart MacDonald, *The History and Philosophy of Art Education* (Cambridge, UK: Lutterworth Press, 1970), 51; female students, Ruth Butler, *Rodin: The Shape of Genius* (New Haven, CT: Yale University Press, 1996), 181–82; "vigorous naturalism," Partha Mitter, *The Triumph of Modernism: India's Artists and the Avant-Garde, 1922–1947* (New York: Oxford University Press, 2007), 173; "New Sculpture," Ana Carden-Coyne, *Reconstructing the Body: Classicism, Modernism, and the First World War* (New York: Oxford University Press, 2009), 139, and Ayral-Clause, 45. Catherine Moriarty, *The Sculpture of Gilbert Ledward* (Aldershot: Lund Humphries/Aldershot, 2003), 27. The third volume of Lanteri's *Modelling: A Guide for Teachers and Students* was published the year JGL met RBP.
24. JGL to NKG, December 4, 1911, GHS MS318/14/158.
25. Jeal, 426–27.
26. Proposal, Shultz and Lawrence, 303; "I must stop," JGL letter fragment, [no date], GHS MS318/15/167(#3246). The letter could also have been written to her mother. "Eager to enjoy," GAG, "As Her Family Knew Her," in Anne Hyde Choate and Helen Ferris, eds., *Juliette Low and the Girl Scouts* (New York: Girl Scouts of the USA, 1928), 57.
27. Evangeline S. Adams, JGL Horoscope, [no date], GHS MS318/15/170.
28. "A sort of outcome," JGL to WWGII, [no date] [August 1911], GHS MS318/14/158(#3094). Many of the girls registered under false names or used initials only. "Partners and comrades," Rose Kerr, *The Story of a Million Girls* (London: Girl Guides Association, 1937), 9–10; Tammy Proctor, *Scouting for Girls* (Santa Barbara, CA: Praeger, 2009), 1, 7. For the masculine appeal of Boy Scouting to girls, see Sally Mitchell, *The New Girl* (New York: Columbia University Press, 1995), 119–24.
29. Proctor, 7, 8.
30. For information on Agnes Baden-Powell, see Helen D. Gardner, *The First Girl Guide* (Stroud: Amberley, 2010); "friendliness," Proctor, 9.
31. In a 1923 interview, JGL stated, "It took one girl four hours to walk over the pass to meetings," so whether it was six hours one way or six hours each way or four hours one way is not clear. JGL Interview, June 24, 1923, NHPC, JGL 1923. New skills, Rose Kerr, "Juliette Low Meets Sir Robert Baden-Powell and the Girl Guides," in Choate and Ferris, 67–68; Shultz and Lawrence, 300–301.

32. Elizabeth Robertson, *The Story of the Girl Guides in Scotland, 1908–2000* (Edinburgh: The Guide Association, 2004), 1; Fife, Doris W. Coyne, *A Kingdom for the Trefoil* (Kirkcaldy: John Davidson & Son, 1979), 12; Rose Kerr, *The Story of the Girl Guides* (London: The Girl Guides Association, 1932), 62. Lady Marjorie began with a (kilted) Boy Scout troop, and at their sisters' insistence started the Girl Guide patrol. Marjorie Dalrymple to Miss Athison, August 25, 1966, NHPC, JGL Gen'l Info-Pubs.
33. "Well and happy," MGL to NKG, September 29, 1911, GHS MS318/6/67; "I have no time," Kerr, in Choate and Ferris, 69; "I like girls," JGL to WWGII, [no date] [August 1911], GHS MS318/14/158(#3094).
34. "To form a patrol," JGL to NKG, December 30, 1911, GHS MS318/14/158; Promise, Proctor, 12–13. For an extensive treatment of Boy Scouting and its ideal of creating high-minded young men fit enough to protect the British Empire, see Michael Rosenthal, *The Character Factory* (New York: Pantheon Books, 1984).
35. Proctor, 14.
36. Robertson, 2.
37. Poem, [no date], JGLB.
38. To ascertain her sailing date, Shultz and Lawrence, 302. *Arcadian* manifest found at the Statue of Liberty–Ellis Island Foundation: www.ellisisland.org. OBP and her father embarked at Jamaica, the penultimate stop, so JGL and RBP were on the ship together for the majority of the journey. See also Olave Baden-Powell, *Window on My Heart* (London: Hodder and Stoughton, 1973), 65–70.

Chapter 12: The Savannah Girl Guides

1. Kisses, Olave Baden-Powell, *Window on My Heart* (London: Hodder and Stoughton, 1973), 66–71. Hereafter cited as OBP, *Window.* Gladys Denny Shultz and Daisy Gordon Lawrence, *Lady from Savannah* (New York: J. B. Lippincott, 1958), 303.
2. "Baden-Powell to Wed," *New York Times*, September 18, 1912.
3. Shultz and Lawrence, 305. For "body building" and "I want girls," see Paul Pressly, "Educating the Daughters of Savannah's Elite," *Georgia Historical Quarterly*, vol. 80, no. 2 (Summer 1996), 255, 256.
4. Hoxie, Pressly, 261; "Love and knowledge," Sallie Margaret McAlpin, "Memoirs of the Formative Days of the Girl Scouts," unidentified, undated clipping, JGLB; Anderson dinner, Shultz and Lawrence, 305–6.
5. A typed "History of Girl Scouts," amended in JGL's handwriting, includes this phrase: "first introduced into America by Juliette Low the organization under the name of Girl Guides and the first patrol of Girl Guides was enrolled in Savannah, Ga, Feb 18, 1912." (The underlining is in the original.) A later—typed—paragraph in the same document begins "In 1912, Mrs. Low had returned to America and started Guides" [sic] in her own city, Savannah, Ga." Around that paragraph, JGL has handwritten "omit." That undated document is in the Georgia Historical Society, GHS MS318/18/214.

   However, in a letter to JDR dated February 28, 1920, JGL typed the following: "I find that I have a plamphlet [sic] copyrighted the year 1910. you [sic] know I did start Girl Guides in 1910 but it was the following year, that I began to get the public into the work. . . ." That document is at the NHPC (JGL, Corresp 1920) along with a letter from JGL to Clara Lisetor Lane dated July 30, 1919, in which JGL states: "In 1910 I enrolled the first patrol of Girl Guides in Savannah, Georgia." (NHPC, JGL Corresp 1918–1919. JGL misspelled her name Liseter Lane.)

On March 12, 1912, JGL wrote to her sister Mabel, stating she was "deep in Girl Guides," but did not mention anything about what surely would have been the momentous event of enrolling the first troop. A copy of that letter is at the JGLB.

6. "Those Eventful Days in Early March, 1912," March 11, 1965, 1–3, JGLB. Page Anderson's mother was also named Page Anderson.
7. "Boy to Greet Baden-Powell," *New York Times*, January 30, 1912; RBP to JGL, February 22, 1912, GHS MS318/18/200. On March 6, 1912, RBP suggested Mrs. Charles B. Alexander. See his letter to JGL of that date, copy in JGLB. See, for one example, the lack of salutation, RBP to JGL, March 23 [1912], JGLB.
8. JGL to MGL, March 12, 1912, copy in JGLB. Daisy shared credit for the revision of the book with Hoxie in her letter to her mother. Shultz and Lawrence, 320, state that Daisy adapted Agnes Baden-Powell's handbook and that Hoxie wrote the chapters on woodcraft and camping and edited the rest.

   Pressly, 262 (n. 21), gives credit to the "committee of women" centered on Pape, including her friends Hortense Orcutt and Jane Judge but also Hoxie. He cites the reminiscences of both Pape and Edith Johnston. The full title of ABP's 1912 manual was *The Official Handbook for Girl Guides or How Girls Can Help Build the Empire*. The copy she inscribed to Daisy reads "to my dear friend Mrs. Low," JGL's *Handbook* at JGLB.
9. Juliette Low and W. J. Hoxie, *How Girls Can Help Their Country* (New York: Knickerbocker Press, 1913). This was the first U.S. handbook published. There were exceptions to every rule, especially in the early days: Mildred Guckenheimer was a nineteen-year-old captain.
10. "Publisher's Column," *Kindergarten News* 6, no. 1 (January 1896), 37. Nina Pape listed the following as the original group of advisers: "Miss Elizabeth Beckwith, Commissioner, Members, Mrs. Robert Billington, Mrs. J. F. C. Myers, Mrs. B. P. Axson, Mrs. W. W. Gordon, Miss Lenora Amorano, Miss Hortense Orcutt, Miss Nina Anderson Paper, Miss Lina Woodbridge, Treas, Miss Sallie McAlpin, Exec, Sect'y (Director). Two prospective Captains, Mrs. J. R. Anderson & Miss Marjorie Van Diviere with Mr. J. Hoxie, a former Harvard graduate and a lover of birds & nature to help us with the original Guide or Scout book," Nina Anderson Pape to Katherine O. Wright, August 15, 1937, JGLB.

    Pressly, 260, describes these women as mostly all connected to the Pape School, although three worked with the Free Kindergarten Association. The kindergarten movement began before the Civil War. It was spearheaded in the United States by women who sought to ameliorate the disadvantages of poverty and to assist the assimilation of immigrants to America while emphasizing fun and providing a wholesome learning atmosphere for young children.
11. More precisely, Savannah Female Orphan Asylum Girl Guide Patrol might have been the first Girl Guide patrol formed in the United States as a direct idea from Juliette Low. The Savannah Female Orphan Asylum Girl Guide Patrol is listed first in "The First Girl Guide Register," JGLB. "The Register," however, is not a

perfect source of information, as too many uncertainties surround the entries it contains, phone interview, Katherine Keena, January 4, 2011. Curiously, in April a troop formed south of town, where Gordon Hoxie was superintendent at the Bethesda Home for Boys, which clearly at the time in some way succored girls, too. Nina Beckett led the Bethesda patrol. On the Bethesda troop, Keena to author, January 7 and February 1, 2011; for Hoxie, Walter G. Fargo, "Walter J. Hoxie," *Wilson Ornithological Society Journal*, vol. 46, no. 3 (September 1934), 180.

12. "Those Eventful Days," p. 5. Nina Anderson Pape stated that all the members of JGL's advisory committee were present as well. Pape to Katherine O. Wright, August 15, 1937, JGLB.
13. Nina Pape lists the following as charter members: Daisy Gordon, Harriet Stewart, Elsie Espey, Florence Crane, Elizabeth Purse, Elizabeth Steele, Walton Bremer, G. Driscoll, Martha Randolph, Page R. Anderson, Anne C. Read, Cecilia Garrod, Jean Cunningham, Clarissa Gaines, Helen Brigham. Next to the following names she has written a question mark: Eleanor Taylor, Ellen Knox, Helen Menzies. Next to the following she has written "no": Anne Hopkins, Edith Battey. From Nina Anderson Pape's 1935 Diary, Nina Anderson Pape Papers, GHS MS605/1/Item 6.

    In 1936 and 1937, the following women attested to their presence as "charter members of the Girl Guides" on March 12, 1912. The numbers following denote the order in which the girls were enrolled. White Rose Patrol: Martha Randolph Stevens (6), Anne Read Charlton (7), Eleanor Taylor Farie (8), Jean Cunningham Reade (3), Page R. Anderson Platt (1), Cecilia Garrard (5), Clarissa Gaines Lambert (4), and Helen Brigham Gadebusch (2). In the Carnation Patrol: Daisy Gordon Lawrence, Elizabeth Skeele Klein, Berenice Fetzer Alnutt, Harriet Stewart Rowland, Eslie Espy Frank, Marian Corbin Aslakson, Florence Crane Norvell, Gertrude Porter Driscoll, and Walton Brewer Nance. Harriet Stewart was the first girl to sign her name, after JGL wrote her niece's name. From "Those Eventful Days," 3, 4.

    City of Savannah Testimonial, February 12, 1926, JGLB. Since 1932, the Girl Scouts officially celebrate March 12, 1912, as the date of the founding.
14. "Character and intelligence," JGL, "History of Girl Scouts," JGLB; NKG to JGL, March 17 [no year], GHS MS 318/42/3 (Addenda 6). African American involvement, author interview with Katherine Keena, January 4, 2010. Mamie's last name is unknown. The ethnically rich troop was led by Henrietta Falk.
15. Helen Holmberg, "From Girl Scout to Sister," copy of clipping from the *Dubuque Witness*, March 9, 1950, JGLB.
16. "Girl Guides in Thrilling Games," *Savannah Morning News*, March 27, 1913, and "Fast Basketball by Girls' Teams," *Savannah Morning News*, March 29, 1913, clippings at JGLB. Curtains, McAlpin, "Memoirs."
17. The information on the early days of Guiding in Savannah comes from McAlpin, "Memoirs," and Shultz and Lawrence, 305–7.
18. McAlpin, "Memoirs."
19. WWGII to JGL, May 14, 1912, JGLB.
20. James McNally to NKG, March 7, 1912, GHS MS318/6/70; WWGII to NKG, March 1, 1912, GHS MS318/6/70. Taft was a Republican. WWGII was a Democrat. Their mutual work for the Yale alumni association trumped their different political philosophies.

21. Alice's wedding, EGP to MGC, April 7, 1912, CFP MS2800/16/14, Anne Hyde Choate to MGC, April 14 [1912], CFP MS2800/16/14. "We live so far apart," JGL to MGC, January 31, 1910, JGLB. The first reunion with Mary and Abby together in Cooperstown since before they were all married happened in the fall of 1910. The three old friends spent three days together on the occasion of Mary and Hyde's silver wedding anniversary.
22. Liberty Hyde Bailey, *The Outlook to Nature* (New York: Macmillan, 1905), 8; Susan A. Miller, *Growing Girls* (New Brunswick, NJ: Rutgers University Press, 2007), 4.
23. Lina Beard and Adelia Belle Beard, *How to Amuse Yourself and Others: The American Girls Handybook* (New York: Scribner's, 1887); Daniel Carter Beard, *The American Boys Handybook: What to Do and How to Do It* (New York: Scribner's 1882).
24. Each of Lina Beard's annual entries in *Woman's Who's Who of America* contained that phrase, "the sister organization of the Boy Scouts." See, for example, the 1914–1915 issue, John W. Leonard, ed. (New York: American Commonwealth Company, 1914), 87. Adelia Beard's entries contain the same phrase; see page 86 of the 1914–1915 issue. For her plans, see also "'Girl Pioneers,' New Club," *New York Times*, February 8, 1912. "Brave, upright," Lina Beard, "Girl Pioneers," *The Outlook* 101, no. 5 (June 1, 1912), 275.
25. "Girl Pioneers, Hurrah!" *New York Times*, June 8, 1911. "Founder," "Says She Founded the Girl Scouts," *New York Times*, April 14, 1924. The Girl Pioneers of America was a short-lived amalgamation of these groups.
26. Miller, 17.
27. "Very interesting fact," Hartley Davis and Mrs. Luther Gulick, "The Camp Fire Girls," *The Outlook*, vol. 101, no. 4 (May 25, 1912), 182; "strictly home-based," Miller, 21; "primitive hearth," Davis and Gulick, 182; Jennifer Helgren, "'Homemaker' Can Include the World," in Jennifer Helgren and Colleen A. Vasconcellos, *Girlhood* (New Brunswick, NJ: Rutgers University Press, 2010), 306.
28. JGL to Charlotte Gulick, [no date] [April 1912], GHS MS318/18/200(#3745); Miller, 26–28.
29. JGL to Edith Johnston, [no date], GHS MS318/18/210.
30. "Boy to Greet Baden-Powell," *New York Times*, January 30, 1912; "Taft Reviews Boy Scouts," *New York Times*, February 4, 1912. The Girl Pioneers were started by Evelyn Wotherspoon Wainwright, wife of Rear Admiral Richard Wainwright. "Roosevelt Luncheon Today," *New York Times*, February 11, 1912; Theodore Roosevelt, "A Message to All the Boys of America," in Walter P. McGuire and Franklin P. Mathiews, eds., *The Boy Scouts Yearbook* (New York: Appleton, 1915), 46–47. Annual BSA dinner, "Baden-Powell Here Again," *New York Times*, February 3, 1912.
31. EGP quoted in Anastatia Hodgens Sims, "Juliette Gordon Low," in Ann Short Chirhart and Betty Wood, eds., *Georgia Women*, vol. 1 (Athens: University of Georgia Press, 2009), 377. "Camp Fire was the most popular organization for girls in the United States until 1930, when Girl Scout membership surpassed its own" (Helgren, 306). "Crowds Cheer Taft as He Leaves City," *New York Times*, March 5, 1913. "Collecting, adapting," JGL to NKG and WWGII, April 12 [1912], NHPC, JGL Corresp 1920-Diary.
32. Publisher, JGL to NKG, June 25, 1912, JGLB; NKG to JGL, July 8, 1912, JGLB; Nellie Kinzie Gordon, *Narrative of the Massacre at Chicago*, 2nd ed. (Chicago:

Fergus, 1914). "History of the Girl Scouts," undated and corrected by hand by JGL, GHS MS318/18/214.

33. Macaw, JGL to NKG, June 25, 1912; bust, JGL to NKG, July 20, 1912, both JGLB.
34. JGL to WWGII, May 22, 1912, JGLB.
35. JGL to NKG and WWGII, May 9, 1912, NHPC, JGL Corresp to Diary. Heroic deeds, like NKG's assistance to the Goshen veterans, could be recorded, without public censure, in newspapers.
36. Evangeline S. Adams, JGL Horoscope, 12, [no date], GHS MS318/15/170.
37. See H. W. Bell to GAG, September 12, 1912, GHS MS318/6/74; "Distinguished Savannahian Passes Away," *Savannah Press*, undated clipping [c. September 12, 1912]; "Gen. Gordon Died in West Virginia," undated, unidentified clipping, GHS, BioFile "Gordon"; "William Washington Gordon," *Confederate Veteran*, vol. 20, no. 11 (November 1912), 526–27. For the African American encomium, see untitled clipping, *Savannah Tribune*, September 14, 1912, GHS MS318/11/122. Yet Willie Gordon was buried, at his request, in his Confederate uniform coat and with his sword. The Daughters of the Confederacy and the Children of the Confederacy sent flowers to the funeral.
38. "Glorious heritage," Eliza Gordon Stiles to GAG, [no date], GHS MS318/6/75; "lost, in Papa," Shultz and Lawrence, 314. MGL to JGL, September 11, 1912, and October 15, 1912, GHS MS318/14/159.
39. Shultz and Lawrence, 313.
40. Nina Pape 1935 Diary.
41. "Baden-Powell's Fiancee 22," *New York Times*, September 22, 1912. RBP was born in 1857. OBP was born in 1889. Wedding ceremony, OBP, *Window*, 90–91; "Gen Baden-Powell Married," *New York Times*, October 31, 1912. Christmas, Shultz and Lawrence, 315.
42. "Stupor," Shultz and Lawrence, 314; Evangeline S. Adams, JGL Horoscope, 12, [no date], GHS MS318/15/170; "luxury of woe," JGL to MGC, March 8 [1888], CFP MS2800/8/15; Job, 42:10.

Chapter 13: The Excitement of Girl Scouting

1. "Reception at Girl Guides' Quarters," *Savannah Press*, December 10, 1912; "Reception at Guides' Headquarters," *Savannah News*, December 8, 1912; "Proficiency Badge Awarded," *Savannah Press*, January 25, 1913; "'Keep Off the Grass,' Girl Guides' Request," *Savannah News*, January 10, 1913, all JGLB.
2. "New Plans of Girl Scouts," unidentified, undated clipping [1913], JGLB; Edith D. Johnston to EGP, June 17, 1913, NHPC, JGL Bio Info to Corresp 1920. Classes, Edith D. Johnston to JGL, February 18, 1913, NHPC, JGL Bio Info to Corresp 1920; "Play Festival a Great Success," *Savannah News*, May 7, 1913, clipping, JGLB.
3. Rose Kerr, *The Story of the Girl Guides* (London: The Girl Guides Association, 1932), 35 (quote), 34.
4. James West to OBP, August 26, 1922, GHS MS318/18/207.
5. Juliette Low and J. W. Hoxie, *How Girls Can Help Their Country* (New York: Knickerbocker Press, 1913), 121, and first page of the foreword.
6. JGL 1916 Speech, GHS MS 318/18/211.
7. Allen Warren, "Popular Manliness: Baden-Powell, Scouting, and the Development of Manly Character," in *Manliness and Morality*, J. A. Mangan and James Walvin, eds. (New York: St. Martin's Press, 1987), 200.

8. "165 Scouts," Edith D. Johnston to EGP, June 17, 1913, NHPC, JGL Bio Info to Corresp 1920; office set-up, Edith D. Johnston to JGL, June 8, 1913, NHPC, JGL Bio Info to Corresp 1920; JGL to Cora Neal, [no date] [1914], NHPC, JGL Corresp 1914. The ideal of eight girls and one captain to a patrol seldom worked out in practice. More important to Daisy was the simple fact that girls and women were involved.
9. For example, "Eleanor puts my return being necessary on the score or Girl Scouts needing me, but they don't. I've fixed them up for 3 months," JGL to GAG, June 19, 1913, GFP MS2235/SHC/259.
10. Edith D. Johnston to EGP, June 17, 1913, NHPC, JGL Bio Info to Corresp 1920.
11. Edith D. Johnston, "Juliette Low Brings Girl Scouting to the U.S.A.," in Anne Hyde Choate and Helen Ferris, *Juliette Low and the Girl Scouts* (New York: Girl Scouts, 1928), 87–88, 90.
12. JGL to Sophie Meldrim, July 3, 1913, GHS MS318/14/159; James E. West to Edith D. Johnston, July 9, 1913, NHPC, JGL Bio Info to Corresp 1920; "met every demand," Anne Hyde Choate, "Girl Scouting Gets Under Way," in Choate and Ferris, 103.
13. JGL to Cora D. Neal, [no date] [1914], NHPC, JGL Corresp 1914; NKG to JGL, [no date] [1914], GHS MS318/42/26.
14. Radium, MGL to NKG, June 28, 1913, GFP MS2235/SHC/259. Book review of *The Treatment of Gout and Rheumatism with Radium*, in *American Journal of the Medical Sciences*, vol. 141, no. 6 (June 1911): 911; Joseph Muir, "Radium for Gout," *New York Times*, October 5, 1913. Wilhelm His, "The Treatment of Gout and Rheumatism by Radium," *British Medical Journal*, February 4, 1911: 243–46. Her treatment is an extrapolation from NKG's twenty-four radium treatments in November 1913. NKG saw that JGL's treatments worked and thus followed her example. NKG to GAG, November 7, 1913, GFP MS2235/SHC/264. "Gouty rash," JGL TO NKG, June 19, 1913, GFP MS2235/SHC/259.
15. Nevill M. Smyth to JGL, June 20, 1913, GFP MS2235/SHC/259.
16. The September Bennett Cup Competition was won by Maurice Prevost flying 125 mph. See "Aeronautics," in Frank Moore Colby, et al., eds., *New International Yearbook* (New York: Dodd, Mead, 1914), 4. JGL's "delicious experience" written on Nevill M. Smyth to JGL July 18, 1913, GFP MS2235/SHC/260; "Ladies Day at Herndon," *Flight*, July 13, 1912, 1. Spratt and Smyth flew together at Herndon. See, for example, "British Deperdussin School," *Flight*, June 7, 1913.
17. Grace's Guide states that Smyth earned his license on July 16, 1913, http://www.gracesguide.co.uk/wiki/1913_Aviators_Certificates_-_UK.
18. JGL to NKG, June 12, 1913, GHS MS318/14/159; "Last Court of Season," *Montreal Gazette*, June 12, 1913.
19. Thanks Badge, JGL to NKG, July 3, 1913, GFP MS2235/SHC/260; "Honored Girl Guides," *Savannah News*, August 8, 1913. On ABP's troubles, see Helen D. Gardner, *The First Girl Guide* (Stroud: Amberley, 2010), especially 72–92.
20. Ready to leave, JGL to NKG, June 23, 1913, GHS MS318/14/159; Lochs plans, JGL to NKG, June 19, 1913, GFP MS2235/SHC/259; "who loves," JGL to NKG, July 8, 1913, GFP MS2235/SHC/260.
21. Edith D. Johnston to JGL, July 14, 1913, NHPC, JGL Bio Info to Corresp 1920.
22. Edith D. Johnston to JGL, September 11, 1913, NHPC, JGL Corresp 1913.
23. For the directors, see *The Book of Camp Fire Girls* (New York: Camp Fire Girls, 1914), 8. Parish, EGP to JGL, May 24, 1913, GFP MS2235/SHC/259.

24. NKG to Mrs. Axson (probably Margaret Callaway Axson of Savannah, who was married to Ellen's first cousin Palmer), May 8, 1913, GHS MS318/7/77; Ellen Axson Wilson to JGL, May 21, 1913, GHS MS318/18/201.
25. Information on the visit to Garrett and Wilson from NKG to MGL, May 5, 1913, GHS MS318/7/77.
26. JGL to Montague Gammon, March 20, 1917, NHPC, JGL Bio-1920. E. H. (Ted) Coy purchased the pearls for his wife, Sophia (Katherine Keena to author, April 16, 2011).
27. JGL to NKG (fragment), [no date] [April 1914], GHS MS318/15/160; NKG to JGL (fragment), [no date] [April 1914], JGLB.
28. Edith D. Johnston to JGL, May 1, 1914, NHPC, JGL Corresp 1914; Cora Neal to JGL, November 11, 1914, NHPC, JGL Corresp 1914; MGL to GAG, December 5, 1913, GFP MS2235/SHC/265; NKG to JGL, May 23, 1914, GHS MS318/42/25.
29. ALH to MGC, September 20 [1914], CFP MS2800/21/14.
30. "George Hyde Clarke," *New York Times*, August 2, 1914; Anne Clarke Logan and Karin Lodensky Nelson, *The Ladies of Hyde Hall* (Cooperstown, NY: Hyde Hall, 2009), 72–73; author interview with Douglas Kent, December 15, 2010.
31. "Laying in stores," JGL to MGL, August 4, 1914, GHS MS318/15/160; JGL to MGL, [no date] [December 1914], GHS MS 318/15/161.
32. On the refugees, see JGL to MGL, October 30 [1914], GHS MS318/5/160; NKG to JGL, January 6, 1915, GHS MS318/42/27; Carrie Kipling to NKG, December 31, 1914, CFP MS2800/SHC272, and Barbara McLaren, *Women of the War* (New York: George H. Doran Company, 1918), chap. 28. "If you can't keep," NKG to JGL, November 30, 1914, GHS MS318/42/26.
33. "Prepared by Frank B. Morse," 1914, NHPC, JGL Corresp July–Dec 1914. Boardman's mother was a patron.
34. JGL to MGL, October 30 [1914], GHS MS318/5/160; revising the handbook, JGL to Cora Neal, October 11, 1914, NHPC, JGL Corresp July–Dec 1914.
35. JGL to Edith D. Johnston, November 17, 1915, GHS MS318/18/202.
36. Raising funds, Edith D. Johnston to JGL, April 24, 1915, NHPC, JGL Bio-1920; "Plan for Girl Scouts," *Savannah News*, October 9, 1915, clipping, JGLB. "Arouse the spirit," "Girl Scout Magazine," *Savannah Press*, January 2, 1915, JGLB. RBP's permission, JGL to Edith D. Johnston, November 17, 1915, GHS MS318/18/202.
37. Bankruptcy, JGL to GAG, January 8, 1915, GFP MS2800/SHC/273; "torpedo," JGL to Edith D. Johnston, January 27, 1915, GHS MS318/18/202; *Lusitania*, MGL to GAG, February 14, 1915, GFP MS2800/SHC/273.
38. "Girl Scouts Not Camp Fire Girls," *New York Times*, March 10, 1915; "Injustice to Girl Scouts," *Savannah News*, March 14, 1915, clipping, JGLB; RWP to GAG, March 20, 1915, GFP MS2800/SHC/274; RWP to JGL, April 13, 1915, GHS MS318/18/202; Number of Girl Scouts, "Girl Scouts at Home and Abroad," *Savannah News*, February 14, 1915, clipping, JGLB; Number of patrons, Juliette Low, *How Girls Can Help Their Country*, v–vi.
39. Organization, Low, *How Girls Can Help Their Country*, 2; JGL to NKG, June 11, 1915, GHS MS318/18/202; "Other 'Firsts' of the Girl Scouts," March 12, 1965, JGLB; Girl Scouts, Inc, *Highlights in Girl Scouting, 1912–2001* (New York: GSUSA, 2002), 6.
40. JGL to MGL, [no date] [May 1915], GHS MS318/15/162.

41. BSA convention, "Girl Scouts at Home and Abroad," *Savannah News*, February 14, 1915; "Girl Scouts Guests on Outing," *Savannah Press*, June 28, 1915, both clippings from JGLB.
42. Birthday, Shultz and Lawrence, 336; NKG to Madame Le Beau, June 19, 1915, GFP MS2800/SHC/275. On the Acousticon, JGL diary letter to NKG, June 28, 1915, GFP MS2800/SHC/275. On the other hand, there is a letter fragment, undated, from NKG to an unknown recipient that states, "Tell Daisy I got back the Acousticon from Boston. I tried it and think it is a 'damned fraud,'" GHS MS318/42/31.
43. Anne Hyde Choate, "Girl Scouting Gets Under Way," in Choate and Ferris, 96; Shultz and Lawrence, 336–37.
44. ALH's note, ALH to GAG, March 29, 1927, GHS MS 318/8/97; "saw Abby," JGL to MGC, July 20, 1915, JGLB.
45. "Two Hundred Americans Killed in Submarine Attacks," *Current History* 5, no. 2 (November 1916), 990–91.
46. "Full of," MGL to NKG, June 29, 1915; tea, JGL diary letter to NKG, June 28, 1915, both from GFP MS2800/SHC/275. Undated, unidentified newspaper clipping of deaths of Edward Henry Leigh and Chandos Leigh, attached to Nevill Smyth to JGL, July 11, 1915, JGLB. Kipling boy, American Consular Service (Berlin) to JGL, October 23, 1915, and JGL to WWGIII, November 2, 1915, both JGLB.
47. JGL 1916 Speech, GHS MS318/18/211.
48. OBP, Gardner, 91; "Clever but thoroughly Victorian," Tammy Proctor, *Scouting for Girls* (Denver: Praeger, 2009), 33–34 (quote from 33).
49. "Right arm," JGL to Edith D. Johnston, October 4, 1915, GHS MS318/18/202; "study the present war," "Richard Wayne Parker," William E. Sackett, ed., *New Jersey's First Citizens* (Paterson, NJ: Scannell, 1917), 387; NKG to JGL, July 27, 1915, GHS MS318/42/27; "R. Wayne Parker Put in an Asylum," July 20, 1915; NKG to JGL, August 17, 1915, GHS MS 318/42/28. Risk of Atlantic crossing, JGL to Edith D. Johnston, October 4, 1915, GHS MS318/18/202. Representative Parker served unbroken in the 51st through the 61st Congresses (1895–1911). He was reelected for the 63rd through the 65th (1914–1919) and again for the 67th (1921–1923).
50. RBP to JGL, September 29, 1915, GHS MS318/18/202; JGL to Cora Neal, [no date] [1914], NHPC, JGL Correspondence 1914. "Growth of Girl Scouts," unidentified clipping, September 15, 1915, JGLB. However, "Guides in America," *Girl Guides Gazette*, August 1915, states that Girl Scout membership was "now approximating three thousand six hundred girls." Badges, "Mrs. Low's Talk on Girl Scout Work," *Savannah Press*, March 1916, typescript, JGLB. "Plan Senior Scouts," *New York Times*, May 3, 1916; mascot, "Service the Slogan of the Girl Scouts," *New York Times*, June 18, 1916. The mother was actually seventeen years old.
51. JGL to Edith D. Johnston, December 5, 1915, JGLB; "Mrs. Low's Talk on Girl Scout Work," *Savannah Press*, March 1916, typescript, JGLB; NKG to JGL, April 1, 1916, GHS MS318/42/29; NKG to JGL, dated Easter Tuesday [April 25], 1916, GHS MS318/42/29. The new heaquarters was 17 West Forty-second Street. "Girl Scout Offices Soon to Open Here," *New York Times*, April 16, 1916; Ted Dickson, Jr., "An International Movement Is the Organization of Girl Scouts, Which,

Organized by Mrs. Low, Has Extended to Several Countries," *Savannah News,* May 7, 1916, clipping, JGLB. Gammon's title became chief executive.

52. "Service the Slogan of the Girl Scouts," *New York Times,* June 18, 1916; ABP to JGL, June 22 [1916], NHPC, JGL Bio to Corresp 1912; sales figure, JGL to MGL, October 31, 1916, GHS MS318/15/162.
53. JGL to Montague Gammon, July 21, 1916, NHPC, Corresp 1915–1916.
54. "A house for relatives," NKG to WWGIII, October 16, 1916, GHS MS318/7/83. Her partner in this enterprise was Violet Stuart Wortley, Mary Low's sister-in-law. Seven homes, "Mrs. W. W. Gordon Returns from London," *Savannah Morning News,* November 7, 1916, GHS Scrapbook MS 318/5637; 56th birthday, JGL to WWGIII, October 31, 1916, GHS MS18/15/162.
55. "Rag doll," NKF to MGL, November 13, 1916; "successful," NKG to MGL, November 9, 1916, both from GHS MS318/7/83.
56. Montague Gammon to JGL, March 2, 1917, NHPC, JGL Bio-1920; "Many Joining Girl Scouts," *New York Times,* February 11, 1916.
57. Self-description from NKG to Mary Wolcott Durham, November 16, 1916, GHS MS318/43/addenda 6/folder 2. "Woman Pioneer Reported Dying," *Chicago Tribune,* February 13, 1917; "John Kinzie's Granddaughter Dies in South," *Chicago Tribune,* February 23, 1917; "I just want," Shultz and Lawrence, 346–47.

Chapter 14: Good Deeds

1. "Sort of break down," JGL to Montague Gammon, March 2, 1917. See also JGL to Gammon, March 8, 1917, both from NHPC, JGL Bio-1920. "Woodland air," JGL to Miss Wilkins, March 10, 1917, NHPC, JGL Bio-1920; Gladys Denny Shultz and Daisy Gordon Lawrence, *Lady from Savannah* (New York: J. B. Lippincott, 1958), 348–49.
2. NKG to JGL, dated Easter Tuesday [April 25], 1916, GHS MS 318/42/29.
3. JGL to Montague Gammon, April 14, April 15, April 18, and July 5, 1917, all NHPC, JGL Bio-1920.
4. Urging to work together, JGL to AHC, [no date] [1917], ("You will, I know, like Prof. Elsom."); salute controversy, JGL to Montague Gammon, March 28, 1917; Gammon to JGL, March 29, 1917; Gammon family patrol, Gammon to JGL, April 7, 1917; pins, JGL to Gammon, April 10, 1917, all from NHPC, JGL Bio-1920.
5. Uniforms, Montague Gammon to JGL, April 11, 1917; "take the responsibility," Gammon to JGL, June 18, 1917. JGL directed that funds be sent to Agnes Baden-Powell twice in 1917. Was it for her assistance with the handbook revisions, or was it a kind of royalty? See Gammon to JGL, April 4, 1917 (£50) and JGL to Gammon, July 17, 1917 ($150). For bill paying, see, for example, JGL to AHC, March 31, 1917, all from NHPC, JGL Bio-1920.
6. Publicity, Charles Pathe films: JGL to Montague Gammon, date illegible ("Please wait until we meet before again trying"), 1917; Gammon to JGL, July 13, 1917; clipping service, Gammon to JGL, May 15, 1917; fifty letters, JGL to Gammon, February 12, 1917; cape design, JGL to Gammon, April 14, 1917, all from NHPC, JGL Bio-1920. Because it was deemed inappropriate and disrespectful to wear the flag, this was not done.
7. GSUSA "Information Pamphlet" (1917) NHPC, JGL Bio-1920. It explained that all Girl Scouts and leaders had to adhere to the Promise and Laws. Girls paid

annual dues of twenty-five cents. They could purchase the handbook for thirty cents. The leader's manual sold for a quarter. Badges, when earned, cost between five and fifteen cents, and uniforms could be homemade or ordered from national headquarters.

8. "$150.00," Montague Gammon to JGL, April 9, 1917; "$412.00," Gammon to JGL, June 19, 1917; "$601.65," Gammon to JGL, June 29, 1917; "to assist in the promotion," Gammon to JGL, April 13, 1917, all NHPC, JGL Bio-1920. RBP to JGL, February 16, 1918, GHS MS318/18/205. Surplus, Gammon to JGL, June 19, 1917, NHPC, JGL Bio-1920.
9. JGL to "Dear Captain," May 22, 1917, NHPC, JGL Bio-1920. The Boy Scouts of America awarded Jenks their highest award in 1926 for this. Occoneechee Council, BSA, http://www.ocscouts.org/scoutsource/Awards/SilverBuffalo.aspx.
10. Montague Gammon to JGL, April 13, 1917; seventy new Girl Scouts; JGL to Gammon, July 5, 1917, both NHPC, JGL Bio-1920.
11. RBP to JGL, June 14, 1917; "English Girl Guides Orderlies to General Pershing," press clipping, both NHPC, JGL Bio-1920.
12. "Appeal to Women to Aid in Making Registration Day a Public Festival," Committee on Public Information, *Official Bulletin,* vol. 1, no. 14 (May 25, 1917): 5. See also "Women Unite for Service," *New York Times,* May 27, 1917; and JGL to AHC, [no date] [1917], NHPC, JGL Bio-1920 ("You will, I know, like Prof. Elsom.") "Linked up," JGL to MGL, letter fragment, [no date] [1917], GHS MS318/18/204.
13. JGL to "Dear Captain," August 22, 1917; APL to JGL, August 22, 1917, both from NHPC, JGL Bio-1920.
14. Mrs. Theodore Price, "Girl Scouts," *The Outlook,* vol. 118, no. 10 (March 6, 1918): 367; "American Girl Scouts," *Girl Guides' Gazette,* vol. 5, no. 54 (June 1918), 85. APL and JGL to Girl Scout Captains, August 29, 1917, JGLB.
15. APL and JGL to Girl Scout Captains, August 29, 1917, JGLB; Herbert Hoover to JGL, October 3, 1917, GHS MS318/18/204.
16. "Red Cross Gains New Auxiliaries," *New York Times,* November 19, 1917.
17. Mrs. Theodore H. Price, "Girl Scouts," *The Outlook,* vol. 118 (March 6, 1918), 367; trench candles, Daniel J. Sweeny, ed., *History of Buffalo and Erie County, 1914–1919* (Buffalo: Committee of One Hundred, 1920), 379. Philadelphia, Price, "Girl Scouts," 367; Washington, "American Girl Scouts," *Girl Guides' Gazette,* vol. 5, no. 54 (June 1918): 85; pickling and drying, Carl Vrooman to JGL, June 5, 1918; Canning Club girls, O. B. Martin to JGL, June 5, 1918, both GHS MS318/18/205.
18. APL to JGL, December 4, 1917, NHPC, JGL Bio-1920; Anne Beiser Allen, *An Independent Woman* (Westport, CT: Greenwood Press, 2000), 90.
19. Edith Benham to JGL, October 16, 1917, GHS MS318/18/204.
20. JGL to MGL, letter fragment, [no date] [1917], GHS MS318/18/204; for Edith Wilson's later awards, see, for example, "President's Wife Presents Golden Eaglet to Cleverest Girl Scout," *Fort Wayne News Sentinel,* April 13, 1918; Edith Benham to JGL, June 18, 1918, GHS MS318/18/205; and "Girl Scouts to Open $100,000 Drive," *New York Times,* September 26, 1919. Elsewhere, JGL stated that she was to award the first Golden Eaglet ever in a letter to Gammon in June 1917. The ceremony was to have been in New Bedford, Massachusetts. See JGL to Montague Gammon, June 28, 1917, NHPC, JGL Bio-1920.

21. "President's Wife Gives Colors Here to Girl Scout Unit," *Philadelphia Inquirer,* June 27, 1918.
22. Constitution verified, Lillian S. Williams, *A Bridge to the Future* (New York: Girl Scouts of the USA, 1996), 10. Katherine and Winifred Quinan were among the founders of the Catholic Lily of the Valley troop. See Helen Holmberg, "From Girl Scout to Sister," copy of clipping from the *Dubuque Witness,* March 9, 1950, JGLB; for anti-Catholic sentiment in the YWCA, see JGL to AHC, September 8, 1918, NHPC, JGL Bio-1920. "In institutions," "American Girl Scouts," *Girl Guides' Gazette,* vol. 5, no. 54 (June 1918): 85. Native American and Mexican American troops, Williams, 11.
23. JGL to Montague Gammon, January 12, 1917, NHPC, JGL Bio-1920.
24. JGL to Montague Gammon, January 12, 1917, NHPC, JGL Bio-1920. Baden-Powell's biographer tells a more nuanced and sympathetic story: Tim Jael, *Baden-Powell* (New Haven, CT: Yale University Press, 2001), 492–93. See also Tammy Proctor, *On My Honor* (Philadelphia: American Philosophical Society, 1992), 144–46.
25. See, for one particularly unsavory example of NKG's racism, NKG to JGL, [no date] [January 1917], JGLB. The letter begins, "I sent a lot of mail to H. Park yesterday." "Bound in the end," JGL to Montague Gammon, January 4, 1917, NHPC, JGL Bio-1920.
26. Philadelphia council, Montague Gammon to JGL, June 29, 1917; hire a shipper, JGL to Gammon, June 2, 1917, both NHPC, JGL Bio-1920.
27. "Size 36," JGL to Montague Gammon, date illegible ("Please wait until we meet before again trying."), 1917, NHPC, JGL Bio-1920; loved her uniform, Josephine Daskam Bacon, "Here and There with Juliette Low in Girl Scouting," in *Juliette Low and the Girl Scouts,* Choate and Ferris, eds. (New York: Girl Scouts, 1928), 134. Nevertheless, Daisy's upbringing and class dictated that women not be conspicuous. According to Katherine Keena, Anne Hyde Choate told how sometimes while traveling Daisy thought it best to appear less obvious, so she would wrap herself in a large scarf like a shroud—believing this would make her less noticeable! (Katherine Keena to author, April 16, 2011.)
28. Gimbel Brothers advertisement, *New York Times,* April 14, 1918; steady income, APL to JGL, December 6, 1917; middling success, JGL to Miss Horowitz, [no date] [1917], NHPC, JGL Bio-1920.
29. Second drive, Price, "Girl Scouts," *The Outlook* 118, no. 10 (March 6, 1918): 367; third and fourth drives, Juliette Low, "Girl Scouts as an Educational Force," Department of the Interior Bulletin No. 33 (Washington, DC: Government Printing Office, 1919), 7; "Liberty Bond Medals to Girls," *New York Times,* June 23, 1918. "$24,000," JGL to "Beachy," July 4, 1918, JGLB.
30. Philander P. Claxton to JGL, August 27, 1918, and JGL to Claxton, September 14, 1918, GHS MS318/18/205. Number of Girl Scouts, Anastatia Hodgens Sims, "Juliette Gordon Low," in Chirhart and Wood, eds., *Georgia Women*, vol. 1 (Athens: University of Georgia Press, 2009), 385. Honorary committee work, JGL to F. C. Holmes, August 1, 1920; John O'Ryan to JGL, March 3, 1920; and Laurence LaTourette Driggs to JGL, November 14, 1920; all GHS MS318/18/206. JGL to F. C. Holmes, August 1, 1920, NHPC, JGL Bio-1920. Driggs to JGL, November 14, 1920, NHPC, JGL Bio-1920. Driggs, see "Just a Word," *The Independent,* vol. 95, no. 3637 (August 17, 1918): 206. America's Gift to France acceptance, JGL to JDR, March 10, 1920, NHPC, JGL Bio-1920.

31. "Fieldwork," JGL to ALP, October 1, 1917, NHPC, JGL Bio-1920; JGL to Mabel Wheeler Daniels, November 9, 1918, Mabel Wheeler Daniels Papers, MC266/1/10, Arthur and Elizabeth Schlesinger Library on the History of Women in America, Radcliffe Institute for Advanced Study.
32. "The simplest method," JGL to Montague Gammon, date illegible ("Please wait until we meet before again trying."), 1917; handbook, JGL to Dorris Hough, August 29, 1918; for Storrow's early tie, see JGL to Mrs. Dennent [?], May 19, 1917, NHPC, JGL Bio-1920; for the letter itself, Helen Storrow to JGL, October 15, 1918, all from NHPC, JGL Bio-1920. See also Proctor, *Scouting for Girls,* 39.
33. There were 41,225 Girl Scouts on March 1, 1919. This figure does not include Brownies (Low, *Girl Scouts as an Educational Force,* 3).
34. Jeffery K. Tauenberger and David M. Morens, "1918 Influenza: The Mother of All Pandemics," *Emerging Infectious Diseases,* vol. 12, no. 1 (January 2006), Centers for Disease Control and Prevention Web site, http://www.cdc.gov/ncidod/EID/vol12no01/05-0979.htm. "Has interfered with," Augusta B. Hartt to JGL, October 29, 1918; "to the little anemic," Edna Mary Colman to JGL, December 12, 1918 (received); "Diet Kitchen," Edna Mary Colman to JGL, [no date] [1918], all from NHPC, JGL Bio-1920.
35. Low, *Girl Scouts as an Educational Force,* 3.
36. Rose Kerr, "Girl Guides," in Choate and Ferris, 71–72.
37. Ibid., 72.
38. Ibid., 72–73.
39. Shultz and Lawrence, 354.
40. "Everyone dances," JGL to Daisy Doots Gordon, January 14, 1919, GHS MS318/14/163.
41. JGL to Daisy Gordon, March 24, 1919, GHS MS318/15/163.
42. JGL to Harold Pratt [?], [no date] [1919], GHS MS318/18/205.

Chapter 15: Girl Scouting in the Roaring Twenties

1. JGL to MGL, May 2, 1915, GHS MS318/15/161. Edith Johnston noted on January 24, 1915, that she "wrote . . . to Miss Mildred Cunningham declining to have the Girl Scouts endorse woman's suffrage." Edith D. Johnston, Secretary, Diary, January 24, 1915, JGLB. (Hereafter cited as Johnston Diary.) Cunningham was the second vice president of the Equal Suffrage Party of Georgia. See Ida Husted Harper, *The History of Woman Suffrage, 1900–1920*, vol. 6 (New York: NAWSA, 1922), 135. NKG quote from "Not a Sympathizer of Equal Suffragists," 1914 clipping from scrapbook 5636, box 35, in GHS MS318.
2. "The more Girl Scouts," Janet Hobson, "A History of the Kalamazoo Girl Scouts No. 44," undergraduate paper for the history seminar, Kalamazoo College, January 1953, 6, http://dspace.nitle.org/bitstream/handle/10090/18260/hobson.pdf?sequence=1. RBP quote, Tim Jeal, *Baden-Powell* (New Haven, CT: Yale University Press, 2001), 491; "who make themselves," JGL to JDR, September 20, 1919, NHPC, JGL Bio-1920. The term "flapper" was used to denote a young society woman in England in the 1910s; see, for example, "Plan to Repatriate Belgian Refugees," *New York Times,* January 16, 1915.
3. Antidote, Tammy Proctor, *Scouting for Girls* (Denver: Praeger, 2009), 27; "Harding Gives Praise to Work of Girl Scouts," *New York Times,* November 8, 1920; Camps, JDR to JGL, July 9, 1925, NHPC, JGL 1925; "the girls will decide,"

Gladys Dennys Shultz and Daisy Gordon Lawrence, *Lady from Savannah* (New York: J. B. Lippincott, 1958), 357.

4. JGL to Mr. Daniels, April 26, 1919, GHS MS318/18/205.
5. "The boy and girl scout," "Sees the Boy Scout a Force for Peace," *New York Times,* May 13, 1919; model for Scouting, "Praises 3,000 Girls for Work in War," *New York Times,* May 19, 1919; "to get all girls," JGL to WWGIII, March 1, 1919, GHS MS318/15/163.
6. International Council, JGL to WWGIII, March 1, 1919, GHS MS318/15/163; "6,000 Girl Scouts in Fund Parade," *New York Times,* November 7, 1920; assimilation, JGL to JDR, May 18, 1920, NHPC, JGL Bio-1920; JGL, "For Those Who Wish to Design an International Flag . . . ," NHPC, JGL 1925; JGL to Marjorie Edgar, July 21, 1921, NHPC, JGL 1921.
7. One of three Americans, Katherine Keena to author, April 16, 2011.
8. Rudyard Kipling to Stanley Baldwin, September 23, 1919 (p. 569); weather, Kipling to Frank N. Doubleday, September 16, 1919 (p. 568), in Thomas Pinney, ed. *The Letters of Rudyard Kipling,* vol. 4 (Iowa City: University of Iowa Press, 1999).
9. Dorris Hough, "Juliette Low Goes Camping," in *Juliette Low and the Girl Scouts,* Anne Hyde Choate and Helen Ferris, eds. (New York: Girl Scouts, 1928), 113. The man was a peddler, according to Hough. There is no date attached to this story.
10. JDR to JGL, February 13, 1920, NHPC, JGL Bio-1920. She gave the name of the artist as Monsieur Jouniaux, a Belgian. JGL said that she "consulted" with RBP before taking the title of founder. See JGL, "The Girl Scouts," [no date], on Hutton Park stationery, JGLB. In 1925 the Executive Board passed a motion that JGL should be given the title "Founder in America" or "Founder in the United States," so as not to be confused with RBP (JGL to JDR, January 20, 1925; JDR to JGL, January 24, 1925, both NHPC, JGL 1925). The picture is now at the JGL Birthplace and Historic Site in Savannah.

    Rose Kerr, "Juliette Low Meets Sir Robert Baden-Powell . . . ," in Choate and Ferris, 77. In 1920 Anne Hyde Choate served as president; first vice president was Helen Storrow and second vice president was Lou Henry Hoover; Edith Macy chaired the Executive Board, of which former First Daughter Eleanor Wilson McAdoo was a member.
11. "Hers was often," Dorris Hough, Draft of Memoir ("I first met Mrs. Low . . .), November 11, 1952, NHPC, Gen'l Info-Pubs; Publicity, "Assistant Director" to JGL, May 11, 1920, NHPC, JGL Bio-1920; First Lady, JGL to JDR, April 21, 1921, NHPC, JGL 1921; membership cards, JGL to JDR, November 29, 1920, NHPC, JGL Bio-1920. For policy, see JGL to JDR, August 14, 1922, NHPC, JGL 1922; JGL, "Brownie Handbook," [no date] [1922], NHPC, JGL 1922; JGL letter fragment ("get the local chairman for different cities . . ."), NHPC, JGL 1921. For dues and the rationale, see JGL to JDR, April 13, 1921, and April 29, 1921, both NHPC, JGL 1921. "Every part of the organization," Anne Hyde Choate, "Girl Scouting Gets Underway," in Choate and Ferris, 102–3.
12. Jane Deeter Rippin, "A Constructive Program for Girl's Work," *Public Welfare,* vol. 3, no. 8 (January 1921), 687–88; "Merging Social Agencies in Philadelphia," *The Survey,* vol. 37 (January 13, 1917), 433; Mary Aickin Rothschild, "Jane Deeter Rippin," *Notable American Women,* Sicherman and Green, eds. (Cambridge, MA: Belknap Press, 1980), 579–80; "Mrs. Rippin Is Dead," *New York Times,* June 3, 1953. The Rockefeller Foundation donated "a new

bookkeeping system" to handle large amounts of money. See JDR to JGL, September 23, 1921, NHPC, JGL 1921.

13. An example of venting, JGL to JDR, February 28, 1920; personnel preferences, JGL to JDR, February 9, 1920; JDR's complaints, JDR to JGL, September 11, 1920; field captains reports, JGL to JDR, March 10, 1920; "I can't tell you how much," JGL to JDR, February 28, 1920, all from NHPC, JGL Bio-1920.
14. "Mrs. Storrow Dies," *New York Times,* November 12, 1944; "ran an almost military," Proctor, 39; JDR to JGL, September 21, 1920; JDR to JGL, December 31, 1920; "seems to suggest things," JDR to JGL, December 20, 1920; JGL to JDR, May 23, 1919, all from NHPC, JGL Bio-1920.
15. *Scouting for Girls* (New York: Girl Scouts, Inc., 1920).
16. Rally, JGL to JDR, June 30, 1920; for Katie Low, JGL to JDR, October 1, 1920, both NHPC, JGL Bio-1290. When Katie Low became involved with Camberwell—and whether JGL facilitated that or vice versa—is unclear.
17. Polish delegate, Rose Kerr, "Juliette Low Meets Sir Robert Baden-Powell," in Choate and Ferris, 73; Danish woman, JGL to JDR, July 30, 1920, NHPC; "will help the international," JGL to JDR, July 30, 1920; "quite an international breeze," JDR to JGL, September 11, 1920; representative from the Netherlands, Matilde Cyfer Van Wyngaarder to JGL, October 4, 1920; urge women, JGL to JDR, November 17, 1920, and JGL to Sheelah Essex Reade (Chairman of the International Council), November 29, 1920, all from NHPC, JGL Bio-1920.
18. "Pneumonia jackets," JGL to JDR, February 9, 1920, NHPC, JGL Bio-1920; "and work up," Dorris Hough, draft of memoir ("I first met Mrs. Low . . ."), November 1, 1952, NHPC, Gen'l Info-Pubs; "prominent women," JGL to Dorris Hough, March 11, 1920, NHPC, JGL, Bio-1920. Hough was the field secretary for the South. Arthur advised her to attend, JGL to Dorris Hough, March 17, 1920, NHPC, JGL, Bio-1920.
19. JGL to Jane Addams, April 5, 1920. JGL did not receive a reply in time to stay there. See JGL to Miss Howells, April 12, 1920; "an inspecting general," JGL to JDR, April 15, 1920, all from NHPC, JGL, Bio-1920.
20. "To encourage," JGL to JDR, June 30, 1920, NHPC, NHPC, JGL, Bio-1920; "Air Safer Than Street in 1940, Aviatrice Says," *Chicago Tribune,* October 22, 1922. "It is the most thrilling," JGL to Daisy Gordon, August 14, 1919, GHS MS318/15/164.
21. "Drive for Girl Scouts, *New York Times,* September 19, 1920; "thousands of girls," JDR to JGL, December 14, 1920, and "men's committee," JDR to JGL, September 11, 1920, both from NHPC, JGL Bio-1920. For nationwide publicity, see JDR to JGL, December 14, 1920, NHPC, JGL Bio-1920, and Jeanne Stevens to JGL, April 23, 1921, NHPC, JGS 1921; Cleveland Dodge, JDR to JGL, February 26, 1920, NHPC, JGL Bio-1920. Helen Storrow went in with another person to donate $500. The necessary number was reached in 1921, JDR to JGL, March 21, 1921, NHPC, JGL 1921. For Daisy's donation, see JGL to JDR, December 13, 1920, NHPC, JGL Bio-1920.
22. "Flies at 70 to Aid Scouts," *New York Times,* November 5, 1920. "6,000 Girl Scouts in Fund Parade," *New York Times,* November 7, 1920. "Give Camp to Girl Scouts," *New York Times,* November 10, 1920.
23. "Please let the function," JGL to JDR, October 1, 1920, NHPC, JGL Bio-1290; "a compact little woman," Arthur Gordon, "My Aunt Daisy Was the First Girl

Scout" (1956), NHPC, JGL Gen'l Info-Pubs; "The deliberate cultivation," "To You, Girl Scouts, from Your Friend, Juliette Low," in Choate and Ferris, 211; birthday, JGL to Emma Hale, October 26, 1920, NHPC, JGL Bio-1290. The local troop was from New Bedford, Massachusetts.

24. Speech topics, JDR to JGL, December 31, 1920, NHPC, JGL Bio-1920. "I could not give," JGL to Dr. Bryant, January 3, 1921; "three hundred council members," JDR to JGL, February 9, 1921; put Kerr to work, JGL to JDR, February 24, 1921, all from NHPC, JGL 1921.
25. JGL to JDR, January 25, 1921; JGL to JDR, January 28, 1921; NHPC, JGL 1921.
26. "Clipping from N.Y. Herald," included with press release from Savannah Girl Scout Headquarters, [no date] [1921], NHPC, JGL 1921. Neal to assist with wrestling match, JGL to JDR, April 1, 1921; and for three months, JGL to Miss Harris, April 1, 1921, both NHPC, JGL 1921. For the warm Catholic response, Joseph D. Mitchell to JGL, [no date] [1921], GHS MS318/15/164.
27. "I know Northerners," JGL to JDR, December 1, 1921, and JDR to JGL, December 22, 1921, both NHPC, JGL 1921. Hiring Atlanta film company, JGL to JDR, December 11, 1921, NHPC, JGL 1921; Josephine Daskam Bacon, "Here and There with Juliette Low," in Choate and Ferris, 138.
28. "Report of the Girl Scouts 1921," NHPC, JGL 1921. James West was still the Chief Scout Executive. He was not invited.
29. Proctor, 40–42.
30. "The risk of sunstroke," JGL to Dorris Haugh, [no date] [1921], NHPC, JGL 1921; "Imagine yourself," JGL to JDR, June 6, 1921, NHPC, Corresp-1921.
31. Dorris Hough, draft of memoir ("I first met Mrs. Low . . .), November 11, 1952, NHPC, Gen'l Info-Pubs. Hough served as head of the Southern region, which included Camp Juliette Low.
32. Dorris Hough, "Juliette Low Goes Camping," in Choate and Ferris, 110; hiring JDR's husband, JGL to JDR, February 25, 1922, JDR to JGL, March 2, 1922, and JGL to JDR, March 17, 1922, all NHPC, JGL 1922. "Another [bank] failure," JGL to JDR, March 17, 1922; "$20,000," JGL to Miss Chisholm, May 24, 1922, both NHPC, JGL 1922. Jane promised," JDR to JGL, March 31, 1922, NHPC, JGL 1922.
33. "Miss Archbold Married," *New York Times,* June 16, 1906; "Anne Archbold, Sportswoman, 94," *New York Times,* March 28, 1968; U.S. Department of the Interior, National Park Service, National Register of Historic Places Nomination Form, December 22, 1994, http://pdfhost.focus.nps.gov/docs/NRHP/Text/94001595.pdf. Archbold was the daughter of a Standard Oil magnate and philanthropist, and Foxlease would be only one of several large donations she would make in her long life. Castle Saunderson became a campsite for Scouting Ireland in 2010.

    OBP to JGL, February 17, 1922, NHPC, JGL 1922; "little bungalow," JGL to JDR, September 25, 1922, NHPC, JGL 1922, Kerr, "Juliette Low Meets Sir Robert Baden-Powell," in Choate and Ferris, 75; "too cunning," JGL to Margaret Gordon, September 13, 1922, GHS MS318/15/164.
34. Japanese dilemma, JGL to JDR, July 6, 1922; instructed Jane, JGL to JDR, September 6, 1922, both from NHPC, JGL 1922.
35. JGL to JDR, June 6, 1921, NHPC, JGL 1921; "Girl Scouts Off to Camp," *New York Times,* July 17, 1921; tales, see Shultz and Lawrence, 24–25, 358-359.

Chapter 16: Making New Friends Internationally

1. Juliette Gordon Low, Patent for "Liquid Container for Use with Garbage Can or the Like," U.S. Patent No. 1,124,925, January 12, 1915.
2. Girl Guide Annual Report, 1917, GGHUK. "One picks up a paper," Anne Patricia Thomson to Miss Mander, September 15, 1923, NHPC, JGL 1923. Miss Mander was the Corresponding Member to the International Council. The letter was sent to her from Thomson, who was a Guide in China. Translation, JGL to JDR, November 2, 1923, NHPC, JGL 1923; Antonia Lindenmyr to JGL, September 8, 1926, NHPC, JGL 1926.
3. JGL to Antonia Lindenmyr, September 30, 1926; JGL to JDR, October 22, 1926, both NHPC, JGL 1926.
4. JGL to Lou Henry Hoover, c. January 25 [1926], GHS MS 318/18/209.
5. JGL to JDR, April 3, 1923; JGL to "Dear Sir," May 8, 1923; JGL to Miss Harris, June 16, 1923, all NHPC, JGL 1923.
6. B. Monroe MacDowell to JDR, May 17, 1923; MacDowell to JGL, May 12, 1923, both NHPC, JGL 1923.
7. Golden Eaglet requirements, *Scouting for Girls* (New York: Girl Scouts, 1920), 535. "A fair way," JGL to Dorris Hough, September 29, 1923; "A matter of principle," JGL to Birdsall Edey, October 20, 1923; *Field News*, Birdsall Edey to JGL, October 5, 1923, all from NHPC, 1923. They began with the December issue. JGL's column ran in November.
8. "I am certain," JGL to Birdsall Edey, September 19, 1923, NHPC, JGL 1923. Agnes M. Schier to JGL, [no date] [1920s], JGLB. For Schier's Girl Scouting work, see Janet Hobson, "A History of the Kalamazoo Girl Scouts No. 44" (undergraduate paper, History Seminar, Kalamazoo College, January 1953), 20–22, http://dspace.nitle.org/bitstream/handle/10090/18260/hobson.pdf?sequence=1.

   Lillian Plotkin to JGL, February 3, 1927, JGLB. RBP felt that "if once you made an exception it would be difficult to draw the line and the golden eaglet would lose its value." RBP to JGL, July 25, 1924, GHS MS318/18/208. See also Carrie F. Wagner to JGL, February 5, 1924, JGLB. Wagner had two disabled girls who should be allowed to try for the honor. Girl Scouts earning the Golden Eaglet, Katherine Keena to author, January 24, 2011. Wedge, JGL to Anne Hyde Choate, December 7, 1925, NHPC, JGL 1925.
9. "Knocked out," JGL to GAG, April 22, 1924, GHS MS318/15/165; "a slight operation," JGL to JDR, February 2, 1924 ("Probably you have expected . . ."), NHPC, JGL 1924; Shultz and Lawrence, 361, state that the cancer appeared first in 1923, diagnosed by Dr. Stuart McGuire, in Richmond, Virginia. Of course, the origins of cancer are seldom clear, but it is worth remembering that a decade earlier, Daisy had a series of gout treatments of highly toxic, cancer-causing radium.
10. JGL to JDR, March 11, 1924, NHPC, JGL 1924.
11. Louise James Bargelt, "Leaders Arrive for Girl Scouts' National Rally," *Chicago Tribune*, April 27, 1924. The *Tribune* reported Girl Scout membership at 160,000. "Does far more at present," JGL to JDR, March 19, 1924, NHPC, JGL 1924. Anne Beiser Allen, *An Independent Woman* (Westport, CT: Greenwood Press, 2000), 94. As usual, JGL contributed funds, $1,000 in August. JGL to JDR, August 22, 1924, NHPC, JGL 1924.

12. "More than 1,000,000," "Cookies for Mrs. Coolidge," *New York Times,* October 12, 1923; "Mrs. Coolidge Greets Girl Scouts," *New York Times,* October 18, 1923. "They were thrilled," JGL to Helen Ferris, October 19, 1923, and "decentralization," JGL to JDR, November 19, 1923, both from NHPC, JGL 1923. "The History of Girl Scout Cookies," GSUSA Web site, http://www.girlscouts.org/program/gs_cookies/cookie_history/early_years.asp.
13. JGL to Edith Macy, May 8, 1924, NHPC, JGL 1924.
14. "Displays," JGL to Edith Macy, July [22], 1924, NHPC, JGL 1924. See also JGL to Helen Ferris, July 26 [1924], NHPC, JGL 1926. JGL, AHC, and Mrs. Hartt "agreed that we would again invite them to U.S. for the 1926 meeting." JGL to Helen Ferris, July 26 [1924], NHPC, JGL 1926.
15. JGL to JDR, [no date] (received March 13, 1924), NHPC, JGL 1924.
16. Margaret Leigh Graves, "In Proud Memory of My Aunt Juliette Gordon Low," NHPC, JGL Gen'l Info-Pubs.
17. MGL to GAG, [no date] [December 1924], GHS MS318/8/91.
18. "Really was the pivot," JDR to JGL, February 10, 1925, JGLB; "Mourn Mrs. V. Everit Macy," *New York Times,* February 3, 1925. According to Allen, 94–95, Hoover got up a fund to support Arnold because the presidency was not a salaried office. "Mrs. Macy Dies Suddenly," *New York Times,* February 2, 1925. "There is only one," JGL to JDR, February 6, 1925, NHPC, JGL 1925.
19. "A permanent training center," JDR to JGL, February 28, 1925; "I feel so often," JDR to JGL, March 10, 1925, both JGLB. This was a second confidential letter on the same topic.
20. JDR's task, JDR, "Her Dream Comes True," in Choate and Ferris, eds., *Juliette Low and the Girl Scouts* (New York: GSUSA, 1928), 164–65. The timing is not clear for these events. In "Her Dream Comes True," JDR wrote that JGL broached, in the spring of 1925, the idea of the World Camp in the United States and at Camp Edith Macy, and that the Executive Board concurred a week later, and the course was set. However, as late as the end of September 1925, JDR wrote JGL (September 28, 1925, NHPC, JGL 1925) that it would be grand to host the World Camp in 1926, "but if plans do not work out for it, perhaps it will be just as well to postpone it until the next meeting, and then Camp Edith Macy will be really ready to receive its International guests." So it is difficult to know when JGL disclosed her cancer to the national director.
21. RBP's foreword to the 1920 Girl Scout manual touted Girl Scouts and Guides as facilitators to world peace and the success of the League of Nations.
22. Girl Scout business, JGL to Helen Ferris, February 5, 1925, NHPC, JGL 1925; Sybil Gordon Newell to JGL, March 2, 1925, JGLB; JGL to JDR, March 22, 1925, NHPC, JGL 1925. Richmond and Dr. McGuire, JGL to JDR, March 22, 1925, NHPC, 1925. Savannah business, Helen Ferris to JGL, February 16, 1925, JGLB; JGL to JDR, March 22, 1925, NHPC, JGL 1925.
23. "Approximately six months," Ruth McGuire, "As I Remember Juliette Low," October 8, 1950, NHPC, JGL, Gen'l Info-Pubs; remembering horoscope, JGL to GAG, July 28, 1924, GHS MS318/15/165; "could only guess," Peggy Leigh Graves, "In Proud Memory of My Aunt, Juliette Gordon Low," NHPC, JGL Gen'l Info-Pubs.
24. Richmond camp, JGL to JDR, June 5, 1925, NHPC, JGL 1925; Ruth McGuire, "As I Remember Juliette Low," October 8, 1950, NHPC, JGL, Gen'l Info-Pubs; Shultz and Lawrence, 374.

25. Seeing many friends, JGL to Mr. Newell, August 7, 1925, NHPC, JGL 1925. Rudyard Kipling to Elsie Bambridge, August 5, 1925, in Thomas Pinney, ed. *The Letters of Rudyard Kipling*, vol. 5 (Iowa City: University of Iowa Press, 2004), 249. In his condolence note to GAG, Kipling emphasizes that they were in formal dinner attire and that he was laughing so hard he could hardly net the fish. Rudyard Kipling to GAG, October 14, 1928, NHPC, JGL Death-Condolences.
26. "Not to be an object," JGL to GAG, March 20, 1925, GHS MS 318/15/166; "Personally, I will lie," MGL to GAG, April 26, 1925; "It makes me sick," MGL to GAG, April 5, 1925, both from GHS MS318/8/95. Ruth McGuire, "As I Remember" NHPC.
27. "I have $5,000," JDR to JGL, July 15, 1925, NHPC, JGL 1925. "I won't be here," Shultz and Lawrence, 366. The date of that comment is not clear. JGL to Sheelah Essex Reade, July 17, 1925, NHPC 1925. "We should cultivate," JGL to Katharine Furse, July 18, 1925, NHPC, 1925. Furse was the head of the Sea Guides, a branch devoted to boating and water activities. Badges, JGL to Leila B. Delano, October 15, 1925; Sibyl Gordon Newell to JGL, November 20, 1925, both NHPC, JGL 1925.
28. JGL to JDR, November 28, 1925; endowment, JDR to JGL, November 30, 1925, both NHPC, JGL 1925.
29. "Every 2 or 3 weeks," AHC to JGL, February 25, 1925, JGLB. Visits, JGL to AHC, December 7, 1925, NHPC, JGL 1925; JGL to JDR, March 10, 1926, NHPC, JGL 1926; JGL to AHC, December 7, 1925, NHPC, JGL 1925.
30. "Throngs of people," "Public Ceremonial in Georgia Day in Honor Founder of Girl Scouts," unidentified newspaper clipping (1926), JGL Scrapbook. "City Pays Honor to Juliette Low," unidentified clipping (February 12, 1926), both JGLB. The testimonial scroll dates the founding of the Girl Scouts in Savannah to March 9, 1912, JGLB. The Savannah Girl Scouts chipped in seventy-five cents apiece to present the founder with flowers, Girl Scout Council of Savannah Board Minutes, February 11, 1926, Archives of Girl Scouts of Historic Georgia, Girl Scout First Headquarters, Savannah.
31. "A gem," from "Dear Caroline," unidentified clipping, February 11, 1926, NHPC, JGL 1926. The ball was held before the eleventh; see above clipping and JGL to Sarah L. Arnold, February 11, 1926, NHPC, JGL 1926; "gas stoves," JGL to Leila B. Delano, February 13, 1926, NHPC, JGL 1926; Shultz and Lawrence, 367–69.
32. "As stuffy as," JGL to Leila B. Delano, February 24, 1926. On March 1, 1926, she told JDR she had the flu, also. "Big Board of Directors," JDR to JGL, February 26, 1926; what should be taught, JGL to Sarah L. Arnold, March 4, 1926; "the dispenser of hospitality," JGL to Leila B. Delano, March 27, 1926, all from NHPC, JGL 1926. "End the dictatorship," JGL to Lou Henry Hoover (unsent), May 31 [no year], GHS MS318/18/209.
33. From her bed, JGL to JDR, April 17, 1926; "the advice of," JGL to Sarah L. Arnold, April 20, 1926, both NHPC, JGL 1926.
34. Leila B. Delano to JGL, May 3, 1926, NHPC, JGL 1926. Grace Coolidge accepted the honorary presidency in October 1923 (copy of Executive Board Minutes, October 1923, NHPC, JGL 1923) and became a Tenderfoot in 1925. Juliette Low pinned on the badge. "Mrs. Coolidge a Tenderfoot Scout," *New York Times*, June 6, 1925.

35. Sheelah Essex Reade, "The International Conference in the United States of America," *Girl Guide Gazette,* August 1926: 238–42 (quote from 239), GGHUK; "World Camp for the Girl Scouts," *New York Times,* April 25, 1926. "A Thinking Day," *The Council Fire* 11, no. 4 (February 1927), GHS MS318/8/96. Presenting badges, JGL to JDR, May 8, 1926, NHPC, JGL 1926.
36. Essex Reade, "The International Conference . . . ," GGHUK, and JGL to Lou Henry Hoover, January 20, 1926, GHS MS318/18/209. "It is not given," JDR to JGL, May 24, 1926, NHPC, JGL 1926.
37. Sesquicentennial, JGL to JDR, June 21, 1926; "awfully pleased," JGL to JDR, July 7, 1926, both NHPC, JGL 1926.
38. National Register of Historic Places Registration Form: Gordonston, GHS Vertical File, "Neighborhoods—Gordonston." For JGL's answer to GAG, see GAG, "Address by G. Arthur Gordon," April 30, 1955, NHPC, JGL Gen'l Info-Pubs.
39. Rudyard Kipling to Elsie Bambridge, August 14, 1926, Pinney, vol. 5, p. 309. Graves, "In Proud Memory . . . ," NHPC.
40. "Medicine: Cancer Cure?," *Time,* June 4, 1923; "Medicine: Cancer," *Time,* February 1, 1926; Graves, "In Proud Memory . . . ," NHPC. "The best that can be said," Irvine Loudon, Review of *William Blair-Bell: Father and Founder* by John Peel, in *Medical History* 31, no. 3 (July 1987): 364.
41. Sixty-sixth birthday, JGL to MGL, October 30, 1926, GHS MS318/15/166. Mabel has handwritten on this letter "after her operation in London." "No internal trouble," JGL to MGL, November 2, 1926, GHS MS318/15/66.
42. "Illogical," JDR to JGL, November 3, 1926, NHPC, JGL 1926; badges and camp, JDR to JGL, December 18, 1926, NHPC, JGL 1926; AHC to JGL, June 16, 1925, GHS MS318/18/208.
43. Shultz and Lawrence, 376–77. This is the only example of her associating with a number of people similarly hearing impaired.
44. JGL to JDR, December 7, 1926, NHPC, JGL 1926; Girl Scout executive committee to JGL, January 11, 1927, NHPC, JGL 1927.
45. JGL to MCC, January 16, 1927, NHPC, JGL 1927. The death certificate lists the cause of death as liver cancer, with breast cancer as the secondary cause; "peacefully," Inez Oliveros to JDR, January 21, 1927, NHPC, JGL Corresp-1927; "Mrs. Low, founder of Girl Scouts, Dies," *New York Times,* January 18, 1927.

Epilogue: "Long Live the Girl Scouts!"

1. Inez Oliveros to JDR, January 21, 1927, NHPC, JGL Corresp-1927; see also Archives of Girl Scout First Headquarters, "Funerary Documents," [no date].
2. Rudyard Kipling to GAG, October 14, 1928, NHPC, JGL Death-Condolences. ALH to GAG, March 29, 1927, GHS MS 318/8/97.
3. Rose Kerr, *The Story of the Girl Guides* (London: The Girl Guides Association, 1832), 62; GAG, "As Her Family Knew Her," 59, and Rowland Leigh, "Our Delightful Companion," both from Anne Hyde Choate and Helen Ferris, eds., *Juliette Gordon Low and the Girl Scouts* (New York: Girl Scouts, 1928), 143.
4. Eleanor Nash McWilliam, "Adventuring in Egypt," in Choate and Ferris, 159.
5. MGL to GAG, June 28, 1924, GHS MS318/8/95.
6. GAG, "As Her Family Knew Her," in Choate and Ferris, 59.
7. Rose Kerr to RBP, April 3, 1927, GHS MS318/8/97; Rudyard Kipling to GAG, October 14, 1928, NHPC, JGL Death-Condolences.

8. JGL, "The Girl Scouts," [no date] [1926], on Hutton Park stationery, JGLB.
9. JGL to JDR, June 15, 1926, NHPC, JGL 1926.
10. GAG, "Address by G. Arthur Gordon," April 30, 1955, NHPC, JGL Gen'l Info-Pubs.
11. JGL to MGC, April 10, 1884, CFP, MS2800/6/12.
12. JGL draft speech, c. 1917 ["In April 1916 we have had to change headquarters . . . "], JGLB.

Bibliography

Archival Sources

Arthur and Elizabeth Schlesinger Library on the History of Women in America, Radcliffe Institute for Advanced Study, Harvard University, Cambridge, Massachusetts
Mabel Wheeler Daniels Papers, MC266
The British Library, London, England
Division of Rare and Manuscript Collections, Cornell University Library, Cornell University, Ithaca, New York
George Hyde Clarke Family Papers, MS2800
Georgia Historical Society, Savannah, Georgia
Gordon Family Papers, MS318
Nina Anderson Pape Papers, MS605
Edith D. Johnston Papers, MS433
Girl Scouts of Historic Georgia, Archives, Savannah, Georgia
Pioneer Troop Records
Juliette Gordon Low Birthplace, Girl Scout National Center, Savannah, Georgia
Correspondence
All letters dated 1868–1910 are found in box 2.
All letters dated 1911–1927 are found in box 3.
Edith D. Johnston Diary (February 1, 1915–April 22, 1915)
National Historic Preservation Center, Girl Scouts of the USA, New York City
Low, Juliette Gordon, Biographical Information to Correspondences—1920
Low, Juliette Gordon, Correspondences—1920 to Diary
Low, Juliette Gordon, General Information to Publications
Baden-Powell, Lady, Biographical Data to Correspondences, 1912–1976
Baden-Powell, Lord and Lady
Scottish National Archives, Edinburgh, Scotland

Southern Historical Collection, Wilson Library, University of North Carolina at Chapel Hill
Gordon Family Papers MS2235

Interviews

Bohlin, Stephen. Director, Andrew Low House, Savannah, Georgia. May 13, 2009.

Howard, Todd. Head Huntmaster, Pine Hill Plantation, Donalsonville, Georgia. October 1, 2010.

Keena, Katherine Knapp. Juliette Gordon Low Birthplace and National Historic Site, Savannah, Georgia. Various dates between May 2009 and May 2011.

Kent, Douglas. Friend of Anne Hyde Choate. September 6, 2010, and December 15, 2010.

Lotz, Stacy. Art professor and metalworker, Monmouth College, Monmouth, Illinois. December 11, 2010, and December 15, 2010.

Prull, Susanna E. Preservation Services Representative, Preserve Rhode Island and Lippitt Mansion. August 25, 2010.

Varnadoe, James. Docent, Juliette Gordon Low Birthplace and Historic Site. May 14, 2009.

Primary Sources

Allen, Peter. *Lectures on Aural Catarrh: The Commonest Forms of Deafness and Their Cure*. London: J. & A. Churchill, 1874.

Baden-Powell, Olave. *Window on My Heart: The Autobiography of Olave, Lady Baden-Powell G.B.E.* As told to Mary Drewery. London: Hodder and Stoughton, 1973.

Baden-Powell, Robert, *Aids to Scouting for N.-C.Os. and Men*. London: Gale & Polden, 1899.

Baden-Powell, Robert. *The Matabele Campaign*. London: Methuen and Company, 1897.

———. *Pig-Sticking, or Hog Hunting: A Complete Account for Sportsmen or Others*. London: Harrison and Sons, 1889.

———. *Scouting for Boys*. Elleke Boehmer, ed. New York: Oxford University Press, 2004.

Bailey, Liberty Hyde. *The Outlook to Nature*. New York: MacMillan, 1905.

Bales, Richard M., ed. *History of Providence County, Rhode Island*. Vol. 2. New York: W. W. Preston, 1891.

Beard, Daniel Carter. *The American Boys Handybook: What to Do and How to Do It*. New York: Scribner's, 1882.

Beard, Lina, and Adelia Belle Beard. *How to Amuse Yourself and Others: The American Girls Handybook*. New York: Scribner's, 1887.

Black, Adam, and Charles. *Black's Picturesque Tourist of Scotland*. Vol. 1, 13th ed. Edinburgh: R. and R. Clark, 1857.

Brayton, Mary Clark, and Ellen F. Terry. *Our Acre and Its Harvest*. Cleveland: Fairbanks, Benedict & Co., 1869.

Campbell, Duncan. *The Lairds of Glenlyon: Historical Sketches*. Perth: S. Cowan, 1886.

Campbell, Lady Colin. [Gertrude Elizabeth Campbell.] *Etiquette of Good Society*. London: Cassel & Company 1893.

Crowe, Eyre. *With Thackeray in America*. New York: Charles Scribner's Sons, 1893.

Daniel, Lizzie Cary. *A Confederate Scrapbook*. Richmond, VA: J. L. Hill Printing Company, 1893.

Dalby, William B. *Lectures on Diseases and Injuries of the Ear*. Philadelphia: Lindsay & Blakiston, 1873.

———. "On the Management of Perforations of the Membrana Tympani." *British Medical Journal* 1, no. 1367 (March 12, 1887): 565–66.

Dawes, Charles G. *Journal as Ambassador to Great Britain*. New York: Macmillan, 1939.

Dodworth, Allen. *Dancing and Its Relation to Education and Social Life*. New York: Harper and Brothers, 1885.

Duncan, A. McC. *Roll of Officers and Members of the Georgia Hussars*. Savannah: The Morning News Printer, [no date].

Escott, T.H.S. "A Foreign Resident." *Society in London*. London: Chatto, Windus, Piccadilly, 1885.

Gordon, Eleanor Lytle Kinzie. *John Kinzie: The "Father of Chicago."* No publisher, 1910.

———. *Narrative of the Massacre at Chicago*, 2nd ed. Chicago: Fergus, 1914.

Gordon, John Brown. *Reminiscences of the Civil War*. New York: Charles Scribner's Sons, 1903.

Greville, Frances Evelyn (Countess of Warwick). *Life's Ebb and Flow*. New York: W. W. Morrow, 1929.

Henry, Josephine K. "Lady Florence Douglas Dixie: Philosopher, Author, Social Reformer, and Humanitarian." *The Liberal Review* 2, no. 6 (July 1905): 336–42.

Houghton, Jacob, and T. W. Bristol. *Reports of William A. Burt and Bela Hubbard, esqs., on the Geography, Topology, and Geology of the . . . South Shore of Lake Superior for 1845*. Detroit: Charles Willcox, 1846.

Howe, M.A. DeWolfe, ed. *Home Letters of General Sherman*. New York: Charles Scribner's Sons, 1909.

Jeakes, Thomas J. "Notes: Threads and Cords." In *Notes and Queries: A Medium of Intercommunications for Literary Men, General Readers*, no. 269 (February 21, 1891): 141–42.

Kerry, Charles. *Smalley in the County of Derby, Its History and Legends*. London: Bemrose and Sons, 1905.

Kinzie, Juliette Magill Augusta. *Wau-bun: The 'Early Day' in the Northwest*. Chicago: D. B. Cooke & Company, 1857.

Lee, F. D., and J. L. Agnew. *Historical Record of the City of Savannah*. Savannah: J. H. Estill, 1869.

Leigh, Edward Chandos. *Bar, Bat, and Bit: Collections and Experiences*. London: John Murray, 1913.

Leigh, Frances Butler. *Ten Years on a Georgia Plantation Since the War*. London: Richard Bentley and Son, 1883.

Lewis, Samuel. *A Topographical Dictionary of Scotland*. Vol. 1. London: S. Lewis and Company, 1851.

Low, Juliette. "Girl Scouts as an Educational Force." *Bureau of Education Bulletin*, no. 33. Washington, DC: Government Printing Office, 1919.

———, and W. J. Hoxie. *How Girls Can Help Their Country: Handbook for Girl Scouts*. New York: Knickerbocker Press, 1913.

McGuire, Walter P., and Franklin P. Mathiews, eds. *The Boy Scouts Yearbook*. New York: Appleton, 1915.

McKinley, Carl. *A Descriptive Narrative of the Earthquake of August 31st 1886*. Charleston, SC: Walker, Evans, and Cogswell Co., 1887.

McLaren, Barbara. *Women of the War.* New York: George H. Doran Company, 1918.

Martineau, Harriet. *Society in America*. Vol. 1. London: Saunders and Otley, 1837.

Miller, Joaquin. *An Illustrated History of the State of Montana*. Chicago: The Lewis Company, 1894.

Mission Hymnal. New York: Bigelow & Main, 1885.

"Mr. Smalley on English Society." *Review of Reviews*. Albert Shaw, ed. Vol. 15 (January–June 1897): 78–79.

Modjeska, Helena. *Memories and Impressions of Helena Modjeska: An Autobiography*. New York: Macmillan, 1910.

Mordaunt, Charles. *Annals of the Warwickshire Hunt, 1795–1895*. Vol. 1. London: Sampson, Low, Marston and Company, 1896.

Norton, Caroline Sheridan. *Stuart of Dunleath*. Vols. 1–3. London: Colburn and Company, 1851.

Politzer, Adam. *A Text-Book of the Diseases of the Ear and Adjacent Organs*. William Dalby, ed. Philadelphia: Lea Brothers, 1894.

Reed, Walter, Victor C. Vaughan, and Edward Shakespeare. *Report on the Origin and Spread of Typhoid Fever in U.S. Military Camps During the Spanish War of 1898*. Vol. 1. Washington, DC: Government Printing Office, 1904.

Rippin, Jane Deeter. "A Constructive Program for Girl's Work." *Public Welfare* 3, no. 8 (January 1921): 687–88.

Sackette, William E., and John J. Scannell. *Scannell's New Jersey First Citizens*. Vol. 1. Paterson, NJ: J. J. Scannell, 1917.

Sage, Mrs. Russell (Margaret Olivia Slocum). *Mrs. Emma Willard and Her Pupils or Fifty Years of Troy Female Seminary 1822–1872*. New York: Mrs. Russell Sage, 1898.

Scharf, John Thomas. *History of Baltimore City and County, from the Earliest Period to the Present*. Philadelphia: Louis Everts, 1881.

Sherman, William Tecumseh. *Memoirs of General W. T. Sherman*. New York: Penguin, 1990 [1875].

Shorthand: A Scientific and Literary Magazine. Vol. 3. London: James Wade, 1889.

Spielmann, Marion Harry. *British Sculpture and Sculptors of Today*. London: Cassell and Company, 1902.

Stretton, Hesba (Sarah Smith). *Hester Morley's Promise*. 2. Vols. London: Henry S. King & Company, 1873.

Stronach, Alice. "Women's Work in Social Settlements." *Windsor Magazine* 36 (June–November 1912): 403–14.

Sweeny, Daniel J., ed. *History of Buffalo and Erie County, 1914–1919*. Buffalo: Committee of One Hundred, 1920.

Waddington, Mary King. *Letters of a Diplomat's Wife, 1883–1902*. New York: Charles Scribner's Sons, 1903.

Welles, Gideon. *Diary of Gideon Welles*. 2 Vols. Boston: Houghton Mifflin Company, 1909.

Wells Newell, William, ed. *Current Superstitions: Collected from the Oral Tradition of English Speaking Folk*. Vol. 4. Boston: Houghton-Mifflin, 1896.

Wilson, James Grant, and Frederick Stoever Dickson. *Thackeray in the United States, 1852–53, 1855–56*. Vol. 1. London: Smith, Elder and Company, 1904.
Young, Filson. *The Relief of Mafeking: How It Was Accomplished by Mahon's Flying Column*. London: Methuen, 1900.

Secondary Sources

Abler, Thomas S. *Cornplanter: Chief Warrior of the Allegany Senecas*. Syracuse, NY: Syracuse University Press, 2007.
Allen, Anne Beiser. *An Independent Woman: The Life of Lou Henry Hoover*. Westport, CT: Greenwood Press, 2000.
Anderson, Mrs. Clarence Gordon. "Eleanor Kenzie Gordon." *Georgia Historical Quarterly* 42, no. 2 (Winter 1958): 163–69.
Anderson, H. Allen. *The Chief: Ernest Thompson Seton and the Changing West*. College Station: Texas A&M University Press, 2000.
Andreas, Alfred Theodore. *History of Chicago*. Vol. 1. Chicago: A. T. Andreas, 1884; reprint New York: Arno Press, 1975.
Ayral-Clause, Odile. *Camille Claudel: A Life*. New York: Harry N. Abrams, 2002.
Bagnall, Ralph. "Girl Scouts Founder Was Also a Woodworker." *Woodworker's Journal*. June 2007: 22–24.
Bailey, Anne J. *War and Ruin*. Wilmington, DE: Scholarly Resources, 2003.
Barber, Edwin Atlee. "The Pioneer of China Painting in America." *New England Magazine* 19, no. 1 (September 1895): 33–49.
———. *The Pottery and Porcelain of the United States*. New York: G. P. Putnam's Sons, 1901.
Baynton, Douglas C. *Forbidden Signs: American Culture and the Campaign Against Sign Language*. Chicago: University of Chicago Press, 1996.
Bearss, Edwin C. "The White River Expedition, June 10–July 16, 1862." *Arkansas Historical Quarterly* 21, no. 4 (Winter 1962): 305–62.
Beckett, J. V. *The Aristocracy in England*. Oxford: Basil Blackwell, 1986.
Biegert, Melissa. "Woman Scout: The Empowerment of Juliette Gordon Low, 1860–1927." Ph.D. dissertation, University of Texas at Austin, May 1998.
Birdsall, Ralph. *The Story of Cooperstown*. Cooperstown, NY: A. H. Crist Company, 1920.
Block, Nelson R., and Tammy Proctor, eds. *Scouting Frontiers: Youth and the Scout Movement's First Century*. Newcastle-upon-Tyne: Cambridge Scholars Publishing, 2009.
Bogue, Margaret Beattie. "As She Knew Them: Juliette Kinzie and the Ho-Chunk, 1830–1833." *Wisconsin Magazine of History* 85, no. 2 (Winter 2001–2002): 44–57.
Bolton, Peter. *The Naples of the Midlands: Wellesbourne, 1800–1939*. Wellesbourne, UK: Local Time, 2007.
Bowditch, Eden Unger. *Baltimore's Historic Parks and Gardens*. Chicago: Arcadia, 2004.
Bragg, William Harris. *De Renne: Three Generations of a Georgia Family*. Athens: University of Georgia Press, 1999.
Bryant, William O. *Cahaba Prison and the Sultana Disaster*. Tuscaloosa: University of Alabama Press, 1990.
Butler, Edward H. *The Story of British Shorthand*. London: Pitman, 1951.

Butler, Ruth. *Rodin: The Shape of Genius*. New Haven, CT: Yale University Press, 1996.

Callen, Anthea. *Angel in the Studio: Women in the Arts and Crafts Movement 1870–1914*. London: Astragal Books, 1979.

Cannadine, David. *The Decline and Fall of the British Aristocracy*. New York: Doubleday, 1992.

Carden-Coyne, Ana. *Reconstructing the Body: Classicism, Modernism, and the First World War*. New York: Oxford University Press, 2009.

Cayleff, Susan E. *Wash and Be Healed: The Water-Cure Movement and Women's Health*. Philadelphia: Temple University Press, 1987.

Choate, Anne Hyde, and Helen Ferris, eds. *Juliette Gordon Low and the Girl Scouts: The Story of an American Woman, 1860–1927*. New York: Girl Scouts, 1928.

Clancy, Jacqueline E. "Hell's Angel: Eleanor Kinzie Gordon's Wartime Summer of 1898." *Tequesta* 43 (2003): 37–61.

Clark, John B. *The Volkmar Legacy to American Art Pottery*. Greenwich, CT: Bruce Museum, 1985.

Clements, Kendrick A. "The New Era and the New Woman: Lou Henry Hoover and 'Feminism's Awkward Age.'" *Pacific Historical Review* 73, no. 3 (August 2004): 425–61.

Cogswell, Elizabeth Wayland Agee. "The Henry Lippitt House: A Document of Life and Taste in Mid-Victorian America." Master's thesis. University of Delaware. 1981.

Coker, Folarin. *A Lady: A Biography of Lady Oyinkan Abayomi*. Ibadan, Nigeria: Evans Brothers, 1987.

The Cooperstown Centennial Celebration, 1907. Cooperstown, NY: *Otsego Republican*, 1907.

Cornell, George L. "The Influence of Native Americans on Modern Conservationists." *Environmental History Review* 9, no. 2 (Summer 1985): 104–17.

Coulter, E. Merton. *Wormsloe: Two Centuries of a Georgia Family*. Athens: University of Georgia Press, 1955.

Coyne, Doris W. *A Kingdom for the Trefoil: A History of Guiding in Fife*. Kirkcaldy: John Davidson & Son, 1979.

Cronin, Patricia. *Harriet Hosmer: Lost and Found*. Milan: Charta, 2009.

Danckers, Ulrich, and Jane Meredith. *A Compendium of the Early History of Chicago*. River Forest, IL: Early Chicago, Inc., 2000.

Davis, Richard Harding. *Real Soldiers of Fortune*. New York: Charles Scribner's Sons, 1912.

Dean, Patty. "'Unique and Handsome': Cass Gilbert's Designs for the Montana Club." *Drumlummon Views* 1, nos. 1–2 (Spring/Summer 2006): 154–76.

Doolittle, Duncan H. *A Soldier's Hero: General Sir Archibald Hunter*. Narragansett, RI: Anawan Publishing Company, 1991.

Dorris, Jonathan Truman. *Pardon and Amnesty Under Lincoln and Johnson: The Restoration of the Confederates to Their Rights and Privileges, 1861–1898*. Chapel Hill: University of North Carolina Press, 1953.

Downard, William L. "William Butler Ogden and the Growth of Chicago." *Journal of the Illinois State Historical Society* 75, no. 1 (Spring 1982): 47–60.

Durham, Roger S. *Guardian of Savannah*. Columbia: University of South Carolina Press, 2008.

Dyer, John P. "Northern Relief for Savannah During Sherman's Occupation." *Journal of Southern History* 19, no. 4 (November 1953): 457–72.

Fargo, William G. "Walter John Hoxie." *Wilson Ornithological Society Journal* 46, no. 3 (September 1934): 169–96.

Gardner, Helen. *The First Girl Guide: The Story of Agnes Baden-Powell*. Stroud, UK: Amberley Publishing, 2010.

Gould, Lewis L. *The William Howard Taft Presidency*. Lawrence: University Press of Kansas, 2009.

Grace, Pierce A. "Doctors Differ Over the German Crown Prince." *British Medical Journal* 305 (December 19–26, 1992): 1536–38.

Green Bay Branch of the AAUW. "Dreamers and Doers: Women of Northeast Wisconsin." *Voyageur: Historical Review of Brown County and Northeast Wisconsin* 21, no. 2 (Winter/Spring 2005): 56–59.

Haeger, John D. "The American Fur Company and the Chicago of 1812–1835." *Journal of the Illinois State Historical Society* 61, no. 2 (Summer 1968): 117–39.

Hamilton, Elizabeth. *The Warwickshire Scandal*. Oxford: Macmillan/Pan, 1999.

Hanley, Clive. "Juliette Gordon Low and Wellesbourne House." http://evergreen.zenfolio.com/f301845861.

Harper, Ida Husted. *The History of Woman Suffrage, 1900-1920*. Vol. 6. New York: NAWSA, 1922.

Harwell, Christopher Lee. "William Henry Stiles: Georgia Gentleman-Politician." Ph.D. dissertation, Emory University, 1959.

Headwaters Heritage History. Butte, MT: Three Forks Area Historical Society, 1983.

Helgren, Jennifer. "'"Homemaker" Can Include the World': Female Citizenship and Internationalism in the Postwar Camp Fire Girls." In *Girlhood: A Global History*. Jennifer Helgren and Colleen A. Vasconcellos, eds. New Brunswick, NJ: Rutgers University Press, 2010: 304–22.

Henken, Elissa R. "Taming the Enemy: Georgian Narratives About the Civil War." *Journal of Folklore Research* 40, no. 3 (September–December 2003): 289–307.

Hibbert, Christopher. *The Royal Victorians: King Edward VII, His Family and Friends*. New York: J. B. Lippincott Company, 1976.

Higginbothom, Peter. *Workhouses of the Midlands*. Stroud, UK: Tempus, 2007.

Hillcourt, William, with Olave, Lady Baden-Powell. *Baden-Powell: The Two Lives of a Hero*. New York: G. P. Putnam's Sons, 1964.

History of Chicago. Chicago: Chicago Historical Publishing Company, 1889.

Holbrook, Bertha A. "The Old Indian Agency House at Portage." *Wisconsin Magazine of History* 29, no. 1 (September 1945): 32–42.

Hood, Susan. "The Famine in the Strokestown Park House Archive." *Irish Review* 7/8 (Winter 1995): 109–17.

Hughes, Nathaniel C., Jr. *General William J. Hardee*. Baton Rouge: Louisiana State University Press, 1965.

Hunter, Archie. *Kitchener's Sword-Arm: The Life and Campaigns of General Sir Archibald Hunter*. New York: Sarpedon, 1996.

———. *Power and Passion in Egypt: A Life of Sir Eldon Gorst, 1861–1911*. London: I. B. Tauris, 2007.

Inness, Sherri A. *Delinquents and Debutants: Twentieth-Century American Girls' Culture*. New York: New York University Press, 1998.

Jabour, Anya. *Topsy-Turvy: How the Civil War Turned the World Upside Down for Southern Children*. Chicago: Ivan R. Dee, 2010.

James, Lawrence. *Raj: The Making and Unmaking of British India*. New York: St. Martin's Press, 1997.

Jeal, Tim. *Baden-Powell: Founder of the Boy Scouts*. New Haven, CT: Yale University Press, 2001.

Johnson, Charles J., Jr. "Nineteenth Century Savannahians on the National Scene." *Bonaventure Historical Society Bulletin* 14, no. 4 (October–December 2008): 1–5.

Jones, Charles C., Jr. *The Siege of Savannah*. Albany, NY: Joel Munsell, 1874.

Jonnes, Jill. *Eiffel's Tower*. New York: Viking, 2009.

Keppel-Jones, Arthur. *Rhodes and Rhodesia: The White Conquest of Zimbabwe, 1884–1902*. Toronto: McGill-Queen's Press, 1983.

Kerr, Rose. *The Story of the Girl Guides*. London: The Girl Guides Association, 1932.

Kerr, Rose, ed. *The Story of a Million Girls: Guiding and Girl Scouting Round the World*. London: The Girl Guides Association, n.d.

Kimmel, Michael S. "Men's Responses to Feminism at the Turn of the Century." *Gender and Society* 1, no. 3 (September 1987): 261–83.

Knight, Lucian Lamar. *A Standard History of Georgia and Georgians*. Vol. 5. Chicago: Lewis Publishing Company, 1917.

Larkin, Susan G. "A Delicious Day: Robert Weir's *Greenwich Boat Club*." *American Art Journal* 33, nos. 1 & 2 (2002): 20–23.

Lasch, Christopher. *Haven in a Heartless World: The Family Besieged*. New York: W. W. Norton, 1995.

Leonard, John William, ed. *Woman's Who's Who of America*. New York: American Commonwealth Company, 1914.

Leslie, Anita. *The Marlborough House Set*. New York: Doubleday, 1973.

Lippitt, Henry F. *Jeanie Lippitt and the Mastery of Silence*. Los Angeles: Henry Lippitt, 1974.

———. *The Lippitt Family: A Collection of Notes and Items of Interest by One of Its Members*. Los Angeles: Henry Lippitt, 1959.

Lippitt, Marian Almy. *I Married a New Englander*. Los Angeles: Ward Ritchie Press, 1947.

Logan, Anne Clarke, and Karin Lodinsky Nelson. *The Ladies of Hyde Hall*. Cooperstown, NY: Hyde Hall, Inc., 2009.

Longford, Elizabeth, ed. *Louisa, Lady in Waiting: The Personal Diaries and Albums of Louisa, Lady in Waiting, to Queen Victoria and Queen Alexandra*. New York: Mayflower Books, 1979.

Loudon, Irvine, "Review of *William Blair-Bell: Father and Founder* by John Peel." *Medical History* 31, no. 3 (July 1987): 364.

Lovell, Caroline Couper. *The Light of Other Days*. Macon, GA: Mercer University Press, 1995.

McCardie, W. J. "Lawson Tait, A Pioneer in Certain Methods of Anaesthesia." *British Journal of Anaesthesia* 3, no. 2 (1925): 76–79.

MacDonald, Stuart. *The History and Philosophy of Art Education*. Cambridge, UK: Lutterworth Press, 1970.

McIlvaine, Mabel, ed. *Reminiscences of Early Chicago*. Chicago: Lakeside Press/R. R. Donnelley & Sons, 1912.

McKay, W. J. Stewart. *Lawson Tait: His Life and Work*. London: Bailliere, Tindall and Cox, 1922.

Macleod, David I. "Act Your Age: Boyhood, Adolescence, and the Rise of the Boy Scouts of America." *Journal of Social History* 16, no. 2 (Winter 1982): 3–20.

———. *Building Character in the American Boy: The Boy Scouts, YMCA, and Their Forerunners, 1870–1920.* Madison: University of Wisconsin Press, 1983.

Manahan, Nancy, ed. *On My Honor: Lesbians Reflect on Their Scouting Experience.* Northboro, MA: Madwoman Press, 1997.

Mangan, J. A., and James Walvin, eds. *Manliness and Morality: Middle-Class Masculinity in Britain and America, 1800–1940.* New York: St. Martin's Press, 1987.

Mayer, Dale C., ed. *Lou Henry Hoover: Essays on a Busy Life.* Worland, WY: High Plains Publishing, 1994.

Mayo, William J. "Radical Operations for the Cure of Cancer of the Second Half of the Large Intestine, Not Including the Rectum." *Transactions of the Sections [of the AMA] on Obstetrics, Gynecology, and Abdominal Surgery.* (1916): 163–76.

Miller, Edward A. *Lincoln's Abolitionist General: The Biography of David Hunter.* Columbia: University of South Carolina Press, 1997.

Miller, Susan. *Growing Girls: The Natural Origins of Girls' Organizations in America.* New Brunswick, NJ: Rutgers University Press, 2007.

Mitchell, Sally. *The New Girl: Girls' Culture in England, 1880–1915.* New York: Columbia University Press, 1995.

Mitter, Partha. *The Triumph of Modernism: India's Artists and the Avant-Garde, 1922–1947.* New York: Oxford University Press, 2007.

Mobley, Joe A. *Weary of War: Life on the Confederate Homefront.* Westport, CT: Praeger Press, 2008.

Moriarty, Catherine. *The Sculpture of Gilbert Ledward.* Aldershot: Lund Humphries, 2003.

Morris, Brian. "Ernest Thompson Seton and the Origins of the Woodcraft Movement." *Journal of Contemporary History* 5, no. 2 (1970): 183–94.

Moss, Michael E., ed. *Robert W. Weir of West Point: Illustrator, Teacher and Poet.* West Point, NY: United States Military Academy, 1976.

Myers, Robert Manson, ed. *The Children of Pride: Selected Letters of the Family of the Rev. Dr. Charles Colcock Jones from the Years 1860–1868.* New Haven, CT: Yale University Press, 1972.

Myers, Ruth, et. al. *Headwaters Heritage History.* Butte, MT: Three Forks Area Historical Society, 1983.

Nelson, Dana D. "Introduction." In *Principles and Privilege: Two Women's Lives on a Georgia Plantation.* Frances A. Kemble and Frances A. Butler Leigh. Ann Arbor: University of Michigan Press, 1994.

Oppenheim, Janet. *Shattered Nerves: Doctors, Patients, and Depression in Victorian England.* New York: Oxford University Press, 1991.

Parkes, Kineton. *Sculpture of Today.* Vol. 1. London: Chapman and Hall, 1921.

Perry, Elisabeth Israels. "From Achievement to Happiness: Girl Scouting in Middle Tennessee, 1910s–1960s." *Journal of Women's History* 5, no. 2 (Fall 1993): 75–94.

Pierce, Bessie Louise. *A History of Chicago.* Vol. 1, *The Beginning of a City, 1673–1848.* New York: Alfred A. Knopf, 1937.

Pinney, Thomas, ed. *The Letters of Rudyard Kipling.* 6 vols. Iowa City: University of Iowa Press, 1990–2004.

Pressly, Paul. "Educating the Daughters of Savannah's Elite: The Pape School and the Progressive Movement." *Georgia Historical Quarterly* 80, no. 2 (Summer 1996): 246–75.

———. "The Northern Roots of Savannah's Antebellum Elite, 1780s–1850s." *Georgia Historical Quarterly* 87, no. 2 (Summer 2003): 157–200.

Price, Leah. "Diary." *London Review of Books* 30, no. 23 (December 4, 2008): 43.

———, and Pamela Thurschwell, eds. *Literary Secretaries/Secretarial Culture*. Burlington, VT: Ashgate Publishing Company, 2005.

Prince, Richard E. *Central of Georgia Railway and Connecting Lines*. Salt Lake City: Stanway-Wheelwright, 1976.

Proctor, Tammy. *On My Honour: Guides and Scouts in Interwar Britain*. Philadelphia: American Philosophical Society, 2002.

———. *Scouting for Girls: A Century of Girl Guides and Girl Scouts*. Denver: Praeger, 2009.

Pullar, Philippa. *Gilded Butterflies: The Rise and Fall of the London Social Season*. London: Hamish Hamilton, 1978.

Quaife, Milo M. "Documents: The Chicago Treaty of 1833." *Wisconsin Magazine of History* 1, no. 1 (September 1917): 287–303.

Randall, Isabel F. *A Lady's Ranch Life in Montana*. Richard L. Saunders, ed. Norman: University of Oklahoma Press, 2004.

Robertson, Elizabeth. *The Story of the Girl Guides in Scotland, 1908–2000*. Edinburgh: The Guide Association, 2004.

Robertson, Mary, ed. "Northern Rebel: The Journal of Nellie Kinzie Gordon, Savannah, 1862." *Georgia Historical Quarterly* 70, no. 3 (Fall 1986): 477–517.

Robins, Ashley H., and Steve L. Sellars. "Oscar Wilde's Terminal Illness: Reappraisal After a Century." *The Lancet* 356 (November 25, 2000): 1841–43.

Rosenthal, Michael. *The Character Factory: Baden-Powell and the Origins of the Boy Scout Movement*. New York: Pantheon Books, 1984.

———. "Knights and Retainers: The Earliest Version of Baden-Powell's Boy Scout Scheme." *Journal of Contemporary History* 15, no. 4 (October 1980): 603–17.

Rothschild, Mary Aickin. "To Scout or to Guide?: The Girl Scout–Boy Scout Controversy, 1912–1941." *Frontiers: A Journal of Women's Studies* 6, no. 3 (Autumn 1981): 115–21.

Russell, Preston, and Barbara Hines. *Savannah: A Story of Her People Since 1733*. Savannah, GA: Frederic C. Beil, 1992.

Ryan, Jennifer Guthrie, and Hugh Stiles Golson. *Andrew Low and the Sign of the Buck*. Savannah, GA: Frederic C. Beil, 2011.

Saxton, Martha. "The Best Girl Scout of Them All." *American Heritage* 33, no. 4 (June/July 1982): 38–46.

Schriner, Gertrude, and Margaret Rogers. *Daisy's Chicago Heritage*. Elk Grove Village, IL: Girl Scout Council of Northwest Cook County, 1976.

Schultz, Rima Lunin. *The Church and the City: A Social History of 150 Years at St. James, Chicago*. Chicago: The Cathedral of Saint James, 1986.

Sebba, Anne. *American Jennie: The Remarkable Life of Lady Randolph Churchill*. New York: W. W. Norton, 2007.

Segal, Eric J. "Norman Rockwell and the Fashioning of American Masculinity." *Art Bulletin* 78, no. 4 (December 1996): 633–46.

Shepherd, John A. *Lawson Tait: The Rebellious Surgeon, 1845–1899*. Lawrence, KS: Coronado Press, 1980.

Shultz, Gladys Denny, and Daisy Gordon Lawrence. *Lady from Savannah: The Life of Juliette Low*. Philadelphia: J. B. Lippincott, 1958.

Simpson, Brooks D. and Jean V. Berlin, eds. *Selected Correspondence of Sherman's Civil War.* Chapel Hill: University of North Carolina Press, 1999.

Sims, Anastatia Hodgens. "Juliette Gordon Low: Late Blooming Daisy." In *Georgia Women: Their Lives and Times.* Vol. 1. Ann Short Chirhart and Betty Wood, eds. Athens: University of Georgia Press, 2009: 370–89.

———, and Katherine Knapp Keena. "Juliette Low's Gift: Girl Scouting in Savannah, 1912–1927." *Georgia Historical Society* 94, no. 3 (Fall 2010): 372–87.

Smith, Anna Habersham Wright. *A Savannah Family, 1830–1901.* Milledgeville, GA: Boyd Publishing, 1999.

Smith, Phyllis. *Bozeman and the Gallatin Valley: A History.* Helena, MT: Twodot, 1996.

Snowden, James Ross. *The Cornplanter Memorial: An Historical Sketch of Gy-ant-wachia—The Cornplanter, and of the Six Nations of Indians.* Harrisburg, PA: Singerly & Myers, 1867.

Stefanco, Carolyn. "Poor Loving Prisoners of War: Nelly Kinzie Gordon and the Dilemma of Northern-Born Women in the Confederate South." In *Enemies of the Country: New Perspectives on Unionists in the Civil War South.* John C. Inscoe and Robert C. Kenzer, eds. Athens: University of Georgia Press, 2001: 148–171.

Stewart, Alexandra. *Daughters of the Glen.* Aberfeldy: Leura Press, 1986.

Stewart, Charles W., ed. *Official Records of the Union and Confederate Navies in the War of the Rebellion.* Washington, D.C.: U. S. Government Printing Office, 1910.

Stronach, Alice. "Women's Work in Social Settlements." *Windsor Magazine* 36 (June–November 1912): 403–14.

Sturdevant, Lynda M. "Girl Scouting in Stillwater, Oklahoma: A Case Study in Local History." *Chronicles of Oklahoma* 57, no. 1 (1979): 34–48.

Swenson, John F. "John H. Kinzie." *Early Chicago.* http://www.earlychicago.com/encyclopedia.php?letter=K.

Testi, Arnaldo. "The Gender of Reform Politics: Theodore Roosevelt and the Culture of Masculinity." *Journal of American History,* March 1995: 1509–33.

Thomson, St. Clair. "Great Medical Victorians." *British Medical Journal* 3 (December 1938): 1165.

Turk, Diana B. *Bound by a Mighty Vow: Sisterhood and Women's Fraternities, 1870–1920.* New York: New York University Press, 2004.

Van Cleve, John Vickrey, ed. *Deaf History Unveiled: Interpretations from the New Scholarship.* Washington, DC: Gallaudet University Press, 2002.

Vincent, John, ed. *The Diaries of Edward Henry Stanley, 15th Earl of Derby (1826–1893).* Oxford: Leopard's Head Press, 2003.

Wade, Eileen K. *Olave Baden-Powell: The Authorized Biography of the World Chief Guide.* London: Hodder and Stoughton, 1971.

Wallenstein, Peter. "Rich Man's War, Poor Man's Fight: Civil War and the Transformation of Public Finance in Georgia." *Journal of Southern History* 50, no. 1 (February 1984): 15–42.

Warlick, Roger K. *As Grain Once Scattered: The History of Christ Church, Savannah, Georgia 1733–1983.* Columbia, GA: The State Printing Company, 1987.

Warren, Allen. "Sir Robert Baden-Powell, the Scout Movement and Citizen Training in Great Britain, 1900–1920." *English Historical Review* 101, no. 399 (April 1986): 376–98.

Weinbren, Daniel. "Against *All* Cruelty: The Humanitarian League, 1891–1919." *History Workshop Journal*, no. 38 (1994): 86–105.

Weintraub, Stanley. *Edward the Caresser: The Playboy Prince Who Became Edward VII.* New York: Free Press, 2001.

Weir, Irene. *Robert W. Weir, Artist.* New York: House of Field–Doubleday, 1947.

Welter, Barbara. "The Cult of True Womanhood, 1820–1860." *American Quarterly* 18, no. 2 (Summer 1966): 151–74.

Williams, George C., and Charlotte Crabtree. "Women Metalworkers in the American South." *Women of Metal: The 49th Annual Washington Antiques Show.* Washington, DC: The Thrift Shop, 2004: 136–41.

Williams, Lillian S. *A Bridge to the Future.* New York: Girl Scouts of the U.S.A., 1996.

Williams, Mentor L. "John Kinzie's Narrative of the Fort Dearborn Massacre." *Illinois State Historical Journal* 46 (Winter 1953): 343–62.

Wilson, Adelaide. *Historic and Picturesque Savannah.* Boston: Boston Photogravure Company, 1889.

Witt, David. *Ernest Thompson Seton: The Life and Legacy of an Artist and Conservationist.* Layton, UT: Gibbs Smith, 2010.

"Women Metal Workers." *The Art Record: A Weekly Illustrated Review of the Arts and Crafts* 2, no. 27 (August 24, 1901): 787–98.

Wood, Winsor. "Daisy's Life." Stuart Hall School Web site. http://www.stuart-hall.org/content/view/35/196/.

Young, Nancy Beck. *Lou Henry Hoover: Activist First Lady.* Lawrence: University Press of Kansas, 2004.

Index